Iraq

A HISTORY

Iraq

A HISTORY

JOHN
ROBERTSON

ONEWORLD

A Oneworld Book

First published by Oneworld Publications, 2015
Reprinted, 2015

ISBN 978-1-85168-586-8
ISBN 978-1-78074-419-3 (eBook)

Typeset by Tetragon, London
Printed and bound in Great Britain by
TJ International Ltd, Padstow, Cornwall

Oneworld Publications
10 Bloomsbury Street
London WC1B 3SR
England

Stay up to date with the latest books,
special offers, and exclusive content from
Oneworld with our monthly newsletter

Sign up on our website
www.oneworld-publications.com

For my parents, Ursula and Martin, who
lit my path to learning

and

for Nina and Jenny, who light my life with
their love.

Contents

Contents

Contents

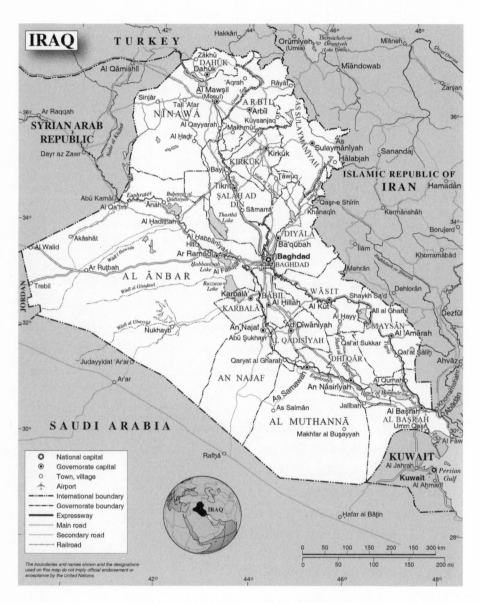

MAP 1. *Iraq (courtesy, United Nations)*

Foreword

I STARTED THIS PROJECT not long after a coalition of military forces of the United States, Great Britain, Australia, and Poland launched its invasion of Iraq in 2003. I had hoped then to produce something that might help my fellow U.S. citizens, and other interested Western readers, to better understand the history and significance of a country that, as many years of university teaching had made plain to me, most of them knew little about. Even more, I hoped this book might provoke them to ponder the history and the humanity of the proud people of Iraq. The last coalition troops departed from Iraq in December, 2011; the mainstream Western media mostly moved on; most of the reading public have closed the book on Iraq, even though, as I write these words in August 2014, the consequences of the Western invasion and occupation continue to play out and Iraq seems headed toward de facto partition and possible dissolution. If what I present here gets some of them, and others, to reopen that book, my time will have been well spent.

I owe so much to so many. In particular, to the giants of scholarship and journalism upon whose shoulders I have serially perched in researching and writing this book. My students have provided inspiration, both in their need and, more importantly, in their stimulating my quest for expertise and for figuring out what might help me to convey to a wider, mostly non-specialist audience something of the depth, complexity, and significance of Iraq's long history.

My thanks go to Central Michigan University (C.M.U.) for providing me the opportunity to develop and teach a variety of courses on the history of the Middle East. Having started out my career at C.M.U. guided by a job description that called for me to teach Western Civilization courses as well as a survey course on the Ancient Near East, I was blessed by a series of deans and History Department chairs and colleagues who, without exception, supported my decision to develop new courses, both undergraduate and graduate, on the "classical" as well as the modern Middle East. As my teaching load became more diverse and demanding, my department chairs assigned me graduate teaching assistants whose help was indispensable in freeing time for me to acquire the new expertise I needed.

The writing of this book benefited immensely from a semester's sabbatical research leave in spring 2011, as well as the decision of C.M.U.'s College of Humanities and Social and Behavioral Sciences, led by Dean Pamela Gates, to give me a reduced teaching assignment in spring 2010.

I am immensely grateful to my Assyriological colleague Dr. Barbara Nevling Porter for her suggestions and comments on a portion of the book – and for much-needed encouragement. I also want to thank Prof. Eleanor Robson for her support and her willingness to help as I was finalizing illustrations for this book. I am likewise immensely grateful to all of the instructors, mentors, and colleagues who, over quite a few years, took on a graduate student who initially was completely untutored in the history of either ancient Mesopotamia or modern Iraq and boosted him along a path and process that eventually enabled him to attempt a book such as this. Specifically, I wish to thank James Muhly, Erle Leichty, Ake Sjoberg, Barry Eichler, Chris Hamlin, Norman Yoffee, Jack Sasson, Martha Roth, Richard Zettler, and Thomas Holland. I also will be forever grateful to Amin Banani, Amal Rassam, and Afif Lutfi al-Sayyid Marsot. They surely have long forgotten me by now, but it was their tutelage during an NEH/AASCU seminar on the Modern Middle East hosted by the University of Michigan in 1984 that truly set me on the path to teaching, research, and writing on the post-antiquity history of the region. I am also very grateful indeed for the comments and contributions of the anonymous reviewer provided by my publisher. It should go without saying that any errors or infelicities in what I have produced are entirely my own responsibility.

I cannot express strongly enough my gratitude for the opportunity to have this book published by such an outstanding publisher, and for their unfailing patience when I needed deadline extensions to deal with challenges both professional and medical. I want to thank Novin Doostdar, Kate Kirkpatrick, Paul Boone, James Magniac, and Paul Nash for all of their help. And I especially want to thank Fiona Slater, who provided superb, spot-on critique and suggestions as I completed revisions of the book's last draft. Anthony Nanson did a superb job of amending and improving my sometimes labored prose, and Kathleen McCully's close proofreading caught several potentially embarrassing mistakes. Many thanks to them as well.

Finally, I could never have completed this project without the patient support and help, gentle nudging, and occasional "just do it!" from my wife, Dr. Nina Nash-Robertson. In the time during which I researched and wrote this book, she led and conducted C.M.U's choral ensembles on performance tours of Ireland, France, and China, as well as a performance in Carnegie Hall – not to mention countless other performances nearer home. She also nursed and sustained me through major injuries and two hip replacements. Nonetheless, she found time to read my drafts and provide valuable suggestions and corrections. What I owe her, in the course of both this project and our more than thirty years together, is beyond any possible recompense.

INTRODUCTION

THE GLORY AND THE CURSE
OF IRAQ'S PAST

We enter histories through the rubble of war

ARUNDHATI ROY
An Ordinary Person's Guide to Empire

B EFORE EARLY 1991, most Europeans and Americans knew little
and likely cared even less about Iraq or its people. They may have
been aware that Iraq had lately been at war for eight years with the Islamic
Republic of Iran. They certainly had heard about Iran's fundamentalist
Islamist regime, led by the West's recently deceased bogeyman-in-chief,
the Ayatollah Ruhollah Khomeini, the Iranian mullah whose followers
had seized the U.S. embassy in Tehran in 1979 and had then held its
occupants hostage for a year and a half. Americans had been enraged
and humiliated by that event, so in Iraq's war with Iran they likely had
hoped that the Iraqis (whose leader, Saddam Hussein, had just begun
to blip on their radar screens) would clobber Iran and thereby defang
or even eliminate the Ayatollah. If they'd made the unlikely decision to
pay closer attention during the war, they may have learned that their
President, Ronald Reagan, had dispatched envoys and pledged U.S.
assistance to Saddam, even though Saddam's unprovoked invasion of
Iran had started the war in the first place. They may also have read that

1

tens of thousands on both sides were killed on the battlefield and in cities and towns. But they probably would have gotten that information only in passing, after flipping through their newspapers to the middle or back pages, to which the editors had relegated terse reports of the faraway conflict. Many readers would have chalked it up as Arabs killing each other; sadly, many were – and remain – unaware that most Iranians are Persians or maybe Turks, not Arabs.

Saddam Hussein's surprising, immensely fateful decision to invade and occupy Kuwait in the summer of 1990 began to change much of that. Overnight, Saddam went from being an anti-Iran semi-proxy for American interests in the Persian Gulf region to a dangerous foe who was rapidly transformed into the epitome of state-sponsored barbarity and the face of evil incarnate. Twelve years later the U.S. President would proclaim Saddam's Iraq to be a charter member of an "Axis of Evil."

In January 1991, under a new president, George H. W. Bush, the United States led the first of what would be two military expeditions against Iraq. The first expedition, Operation *Desert Storm*, involved a coalition of many allies, but relied on the U.S.'s overwhelming military power to drive Saddam's forces from Kuwait. However, in a fateful decision of unexpected consequence for both Saddam's Iraq and his own son George, Bush opted not to send U.S. forces into Iraq itself. For the next twelve years, Iraq was throttled by further, more limited military strikes as well as crippling, arguably catastrophic economic sanctions.

Manipulating popular outrage, paranoia, and misdirected thirst for revenge in the wake of the "9/11" (11 September 2001) al-Qaeda terror attacks on New York and Washington, D.C., and with the robust political and military support of British Prime Minister Tony Blair, in March 2003 President George W. Bush set in motion the second military expedition against Iraq. With it came the "shock and awe" of the full-scale military invasion and subsequent occupation of Iraq by vastly superior American and British forces supplemented by smaller contingents furnished by countries of the so-called "coalition of the willing." The declared purpose of the grandiosely, yet unprophetically, named Operation *Iraqi Freedom* was to liberate the Iraqi people by forcing "regime change." The coalition forces quickly ousted and later captured Saddam, trapped and killed his two sons, and installed an American proconsul to administer the occupation of Iraq. The years that followed were marked by violent insurgency, resistance to foreign occupation, and civil war, as well as the crafting of a new constitution for Iraq, the electing of local and national officials, and the installing of a new Iraqi-led government.

What some historians have already begun to term the Iraq War of 1991–2011 officially came to an end when the last U.S. forces were withdrawn from Iraq in December 2011. With the troops home, the erstwhile invaders have begun to thrust Iraq deep down their collective memory hole. Except for that slim portion of their populaces whose lives were directly affected by the military adventure, as either combatants or members of combatants' families, Iraq matters little to them. In that sense, things have come full circle, back to 1990, before Saddam Hussein launched his invasion of Kuwait.

Except that Iraq still does matter. And long from now, whether a unitary state named "Iraq" endures or not, it will continue to matter. One of the purposes of this book is to explain why. To do that means reaching far back into Iraq's past, to when there was no "Iraq." In fact, the "Iraq" part of Iraq's history is but a small, late contributor to why Iraq is important to all of us in the West today and why it has been important to Western civilization for thousands of years.

When American and British soldiers marched off to fight in Iraq in 2003, their ears rang with rousing exhortations, and they arrived with lofty expectations. They came as standard-bearers of self-proclaimed great countries, cradles of liberty, freedom, and democracy, countries that were the embodiment of "good" and "civilization." Their assigned mission was to liberate an enslaved nation, to pierce the gloom and lift the fortunes of people who had become collectively shrink-wrapped in tyranny, oppression, poverty, even barbarism. Some among the American soldiers, at least, believed that their mission was of an even higher order: to fight as warriors in a new crusade, one sanctioned by divine purpose, for they had been told from childhood that their country and its purposes and projects were exceptional and unconditionally blessed by God Almighty.

Once in Iraq, they were confronted with a largely barren and bleak landscape blistered by intense heat and seared by sandstorms. Its inhabitants struggled to survive under a dilapidated infrastructure, their cities and towns fouled with pools of open sewage. Much of this was the consequence of the war twelve years earlier and the economic sanctions that had followed. Many of the soldiers chose to lump together these miserable Iraqis as "Arabs" (or perhaps "A-rabs"), or as "rag-heads," "towel-heads," "Ali Babas," "hajjis," or "sand niggers" – monikers they might have picked up from veterans of the 1991 *Desert Storm* expedition. Most of them assumed that Iraqis were all Muslims – and thereby, in the eyes of some, devotees of a false, not truly civilized religion that preached fanaticism and instilled terrorist inclinations in its practitioners. And to compound the "otherness" of the Iraqis, their commander-in-chief had assured them – after the Central Intelligence Agency had assured him – that there was indisputable, "slam-dunk" proof that these fanatics possessed "weapons of mass destruction" that Saddam Hussein had been stockpiling for years and that they would soon discover and destroy, thereby safeguarding the welfare of their own country and all the world's civilized peoples.

Spurred thus by certainty of the righteousness of their mission, these soldiers did quickly defeat the Iraqi military – the mission was accomplished. Yet, soon after the beginning of their occupation of Iraq, many were astonished that the reportedly backward, impoverished Iraqi people, so greatly in need of the blessings of the freedom and democracy the soldiers had come to bestow, were becoming ungrateful, even hostile, to their liberators.

Perhaps the soldiers' teachers in school or Bible camp, or the television programs they'd viewed on the National Geographic Channel, or the Discovery Channel, or the BBC, had imparted to them some idea of what Iraq was like. They may have received some superficial, romanticized notion of Iraq as an exotic, biblical place that still had some old ruins, a place where once upon a time there had been some really ancient civilizations that were now completely dead and long forgotten except by ivory-towered historians or maybe in some goofy animated feature from Disney or a grainy documentary on YouTube. Why should anyone care about this stuff now? For that matter, why should Iraqis care?

Imagine, then, how astonished these liberators might have felt if they'd known that the sullen "hajjis" staring at the Humvees and Bradley Fighting Vehicles patrolling their streets felt richly entitled to see themselves, and not the Westerners, as the more truly civilized people. In 2003 many Iraqis were well aware – and had in fact been purposefully reminded in the time of Saddam Hussein – that they were the heirs of great civilizations that were incomparably older than that of this newest bunch of occupiers. Moreover, their long history featured a diversity, a profound richness and intricacy, a continuity, and a longevity of culture, literature, and religious expression that these occupiers could scarcely hope to comprehend or to appreciate. These newest invaders were but the latest in a long series of intruders who had punctuated the millennia of their history since antiquity but who had almost always been subsumed into the land's long-established populations and had ended up embracing and enriching its ancient traditions.

Like the invaders of centuries past, these new arrivals had been enticed by much the same thing: the wealth, and the resulting power, they might gain from control of Iraq's natural resources and geographical situation, especially when these were harnessed to the industriousness and ingenuity of Iraq's people. For thousands of years, that wealth had been derived mostly from two sources: the immense harvests yielded by

5

the irrigated floodplain of the two great rivers that traversed the land – the Tigris and the Euphrates – and the far-flung, hugely lucrative commerce for which Iraq had long been both a crossroads and a terminus. In more recent times, invaders had come in quest of the power to be gained from another resource – Iraq's vast underground deposits of oil. Thus, Iraq's natural bounties had often been a curse. They attracted would-be conquerors like a magnet; they led greedy rulers, both indigenous and alien, to over-reach in their efforts to maximize agricultural wealth, which led to ruin; and in recent decades the wealth derived from oil had been used by dictators to mollify a sometimes restive population, which had retarded political development and social progress.

Yet, that natural bounty had also been the engine that had repeatedly propelled Iraq to pinnacles of political power, social and cultural sophistication, and scientific and technological advance, as well as territorial conquest and imperial glory. The Anglo-American invaders of 2003 could take justifiable pride in their home countries' histories of democracy and human rights. Yet, democratic values and the rule of law had hardly been strangers to Iraq's history.[1] The Iraqi people dwell in a landscape redolent with reminders that their land was the cradle of civilization: where human society's first cities, scripts, and literature arose; where principles of governance by established law first took root, long before England's Magna Carta or the United States' Constitution; and where the world's earliest empires had their genesis, long before Britannia ruled the waves or the American intelligentsia wrote of a Pax Americana or the "end of history."

Those soldiers who had been raised in the monotheistic traditions of Judaism and Christianity might have been surprised to learn that they had been sent to fight in a land that had once nurtured the largest and most prosperous Jewish community in the Middle East, with roots extending at least as early as the sixth century BCE. Ancient Christian communities had thrived there as well, with roots and traditions much closer to the customs of the time of Jesus than were those of their

Presbyterian, Baptist, Anglican, or Roman Catholic congregations back home. Those relatively few soldiers among them who were familiar with or adherents of the latest of the great monotheistic traditions, Islam, recognized immediately that they had been deployed to a predominantly Muslim land. But they may not have known that Iraq had once been the heart of a great Muslim-ruled empire whose emperor, the caliph in Baghdad, was recognized as the sovereign of a vast domain that stretched from Iran in the east, across Egypt and North Africa, to Spain in the west. The commanders of troops deployed to Iraq's southern regions or around Baghdad may have informed those troops that many of the Iraqis they would encounter were a type of Muslim called Shi'ites, but they likely would neither have known nor have appreciated that Iraq is the heart of Shi'ism or that the hallowed resting places of Shi'ism's greatest saints are located there.

Those soldiers who felt more at ease in a secular humanist tradition – or had heard of or seen movies about some of the popular tales about the Middle East – might have heard of Baghdad as the storybook setting of *The Thousand and One Nights*, or might at least have heard of characters like Sindbad, Aladdin, and Ali Baba. But they may not have known that the celebrated Arab caliph Harun ar-Rashid, whose court in Baghdad is the setting of many of those stories, had presided over a flowering of commerce, the arts, and architecture at a time when London and Paris were relatively backward towns mired in squalor. Nor might they have known that the caliphs at Baghdad had been patrons of tremendous scientific advance and intellectual ferment at a time when the founding of the universities at Oxford and Cambridge was still centuries in the future, or that when the scholars of those esteemed universities and their colleagues elsewhere in Europe made their great advances in knowledge they were building on foundations already laid with the help of Arab and Persian scientists and translators who had preserved the learning of the ancient Greeks and Romans. Iraq, they would have been surprised to learn, was a wellspring of the

Renaissance and may justifiably be regarded as a birthplace of modern "Western civilization."

Finally, whatever their lack of awareness of Iraq's brilliant past and its contributions to civilization, these soldiers were to learn almost immediately upon arriving in Iraq that a majority of the Iraqi people share a political identity and culture that are not exclusively Iraqi, but Arab, and that as Arabs they feel an identity and affinity with Arabs throughout the Middle East. They may have also assumed that "Arabness" is a primordial element in the make-up of many Middle Eastern people. They might have been surprised to know then that the designation "Arab" had long been a pejorative term for a Bedouin, an uncivilized camel-riding, sheep- and goat-herding nomad. Only in the twentieth century, largely as a response to domination by foreigners both Turk and European, had there emerged a positive connotation of "Arab" as an honorable badge of ethnic identity and solidarity, and of "the Arabs" as a "nation" whom the Western powers had wrongfully fragmented after World War I, but who believed themselves to be as much entitled to political sovereignty, self-determination, and self-government as was any European or American nation. The ferocity and tenacity of the resistance that the young occupiers encountered from the Arabs of Iraq may have tipped them off to Iraq's historical role at the heart of this notion of Arab nationalism, which has pulsed in resistance to domination by European and American colonial interests since 1920.

They would have been warned about the "evil-doing" Baath Party, yet would not have known that many had embraced the Baath Party not as a tool for political domination but as a force to galvanize Arab national pride and identity and thereby help Iraq become truly independent of longstanding European influence. All too often in history, movements that have taken sail in potentially liberating and empowering political ideologies have had that sail collapsed by the failings of the individuals who led them. Just as the demise of the socialist system embraced by the revolutionary founders of the Soviet Union can be assigned to the brutality of the Communist regimes of Josef Stalin and his successors, the Arab nationalism for which Iraq was profoundly responsible was blighted by the rise of Saddam Hussein to leadership of the Baath Party. The Iraqi people have paid a devastating price for that.

In this book, we will traverse the long span of Iraq's history, from prehistoric beginnings to the early twenty-first century. But this is not intended to be a simple, superficial, chronicling romp through Iraq's history from Stone Age to Saddam. Much of my purpose here is to draw attention to Iraq's too often overlooked historical role as a cradle of seminal advances in human endeavor, and to the debts that civilization – both in the West and all over our planet – owes to Iraq's historical experience. We will focus on how Iraq's past has played a vital role in shaping the world.

My most fundamental premise here is: Iraq matters. By the end of this book, I hope to have made it abundantly evident that after more than twenty years of war against Iraq, we in the West walk away, turn the page, and consign Iraq to the category of "been there, done that," only to our own detriment. Iraq still matters *now*. Its future – especially, the struggle of its long-suffering people to overcome the devastation and chaos of recent decades – ought to matter to us all.

I will argue further, however, that examining Iraq's long history through different prisms can illuminate other themes and aspects of global history. One of those prisms casts the historical trajectories of the West, on the one hand, and Iraq, on the other, into sharp contrast. Great catastrophes not of Iraq's or Iraqis' own making have often, almost regularly, punctuated and cursed the history of Iraq, arguably much more so than the history of most of Europe, and incomparably more so than that of the United States, except perhaps from a Native American perspective. Since as far back as the third millennium BCE, Iraq has suffered disruption and at times catastrophe at the hands of alien migrants, foreign invaders, and conquerors, from mountain tribesmen sweeping into the Mesopotamian floodplain around 2250 BCE, to Alexander the Great's phalanxes in the fourth century BCE, to the Mongol Khan Hulegu's horde in 1258, to the European and American occupations from World War I to Operation *Iraqi Freedom*. This millennia-long history of recurring invasion and devastation represents repeated strikings at the lure that Iraq's native resources have dangled before conquerors' eyes. Yet, these same resources have made Iraq the cradle of great civilizations. From the Sumerians and Babylonians of ancient Mesopotamia to the Arabs and Kurds of present-day Iraq, many peoples have taken their illustrious, even glorious, though often doomed, turn in rocking that cradle.

1

PLACES, PEOPLES, POTENTIALS
The Enduring Foundations of Life in Iraq

I N HIS BESTSELLING BOOK, *Guns, Germs, and Steel,* Jared Diamond posited that the rise of the Western European nations was deter-mined by their peculiar advantages of geography, climate, and resource availability. Similarly, the respected French historian Fernand Braudel and others of what became known as the Annales school of historical thought believed that the histories of human societies were constrained by underlying long-term structures of geography and climate, all of which tended to narrow the options available to human societies as they developed their specific political and social-economic systems. This kind of approach to history smacks of geographical determinism, and most modern historians have tended to be a bit wary of it. Nonetheless, it seems safe to say that the distinctive geography and relatively limited natural resources of the region corresponding to modern-day Iraq have been crucial in shaping its history and civilization, from antiquity to the present day. Therefore, an understanding of the possibilities created, and the constraints imposed, by aspects of Iraq's physical and human geography is essential if we are to navigate the deeper currents that have flowed throughout Iraq's history.

My use of a hydrological metaphor here is intentional. The first point to be made about Iraq's geography has to do with the names applied to the country today and in the past. Before about 1920 there was no country called Iraq. However, the name "Iraq" – perhaps derived from the Persian word *eragh*, or "lowland," which characterizes the floodplain and marshes of the lower Tigris–Euphrates basin – had been applied to the region historically. In traditional Arab nomenclature for the geography of the Middle East, the region was referred to as *bilad al-Iraq* (land of the river banks), in contrast to *bilad al-Sham* (land of the north, or Syria) and *bilad al-Yaman* (land of the south, or the Arabian Peninsula).[1] For reasons we will explore later, an internationally recognized country designated "Iraq" was created a few years after the end of World War I under the auspices of the new League of Nations, but mainly at the instigation of Great Britain and France, the European powers that by 1918 had defeated the Ottoman empire, which had ruled the region since the sixteenth century. Before the creation of the modern country of Iraq, the region had been referred to by a number of geographical names that reflected the languages of the many peoples who had occupied or conquered the region. But since the era of classical Greco-Roman antiquity, Europeans had customarily referred to the region as "Mesopotamia" – an ancient Greek term meaning the land "between the rivers." Those two rivers are the Tigris, to the east, and the Euphrates, to the west. Both of them originate in the mountains of Anatolia – what is today Turkey – from which they flow south. Today, they conjoin in southern Iraq into a single watercourse, the Shatt al-Arab, which then flows into the Persian (or, as preferred by many in the Arab world, Arabian) Gulf. In antiquity, the two rivers flowed separately into the Gulf. Broadly defined, Mesopotamia is both more and less than the area defined by the borders of modern Iraq. As the land between these two rivers, it includes neither the western desert of modern Iraq nor the Zagros Mountains and their foothills to the east. But Mesopotamia extends on its northern and northwestern boundaries well outside the area of what is today Iraq, into western Syria and southern Turkey, while in the south the lowlands of southern Mesopotamia merge into the region of Khuzistan, in southwestern Iran, east of the Tigris.

To extend our hydrological metaphor, we can navigate the currents of Mesopotamia's history from as early as about 4000 BCE. As the following chapters illustrate, the continuing flow of that history is dominated largely by the hard-won but enduring successes of human beings in harnessing the potentials that the Tigris and Euphrates bestowed.

We can organize a discussion of Iraq's physical geography and its impact on Iraq's history by concentrating on a few themes. First, the Tigris and Euphrates rivers and their floodplain have been central to Iraq's history. Second, Iraq has a limited and uneven distribution of raw materials and natural resources, which has had major consequences for Iraq's history. Finally, the region has historically been relatively accessible, and thus vulnerable, to invaders or migrants from the bordering uplands and deserts, and from areas much more distant.

THE "LAND BETWEEN THE RIVERS"

Perhaps the most memorable sentence left to us by the Greek historian Herodotus, the so-called "father of history," is his marvelously succinct description of the land of Egypt: "the river's gift." The river, of course, was the Nile. However, he might equally have described Mesopotamia, especially its southern extension, as "the rivers' gift," for none of the achievements chalked up by Iraq's ancient civilizations – not to mention those of its later Arab conquerors and their successors ruling from Baghdad – could have been made without the gift of the irrigation waters provided by the Tigris and the Euphrates. Irrigation made life possible. Without it, southern Iraq could never have supported a Baghdad, or a Babylon, or even a small town. Parts of northern and northwestern Iraq, from around the latitude of the modern city of Samarra northward, and especially in the piedmont and mountainous regions near and east of the Tigris, receive enough annual precipitation to sustain agriculture. Fifty-some years ago American archaeologists unearthed some of Iraq's earliest farming villages, dating as early as 6000 BCE, in the mountain foothill regions of northern Iraq (today's Kurdish region), where the rainfall was adequate for what has been ever since a precarious agricultural economy. Southern Iraq, on the other hand, does not receive enough rainfall to support farming, nor, since the beginning of Iraq's history, has it ever done. One of the most remarkable achievements of Iraq's Neolithic inhabitants occurred around 5500 BCE, in the region of what is now Samarra along the Tigris, when enterprising farmers, evidently hoping, or desperate, to expand their settlements southward into an area where rainfall was only marginally sufficient for agriculture, began to experiment with digging small-scale trenches to channel water from the Tigris to their fields. We must count these simple farmers among the most important pioneers in human history, for though such small-scale, essentially local systems would continue to be used along the rivers for millennia, their descendants would develop their innovations into large-scale irrigation that would allow southern Iraq to become, as the esteemed archaeologist Robert M. Adams beautifully phrased it, the "heartland of cities" – the birthplace of the world's earliest urban societies.

By about 4000 BCE, these earliest cities were starting to emerge in the marshes and floodplain of the Tigris–Euphrates river system of southern Iraq, the region that became known to later Arab populations as the "Sawad." The next chapter will elaborate in more detail the immense cultural achievements of these and later cities in the region. But it should be emphasized from the outset that those cities, their teeming populations, and their glorious successes were possible only because of the tremendous agricultural productivity of the irrigated floodplains – as well as the toil and sweat of the many thousands of teams of mostly unnamed and unsung laborers who dug and maintained the irrigation networks and plowed, sowed, and harvested the fields. The many scribes (in truth, bureaucrats) who administered the great agricultural estates of the temples and palaces of ancient Iraq kept meticulous records of these teams: their overseers and numbers, the amount of land they plowed, the number of draft animals assigned to pull their plows, how much seed they sowed. Such mundane data have provided modern scholars enough information to calculate that the yields, mostly in barley and wheat, of ancient southern Mesopotamia's vast irrigated acreages compare favorably with those of the modern Midwestern United States and Canada. The harvests from these estates vastly exceeded what was needed to feed the population. The political power, the military conquests, the imperial bureaucracy, the temple–palace–mosque-building of Mesopotamian rulers from earliest times until the bounty of oil could be harvested in the twentieth century – all of this was predicated on the rulers' ability to control and spend the vast agricultural surplus that the Tigris and Euphrates made possible.

The rivers' blessings, however, could also become the rivers' curse. The curse sometimes sprang from what Iraq's early inhabitants might have perceived as the rivers' own fickleness – or perhaps as the anger of the gods or God who dictated the rivers' behavior. Of the two rivers, the Tigris tends to have a deeper bed and therefore flows faster, making it less usable for early irrigation technology. The Euphrates, on the other hand, tends to have a shallower bed and thus flows more slowly. This made it more easily tapped for irrigation, but it also gives it a greater propensity to meander or even shift its bed to a new course. This in turn brought the possibility that communities that had sited themselves close to the river would find themselves deprived of access to the watercourse that had sustained them, and thus forced to abandon their settlement and relocate, with all the attendant suffering. The slow current of the irrigation channels that were dug off from the rivers also exacerbated the destructive effects of the water-borne silt that was constantly being deposited in the channels' beds. Preventing these channels from clogging required regular dredging operations, involving thousands of man-hours of back-breaking labor. Historically, rulers who neglected this task – or were prevented by circumstances from attending to it properly – sapped the wealth-producing potential of the irrigation system and, with it, the ruler's own power and their ability to withstand external threats.

A ruler might also unwittingly diminish his power by trying to extract too much wealth from the land he controlled. In traditional agricultural systems, those who manage land know that it must be allowed to lie fallow on a regular basis so that it can be recharged with nutrients and renew its fertility. In irrigation regimes such as that in southern Iraq's floodplain, this also entails not irrigating that land in order to prevent it getting saturated. Over-irrigation, on the other hand, can raise the level of the underlying ground water high enough for the salts in the soil to leach upwards through capillary action. The fields then become encrusted with salt – "salinization" – which over time renders them useless for cultivation. In modern times, farmers have been able to make use of motor-powered pumps to rid the fields of excess water and thereby deter salinization. Pre-modern farmers – and pre-modern rulers of Iraq – had no access to such technology. From as early as 2000 BCE, we find evidence of declining grain yields that probably were caused by salinization resulting from over-irrigation and failure to let the land lie fallow.[2] This problem recurred regularly down to the modern era, with often serious consequences for food production and rulers' power.

As I have indicated, the tendency of rivers and irrigation channels to become clogged with silt required persistent managing throughout Iraq's history in order to maintain productivity. Such silt deposition, over time, would also raise the level of the channels significantly higher than that of the surrounding fields. Those fields – and the settlements they supported – were then protected from the rivers' force only by the levees of heaped-up soil along the sides of the channels.

Of the ancient dwellers whose cities and towns clung to the rivers and channels that coursed through the floodplain, the vast majority never saw – perhaps never even knew of – the mountains from which the two great rivers flowed. Nor would they have seen the snows that blanketed the mountains in the winter, only to melt as winter broke, engorging the rivers as they coursed inexorably toward the floodplain. But when those mountain waters arrived in the spring they could do so with tremendous force that breached the levees along the irrigation channels, a fearsomeness the pre-modern inhabitants of the floodplain might easily ascribe to the anger of fickle, inexplicably vengeful gods. For the ancient Egyptians, the annual summer flooding of the Nile brought the promise of life and abundance – the resurrection of the land. For the people of ancient Iraq, the spring floods brought the ruin of their fields and the destruction of their settlements. One of the recurring themes in the literature of ancient Mesopotamia is that of a Great Flood sent by the gods to devastate the earth and punish humankind. Most schoolchildren in Europe and America are taught the story of Noah, whom God commanded to build a great ship (the "ark") and who, in it, was able to ride out the Great Flood that God sent to punish humankind. How many of them are told that that story was borrowed by the biblical writers from ancient Mesopotamian precursors? One of them, the *Epic of Gilgamesh*, relates the story of a man named Utnapishtim, who tells Gilgamesh of the Great Flood that Enlil, the most powerful god of early Mesopotamia, sent to destroy evil humankind. Utnapishtim and his family were warned by a friendlier god and rode out the Flood in a boat that the god told Utnapishtim to build. Although some have speculated that the origins of these tales of a Great Flood lie in the cataclysmic flooding of the Black Sea during a prehistoric episode of global warming as the last Ice Age ended, most scholars believe that these stories were inspired by ancient memories of the disastrous spring floods that "covered the earth," as far as the early dwellers in the Tigris–Euphrates floodplain were concerned.

On balance, though, the rivers' assets have far outweighed their liabilities. The rivers and the major irrigation channels that branched from them were crucial arteries of transport and communication in an era when large-scale commerce and transport were much more profitable and efficient – and therefore more frequently used – than was transport by land. The wealth and sophistication of ancient and classical Arab Iraq owed much to the trade that was carried along Iraq's waterways. Nonetheless, irrigation water and agricultural fertility constituted the greatest, most enduring blessings to Iraq from the Tigris and Euphrates – blessings that made Iraq a cradle of ancient cities yet also cursed it with an abundance that, over the millennia, attracted the unwanted attentions of migrants and conquerors.

DISTRIBUTION OF RAW MATERIALS AND NATURAL RESOURCES

Ask anyone on the street to name Iraq's most important natural resource and, unless that person has just landed from Mars, they will respond, immediately, "Oil." Since the discovery of oil in Iraq in the early twentieth century, the West has coveted it. Now that Iraq is known to possess the second-largest proven oil reserves of any country, and tens of millions more barrels are believed to be waiting to be discovered, oil corporations are salivating at the prospect of the wealth and power that access to that oil promises to bestow. In the world of the twenty-first century, why wouldn't that be so? Oil powers much of our modern industrial machinery. Without the gasoline produced from it, modern societies throughout the world would be largely immobilized. Without the plastics produced from oil, we would be bereft of computers and many of our most common household appliances, none of us would have laptops or iPods, children would have fewer toys. Iraq should be a rich country then? Hasn't it always been so?

No. For one thing, before the invention of the internal-combustion engine in the nineteenth century, Iraq's petroleum was of minor importance economically. And after the engine had been invented and the world began to rely on it, most of the oil used to power those tanks, ships, airplanes, and automobiles came from the United States. The oil of the Middle East in general – and Iraq in particular – emerged as a significant economic consideration, and a source of new wealth for Middle Eastern countries, only after World War II. Still, the petroleum of Iraq had had its uses, well back into antiquity. Drilling for oil and pumping it to the surface were neither possible nor desirable in pre-modern times, but standing pools of bitumen could be found in the region of Iraq. Scholars have found words for petroleum products and the mention of uses of them in some of the earliest records of ancient Iraq. Among the more important was as a coating for waterproofing bricks and baskets, mats for roofing, and other utilitarian objects.

Besides the abundant river water, mud, clay, and reeds of Iraq's riverine environments, these limited surface deposits of petroleum substances were one of the few notable raw materials that Iraq possessed. Otherwise, Iraq's raw materials cupboard, at least during the pre-modern era, was pretty bare. Iraq has no major mineral deposits: no copper or tin (the components of bronze, the basic medium of tool and weapons technology in the region from ca. 3500 to almost 1000 BCE); and no iron (which after 1200 BCE replaced bronze as the most important metal of technology). During the Neolithic period, before the development of metalworking, some local stones could be flaked and chipped to produce blades, scrapers, and other implements, but even then the most highly prized raw material for chipped-stone tools, obsidian, had to be brought in from as far away as the region of modern Turkey.

Nor did Iraq possess major forests to provide the long, sturdy timbers necessary for large-scale building construction. In ancient times some trees suitable for such purposes grew in the higher elevations of the Zagros Mountains to the east and northeast of the lowland floodplains. By the end of antiquity, though, those had begun to disappear after centuries of exploitation, compounded by the effects of erosion after centuries of grazing by pastoralists' herds of sheep and goats. In any case, those resources were often difficult for the urban dwellers of the floodplain to lay their hands on, since they grew in the territory of tribal highlanders who might not be sympathetic to the lowlanders' needs. Accordingly, from very ancient times the cedars and pines of what are now Syria and Lebanon were targeted by lowland rulers for acquisition by either conquest or trade. One of the more famous stories of Gilgamesh centers on his journey with his boon companion, Enkidu, to the great cedar mountain in the far-off lands west of Mesopotamia, where the two heroes slay the fearsome monster Huwawa, the guardian of the cedar forest, before they can return in triumph with the huge timbers that they felled.

Iraq's dearth of raw materials extends to building stone, especially in the southern region where Iraq's earliest cities and civilization arose. Some local resources of stone were available and were exploited as early as the fourth millennium BCE in one of the monumental buildings in the ancient city of Uruk, Gilgamesh's hometown. But, by and large, the people of ancient southern Iraq had very little building-quality stone to work with, especially compared with the ancient Egyptians, for whom large deposits of limestone, sandstone, and granite were much more accessible. The proof of that has been apparent for thousands of years. The stone resources the Egyptians harvested to build the Great Pyramid of Khufu at Giza were right at the site, and the magnificent temples at Thebes, Edfu, and other sites in the Nile Valley demonstrate that the Egyptians were blessed with abundant resources in building stone – and knew how to use them. It is for this reason – as well as the hieroglyphic inscriptions on those stone temples and tombs – that the world never lost sight of the ancient Egyptians even long after the pharaohs had ceased to rule there.

In northern Iraq, in their capitals along the Tigris, the rulers of the ancient kingdom and empire of Assyria did have access to stone with which to decorate their palaces. When the sculpted reliefs that lined their palace corridors and the huge sculpted figures that guarded them were discovered by British and French archaeologists in the 1840s, the world was dramatically reminded that ancient Mesopotamia had spawned a civilization as grand as Egypt's. But for the most part the people of Mesopotamia/Iraq built their houses, villages, temples, and cities from the materials most readily at hand: the mud of the river banks, and the water of the rivers themselves. From at least as early as 6000 BCE, villagers in central Mesopotamia were constructing their houses from a mixture of mud, straw, and water – called "adobe" in the American southwest – that was shaped into bricks which were then dried in the sun before being used in construction. The size and shape of these bricks changed over the millennia, but they became literally the building blocks of the great civilizations of Iraq. When used in major public buildings, they were sometimes baked in kilns to improve durability. Even for the rural villagers of modern Iraq, mud brick is often the construction medium of choice. It can be made from materials readily at hand; it insulates well against the heat of Iraq's summers and the cool temperatures of its winters; and it holds up well against the rigors of the climate. However, the surfaces require periodic re-plastering, and if a mud-brick structure is not maintained regularly it will decay fairly quickly. Over the centuries, a favorite method of rebuilding mud-brick houses has been to demolish the upper courses and then use the lower courses as a foundation for rebuilding. If occupation at a village or town continues over a long time, or is abandoned and then restarted, such rebuilding results in the rising up of a mound as the level of the settlement grows ever higher relative to the surrounding area. The Arabic word for a mound that represents the remains of a human settlement is "tell." It was in such tells that the pioneering archaeologists of the nineteenth century made their spectacular discoveries.

Yet, one of the conundrums of Iraq's early history takes us back to the problem we cited earlier. How did some of the earliest, most powerful civilizations on the planet emerge and flourish in a region so bereft of natural resources? It seems logical to assume that the agricultural wealth of the region had a lot to do with it, and most scholars are agreed that in the earliest periods of Iraq's long history its local rulers were able to export grain, woolen textiles, and perhaps luxury items wrought by specialized craftsmen in return for precious and utilitarian metals and other resources from outside the region. One of the better-known examples of such exchange was discovered in the excavated remains of Kanesh, an ancient city of what is now Turkey, where written records from around 1910 to 1750 BCE document the export of gold and silver to the city of Ashur in what is now northern Iraq. Those shipments of gold and silver were paid for in part by the profits from the sale of textiles that merchants from Ashur had brought to Kanesh, a distance of some one thousand miles, on the backs of donkeys, and then sold to the locals. Even earlier, around 2400 BCE, ships from as far away as Oman and the Indus Valley in Pakistan plied the waters of the Persian Gulf and beyond to bring luxury items made of semi-precious stones like carnelian and lapis lazuli to the ruling elite of southern Mesopotamia. In the 1920s, the British archaeologist and sometime spy Leonard Woolley found hundreds of these items during his excavation of one of the most celebrated archaeological discoveries ever, the so-called Royal Cemetery of the city of Ur.

Since the beginning of history, Iraq has benefited from its location astride important trade routes linking regions as distant as China to the east and the Mediterranean world and Europe to the west. As we will see, when Baghdad began to emerge as the capital of the Arab empire in the eighth century, its location at the nexus of those routes attracted tremendous wealth, derived from international commerce, that made the courts of the Arab caliphs centers of luxury and conspicuous consumption, as well as a magnet for artists, poets, and philosophers. In modern times, Iraq's location at the major source of the world's most lucrative commodity – petroleum – for a few decades allowed its rulers to spend profusely on infrastructure, educational, and medical projects that brought the country to the brink of First World status.

IRAQ'S ACCESSIBILITY AND VULNERABILITY TO EXTERNAL FORCES

Throughout its long history, Mesopotamia/Iraq has suffered repeated episodes of invasion or migration by outsiders, some (like the Mongols) more violent than others, some (like the mountain tribesmen known as Gutians, of the late third millennium BCE) destined to be an ephemeral presence, others (like the Arab armies bearing the new faith of Islam from the Arabian Peninsula in the seventh century CE) destined to dominate the region for centuries. One geographical reason for Iraq's vulnerability to such attacks is that the country's most densely populated areas, which have historically been along the Tigris and Euphrates rivers, have no imposing geographical deterrents to protect them and are relatively easy to invade. Egypt, by contrast, is relatively well buffered in the Nile Valley. If we take the Tigris River in northern Iraq as a starting point and then trace a rough circle clockwise around the modern borders of Iraq, we can spot a number of quarters from which Iraq has been exposed to often hostile, unwelcome foreigners and from which over at least five thousand years a variety of threats have come.

East of the Tigris, in the area of the modern border between Iraq and Iran, lie the foothills and more elevated zones of the Zagros Mountains. Historically, the rain-fed valleys of the Zagros uplands have sheltered small "tribal" villages of hardy farmers as well as pastoral herders of sheep and goats. An enduring theme in the literature of Iraq has been the disdain with which the urbane city-dwellers of the floodplain have treated the bumpkin Zagros hill-people and the desert herders. Yet, from earliest history to recent times, the Zagros hill-people have posed a threat to the great kingdoms and states ruled from the urban capitals in the Mesopotamian floodplain. Around 2200 BCE, the attacks of the Gutians helped bring down the kings of Agade, the capital, not far from modern Baghdad, of what was arguably the world's earliest empire. Almost four thousand years later, the Kurds who came to inhabit this region resisted rule from Baghdad, and even today they are bent on maintaining their autonomy from the central government and perhaps establishing an independent state.

Proceeding southward from the land of the Gutians/Kurds, to what is now southwestern Iran, we come to the region of Khuzistan, extending east from the southernmost portion of the Tigris–Euphrates floodplain. Between 1980 and 1988 this region was the scene of brutal combat between the invading armies of Saddam Hussein and the forces of the Islamic Republic of Iran. As early as 3000 BCE, it was dominated by Susa, a great city that rivalled those of ancient Iraq. In the centuries to follow, this region would fall under the control of a powerful Iranian kingdom called Elam, one of whose kings invaded southern Mesopotamia around 2000 BCE, destroyed its great capital city of Ur, and carried off Ur's emperor into captivity and oblivion. Until Elam's power was snuffed out by the might of the Assyrian rulers of Mesopotamia during the mid-seventh century BCE, its kings frequently tormented the kings of ancient Iraq. When Elam fell, a new threat emerged from this quarter in the person of Cyrus, king of the Persians. Tension continued in this region of Iraq centuries later when Ottoman domination there was contested by the Safavid rulers of Iran. Throughout Iraq's history, its exposure to its southeast has often brought tension and occasionally calamity.

At the southern end of Iraq lies the Persian Gulf, into which the Tigris and Euphrates today flow via the Shatt al-Arab, and flowed separately in ancient times. Near the head of the Gulf, along the waterways, lie extensive marshlands. For millennia, these marshlands have supported small villages of tribal people – the "Marsh Arabs" – who continue to fish, raise water buffalo, and farm on a small scale. The reed houses (*mudhifs*) and boats they use are depicted in artwork dating as early as 3000 BCE. Around 1500 BCE there emerged in this area a mini-state, the Sealands kingdom, whose rulers contended with the kings of Babylon farther upstream. In the eighth and seventh centuries BCE, the marshlands were the seat of uprisings against the Assyrian empire that dominated the era, and among the sculpted stone reliefs that decorate the walls of the Assyrian kings' palaces are scenes of rebels hiding in the marshes. As recently as 1991, the southern marshes sheltered rebels against a powerful ruler: the Arab Shia of Iraq's south when they rose up against Saddam Hussein.

Beyond the marshlands lies the open water of the Persian Gulf. From this quarter have come the invasions that have been most devastating in Iraq's recent history: most recently, the invasion of 2003 and subsequent occupation of Iraq; before that, the 1991 invasion (Operation *Desert Storm*) authorized by the United Nations and led by the U.S.; and before that, in 1914, the British invasion during World War I. But in the preceding centuries, as far back as perhaps 3000 BCE, the Persian Gulf (known in ancient Mesopotamia as the "Lower Sea") was the conduit for traders whose boats brought to the region valuable commodities and luxury goods from as far away as India and China.

To the southwest, west, and northwest of the Tigris–Euphrates floodplain lies the dry, barren expanse of the great Syrian–Arabian desert, the province of nomadic groups who have eked out a living by moving their herds to available water and pasturage. Given its lack of water and cultivable land, this region has never been able to support a major state or kingdom that could threaten the cities and states centered in the floodplain. Nonetheless, at times, raids and tribal migrations emanating from the Arabian peninsula have coursed through it, with major impact on Iraq's history.

THE PEOPLES AND SOCIAL PATTERNS OF IRAQ

Any inventory of a country's resources and potential must list at the top the histories, abilities, and contributions of its peoples, in all their diversity. To catalogue exhaustively all aspects of Iraq's diversity in this regard is too much to attempt in a work such as this. But if we examine even the broader categories, the richness and complexity of Iraq's society become clear. Much has been the product of historical change, migrants and invaders having entered Iraq over the course of thousands of years, often destroying, but just as often settling down and interacting dynamically and fruitfully with the peoples who arrived and settled before them.

Tensions between these groups have pivoted around their different ways of life, which we can define largely on the basis of how groups have sustained themselves and survived – in other words, how they have been organized to feed and shelter themselves.

Anthropologists have identified four basic modes of life that human societies in general have practiced. The earliest were hunter-gatherers, who foraged across the landscape to harvest its naturally occurring food resources – hunting wild animals and gathering wild plants such as nuts, berries, and the wild ancestors of grasses such as wheat and barley. In the 1950s, archaeologists recovered substantial evidence of such people in northern Iraq at a site called Shanidar Cave; much more evidence has been found since. The hunter-gatherer lifestyle was the only way of life that early humans practiced anywhere until around 10,000 BCE, when, starting in the region of modern-day Israel/Palestine and Syria and then in Turkey, Iran, and northern Iraq, some hunter-gatherers, probably faced with a shrinking supply of wild foodstuffs as the region's climate changed after the last Ice Age, began to experiment with planting and cultivating grain and taming animals like sheep and goats – and later pigs and cattle. Over the next few thousand years, there thus emerged the second mode of life: farming groups living in permanently occupied villages, which now spread widely throughout the Middle East. In Iraq, the foothills of the Zagros and Taurus Mountains and the northern plains around the Tigris and Euphrates tended to get enough annual rainfall to support farming. Thus, Iraq became one of the planet's earliest centers of agriculture – one of the first of what would become innumerable contributions of Iraq's people to global civilization.

In time, the village farmers seem to have squeezed out or assimilated the hunter-gatherers, although the farmers continued to avail themselves of wild plants and animals as food sources. By about 6000 BCE, village farmers were moving southward into the Tigris–Euphrates floodplain, where, as we have seen, they became some of the first people ever to devise irrigation technology. By about 4000 BCE, farming villages had spread to most of the areas in Iraq where they are still found today. Until quite recently, the bulk of Iraq's population – especially in the north – was made up of the hard-working inhabitants of these farming villages.

But perhaps two thousand years before then a third mode of life had begun to emerge in Iraq, when some groups began to develop the lifestyle we refer to as "pastoral nomadism," which is based principally on raising herds of what by 6000 BCE human intervention had transformed from wild into domesticated sheep and goats. These groups could only ensure enough food for their livestock by moving them – and moving themselves as well, by foot, by donkey, or, later, by horse – to areas where they could find food according to the season. In summer, this meant taking their herds to the mountain regions and setting up tent camps. In winter, they pulled up stakes, packed their tents, and brought their herds from the highland areas back down to the lowlands.

Here, though, they came into contact with the farming villages. Traditionally, historians and travel writers have made much of the conflict between the "desert and the sown" – and there is some basis for this. Some of the earliest literature from ancient Iraq reveals the disgust that settled peoples felt for the nomads' way of life. Also, nomads' raiding of villages has been a fact of Middle Eastern life for millennia. However, without the products and services that nomads have provided farmers, and vice versa, over those millennia, neither group could have prospered as well as it did. Modern scholars who have researched this relationship tend to focus more on the symbiosis and synergy between the groups, rather than the tensions. From their flocks of sheep and goats, the nomads produced – and provided for the villagers – wool, hides, meat, and milk products to enrich their diets and their lifestyle. The villagers could provide grain and other agricultural products to fill out the nomads' diet. Perhaps more important for the nomads, the villagers permitted them to graze their animals on the stubble of the harvested fields. The farmers got in return the fertilizing of their fields with manure from the livestock. These grazing rights have been important for the nomads, but disputes over such rights between nomads and farmers – or between different nomad groups – have also been a source of tension and conflict.

When tensions fester and conflict erupts within or between these groups, the basic principles by which they have traditionally organized to protect themselves, preserve their prerogatives, and seek justice have by and large been linked to ties of kinship – simply put, "blood ties" or, in journalistic vernacular, the "tribes." The origins of Iraq's many tribes, their histories, and their interrelationships have been fodder for reams of academic studies, and a brief examination can in no way do justice to the complexities and subtleties of those subjects. The most basic concept underlying the idea of the "tribe" is kinship – and, more specifically, shared descent (whether real or imputed) from a common male ancestor, whose existence can sometimes be difficult to validate historically, but with whose name his "descendants" strongly identify. In some historical periods, tribes have come together in "confederations," but on a general, more mundane level, it is as members of the subgroups of the tribe – the "clan" and, below that, the "family" – that rural and pastoral people, and their descendants who have migrated to Iraq's cities, have organized their lives. It is not uncommon to find that most of the inhabitants of a village or the members of a nomad camp-group belong to the same extended family, or to no more than a few of them. In these settings, the need to preserve and protect the solidarity of the kinship group, from family to clan to tribe, is perhaps the single most important social value. Intimately bound up with that need are many other traditional values, among them, honor, manly courage, female sexual virtue, hospitality to strangers, and the obligation to avenge an insult to the group – be it the killing or bodily injury of a member of the group, or the sullying of the group's sexual honor.

One owes one's primary and most abiding loyalty to the blood group –
family, clan, and tribe.

The primacy of that loyalty to the blood group, however, gave birth to
one of the most persistent social and political tensions to have dominated
Iraq's history since the dawning of civilization there. In many ways the
dawning of civilization was the chief cause of that tension, because with
it came the dawn of the first cities: it was in southern Iraq that the first
cities on our planet appeared, starting around 4000 BCE.

With those first cities emerged the last of the anthropologists' four
modes of life: the city-dwellers. The city-dwellers also invented the
planet's first writing. It is mostly from the many centuries of written
records they have produced that historians have recreated Iraq's long
history. But those records tend to reflect and to favor, sometimes
almost exclusively, the interests, attitudes, and perspectives of those
city-dwellers. So their emergence had the effect of shoving the villagers
and nomads to the margins of our historical radar screen.

By about 2700 BCE, ancient Iraq's first cities also became the seats
of power of some of our planet's first kings. One of the most necessary
tasks that confronted those first kings has remained one of the most
difficult for all of Iraq's rulers ever since – to establish and enforce
the dominion of the city-based "state" over the inhabitants of the surrounding countryside. The people of the countryside had long been
accustomed to directing their loyalty to, and looking for leadership
from, local authority as embodied in the family, the clan, and the tribe.
Therein lay a tension that has bedeviled Iraq's history from the very
start. That tension persists even to the present day, as the government
in Baghdad tries to chart a way forward in a country where tribal and
blood ties have long dominated social relations.

The invention of writing in Iraq's first cities also makes it possible
for us to speak of the ethnic and linguistic complexity of Iraq's people
as early as 3000 BCE, and perhaps earlier. Today, accounts of current
events in Iraq are couched in very broad ethnic and religious categories.

Journalists and commentators tend to lump Iraqis into general categories such as Shi'ite Arabs, Sunni Arabs, and Kurds. The minority Turkmen population and, until recently, Yazidis and Mandaeans have received only occasional mention. Iranians, including Persians, are also mentioned as a presence in Iraq, often as outsiders whom some Iraqis perceive as a threat.

As noted earlier, people moving westward from Iran into Iraq have had a major impact on Iraq's history, and those Iranians whom we classify as Persians have played a crucial role in shaping Iraq's history. Most anthropologists today dismiss both the concept and the category of "race" as scientifically useless, but even a few decades ago it was common for experts to expound upon the different "races" of Iraq. More useful is a categorization according to ethnic group, as defined largely by the group's use of a common language and sharing of some important aspects of culture. Using these criteria, the largest group in Iraq's modern population can be identified as the Arabs, largely because they speak the Arabic language, which is the most widely spoken language in the family of languages known as Semitic. Arabs are the dominant ethno-linguistic group across the Middle East today, but from a linguistic standpoint colloquial Iraqi Arabic is markedly different from the Arabic dialect spoken in, say, Egypt. It would be a mistake to assume – as all too many people do – that the Arabs of Iraq are all descended from migrants from what is now Saudi Arabia. People from the Arabian Peninsula were indeed migrating into what is now Iraq by the later centuries BCE. The Arabs who invaded the region as part of the Muslim conquest beginning in the mid-seventh century CE surely changed its demography. But the Arabs of today's Iraq also include descendants of many earlier ethnic groups who came before them but who over the centuries were assimilated into the "Arab" population through their adoption of the Arabic language and other aspects of Arabic culture. Some of those predecessors spoke Semitic languages related to Arabic – among them, the Babylonians and Assyrians, who spoke a language called Akkadian, as well as the Arameans, whose language is still used today in some remote areas of northern Iraq, principally as part of the liturgy of the very old Christian communities there. Some of those predecessors – like the Sumerians, Hurrians, and Kassites, whose languages fell out of use millennia ago – spoke languages completely unrelated to the Semitic language family. In today's Iraq, Arabs comprise perhaps seventy percent of the population. The lack of any recent systematic census makes it impossible to be more precise.

The second-largest component of Iraq's population consists of the Kurds. Kurdish belongs to the Indo-European language family, which means it is related to English, French, and other modern European languages , as well as to Persian (Farsi), the dominant language of Iran. The date of the earliest arrival of the Kurds in Iraq remains a matter of debate, but the Kurds have traditionally linked themselves to the ancient people known as the Medes, who along with the Persians entered and began to dominate Iran sometime around 1000 BCE. The Kurds of Iraq have always been most closely linked to the Zagros Mountain regions of northeastern Iraq, where they have supported themselves as farmers, herders, and townspeople and have insisted on governing themselves according to their own customs and family structures. Historically, the Kurds have fiercely defended their separateness and have strived for autonomy and self-government, often with considerable success. The region of dominant Kurdish population – which some refer to as "Kurdistan" – includes not only this portion of Iraq but also contiguous areas in southeastern modern Turkey, northwestern Iran, and northeastern Syria. The various regimes that historically have ruled all of these modern countries have tended to regard the Kurds as a troublesome minority against whom they have often resorted to persecution and violence to impose their control and quell Kurdish aspirations to self-rule. Since the destruction of Saddam Hussein's regime, which resorted to extreme measures to subjugate them in the late 1980s and early 1990s, the Kurds have been participating in the Iraqi government while insisting on a great deal of political and economic autonomy. Many of them nurture hope for a truly independent Kurdistan.

Although the Kurds have generally been content in their mountain strongholds, the third-largest ethnic minority in Iraq at one time produced rulers who were able to extend their sway throughout the Middle East as well as Central Asia. The Turks first blip onto the historical radar as horse-riding nomads from Central Asia. They were imported by Arab rulers into the area of Iraq in the eighth and ninth centuries CE as mercenaries and slave-soldiers highly prized for their skills and ferocity as horsemen wielding compound bows to deadly effect. By the mid-eleventh century, Turkish tribal armies who came to be identified by the name of one of their great khans (or chieftains), Seljuk, swept into Iraq and across much of the Middle East. After annihilating a Byzantine army in Anatolia in 1071, the Seljuks established a vast though short-lived empire that dominated the Middle East until about 1100 and then hung on in Turkey for many years after. A few centuries after the Seljuk zenith, another Turkish group, likewise named for one of its great early chieftains, Osman, secured control first over northwestern Turkey, then much of southeastern Europe, and eventually most of the Middle East, including Iraq. Their Ottoman empire endured until the end of World War I. The descendants of these Turks who live in Iraq today are known as Turkoman, or Turkmen. Their language, which belongs to the Altaic family of languages, is unrelated to either Arabic or Kurdish. Although they constitute a small minority of the population, the Turkmen of Iraq retain a strong sense of ethnic identity and solidarity.

Finally, though hardly a dominant ethno-linguistic group in Iraq today, the Persians have had a profound influence on the country's history since Iraq's conquest by the great Persian empire-builder Cyrus the Great in 538 BCE. The Persians, along with the Medes, arrived in Iran around 1000 BCE and established themselves as a small kingdom in the area of Fars, in what is now southwestern Iran. In the centuries after Cyrus's conquest, Persian kings, officers, administrators, and scholars played a huge role in shaping the culture and governing of Iraq. Today, the largely Persian religious hierarchy of the modern Islamic Republic of Iran exercises great influence over many of the Shi'ite Muslims of southern Iraq.

Having broached the topic of religion, we must also recognize that Iraq's ethnic diversity is rivalled by the diversity of its religions. Today, the dominant religion among Arabs, Kurds, Turks, and Persians is Islam, but among the predominantly Muslim countries of the world, Iraq is rare in having sizeable populations of both the globally larger Sunni branch of Islam and the globally smaller Shi'a, or Shi'ite, branch. The origins of this crucial division will be examined later. Its consequences for Iraq's history have been both enduring and profound.

No census of Iraq's population has ever differentiated between its Sunni and Shi'ite citizens, but most experts agree that Iraq's Shi'ites outnumber the Sunni, comprising perhaps fifty-five to sixty percent of the total – although many Sunnis reject these numbers and assert themselves to be the larger population. Historically, Iraq also contained large populations who practiced the two other major monotheistic religions, Judaism and Christianity. A more detailed account of the origins and histories of Iraq's Jewish and Christian minorities appears below, but it is useful to note here that a large number of Jews came to Iraq from Palestine from as early as the eighth century BCE and that until only a few decades ago the Jewish community of Iraq was one of the largest and most prosperous in the world. Christian communities emerged in Mesopotamia as early as the first century CE. Down to the present day, Christians have been a vital confessional community in Iraq, although, like the Jews, their numbers have dwindled in recent decades, especially in the wake of the turmoil that beset the country following the 2003 invasion.

Muslim, Jew, and Christian are not the only pieces in the mosaic of Iraq's religious heritage. Ancient sects like the Yazidis, the Mandaeans, and the Shabaks have practiced their respective faiths in Iraq for centuries. When invading Arab tribesmen brought Islam to the area in the seventh century, the Jewish and Christian communities there were in regular and fruitful contact with another religious community, long

settled among them, whose members lived according to the moral pre-
cepts preached many centuries earlier by the Iranian teacher Zarathustra,
whom the West came to know by the Greek form of his name, Zoroaster.
Although their numbers have shrunk over the centuries, Zoroastrian
communities are still to be found in both Iraq and Iran.

Underlying all these monotheistic religions of Iraq are the intermin-
gled strata and persistent residue of thousands of years during which
the people of Iraq worshipped literally hundreds of gods and goddesses.
The origins of those many deities extend deeply into the prehistoric
past, when people often saw their only hope for prosperity, even survival, as intimately bound up with placating the myriad natural forces
that brought feast or famine, luxury or destitution. In the service of
those deities, the earliest Iraqis built cities and temples and conquered
vast empires. They also created artistic masterpieces, devised rituals
that included kernels from which later sprouted modern sciences and
technology, and composed tales and poems that continue to tantalize
and instruct us today.

All in all, the history of Iraq has been mightily influenced by Iraq's
geographical situation – a situation blessed by great agricultural and
commercial potential; constrained by the lack or uneven distribution of
resources like minerals, wood, and precipitation; and endowed with an
abundance of a resource, petroleum, today vital to the prosperity and
power of the world's industrialized nations and therefore coveted by
them. The blessings Iraq's geographical situation has bestowed have also
afflicted Iraq's history, by attracting the envy and unwanted attention
of outsiders intent on claiming those blessings for themselves. Iraq's
geographical location has also provided relatively open corridors by
which outsiders have intruded and been able to impose their control.
Yet the intruders of the past brought a rich ethnic and cultural diversity
that produced Iraq's matrix of long-enduring traditions and ways of life.

2

CRADLE OF CIVILIZATION

We the sons of Mesopotamia, land of the prophets, resting place of the holy imams, the leaders of civilization and the creators of the alphabet, the cradle of arithmetic: on our land, the first law put in place by mankind was written; in our nation, the most noble era of justice in the politics of nations was laid down; on our soil, the followers of the prophet and the saints prayed, the philosophers and the scientists theorized and the writers and poets created.

PREAMBLE TO THE
CONSTITUTION OF IRAQ, 2005

T HESE WORDS FROM IRAQ'S CONSTITUTION make it clear: with all of the strife throttling their country following the demise of Saddam Hussein, the drafters of the republic of Iraq's new constitution looked to a glorious past to find the foundations of a modern national identity and a pride upon which to rebuild a national community shattered by war, invasion, and internal violence. Now, almost ten years after the constitution was promulgated, the success of that rebuilding still hangs in the balance. But, indisputably, the evidence of Iraq's past greatness lies all around.

Among the most frequent topographical features in Iraq, and across much of the Middle East, are the earthen mounds that dot the landscape.

Some are low and of relatively small circumference; others are quite tall and cover hundreds of acres. In the Arab countries of the Middle East, including Iraq, such a mound is known as a "tell." In Iran and Turkey, the most common terms are *tepe* and *huyuk*, respectively. Each tell represents, not a natural geological formation, but the remains of a human settlement, often the result of millennia of building and rebuilding a village, or a town, or a city, with mud brick.

Some of them are still loci of human occupation. One of the most famous tells in the Middle East lies in the heart of the modern city of Erbil in northern Iraq. It contains the remains of perhaps eight thousand years of human habitation. According to some, Erbil may be the oldest continuously occupied settlement on our planet. Most tells, though, stand alone and deserted, stark reminders that no settlement, whatever its size or celebrity, is destined to last forever in the face of environmental change and the forces of history.

At last count, Iraq contained more than ten thousand tells, the vast majority of them unexcavated and at most only cursorily examined by scientific archaeologists. Unfortunately, too many of them have been plundered by the illicit excavators who have been ravaging Iraq's archaeological sites for decades and, especially after the invasion of 2003, robbing us of invaluable clues to Iraq's heritage. Luckily, though, ever since the British soldier-archaeologist Austen Henry Layard and his French contemporary Paul Emile Botta began the modern recovery of Iraq's ancient past in the 1840s, expeditions led by more or less scientific archaeologists – ironically, many of them dispatched from countries whose military forces spearheaded the 2003 invasion that led to the obliteration of so much of Iraq's ancient heritage – have been able to uncover a significant remnant of what were, in their respective eras, among the wealthiest, most powerful, and most sophisticated civilizations on the planet. Because of their discoveries, modern historians have been able to corroborate many of the Hebrew Bible's and ancient Greeks' descriptions of fabulous cities, powerful rulers, and mighty armies that conquered vast empires. We also have been able to learn that, just as the leaders of modern Iraq have asserted in their new constitution, the people of ancient Iraq were indeed "leaders of civilization" and their land was indeed the cradle of the world's first cities, as well as mathematics and astronomy, and the place where humankind's earliest-known laws were written down.

And it all began with the Sumerians...

"HISTORY BEGINS AT SUMER"

Or so, at least, thought Professor Samuel Noah Kramer, a Russian Jewish immigrant to the United States who by the mid-1950s had become one of the scholarly pioneers who made known to a wider audience the tremendous achievements of the early people of Iraq whom we know today as the Sumerians. As Kramer made clear in his books,[1] the Sumerians were responsible for some very important firsts in world history – firsts in which modern Iraqis still take pride.

Where was Sumer, and who were the Sumerians? The ancient name of their homeland is more correctly pronounced "Shumer," not "Sumer," but early on European scholars got into the habit of using the latter term "Sumer," so it is now preferred almost universally. (The name "Sumeria" is incorrect.) The Sumerians themselves were just as likely to refer to their land as simply "the land" (in the Sumerian language, *kalam*) and to themselves as "the black-headed people."

The land of ancient Sumer corresponds to the far southeast of modern Iraq, including the lower floodplain of the Tigris and Euphrates, from Basra to as far northwest as Najaf. The Sumerians' origins remain uncertain. Until fairly recently, this question was the focus of what was long called the "Sumerian Problem" – the problem being to figure out who the Sumerians were, where they came from, and whether they were the original inhabitants of this region of lower Iraq. Several scholars,

MAP 2. *Archaeological sites in Iraq*
(courtesy, the Oriental Institute of the University of Chicago)

including Kramer, believed they had migrated to Mesopotamia, perhaps from India or some other region to the east, but the modern consensus favors a more or less indigenous origin. Some of the uncertainty is tied to the Sumerian language, evidence of which first came to light as a result of pioneering archaeological discoveries made during the late nineteenth century. To this day, Sumerian has not been linked conclusively to any other known language family,[2] which makes it difficult to link the Sumerians to any known ethno-linguistic group. Moreover, it is now clear that people speaking languages other than Sumerian were living in the region early on as well. To the extent that we can equate different languages with different ethnic groups, which is by no means a straightforward assumption, we can assume that the Sumerians shared southern Iraq with other people.

By perhaps as early as 6000 BCE, the marshy area of southernmost Iraq was inhabited by people with a lifestyle similar to that of the Marsh Arabs today, hunting and fishing, as well as harvesting the marshes' vast reed thickets to provide themselves with materials for their houses and other necessities. Exactly how early those people settled there is uncertain. We are not sure how much of that area was covered by the waters of the Persian Gulf during the fifth millennium BCE or when those waters subsided enough for humans to move into the area. Recent studies[3] suggest that early villages were established on "turtleback" mounds that began to emerge as water levels in the south declined. These early settlements would have been linked to each other by boats that plied the waters from mound to mound, thereby building ties of trade and communication. Some of these settlements were probably the earliest nuclei of the cities that emerged later.

Meanwhile, another important development was taking place upstream along the Tigris, in the region of the modern and medieval city of Samarra, where millennia later the Arab conquerors of Iraq were to establish a great capital city. This region marks the northernmost extent of the floodplain. Here, rainfall was and still is insufficient to support agriculture. To overcome this challenge, early villagers devised a brilliant solution, one for which the people of Iraq even now are in their debt: they dug canals to divert the water of the Tigris to their fields. To these ancient villagers (whom archaeologists have named the "Samarrans"; we have no idea what they called themselves), the people of Mesopotamia/Iraq owe the foundations of the prosperity and achievements that are so evident throughout their history, for without the Samarrans' development of basic irrigation technology, Mesopotamia's fertile floodplains could never have supported the great cities that were soon to emerge there.

By 5000 BCE, villages were being established in the semi-marshy regions of the southern floodplain. One of them, Eridu, became revered by the later Sumerians as the most ancient of their cities – and the first city upon which the gods bestowed an institution they believed to be crucial for civilization: kingship. Around 5000 BCE though, Eridu was but a small settlement where people were making a distinctive decorated pottery that archaeologists, before they excavated at the tell of Eridu, first identified in the 1920s while excavating at a nearby site, Tell al-Ubaid. This "Ubaid-style" pottery evidently originated in this region of southern Iraq. At first, archaeologists assumed it to be a more or less local phenomenon. In recent decades we have discovered that by about 4000 BCE people were making and using Ubaid pottery across a region of thousands of square miles, from southern Iraq northwest to the Mediterranean, as well as down the western coast of the Persian Gulf. What this may signify about the nature and extent of the influence that people from southern Iraq exerted across the Middle East at this early date is a topic scholars continue to debate.

In Mesopotamia itself, from the humble beginnings at places like Eridu, humankind was about to make a great leap forward.

THE FIRST CITIES AND THE INVENTION OF WRITING

Not too long after 4000 BCE, Mesopotamia, especially the Tigris–Euphrates floodplain, was becoming what Adams has termed both the "heartland of cities" and the "homeland of cities."[4] We were once fairly certain that the rise of the first cities in Mesopotamia was pretty much exclusive to the southern floodplain, and that upstream, northern Mesopotamia was a backwater at this time. But the destabilization of Iraq in recent years forced archaeologists who had devoted most of their attention there to refocus their efforts elsewhere. Among the beneficiaries was Syria, eastern portions of which lie well within the "Jazira," the "island" between the Tigris and Euphrates. Excavations at Tell Hamoukar and, especially, Tell Brak, just inside the modern Syrian border with Iraq, have uncovered large settlements (at Brak, more than fifty-five hectares in size) with evidence of major trade activity involving, among other commodities, obsidian from Turkey. Especially startling about these discoveries is that these early cities of the north date to the late fifth millennium BCE, which makes them contemporary with urban growth in the southern floodplain, if not older. The finds at Tell Brak thus threaten to alter, perhaps radically, our previous conclusions about the priority of the southern Mesopotamian floodplain in the rise of the first cities.[5] There is a lot that we still do not understand about the origins of city life. More excavation and research are needed, and archaeologists are champing at the bit to resume explorations in Iraq.

Nonetheless, from current knowledge, we can state that soon after 4000 BCE more and larger settlements arose in the southern floodplain, their populations swelling almost exponentially as thousands of people flocked to them from the surrounding countryside. Feeding such population growth likely required that ever larger and more complex irrigation systems be designed and built. Although historians continue to debate whether the need for more irrigation constructions was the cause of the rise of centralized city-based authority, we do begin to see evidence of powerful centralized authority in these cities. This may have been based on religious authority, since some of the earliest large buildings have been identified as temples, or on authority stemming from clan or family prestige; probably on some mixture of the two. However their authority was legitimized, the leaders of these earliest cities controlled and managed great wealth: thousands of acres of cultivated land and thousands of sheep, goats, cattle, and other livestock, all of which involved the work of thousands of people.

The power these leaders accrued in the process became startlingly evident in the nineteenth and twentieth centuries when American and European archaeologists began to excavate the great mounds where these cities were located. Of all these mounds, the tell known as Warka, in southern Iraq – the heart of ancient Sumer – yielded the evidence that best defines the phenomenal advances of this era. The current name "Warka" preserves the ancient name of the great city that once stood here, perhaps the most fabled of all of ancient Sumer's cities: Uruk (called Erech in the Bible). From its founding almost seven thousand years ago to its final abandonment in the third century CE, the life of the city spanned five thousand years – a remarkable achievement in its own right. By 3000 BCE, Uruk was the site of the world's first great city. Its massive fortification wall was about 9.5 kilometers long, enclosing an area of 5.5 square kilometers. Compare this with the enclosed areas of the two most iconic cities of the ancient West: the walls of Athens at its zenith enclosed an area of only 2.5 square kilometers, and Rome, even in the first century CE – three thousand years after Uruk's wall was first built – was only twice as large as Uruk. Its architectural nuclei comprised two great complexes of mud-brick buildings, including temples dedicated to the two great deities of the city: the great sky-god, An, and the goddess of sex and beauty, Inanna, who later came to be known more widely as Ishtar. One of the temples stood on a high mud-brick platform, perhaps designed to elevate the world of the sacred above that of the bustling city. Whatever the reason, this erecting of a sacred structure atop a platform marks the beginning of an architectural evolution that culminated a few centuries later in the distinctively Mesopotamian type of sacred building known as the "ziggurat." A ziggurat consisted of a series of platforms built in layers like a wedding cake, with a monumental exterior stairway, to create a massive high tower. Today, the best-preserved ziggurat is to be found at the ancient city of Ur in southern Iraq. Hundreds of American soldiers had their photos taken there after 2003, since a major U.S. military base was located at the site. But from archaeological excavations and other sources – including Herodotus' account of the city of Babylon as it was more than two thousand years later, and the biblical story of the Tower of Babel, or Babylon – we know that almost all the great cities of ancient Iraq had ziggurats.

These sacred buildings of Uruk were also beautifully decorated, some-times with mosaics made of thousands of small baked-clay cones with the flat ends painted white, black, or red and the pointed ends inserted into mud plaster on the walls to create diagonal, triangular, or zigzag designs. The excavations in the temple complexes of Uruk also yielded spectacular examples of early Sumerian art, including sculpted figures of men (perhaps members of the ruling elite of the city); a sculpted stone head of a woman (the "Lady of Warka") that compares well with the finest work from classical Greek ateliers; and a three-meter-tall stone vase with sculpted scenes depicting aspects of the economic and ritual activities for which the temples were the focus. This vase was tragically smashed during the looting of the National Museum of Iraq after the American conquest of the city in 2003.

Given the splendor and scale of these structures, building them required prodigious effort, organization, and logistical planning. Many thousands of man-hours had to be put in by a huge force of laborers, all of whom had to be recruited – whether by compulsion, payment, or via a sense of civic or sacred duty, we cannot be sure. Their many tasks – from making the thousands of mud bricks to creating the decorative artwork on the buildings' walls– had to be organized, assigned, and managed, over a period of several years, by a hierarchy of managers ranging from the overseer of the overall construction down to the foremen who kept the crews hard at it. While all these laborers and managers were on the job, the temple administrators – who perhaps at this time were also the principal rulers at Uruk and other Sumerian cities – had to be sure they were provided with food, the required tools, and other necessities. How were they to manage all that, to make sure that the right stuff, in the right amounts, got to the right people?

A much-used adage tells us that "necessity is the mother of inven-tion." Out of administrative necessity, these undoubtedly overstressed managers of ancient Uruk came up with some new management tech-nologies, one of which ultimately revolutionized life across the world. In archaeological levels dating to around 3200 BCE, the excavators at Uruk found a number of clay artifacts (we call them "tablets") inscribed with crude picture-signs (pictograms) along with indentations that represent numerical notation. These were simple accounts, records of receipt or expenditure, presumably involving the managers and resources of the temples' estates. Tablets from later archaeological levels at Uruk show that in a relatively short time these "scribes" invented hundreds of such "pictographic" symbols, or signs, which represented and recorded a broad variety of animals, crops, and commodities, both natural and manufactured, as well as men and women ranging in status from slave to high official.[6] With a few centuries of refinement, and as signs came to represent not only things and words but also sounds (mostly syllables), this system of what we call "pictographic writing" evolved into the sophisticated and complex script that we call "cuneiform" – literally (from Latin *cuneus*), "wedge-shaped" writing, because the individual signs in the script are composed of wedge-shaped impressions made by a scribe with a reed stylus on a clay tablet, or, later, of incisions chiseled into a stele or other object of stone.

Another innovation at this time entailed finely carving a distinctive geometric pattern or pictorial image, and eventually the cuneiform signs to indicate the name and title of an official, into the surface of a thumb-sized cylinder of soft stone. Much as the rulers of medieval Europe affixed their official seals onto wax to authenticate a document, early Sumerian officials could roll these "cylinder seals" across the clay sealing of a basket or across a portion of a document recorded on a clay tablet, thereby signifying that a transaction had been authorized. The scenes depicted on these cylinder seals – which continued to be used for centuries – are often exquisitely rendered and have provided us with invaluable clues to the religious rituals and mythologies of the people of ancient Iraq. After the invasion of 2003, these easily hidden and extremely portable seals unfortunately also became prime targets for the treasure hunters who trashed the mounds of Iraq's ancient cities.

The earliest developments of what evolved into the cuneiform script were at Uruk, as far as we can tell, but the new bureaucratic technologies of writing and cylinder seals were rapidly adopted throughout southern Mesopotamia and beyond. Eventually, the use of cuneiform spread throughout the Middle East, to be adopted and adapted by peoples from the Mediterranean shores to the Iranian plateau to write languages completely unrelated to the Sumerian language for which it seems to have been first invented. Cuneiform remained the predominant system of literacy throughout the Middle East, even being used by scribes in the New Kingdom Egyptian royal court in the mid-fourteenth century BCE, until it was slowly superseded by the spread of the much more easily learned alphabetic writing after 1000 BCE. In Iraq, cuneiform continued in steadily diminishing use until shortly after the time of Christ. By as early as 2600 BCE, it had evolved well beyond its original bureaucratic purpose. Beginning in the era of the ancient Sumerian cities, the scribes of earliest Iraq created a record of history, literature, science, mythology, and scholarship that became the foundation of later civilization not only in the Middle East but also in the West.

The invention of cuneiform also brings us to the dawn of "history" in Iraq – at least to the extent that one defines "history" as beginning with the availability of written records. Historians and archaeologists have always felt it necessary to divide (and subdivide and sub-subdivide) the long span of history into manageable bites and chunks that we call "periods." Customarily we have accomplished that by using political events like the establishing of a new dynasty of kings (in England, for example, the Plantagenets, Tudors, and Stuarts) or the conquest of a country by an invader (again, in England, the Anglo-Saxon period, the Norman period) to define dividing lines between periods. Most historians will tell you that such chronological divisions can be rather arbitrary and that imposing them masks a great deal of continuity from one period to the next.

The same problem confronts us when dealing with the history of ancient Iraq. When the decipherment of cuneiform in the mid-nineteenth century opened up thousands of clay tablets to historical inquiry, scholars began to seek dividing points by which they could organize that most ancient history into a sequence of periods. By the later twentieth century, they had arrived at a more or less generally accepted periodization, although the absolute dates of these periods, especially for those earlier than 1000 BCE, remain uncertain and are constantly being reassessed.

Furthermore, the villagers and nomads who lived and died largely outside the purview of city-based rulers were most of the time quite oblivious to such events as the overthrow of rulers and change of dynasties. Many of the people who lived in Mesopotamia during the rule of, say, the celebrated king Hammurabi of Babylon likely never heard of Hammurabi – and they surely did not know they were living during what scholars refer to as the Old Babylonian period. That may seem obvious, but it does say something about how meaningful or relevant are our structures of historical time. Using political-dynastic dividers masks a great deal of continuity between periods in the persistence of basic living conditions and social tensions; among them, for ancient Iraq, the enduring significance of cities as centers of political, economic, and cultural life; the ongoing tensions and symbiosis between the city-dwellers, on the one hand, and the rural villagers and nomadic herders; and the ties of kinship, clan, and tribe that could link city and countryside and often governed how people structured their social and political relationships. All these elements were central to life and history in ancient Mesopotamia and remained so throughout Iraq's history down to the present.

However, even a cursory look at the standard periodization that will be outlined below reveals that this long history is punctuated frequently and definitively by incursions of outsiders. Some of them appear as marauders and then leave; some come onto the scene less violently or abruptly, sometimes seemingly out of nowhere – because our evidence is so fragmentary – but then stay on to govern as new overlords. As a harbinger of history to come, these invaders often enter from the region of what is now Iran. All of these newcomers, we must assume, were motivated by the lure of Iraq's wealth, be that its agricultural bounty in the third millennium BCE or its oilfields in the early third millennium CE.

What follows is a chronology and brief characterization of the major periods in the history of ancient Iraq, from the first "historical" (documented by written records) period to the conquest of Babylon by Cyrus the Great in 539 BCE – the first conquest of Iraq by an imperial power that was centered outside Iraq.

THE EARLY DYNASTIC PERIOD (CA. 2900–2350 BCE)

In the fall of 2007, Iraq was described as "a collection of city-states such as Baghdad, Mosul, Basra, Ramadi, Erbil, and others, each controlled by various warlords with their own militias. And the villages are entirely unprotected."[7] When written records first shed light on Iraq's early history, they reveal a picture of the country not entirely dissimilar from this condition: fragmented, disunited, with various social groups and cities competing for influence and control. This is very important to note. For much of Iraq's history, even from earliest times, the residents of any specific city seem convinced that it is in the natural order of things that their city defend its individual distinctiveness and prerogatives. Consequently, they are often loath to see their city subsumed in a larger state or empire. Even though very early records evince awareness of an overarching geographical and cultural unity called Sumer, there was no overall ruler of Sumer. Instead, the floodplain of southern Mesopotamia was populated by a number of strong-walled city-states, each comprising a city and the surrounding irrigated fields, marshland, and desert. Among the more important cities between 3000 and 2350 BCE were Uruk, Eridu, Ur, Umma, Lagash, Shuruppak, and Kish, but not yet Babylon or Baghdad, neither of which yet existed. Also numbered among the earliest cities of Sumer was the great cult-city of Nippur. Nippur was the city that might claim some status as a "national" center, if only because of the singular importance of its great temples and its chief patron god, Enlil, the most powerful of the many Sumerian gods. According to later sources, especially a difficult source known as the Sumerian King List, each of these early cities – except for Nippur, which never had its own line of kings – was ruled by its own dynasty of rulers. Hence, we call the earliest historical period in Mesopotamia the "Early Dynastic period." The majority of those distant rulers will likely always remain only dimly known to us, even he who stands out above all the others: Gilgamesh, the mighty warrior-hero-king of Uruk whose exploits and legend were to be remembered for millennia, first in individual stories composed by Sumerian bards, then centuries later, and most famously, in the world's first literary epic, the *Epic of Gilgamesh*, the earliest version of which was not composed until almost a millennium after Gilgamesh ruled at Uruk. A few lines near the start of the later standard version of the epic hyperbolically celebrate his heroic qualities:

> Supreme over other kings, lordly in appearance,
>> he is the hero, born of Uruk, the goring wild
>> bull. He walks out in front, the leader,
> and walks at the rear, trusted by his companions.
>> Mighty net, protector of his people,
> raging flood-wave who destroys even walls of stone!
> Offspring of Lugalbanda, Gilgamesh is strong to perfection.[8]

Each of the cities of Sumer had its own temple, sometimes several, its massive ziggurat tower dominating the city skyline and providing, as

Thorkild Jacobsen, a renowned scholar of ancient Sumerian religion, put it, "visible assurance" of the city god's presence and protection. The temple's thick, decorated mud-brick walls served as shelter for the statue of the god whose house the temple was, as well as nerve center of the god's household. Each temple had its own staff of administrators and "priests" and/or "priestesses" who were charged with managing the gods' (temples') estates and performing the highly scripted rituals that kept the resident god fed, clothed, and happy. From all appearances, they took their jobs very seriously. Failure to keep the gods happy brought nasty consequences.

In a number of these early Sumerian cities, temple leaders provided leadership for the city as a whole at first, but by around 2600 BCE leaders with a more military character began to emerge in some cities. Some of them bore the Sumerian title *lugal* (literally, "man great"), which scholars customarily translate as "king." All these cities were by then girdled with massive mud-brick fortification walls. Competition among them was intensifying rapidly as they sought control of water, arable land, and the trade routes that provided access to prized resources that were unavailable on the floodplain, like timber, metals, and semi-precious stones such as lapis lazuli. One of the more celebrated accounts of inter-city war during this time is the Vulture Stele of Eannatum, so called because one of its more graphic scenes depicts vultures flying off with the heads of decapitated enemy soldiers in their talons. In a smaller-scale precursor of the kind of monumental commemoration that Saddam Hussein would erect thousands of years later to commemorate his 1980–88 war with Iran, Eannatum, who ruled the city-state of Lagash around 2450 BCE, set up this public monument to proclaim Lagash's victory over the rival city of Umma as well as, literally, set in stone the conditions he imposed on the vanquished ruler of Umma. In contrast to Saddam's self-glorification, Eannatum ascribed the credit for his victory to the two great patron deities of Lagash, the warrior-god Ningirsu and his mother, the birth-goddess Ninhursag, both of whom are also depicted on the monument and at whose command Eannatum had brought the army of Lagash to the battlefield.

As the self-proclaimed viceroys of their cities' gods, the rulers of these early Sumerian cities shouldered the huge responsibilities of protecting the gods' domain (the city and its surrounding territory) and the gods' houses and households – in other words, the temples and their associated estates, which comprised thousands of head of livestock and thousands of acres of irrigated farmland. As early as the late third millennium BCE, and for centuries to come, rulers' inscriptions and the administrative records of their households testify to kings' devotion to building new watercourses and maintaining old ones to ensure an adequate supply of irrigation water. Ancient Mesopotamian rulers would also have themselves depicted on ceremonial monuments as a patron god's pious and dutiful servant, bearing in a basket the ceremonial first brick for the building of a temple – the construction of which required immense manpower, organization, and material. And not only in mud brick. Rulers had to match the immense size of the gods' temples with sumptuous interior decoration as well as ornamentation, furniture, and ritual vessels and implements made by skilled craftsmen using exotic, expensive materials.

Our best source for envisioning all of this dates to more than two hundred years after the Early Dynastic period. It was left to us courtesy of a later Sumerian ruler, Gudea, who ruled the city-state of Lagash shortly before 2100 BCE. In the late nineteenth century, French archaeologists recovered two large clay cylinders inscribed in cuneiform with a long, detailed account of how Lagash's patron god, Ningirsu, sent Gudea a dream with explicit instructions of how to rebuild and refurbish his temple, and how Gudea then fulfilled Ningirsu's instructions to the letter. He had exotic woods and stones brought to Lagash from the far reaches of the known world:

logs of cedar wood from the cedar hills [probably modern Lebanon], logs of cypress wood from the cypress hills, logs of zabalum wood from the zabalum hills, tall spruce trees, plane trees, and eranum trees. Lord Niĝirsu directed Gudea into the impenetrable mountains of stones and he brought back great stones in the form of slabs. For Lord Niĝirsu, Gudea had ships with ḫauna dock there, and ships with gravel, with dried bitumen...and gypsum from the hills of Madga, cargoes like boats bringing grain from the fields. Great things came to the succour of the ruler building the E-ninnu [Ningirsu's temple]: a copper mountain in Kimaš revealed itself to him. He mined its copper onto rafts. To the man in charge of building his master's house, the ruler, gold was brought in dust form from its mountains. For Gudea refined silver was brought down from its mountains. Translucent cornelian from Meluḫa [probably the Indus Valley region] was spread before him. From the alabaster mountains alabaster was brought down to him. The shepherd was going to build the house with silver, so he sat together with silversmiths. He was going to build the E-ninnu with precious stone, so he sat with jewelers. He was going to build it with copper and tin, so the mother-goddess of the Land directed before him the chief of the smiths. The heavy hammer-stones roared for him like a storm. The dolerite, the light hammer-stones...two...three... like a huge mass of water gushing forth...

He built his master's house exactly as he had been told to. The true shepherd Gudea made it grow so high as to fill the space between heaven and earth, had it wear a tiara shaped like the new moon, and had its fame spread as far as the heart of the highlands. Gudea made Niĝirsu's house come out like the sun from the clouds, had it grow to be like hills of lapis lazuli and had it stand to be marvelled at like hills of white alabaster.[9]

Gudea would have us believe that all these wonderful things were brought to him at his own command or perhaps by the snap of the divine Ningirsu's fingers. In reality, Gudea was able to lay his hands on this marvelous stuff only by dint of the efforts of merchants, caravaneers, sailors, or soldiers who ventured many hundreds of miles to get it, by force or by trade. From the Indus Valley, where the powerful and sophisticated Harappan civilization had taken shape by 3000 BCE, they brought the red carnelian stone. From what is now Afghanistan came the blue lapis lazuli. From the Taurus Mountains came silver; from the Lebanon Mountains, cedar. All of this was carried out, so Gudea would have us believe, for the honor and glory of Lagash's patron god, the protector and benefactor of both him and his city.

But Ningirsu and his divine peers were not the only beings who benefited from all this effort. Although rulers like Gudea were not regarded as gods themselves as the pharaohs of Egypt were, they often claimed divine parentage and special divine favor – and that status certainly brought material rewards.

Nowhere in the early history of Iraq's most ancient cities is this more spectacularly revealed than in the city of Ur. Of all the cities of ancient Sumer, Ur was the only one that people in the West were likely to have heard of before the pioneering archaeological discoveries of the nineteenth century. The book of Genesis identified "Ur of the Chaldees" as the home of the first great Israelite patriarch, Abraham; the Chaldeans being a people who settled in southern Iraq around 1000 BCE. The mound of ancient Ur was the scene of one of the most stunning archaeological discoveries of the twentieth century when the British archaeologist Leonard Woolley, directing excavations for a joint expedition of the University Museum of the University of Pennsylvania and the British Museum, discovered a large cemetery of about two thousand mainly simple burials. But within that cemetery was a group of sixteen stone-built tombs, some of them multi-chambered. Archaeologists still debate just how "royal" were the individuals who were entombed in them, but they are commonly celebrated as the "Royal Cemetery" of Ur. The crushed and decomposed skeletons within them were festooned with evidence of the eminent status of Ur's elite around 2600–2500 BCE. What Woolley identified as the "Great Death Pit" contained the remains of sixty-eight women and six men. All were adorned with jewelry and personal equipment of spectacular luxury, ranging from a golden helmet and dagger to beautifully inlaid and decorated musical instruments. Especially appealing to twentieth-century sensibilities was an inlaid game board. It was reconstructed and marketed as "Ur: The Royal Game of Sumer."

The bodies in the Death Pit lay in neat rows within and outside the stone tomb of a woman identified by an inscribed cylinder seal as a queen named Puabi. Because he could detect no sign that any of the deceased had been dispatched violently, Woolley assumed that all had taken some kind of poison, either willingly or resignedly. However, later reassessment using computed tomography (C.T.) scans and other techniques not available in Woolley's time revealed that all of the deceased were killed by a blow to the side or back of the head with a sharp instrument, and that some of the bodies were then baked and treated with a mercury compound that may have retarded decomposition during lengthy funerary ceremonies.[10] We will never know for certain, but it is tempting to speculate that, like the ancient Egyptian royal officials of the Old Kingdom's Pyramid Age who hoped for the privilege of burial near their king in order to share his eternal afterlife, these royal servants were intended to serve their master or mistress in the hereafter. Queen Puabi herself had been laid to rest in astonishing splendor, wearing an elaborate headdress fashioned from almost ten pounds of gold and featuring:

> gold leaves, gold ribbons, strands of lapis lazuli and carnelian beads, a tall comb of gold, chokers, necklaces, and a pair of large, crescent-shaped earrings. Her upper body was covered in strings of beads made of precious metals and semi-precious stones stretching from her shoulders to her belt, while rings decorated

all her fingers. An ornate diadem made of thousands of small
lapis lazuli beads with gold pendants of animals and plants was
on a table near her head.[11]

Puabi's headdress bears witness to the consummate metallurgical skill
and artistic creativity of the craftsmen who served Ur's royal court
around 2500 BCE. And, as with Gudea's temple project at Lagash a few
centuries later, her headdress along with other luxurious objects found
in the Royal Cemetery show us that even the earliest Sumerian rulers
were able to furnish their craftsmen with exotic, expensive materials
brought from the far corners of the known world: lapis lazuli from
Afghanistan, carnelian from the Indus region, and gold, perhaps from
the Taurus Mountains of southern Anatolia or even from Egypt.

Beyond the Sumerian floodplain were emerging at this very early
time not only trading partners but peoples who in time would con-
tend for power in ancient Iraq. Among them were a people known
as the Hurrians, who were to exercise huge influence on the history
and culture of Syria, Anatolia, and northern Iraq during the early
and middle second millennium BCE. Until recently, most historians
believed that the Hurrians migrated, probably from the region of the
Caucasus Mountains, to the upper reaches of the Tigris and Euphrates
only around 2300 BCE, but new discoveries in Syria at a site called
Tell Mozan (identified as the ancient city of Urkesh, a major Hurrian
capital) suggest the Hurrians may have been present in Syria as much
as a thousand years earlier, which would make their presence in Syria
contemporary with the earliest Sumerian city-states. Our understanding
of their language is as scant as our knowledge of their origins, but we
do know that it is related neither to Sumerian nor to the later Semitic
languages that emerged in the region.[12]

While the Hurrians were establishing themselves to the northwest
of Sumer, other peoples, some of whom were to have a great impact
on the ancient history of Iraq, were establishing themselves to the east,

in the plateaus and foothill regions of what is now Iran. Our sources name several early kingdoms here – some of them as sources of raw and exotic materials coveted by Sumer's ruler elites, others as potential military threats. The kingdom known as Elam and its great capital city of Susa, in what is now Khuzistan, were to prove especially significant in Sumer's later history.

THE AKKAD PERIOD (CA. 2350–2150 BCE)

By far the most important development during this period was the rise of a new ruling family whose elite spoke a non-Sumerian, Semitic language – the earliest for which we have written evidence – and hailed from the region of Akkad, just upstream of Sumer. Its founder was a heroic figure who arose from obscure origins and took for himself the name Sharrukin (literally "true king" – a tip-off that he was in fact a usurper), or Sargon. He and his successors used brute military force to take and then maintain control of all the cities of the Sumerian floodplain. On occasion the kings of Akkad had to quell insurrections led by local leaders of the subjugated Sumerian cities, which throughout their history insisted on their independence and prerogatives.

From their new, as yet undiscovered, capital city, Agade (or Akkad), founded by Sargon himself, the Akkadian kings dispatched their armies on campaigns far into the regions beyond the floodplain, including parts of modern-day Iran and Syria, and perhaps down the coast of the Persian Gulf. Scholars still wrestle with the details of how much land they actually conquered and how they administered it. We know enough to assert that Sargon and his successors opened a new chapter in world history: they were the world's first empire-builders. Throughout the later history of ancient Iraq, Sargon was lionized as a heroic figure, the epitome of all-conquering overlordship, an enduring model to be emulated through the ages. His grandson and perhaps even farther-conquering descendant,

Naram-Sin, would be remembered, however, as a sacrilegious ruler whose offenses fired the wrath of the gods and brought down destruction on his kingdom. The fact that he was also the first, though not the last, ruler of ancient Mesopotamia to call himself a god may have had something to do with later assessments of him as too full of hubris. Whatever Naram-Sin's actual contribution to the demise of his realm – and the evidence suggests that it was slight – by around 2200 BCE the empire of the kings of Akkad was being whittled down in size, partly by mountain-dwellers known as the Guti, or Gutians. "Uncivilized" in the eyes of the city-dwellers, the Guti descended onto the floodplain from the Zagros Mountains. Some ancient accounts assign to the Guti the destruction of the Akkad dynasty, whereas others indicate that kings of Akkad continued to rule a portion of the region for perhaps another fifty years. In any event, the Gutian invasion is the earliest example of a recurring phenomenon in the history of Iraq: a threat from the east swooping in to take over.

THE UR III PERIOD (CA. 2100–2000 BCE)

The chaotic demise of the Akkad dynasty left the region fragmented during a period still poorly understood by historians. But it also witnessed one of the more celebrated reigns of early Sumer's history, that of Gudea, the ruler of Lagash, whose accomplishments as a temple builder I spotlighted earlier. Around 2100 BCE, a warrior-hero from Uruk named Utu-hegal expelled the Gutians in what the sources celebrate as a war of liberation. In the wake of his death, Utu-hegal's subordinate, Ur-namma, set himself up as ruler and founded a new dynasty at the already ancient city of Ur, where he built the ziggurat that we noted as the best-preserved example of this iconically Mesopotamian structure.

As the third dynasty to rule from Ur, the members of the Third Dynasty of Ur ("Ur III"), like the kings of Akkad, at first dominated the cities of the floodplain, but then, especially under Ur-namma's son and successor, Shulgi, they extended their domination to incorporate a substantial area of northern Mesopotamia and western Iran. The Ur III empire was smaller than that of the Akkad kings, but if the hundreds of thousands of clay tablets left to us by successive Ur III royal administrations are any indication, it was tightly administered. The sheer volume of records dating to this period – hundreds of thousands, more than from any other period of Iraq's ancient history – reflects what stands out the most about this brief period: the tremendous energy, productivity, and imagination of a class of individuals who, though we lump them together as "scribes," included scholars, literary composers, and scientists – as well as accountants stationed at various rungs up the administrative ladder. By and large, they were employees of the royal administration or subsidiary administrative offices. The literary works they produced number among the most celebrated written in the Sumerian language, which by this time may have gone out of use as a spoken vernacular. These range from stories about the gods and goddesses to poems that extol with sycophantic praise the might and virtues of the kings. The so-called "praise poems" dedicated to Shulgi tout him as a latter-day Gilgamesh, with whom, in fact, Shulgi encouraged his court scribes to associate him. Consider the following excerpt from the praise poem known as "Shulgi B":

> I am a king, offspring begotten by a king and borne by a queen. I, Shulgi the noble, have been blessed with a favorable destiny right from the womb. When I was small, I was at the academy, where I learned the scribal art from the tablets of Sumer and Akkad. None of the nobles could write on clay as I could. There where people regularly went for tutelage in the scribal art, I qualified fully in subtraction, addition, reckoning and accounting...
>
> When I sprang up, muscular as a cheetah, galloping like a thoroughbred ass at full gallop, the favor of An [the sky-god]

brought me joy; to my delight Enlil [most respected of the gods
of Sumer] spoke favorably about me, and they gave me the sceptre
because of my righteousness. I place my foot on the neck of the
foreign lands; the fame of my weapons is established as far as the
south, and my victory is established in the highlands. When I set
off for battle and strife to a place that Enlil has commanded me, I
go ahead of the main body of my troops and I clear the terrain for
my scouts. I have a positive passion for weapons. Not only do I
carry lance and spear, I also know how to handle slingstones with
a sling. The clay bullets, the treacherous pellets that I shoot, fly
around like a violent rainstorm. In my rage I do not let them miss.

I sow fear and confusion in the foreign land. I look to my
brother and friend, youthful Utu [the sun-god], as a source of
divine encouragement. I, Shulgi, converse with him whenever
he rises over there; he is the god who keeps a good eye on my
battles...I broke the weapons of the highlands over my knees,
and in the south placed a yoke on the neck of Elam. I make the
populations of the rebel lands – how could they still resist my
weapons? – scatter like seed-grain over Sumer and Akkad.

Let me boast of what I have done. The fame of my power is
spread far and wide. My wisdom is full of subtlety. Do not my
achievements surpass all qualifications?[13]

By far the scribes' most abundantly attested assignments are their efforts
to keep extremely detailed tabs on the massive resources that were fun-
neled into the Ur III court and its dependants – and especially to the
temples of the great cult center of Nippur. The vast majority of the clay
tablets remaining to us from the Ur III period are accounting records.
There are literally tens of thousands of them: receipts of materials, deliv-
eries of livestock, accounts of harvests, lists of rations for agricultural
laborers or canal diggers. One tablet – to cite but one example – gives
us an idea of both the size of the royal resource base and the exactness

with which they were recorded. It notes that, during one three-year period of Shulgi's reign, the bureaucrats at one of the royal administrative centers handled "28,601 cattle, 404 deer, 236 wild sheep, 38 horses, 360 onagers, 2931 donkeys, 347,394 sheep, 3880 gazelles, 457 bears, 13 monkeys, and 1 unidentified animal."[14]

Like the Akkad dynasty, however, the Third Dynasty of Ur was brought down by peoples whom the sources characterize as outsiders. From the kingdom of Elam in the east came invaders who captured and sacked the capital city of Ur and carried off into captivity its last king, the unfortunate Ibbi-Sin. The memory of that catastrophe was preserved in another literary masterpiece, "Lamentation over the Destruction of Ur." It tells of how the gods decided to abandon Ur, despite the pleas of its patron god, the moon-god Nanna. The conqueror comes like a great storm, devastating the city, destroying its temples, annihilating its population, inflicting horrors that were to be visited on the people and cities of Iraq all too often in the centuries to follow:

> [Ur's] people littered its outskirts just as if they might have been broken potsherds. Breaches had been made in its walls – the people groan. On its lofty city-gates where walks had been taken, corpses were piled. On its boulevards where festivals had been held, heads lay scattered. In all its streets where walks had been taken, corpses were piled. In its places where the dances of the Land had taken place, people were stacked in heaps. They made the blood of the Land flow down the wadis like copper or tin. Its corpses, like fat left in the sun, melted away of themselves.[15]

From the west, however, arrived a people who were to play an even more significant part in ancient Iraq's history. The sources refer to them as the Amurru, or Amorites, rural tribesmen, many of them nomadic herders of sheep and goats – barbarians in the eyes of the city scribes who wrote about them. Mesopotamian literature generally ridicules

Amorite manners and customs. For example, in the Sumerian myth "The Marriage of Martu," Martu, the god most closely identified with the Amorites, demands that the Sumerian goddess Adjar-kidug, patron goddess of a major city, be given in marriage to him. Adjar-kidug's girlfriend implores her not to marry this uncouth yahoo:

> Now listen, their hands are destructive and their features are those of monkeys; he is one who eats what Nanna forbids and does not show reverence. They never stop roaming about…they are an abomination to the gods' dwellings. Their ideas are confused; they cause only disturbance. He is clothed in sack-leather… lives in a tent, is exposed to wind and rain, and cannot properly recite prayers. He lives in the mountains and ignores the places of gods, digs up truffles in the foothills, does not know how to bend the knee, and eats raw flesh. He has no house during his life, and when he dies he will not be carried to a burial place. My girlfriend, why would you marry Martu?[16]

In the end, though, she does marry him – a union that reflects contemporary awareness of the sometimes symbiotic, sometimes hostile relationship between city-dwellers and rural tribespeople that has been an enduring feature of Iraqi society from the days of ancient Sumer down to the present.

With the end of the Third Dynasty of Ur in about 2000 BCE, the Amorites took over as political kingpins across much of Mesopotamia. It is also at this point in time that the standard chronology of ancient Iraq's history bifurcates to reflect the emergence of separate centers of political power in the south and the north. In the south, from a political and cultural milieu that for more than a thousand years had been dominated by the great Sumerian city-states and the Akkad rulers who followed them, there emerged a new power that was to dominate the region for the next two thousand years: Babylon. Thus, from about 2000 BCE, it is appropriate to refer to southern and central Iraq as "Babylonia" and to its history as "Babylonian." To the north, along the Tigris, another great center of political and commercial power emerged around 2000 BCE: Ashur. Ashur was also the name of the chief god revered in this region. Long after the city of Ashur's importance had been eclipsed by more famous cities such as Nineveh, the region was still known as the "land of Ashur," or "Assyria," and its history and people as "Assyrian." For the next fifteen hundred years, the rivalry between Assyria and Babylonia was to dominate Iraq's history, until the Chaldean rulers of Babylonia vanquished the last of the Assyrian kings, only to be swept up in their turn by newcomers from Persia.

THE OLD BABYLONIAN AND OLD ASSYRIAN PERIODS (CA. 2000–1595 BCE)

This period marks the rise of the Amorites, who brought with them their language, a West Semitic tongue related to the Akkadian spoken by Sargon and his heirs. Their leaders took control of cities throughout the entire region of Iraq (both the southern floodplain and the reaches upstream) and to the north and west, into what is now Syria. Though they now became rulers of city-based kingdoms, these Amorite kings retained a strong sense of their semi-nomadic, tribal origins. Thus, the later document known as the Assyrian King List (a list of the kings of Assyria, beginning with the Amorites) describes the earliest ancestors as the kings "who lived in tents."

Roughly contemporary with the Old Babylonian period but not as well documented by cuneiform texts, the Old Assyrian period witnessed the emergence of Assyria as a political and commercial power. As early as 1950 BCE, elite families of the city of Ashur were engaging in highly profitable caravan-trade operations that linked Ashur with towns and trading posts as far away as what is now central Turkey. In those faraway places the scions of these families established colonies – branch offices of family-owned companies, as it were – where they made deals with local buyers, selling tin and woven textiles that their donkey caravans brought from Ashur and then using the profits to buy locally available gold and silver, which went back to the home offices at Ashur on the return trip. Thousands of years later the inhabitants of what once was Assyria would prosper from the caravan routes of lorries regularly plying roads through the Taurus Mountains between Iraq and Turkey.

About 150 years after this caravan trade had begun, a dynamic, charismatic Amorite chieftain named Shamshi-Adad established himself and his sons by force of arms in several cities, most notably the city of Mari on the Euphrates. Here thousands of cuneiform tablets that French archaeologists have pulled from the ruins of its royal palace since 1935 have yielded a treasure trove of information about the politics, diplomacy, and religious practices of this time. From these cities, Shamshi-Adad and sons ruled a region that extended well beyond Assyria proper along the Euphrates into what is now eastern Syria.

Soon after his death, Shamshi-Adad's kingdom crumbled before the power of the Babylonian ruler Hammurabi. This man is by far the most celebrated monarch of the Old Babylonian period.[17] During his reign (1795–1750 BCE), Babylon first rose to preeminence in ancient southern Iraq. It would remain preeminent throughout almost the rest of antiquity. Hammurabi is especially known today for his famous "Code" of laws. In his own time his power and fame rested on his conquest of the cities of the old Sumerian heartland south of Babylon, as well as cities well upstream along the Euphrates into Syria, where he destroyed the palace at Mari. He was also a tireless administrator of his realm. We possess a number of clay-tablet letters from him to one of his chief officials, a governor of one of the southern cities. He comes across as a hands-on, almost micro-managing boss, keeping a watchful eye on goings-on among his subordinates and ready and willing to step in when he saw fit.

But it is undoubtedly the Code of Hammurabi for which he has been most celebrated – deservedly so, both for the artistic merit of the sculpted diorite stele on which the Code was inscribed and for what it tells us about economic realities, social structure, and ideal standards of justice in ancient Iraq, as well as the qualities of the ideal Babylonian ruler. The stele was discovered in 1901 or 1902 in the ruins of the ancient Elamite capital of Susa, where, hundreds of years after Hammurabi's time, the Elamite king who had recently sacked Babylon took it as a trophy. Owing to the weakness of the Qajar rulers of Iran during the early twentieth century, when Russia and Great Britain dominated Iran's affairs, the French archaeologists who discovered it were able to send it to France, where it still resides in the Louvre in Paris. (Iraq had already lost by then a major portion of its ancient treasures to European and American museums.) The stele is a physically impressive monument: 2.25 meters tall, 1.9 meters in diameter at its base. At its top is sculpted the image of Hammurabi standing reverently before the enthroned sun-god Shamash, the Akkadian deity who was associated with justice and the swearing of oaths. The remainder of the monument is covered with forty-nine columns of beautifully inscribed cuneiform, in the Akkadian language, which the Amorite conquerors had adopted for their royal inscriptions. The text begins with a prologue praising Hammurabi and extolling his many achievements on behalf of the people and the gods whose cities he controls. Hammurabi asserts that the great gods Anu and Enlil,

> for the enhancement of the well-being of the people, named me by my name: Hammurabi, the pious prince, who venerates the gods, to make justice to prevail in the land, to abolish the wicked and the evil, to prevent the strong from oppressing the weak, to rise like the sun-god Shamash over all humankind, to illuminate the land.[18]

There follow 281 legal rulings, with their provisions rendered in an "If… then…" formula. For example, the very first "law" states,

> If a man accuses another man and charges him with a homicide but cannot bring proof against him, his accuser shall be killed.[19]

The laws are organized in groups according to general themes that are remarkably diverse though hardly cover all possible circumstances: murder, manslaughter, assault, larceny, libel, kidnapping, embezzlement, marriage and bride price, divorce, and inheritance. Also included are numerous rulings concerning slaves and the institution of slavery. Hammurabi's laws make clear that Babylonian society distinguished clearly between free, semi-free (or semi-dependent), and slave status and that people of different statuses had correspondingly different rights, prerogatives, worths, and punishments. Another significant feature of Hammurabi's laws is the underlying principle of restitution, what legal experts refer to as "talionic" law: straightforwardly eye-for-an-eye, tooth-for-a-tooth, life-for-a-life justice – at least when the offenses involved free citizens; restitution for death or injury of a slave could be made through monetary compensation. Some see here the impact of tribal custom, not completely unlike the principles, like vendetta for wrongful death, still at work today in Middle Eastern tribal societies. And the parallel with early laws of the Israelites, as recorded in the Bible, is clear.

The rulings in Hammurabi's laws reflect many of the conflicts and tensions of everyday life. When combined with the evidence that archaeologists and Assyriologists (the scholars who specialize in the study of ancient Mesopotamian written records) have recovered, they help us recreate a vivid picture of life in the congested cities of ancient Babylonia. Those cities had distinct neighborhoods, with rich and poor living alongside each other, often at close quarters, in houses that lined networks of narrow, winding lanes, probably not unlike what one can find today in the old quarters of many Middle Eastern cities. One's residence in the local neighborhood contributed to one's social and legal identity, and close family ties mattered more than tribal or clan allegiance. City quarters were supervised by officials who could issue warnings or convene hearings about matters of public concern, such as houses dangerously in disrepair or domestic animals which threatened local residents. Residents of a neighborhood could also be enjoined to watch out for strangers or look into the conduct of a woman who repudiated her husband.

However, the Code of Hammurabi was not – as is often claimed – the world's earliest collection of laws. We have at least two earlier compilations from Mesopotamia. Nor can we be sure that it served as the functioning law of the land. It is mentioned in none of the thousands of other texts dating to this period, and some records of court cases from this time even contain decisions that contradict Hammurabi's laws. Nonetheless, it has been invaluable in helping us understand conditions of life in ancient Iraq. As an exemplar of ideals and principles of law and justice, it is a towering landmark in the history of human achievement.

After Hammurabi's time the details of the early history of Assyria, Babylonia's upstream neighbor and rival, become obscured. For that matter, the history of Babylonia also becomes murky as Hammurabi's great kingdom steadily shriveled under the rule of his descendants. Scholars have discovered that, for reasons that likely involved some major shift in the courses of the Tigris and Euphrates, virtually all the cities of the old Sumerian south were abandoned, perhaps for two hundred years. When the denouement of the Amorite dynasty of Babylonia finally came, it came at the hand of outsiders, as it had for the Akkad and Ur III kings and would again for kings to come. This time the conqueror came not from Iran, but from the north, from a newly arisen kingdom called Hatti. Because earlier scholars mistakenly identified them with a people mentioned in the Bible, we persist in calling these people "Hittites." By 1650 BCE, the rulers of Hatti had taken control in what is now central Turkey. They spoke a language unrelated to Sumerian or to the Semitic Akkadian and Amorite tongues of Hammurabi's Babylonia. Their language is the earliest recorded member of the Indo-European language family. In 1595 BCE, the Hittite king Murshili I led his army down the Euphrates to Babylon and sacked it. But, unlike later conquerors of Iraq, the Hittites quickly abandoned their conquest and returned to their Anatolian homeland.

THE KASSITE AND MIDDLE ASSYRIAN PERIODS (1595 TO CA. 1000 BCE)

Because archaeologists have recovered very few documents relating to this period, the curtain rings down on the Mesopotamian stage during the decades immediately following the Hittite sack of Babylon. But around 1450 BCE, thanks to documents from Egypt, whose pharaohs were beginning to build an empire into the Middle East and wanted to leave a record of it, the curtain comes up again. The cast of characters ruling over Babylonia and Assyria has changed almost beyond recognition. A people called the Kassites, yet another newcomer group with links to Iran, were now in charge in Babylonia, where they had seamlessly taken over the long-established traditions of Mesopotamian kingship. Doing so served them well: they ruled there for about four hundred years, longer than any other Babylonian dynasty. Upstream, meanwhile, Assyria had been reduced to the status of vassal of a new, militarily robust kingdom called Mitanni, whose Hurrian rulers by 1400 BCE held sway over most of Syria and northern Iraq and were contending with the warrior pharaohs of Egypt's New Kingdom for control over coastal Syria and Palestine and the wealth brought through this region's seaports.

About 1350 BCE, a new line of Assyrian kings shed Mitanni's yoke and re-established an independent Assyrian kingdom – the so-called Middle Assyrian kingdom. As an extremely informative archive of

66

diplomatic letters from the Egyptian royal capital of this time reveals, the two Mesopotamian kingdoms of Kassite Babylonia and Assyria were members of what some scholars have termed a Late Bronze Age brotherhood (or "club") of Great Kings that also included the pharaoh of Egypt, the kings of Mitanni and Alashiya (probably Cyprus), and the king of a resuscitated Hatti. From a modern perspective, relations between the two Mesopotamian monarchs were hardly brotherly. One of the letters to the Pharaoh tells us that the Babylonian King was quite peeved upon learning that Pharaoh had accepted the upstart Assyrian ruler into their club. Until the fall of the Kassite kingdom of Babylonia ca. 1140 BCE, relations between the rival Mesopotamian kingdoms were usually hostile, Assyria often holding the upper hand, especially when one of its kings conquered Babylon in the late thirteenth century BCE and made it Assyria's vassal.

TRANSITION TO EMPIRE, CA. 1100–900 BCE

The twelfth century BCE was a time of tremendous political and social chaos and collapse across the entire Middle East from Egypt to Mesopotamia. (It was also a time of significant technological innovation and transition, as bronze – an alloy of copper and tin – was being replaced by iron as the pre-eminent metal used to fashion tools and weapons. The history of technology now transitions from the Bronze Age to the Iron Age.) The turmoil left both the Assyrian and Babylonian kingdoms on the ropes. The Middle East as a whole was buffeted by myriad forces, among them, once again, outsiders – this time the semi-nomadic, tribal peoples whom we know as the Arameans and the Chaldeans. Their origins are obscure, but between 1100 and 900 BCE semi-nomadic, tribal peoples whom we know as the Aramaeans and the Chaldaeans settled down throughout much of Iraq and Syria, and parts of Iran. Their impact proved to be both momentous and enduring.

Marauding bands of Arameans were beginning to intrude into the Assyrian realm by the twelfth century BCE. As time went on, some of them assimilated within the general population of the kingdom, even serving as officials. Elsewhere, Aramean chieftains set up petty kingdoms throughout Syria, Palestine, and Mesopotamia. The cuneiform sources refer to these kingdoms as the "house of" so-and-so. Their rulers were able to enrich themselves by controlling the new caravan routes that were opening up with the advent of the camel, which several centuries earlier had been domesticated in the peninsular homeland of another Semitic people who also begin to pop up on our historical radar screen at about this time: the Arabs. In the centuries to come, however, the Arameans' chief importance was to lie not in their power or their wealth, but in the impact of their migrations and their forced resettlement at the hands of later conquerors, for it was by such means that their language, Aramaic, became the most widespread spoken language throughout the Middle East, including Iraq. It remained so until Aramaic was supplanted by Arabic after the Muslim Arab conquests, which began in the seventh century CE.

Along with the Aramaic language spread a new technology of literacy, the impact of which was eventually to prove revolutionary. By 1000 BCE, the Arameans were adapting for their own use the alphabetic writing system that had been refined by those intrepid seafaring merchants of the Syrian port-cities whom we, courtesy of Herodotus, know as the Phoenicians. (They never called themselves by that name.) The Aramaic alphabet was a purely phonetic, purely consonantal writing system that had many fewer characters than cuneiform and was therefore much easier to learn. In the centuries that followed, the Aramaic alphabet inexorably supplanted cuneiform as the dominant technology of literacy and record-keeping throughout the Middle East. For modern historians this monumental advance in the spread of literacy beyond an elite of scholars and scribes is a mixed blessing. As opposed to the sturdy clay tablets or stone stelae upon which cuneiform documents were inscribed, the Aramaic alphabet was best suited to brush and ink on parchment and papyrus – materials that do not survive nearly as well, or as often, when buried in tells.

When we first encounter the Chaldeans, they, like the Arameans, are settling in petty tribal sheikhdoms in the region of Babylonia. In the seventh century BCE they took over political rule, though only after a long period of bitter rivalry with, and domination by, the kings of a resurgent Assyria. In the Bible we find the Chaldeans mentioned very early on, in Genesis, where Abraham is described as originating from "Ur of the Chaldees." Many centuries later, their name became associated with the Christians of northern Iraq.

THE GREAT "WORLD EMPIRES" (CA. 900–539 BCE): THE NEO-ASSYRIAN AND NEO-BABYLONIAN PERIODS

The next three-and-a-half centuries were the earliest era of Iraq's history about which the modern world had any inkling before the pioneering archaeological discoveries and the decipherment of cuneiform in the mid-nineteenth century. The Hebrew Bible, later Jewish religious texts, and the history authored by Herodotus in the fifth century BCE had been known to the West for centuries, and those works mention the empires ruled by the kings of Assyria and Babylonia beginning in the ninth century BCE. This period marks the beginning of a longer era during which Iraq features as either the seat of an empire or a major component of an empire ruled from elsewhere.

Perhaps no theme is more central to, or enduring in, Iraq's history than that of past imperial greatness. The memories of ancient Iraq preserved in the Bible and the histories written by later Greek historians – and the attitudes and judgments that their authors conveyed – have resounded through the centuries to help shape the West's view of modern Iraq as well.

From the very beginnings of its history and civilization – the world's earliest – Iraq's rulers could command great power, luxury, and status. The memory of this splendid past has by no means been lost among their distant progeny, the citizens of modern Iraq. Since the discovery of her tomb in the late 1920s, several artists have reconstructed likenesses of the celebrated queen of Ur, Queen Puabi – her face and head as well as her headdress, which itself had to be reconstructed from the hundreds of pieces in which it was found. In doing so, they hoped both to serve the interests of science and to revivify a human element of ancient Sumer. During the travails of the post-2003 Anglo-American occupation, at least one Iraqi artist used a likeness of Puabi to remind his fellow citizens that their country was rooted in a long and glorious history. In Baghdad, he painted on one of the many concrete blast-walls erected by the U.S. forces a brilliantly colored portrait of Queen Puabi, with her headdress. From one of the uglier and more inglorious symbols of Iraq's occupation, an ancient queen of Iraq serenely gazed; a vivid reminder to Iraq's people that, like her image, their country would endure.

3

CRADLE OF EMPIRES

TODAY, MANY NATION-STATES look back and gaze proudly upon what they consider their glorious days of empire – times of power and wealth, when their rulers controlled far-flung realms and could enrich both themselves and their homelands with the human and natural resources brought from imperial dominions. No visitor who has spent any time in London, for example, can escape being confronted with the celebration of the British empire in Westminster Abbey, St. Paul's Cathedral, or Trafalgar Square. A visitor to modern Iran may need to travel a bit farther off the beaten path to reach the site of ancient Persepolis, but there they will find the remains of a great palace-city, the capital of the vast Achaemenid Persian empire that Cyrus the Great founded in the sixth century BCE. Although it was built long before the coming of Islam, Persepolis remains a source of great pride to Iranians even in today's Islamic republic. Even more ancient, yet better known to Western tourists than Persepolis, are the remains of Karnak and Luxor, the monumental ceremonial centers of the Egyptian capital at Thebes (which the Egyptians called Waset) during the great imperial age of ancient Egypt's New Kingdom (ca. 1550–1080 BCE), when Egypt's pharaohs ruled much of the Middle East.

The people of modern Iraq can lay claim to an ancient imperial past just as glorious, and no doubt just as filled with brutality and exploitation, as that of any modern nation. As we have seen, the great cities and civilization of ancient Iraq had been flourishing more than two thousand years before Iraq's age of ancient empire. Yet, compared with the vast expanse of palatial architecture at Persepolis or the towering temples of Thebes, the remains of ancient Iraq's imperial heyday are less noticeable today, and correspondingly less known to the Western public. In part this is because the great ceremonial structures of Iraq's Babylonian south were built of mud brick; the passing of millennia has reduced them to heaps of ruins. In the Assyrian north, the great kings of the ninth to seventh centuries BCE built magnificent royal palaces at their imperial capitals, but many of the most evocative and brilliant artworks celebrating their empire – the monumental statues and massive, beautifully sculpted stone reliefs that lined the palace walls – were hauled away by their Western discoverers, to be ensconced as prized possessions of the European and American museums that sponsored them. In more recent decades the Assyrian palaces have been plundered again, by illicit treasure-hunting. In the south, the site of Babylon has been thoroughly trashed: first by Saddam Hussein, who built his own palace and effected restorations there to associate his dictatorship with an ancient era of real greatness; then, after 2003, by the U.S. military, which set up a base directly atop the ancient ruins, their Humvees and tanks crushing Babylonian antiquities still lying underground. Some observers, both Iraqi and American, saw this as a deliberate attempt to sever modern Iraqis from their roots in a great past.

Nonetheless, from the ninth century BCE until the middle of the seventh century CE, Iraq, the original heartland of cities, was also the heartland of what can justifiably be thought of as the first "world empires" – though some might award that distinction to the late third-millennium BCE empire of Sargon of Akkad and his descendants. Vague, poorly informed, extremely biased recollections of those empires are preserved in both the Bible and Herodotus. For centuries these sources were all we had to go on. Even long after the modern archaeological discovery of ancient imperial capitals like Nineveh and Babylon, these prejudicial accounts shape and shade people's perceptions and judgments of Iraq's ancient civilizations, often for the worse.

Until the mid-nineteenth century, we had a very poorly informed understanding of ancient Iraq's age of empire. That understanding paled in comparison with our knowledge of the Roman empire, by then long sanctified as Western civilization's golden age of imperial dominion and sophisticated culture. To this day the Roman empire remains central to the West's sense of its roots and past greatness. The evidence of Iraq's ancient greatness still lay slumbering as late as 1840, undisturbed beneath its ruined mounds. The thousands of tells dotting Iraq's landscape had as yet aroused little interest among the local Arab and Kurdish population, other than as focuses of local legends or places where might be found old objects for which a passing European diplomat or traveler might offer a coin or two. Most of the local inhabitants were Muslims, who customarily viewed the pre-Islamic past as the era of *jahiliyya*, or ignorance of the true religion of Islam, and therefore not worthy of a believer's serious attention.

The vast mounds of Iraq's ancient imperial capitals silently waited until a series of enterprising, sometimes greedy European and American – and Iraqi – explorers were able to organize and lead expeditions into what then were truly the wilds of Mesopotamia. They faced often appalling conditions: exposure to the elements, debilitating or even fatal disease, inadequate food, tainted water, no sanitation. To compound the danger, they also stirred suspicion or even violent hostility from local tribesmen. Austen H. Layard, the most celebrated of these early discoverers, was once robbed, beaten, stripped naked, and left for dead by local brigands, but luckily was able to make his way to a settlement where he recovered.[1] Sometimes the explorers' operations were obstructed by local officials who distrusted the foreigners' motives and resented their presence, or by delays in securing the required official 'firmans' (permits) from the imperial court of the Ottoman sultan in Constantinople, who ruled the Middle East during the nineteenth and early twentieth century.

Why then did they do it? By and large they were well-educated European men, which meant they were well acquainted with what Herodotus and the Bible's authors had to say about magnificent ancient capitals like Babylon and Nineveh.² They also had been schooled in the deeds of the Achaemenid Persian kings Cyrus the Great, Darius, and Xerxes, all of whom pridefully counted Babylon among their possessions. They would have thrilled to Herodotus' accounts of how the brave Greeks of Athens and Sparta had fended off the massive invasion forces that Darius, then Xerxes, had sent against them between 490 and 479 BCE; how the Greeks had smashed the Persian armies and fleets in great victories at Marathon, Salamis, and Plataea. They also knew how the all-conquering armies of Alexander the Great had campaigned across the Middle East and into Mesopotamia, where they defeated the armies of the Persian king Darius III at Gaugamela (near Irbil in modern northern Iraq) in 331 BCE and then marched on to capture Babylon, then Persia and its entire empire, and beyond. The intoxicating romance of discovering great cities made famous in the Bible, and in the process perhaps corroborating some of the biblical accounts, surely lured the explorers as well. Nor were they averse to the prospect of wealth and fame, and the European museums that helped fund their expeditions were eager for a share of whatever spoils these intrepid pioneers might take away.

As brave and determined as they were, however, to refer to these men as "archaeologists" is almost an insult to modern practitioners of the science of archaeology. Archaeologists today prefer limited, carefully planned and executed excavations and often, when possible, non-invasive means of revealing and studying whatever remains of the past lie beneath the ground. Until about 1900, archaeologists such as those whose exploits we are about to spotlight were little more than treasure hunters. Their methods of excavating and then extracting their finds destroyed a huge amount of evidence that modern archaeologists would dearly love to have back. Some of what they found now resides in overseas museums. Some of it lies at the bottom of the Tigris, where two boats that the Frenchman Victor Place filled with artifacts sank in the strong current. The rightful ownership of these treasures of ancient Iraq continues to be debated.

Yet, however flawed their methods of discovery, these pioneers opened a new window – and world – of history. After so many centuries of darkness beneath the mounds of Mesopotamia, the ancient empires of Assyria and Babylon were suddenly thrust into the light, to the wonderment of a modern world that would be stunned by their magnificence – and repulsed by their brutality.

THE REDISCOVERY OF "THE MIGHT THAT WAS ASSYRIA"

Although the locations of the great capital cities of Assyria had been long forgotten, their names were well known to nineteenth-century Westerners. Genesis (chapter 10) tells of Nimrod, a descendant of Noah who was the first to become a mighty warrior. Nimrod had ruled in the land of Shinar (Babylonia), from where he had ventured into Assyria, where he built Nineveh and Calah. Nineveh and several of the great Assyrian emperor-kings also figure in the books of Kings and Chronicles, as well as in the books of several of the Hebrew prophets, which even today shape our views of Iraq as a place cursed by history – not to mention cursed by God. Although the classical Greco-Roman sources show little awareness of the great Assyrian capitals, as early as Herodotus and Ctesias (whose work is preserved in that of the first-century BCE historian Diodorus Siculus) they remember a legendary queen named Semiramis, who wed a great conqueror-king named Ninus (likely a reflection of the name of Nineveh). After Ninus' death in battle,

Semiramis ascended to his throne and in her own right conquered much of Asia as far away as India. She became much better, albeit inaccurately, known in Greek accounts as the builder of Babylon, as well as a wily, ruthless, sexually adventuresome ruler. She was memorialized in these roles in later European art well into the nineteenth century – as in Edgar Degas' painting *Semiramis construisant Babylone* ("Semiramis Building Babylon," ca. 1861) and Rossini's opera *Semiramide*, which had its premiere in Venice in 1823.[3] The legendary Semiramis may possibly be identified with an actual Assyrian queen, Shammuramat, the Babylonian wife of the Assyrian king Shamshi-Adad V (ruled 811–808 BCE) and a powerful figure in her own right who may have acted as regent for her son, Adad-nirari III, when he acceded to the throne.

We owe the initial rediscovery of what the scholar H. W. F. Saggs aptly titled "the might that was Assyria" mainly to two Europeans: an English adventurer and diplomat, Austen Henry Layard, and a French diplomat, Paul-Émile Botta. Perhaps impelled by his cosmopolitan upbringing and education, Layard set out across Asia in 1839 in hopes of a posting in Ceylon (modern Sri Lanka; then part of Britain's vast empire), only to abort that plan en route and bounce around Mesopotamia and Persia for a while. During those early travels, he had opportunity to explore tells at Nimrud and Kuyunjik (near Mosul), two of the great ruin-mounds in the Tigris region of northern Mesopotamia. While at Kuyunjik, Layard met the young diplomat Paul Botta, who at that time was the French vice-consul stationed at Mosul. Botta had begun to explore the Kuyunjik mound in 1842. He now encouraged Layard to undertake his own excavations. After securing the support of the British Ambassador to the Ottoman government at Constantinople, Layard returned to northern Mesopotamia and, between 1845 and 1851, supervised extensive excavations at both Nimrud and Kuyunjik. Botta, meanwhile, began in 1843 to excavate at yet another mound in the region, near the village of Khorsabad. Both men believed they were excavating either at the biblically famous

Assyrian capital Nineveh or in its environs – testimony to the allure of this fabled site specifically, and biblical discovery in general, in nineteenth-century European minds.

Their excavations brought to light, for the first time in more than two thousand years, the Assyrian imperial capital cities of Kalhu (biblical Calah) at Nimrud, Nineveh at Kuyunjik and Nabi Yunus, and the previously unknown (and only briefly occupied) Assyrian royal palace at the capital city of Dur-Sharrukin (modern Khorsabad). Other archaeologists, from both Europe and the United States, followed Layard and Botta to continue and expand these excavations. Together, these explorations produced some of the most astounding – and unexpected – discoveries in the history of archaeology: enormous statues of winged bulls and human-headed guardian figures; thousands of meters of sculpted bas-reliefs, with detailed cuneiform inscriptions, that lined the walls of the royal palaces; and, perhaps the most significant of all, the clay-tablet library of the seventh-century BCE Assyrian king Ashurbanipal, arguably the single most important source for our knowledge of ancient Mesopotamian literature and science. The enduring impact of these discoveries, made in the land of Assyria, is reflected in the fact that the scholarly field of the study of the civilization of ancient Mesopotamia came to be known as "Assyriology," and its practitioners as "Assyriologists." Because of these pioneering discoveries, and the many more that were to follow until the eve of the recent wars that destabilized Iraq and interrupted the work of archaeologists there, historians have been able to fashion a detailed account of the history of ancient Iraq's first great age of empire.

We encountered the Assyrians in the preceding chapter, first, as the enterprising merchant families of the city of Ashur shortly after 2000 BCE; secondly, soon thereafter, during the era of the Amorite king Shamshi-Adad and his successors; and, thirdly, a few centuries later, during the time of the Late Bronze Age "club of the great powers," when the kings of Assyria were competing with the Kassite rulers of Babylonia.

In the later thirteenth century BCE, one of the Assyrian kings even conquered and sacked Babylon – an act that, given Babylon's revered status, was regarded by many as sacrilege, perhaps equivalent to sacking the Vatican or Mecca today. That conquest also led the impressionable Assyrians to import ancient Babylonian religious observances as well as the Babylonian literary dialect of the Akkadian language. Although Assyria had achieved political and military preeminence, Babylon's cultural preeminence was undeniable.

By 1000 BCE, Assyria had sunk into decline, but that decline was brief. In the early ninth century BCE, two mighty warrior-kings, Ashurnasirpal II and Shalmaneser III (whose reigns spanned the period 883–824 BCE), expanded Assyria's conquests to their farthest extent yet, reaching east into Iran, north into Anatolia, west to the Mediterranean, and south to tame the power of Babylon.[4] These early conquests set the stage for the even greater conquests their successors were to achieve during the eighth and seventh centuries BCE. But these two kings also defined a style of imperial rule that, even today, while it awes us with its grandeur, also disgusts us with its brutality; an eerie precedent for what was to follow millennia later under Saddam Hussein, who brashly borrowed from the same imagery the Assyrian kings utilized.

The first of these kings, Ashurnasirpal II (ruled 884–859 BCE), rebuilt and fortified the capital city at ancient Kalhu (Nimrud) in spectacular fashion, erecting temples and a magnificent palace – the opening of which he celebrated with a huge party, so he tells us. The historian A. T. Olmstead once famously referred to Ashurnasirpal's "calculated frightfulness;" H. R. Hall described him as possessing a "ruthless and unsparing nature that beat down all opposition by the method of absolute annihilation," for "no human pity existed in the breast of Ashurnasirpal."[5] They could describe Ashurnasirpal as so fearsome because of the sculpted and inscribed bas-reliefs that Layard and those who followed him found at Nimrud. These reliefs, originally brightly painted, covered the lower portion of the walls of much of the palace, as well as the walls of the temple Ashurnasirpal built to honor the warrior-god Ninurta. [6] They provide some of the starkest, most graphic depictions of Assyrian conquests and the horrors the Assyrians inflicted on recalcitrant conquered peoples. They also vividly depict the onslaughts of Ashurnasirpal's mighty war machine, which was by far the best organized and equipped of its time, with infantry, chariotry, cavalry, and battering rams. Along with the similarly graphic reliefs discovered at Nineveh (dating to more than two centuries later), they also show us that to submit meekly before the might of the Assyrian king was far more prudent than resisting it, because to resist him was to resist the viceroy of the Assyrians' supreme god, Ashur, whose divine wrath the king believed he was justified in meting out as the god's avenging avatar.

The scale of that wrath taxes our ability to imagine it. For example, Ashurnasirpal boasts that, after one city refused to submit,

> I flayed [i.e., skinned alive] as many nobles as had rebelled against me and draped their skins over the pile of corpses; some I spread out within the pile, some I erected on stakes upon the pile...I flayed many right through my land and draped their skins over the walls...
>
> I felled 50 of their fighting men with the sword, burnt 200 captives from them, and defeated in a battle on the plain 332 troops...With their blood I dyed the mountain red like red wool, and the rest of them the ravines and torrents of the mountain swallowed. I carried off captives and possessions from them. I cut off the heads of their fighters and built with them a tower before their city. I burnt their adolescent boys and girls.[7]

Such brutal treatment of recalcitrant subjects persisted as an aspect of Assyrian imperialism down to the end of the empire. One of the later Assyrian kings, Sennacherib, built his palace at the great capital of Nineveh, where Layard discovered bas-reliefs that he estimated might have stretched for two miles if they were lined up in a row. Like Ashurnasirpal's reliefs at Nimrud, these featured graphic depictions with accompanying narratives inscribed in cuneiform. In one of them, Sennacherib relates his destruction of the armies of the kingdom of Elam:

> I cut their throats like lambs. I cut off their precious lives (as one cuts) a string. Like the many waters of a storm, I made (the contents of) their gullets and entrails run down upon the wide earth. My prancing steeds harnessed for my riding, plunged into the streams of their blood as (into) a river. The wheels of my war chariot, which brings low the wicked and the evil, were bespattered with their blood and filth. With the bodies of their warriors I filled the plain, like grass. Testicles I cut off, and tore out their privates like the seeds of cucumbers.[8]

Moreover, the divine justice of Ashur, as meted out by the Assyrian king, was not limited to this world. The bas-reliefs of Sennacherib's grandson, Ashurbanipal, found at his own Nineveh palace, record the Assyrians' destruction of, yet again, the army of Elam at the Battle of Til-Tuba during the seventh century BCE. Besides telling how he fed the dismembered bodies of dead Elamites "to the dogs, swine, wolves, and eagles, to the birds of heaven and the fish of the deep," Ashurbanipal reports his treatment of the dead ancestors of the vanquished Elamite king:

> The sepulchers of their earlier and later kings, who did not fear Ashur and [the goddess] Ishtar, my lords, and who had plagued the kings, my fathers, I destroyed, I devastated, I exposed to the sun. Their bones I carried off to Assyria. I laid restlessness upon their shades. I deprived them of food-offerings and libations of water.[9]

The Elamite king himself was killed in the battle; Ashurbanipal's bas-reliefs depict how amid the battlefield melee an Assyrian soldier decapi-tated him. Afterward, the battle won and the Assyrian conquest of Elam assured, we see Ashurbanipal, his queen, and their servants refresh-ing themselves at an intimate party in a pleasure garden. Overhead, prominently displayed, is a macabre party decoration: the Elamite king's severed head, hung from a tree limb.

The underlying rationale for Assyrian conquest, besides validating the supremacy of Ashur, was to enrich the Assyrian crown and state by exploiting the natural and human resources of conquered lands, which the Assyrians had no qualms about removing to Assyria. Consequently, Assyrian rule did not sit lightly on their subjects, and the history of the Assyrian empire is full of attempts by rebellious vassals to shake off the Assyrian yoke.

It was in this connection that the West's most deeply rooted and longest-enduring images of Assyria came into being, for among the peoples caught up in the Assyrian onslaught were the early Israelites, whose experience of Assyrian rule was memorialized in several books of the Bible. To understand how and why biblical attitudes toward the Assyrians took shape as they did, we need to sketch a skeletal framework of the early history of the Jewish people.

ASSYRIA AND THE BIBLE: CREATING A BOGEYMAN

Scholars have long wrestled with the factuality of the biblical accounts of the early history of the people who came to be known as the people of Israel. Today, most historians would relegate to the realm of legend or mythology the accounts of the ancestral patriarchs Abraham, his son Isaac, Isaac's son Jacob, and the twelve sons of Jacob. Following the era of the patriarchs, which most scholars believe reflects conditions of the early and mid-second millennium BCE, the Bible tells of a period during which the Israelites migrated to Egypt, where they were soon enslaved. This era of bondage ended with the emergence of a charismatic leader named Moses, one of the most central and powerful figures in the history of the Jewish people – and of monotheism in general. Endowed by the Hebrew god Yahweh with the power to work miracles, Moses performed feats that inspired both awe and dread in the Pharaoh, which led him finally to permit the Israelites to leave Egypt. As the book of Exodus famously relates, Pharaoh soon regretted his decision and set out with his army after the Israelites, only to be thwarted when Moses miraculously parted the Red Sea to enable the Israelites to escape and then caused the sea to close over and destroy the pursuing Egyptians. Egyptian records say nothing of such a disaster – one of a number of reasons why scholars doubt that any of it ever took place. The biblical account goes on to describe how Moses led the Hebrews across the Sinai desert to the "Promised Land" – what is today Israel/Palestine. En route, he received from Yahweh, atop Mt. Sinai, the Ten Commandments. Again, historical corroboration of these events from sources outside the Bible is essentially nonexistent.

The Bible then tells how after Moses' death the Israelites, now led by a warrior named Joshua, made their way into Palestine, where they defeated – and in some cases annihilated with a brutality on a par with the Assyrians' methods – many local peoples and thereby established themselves on the land in a process traditionally referred to as the "Hebrew conquest." Although archaeological data render these events more amenable to scientific investigation, we still struggle with the facts of what actually happened. Finally, in the face of the dire threat posed by the Philistines – themselves newcomers, probably from Greece or the Aegean region, to the region that still bears their name, Palestine – the Israelites united under a warrior-chieftain named Saul, who, the Bible says, was anointed by Samuel as the first king to rule over a united Israelite people. After a brief reign, Saul was killed in battle. He was succeeded by a former protégé, David, who was in turn succeeded by his son Solomon. The reigns of these two kings, which probably span the era ca. 1000 to ca. 920 BCE, are commonly regarded as the golden era of the "United Monarchy" of the Israelite people. Modern scholars question the veracity of the biblical accounts that credit David and Solomon with the conquest of a far-flung empire, which they ruled from a magnificent capital at Jerusalem, conquered by David, but most accept the Bible's basic assertion that Jerusalem was the capital of a united Israelite state, whatever its actual size or name might have been at this time. Solomon was also responsible for completing the construction of what became the centerpiece of early Jewish ritual and belief: the great temple at Jerusalem, which in Jewish history is recognized as the "First Temple."

Also by this time there seems to have emerged a tradition that the Israelite people – and Israelite political statehood – consisted of twelve "tribes" descended from the sons of Jacob. The united Israelite kingdom of the era of David and Solomon consisted of two distinct entities. To the north, in a region more blessed with natural resources, was the land of Israel, identified with the territory traditionally associated with the ten northern tribes of the Israelites. To the south, in the territory traditionally associated with the two southern tribes (Judah and the very small tribe of Benjamin), was the land of Judah. The death of Solomon ca. 920 BCE spawned a civil war that left these two regions independent and divided against each other, with Judah and Israel ruled by different lineages of kings from their respective capitals at Jerusalem and Samaria.

Only in the ninth century BCE, in the era of the Assyrian conquests under Ashurnasirpal II and Shalmaneser III, do we see these biblical kingdoms – especially the more powerful and wealthy Israel – emerge into the full light of history.[10] Assyrian records note Ahab, the ruler of Israel, among the leaders of a hostile coalition that Shalmaneser's army fought at the Battle of Qarqar in 853 BCE. On a later Assyrian monument known as the Black Obelisk, amid scenes of tribute being paid from various lands to the Assyrian king, appears Jehu, Ahab's successor, pros- trating himself in submission before Shalmaneser. After Shalmaneser's death in 824 BCE, Assyrian authority in the region declined for a brief spell, during which the rulers of Israel began to reassert their autonomy. But that was soon squelched as the Assyrians began to reimpose their domination after the accession in 744 BCE of the great king Tiglath- pileser III, who embarked upon a major reorganization of the Assyrian imperial administrative system as well as launching new military cam- paigns. Soon he was turning his attention to the ten northern tribes of the kingdom of Israel. The biblical and Mesopotamian accounts of the Assyrian conquest of Israel are often contradictory, but between 733 and 720 BCE, after a series of attacks by Tiglath-pileser III, Shalmaneser V, and Sargon II, Israel's royal capital of Samaria and other major set- tlements were captured, its royal lineage was extinguished, and the kingdom became a province of the Assyrian empire.

Most famously for later history, both the Bible and the Assyrian inscriptions report that by the end of these campaigns the Assyrians had forcibly deported into faraway exile thousands of the people of Israel. Therein lie the origins of one of the more enduring and mysterious lega- cies of ancient Iraq's interaction with the ancient people of the Hebrew Bible: the legends surrounding the Ten Lost Tribes of Israel.[11] The Bible loses sight of these people, but for centuries afterward travelers and explorers, upon encountering a people previously unknown to them, would attempt to identify them as a remnant of the Ten Lost Tribes. When Europeans "discovered" the New World, starting with Columbus's voyage of 1492, they were startled to find there people whom the Bible evidently had not mentioned. Yet, because these Europeans also believed in the inerrancy of the Bible as God's word, and therefore in its iner- rancy as a record of all of God's creation, including the peoples of the world, some among the discoverers were convinced that the people of the New World were the long-vanished Ten Lost Tribes of Israel. More than three hundred years after Columbus made landfall on San Salvador, the legend continued to shape explorers' dreams. When the American explorers Meriwether Lewis and William Clark were preparing for their epic expedition (1804–06) across the newly acquired Louisiana Purchase to the Pacific coast, Lewis met with the respected Philadelphia physician and scientist Dr. Benjamin Rush to discuss with him what they might expect to encounter. Dr. Rush exhorted Lewis to keep an eye out for the Ten Lost Tribes of Israel.[12]

Mass deportation was an expedient the Assyrians commonly forced upon conquered peoples in order to uproot and dispossess them and thereby control and pacify them, as well as provide themselves with labor forces much needed for their state agricultural and construction projects. The Bible claims the Assyrians expelled all of the people of Israel, and until the modern discovery of the Assyrian records of these events this was the last supposedly reliable information about their location. Using the Assyrian records, however, we can track at least some of the Israelite exiles' routes and eventual destinations, in some instances as far away as Iran. We can also calculate the total number of those deported as around forty thousand. According to recent analysis of archaeological findings, that would have been no more than twenty percent – and perhaps as little as ten percent – of the population of Israel. In other words, most of Israel's population was not compelled to leave by the Assyrians, although they did indeed face Assyrian takeover and occupation when the Assyrians incorporated Israel into their empire as the province of Samerina. Possibly as many as eighty thousand of Israel's population fled south to Judah; others simply continued to occupy the lands where they had lived for centuries, though now as subjects of Assyrian overlords. Many of them likely intermarried with other people the Assyrians transplanted there. According to Assyrian records, among these newcomers were thousands of Babylonians and many Arabs, most of whom over time probably adopted the religion of the remaining Israelites and became a part of the Jewish population that would endure in the region for centuries to come.

The memory of Assyrian power and of the destruction and misery that the Assyrian conquests inflicted upon the people of Israel was stamped indelibly in later books of the Hebrew Bible. The Hebrew prophets rail against the wickedness of the city of Nineveh. The book of Jonah says that the prophet Jonah preached there and was frustrated when God refused to destroy the city. Jonah's association with the city in the Muslim tradition is evident even today in the name of one of the tells that comprise the ruins there: Tell Nabi Yunus, or the mound of the prophet Jonah, upon which is located a shrine honoring his grave. The Bible also identifies the Assyrians as God's chosen instrument for the punishment of the kingdom of Israel because it had strayed from God's laws and therefore had called down upon itself God's wrath. Thus, Isaiah 10:5:

> Ah, Assyria, the rod of my anger – the club in their hands is my fury! Against a godless nation I send him, and against the people of my wrath I command him, to take spoil and seize plunder, and to tread them down like the mire of the streets.[13]

With Israel disposed of, it was not long before the Assyrians turned their attention to its southern, less powerful neighbor, Judah, especially after its king Hezekiah decided (in 701 BCE) to rebel against the new Assyrian king, Sennacherib, who had acceded to the throne after his father, Sargon, was killed in battle four years earlier. The consequences of Hezekiah's rebellion are chronicled in both biblical and Assyrian sources, although the two sources relate markedly divergent versions of what happened. Sennacherib's army captured and sacked dozens of Judah's cities and villages, including the well-fortified city of Lachish, whose leaders Sennacherib's palace reliefs in Nineveh show spreadeagled on the ground and being skinned alive. The Assyrian account also claims that more than 200,000 Judahites were sent into exile. Then came the turn of Judah's capital, Jerusalem, which the Assyrians besieged, shutting in Hezekiah, according to Sennacherib's description, "like a bird in a cage."

Sennacherib's account goes on to say that Hezekiah submitted and paid heavy tribute (thirty talents of gold and eight hundred of silver) to save his city from the Assyrians' wrath. The biblical accounts (in 2 Kings and 2 Chronicles), on the other hand, relate a very different outcome: after the prophet Isaiah had reassured a fearful Hezekiah of God's favor, God rescued Hezekiah and Jerusalem by sending an angel to kill all 185,000 soldiers in the Assyrian camp. Nothing in any of the Assyrian sources speaks of an avenging angel, of course, or corroborates such a catastrophe. The Bible goes on to say that Sennacherib was assassinated soon thereafter by his sons – an event the Babylonian sources do confirm, albeit tersely. Thus met his end a great Assyrian king whom, for all his achievements, the Bible reviles as a paramount example of how the God of Israel controls all human destiny and punishes the arrogant:

> Against whom have you raised your voice and haughtily lifted your eyes? Against the Holy One of Israel…Have you not heard that I determined it long ago? I planned from days of old what I now bring to pass, that you should make fortified cities crash into heaps of ruins, while their inhabitants, shorn of strength, are dismayed and confounded; they have become like plants of the field and like tender grass, like grass on the housetops, blighted before it is grown. But I know your rising and your sitting, your going out and coming in, and your raging against me. Because you have raged against me and your arrogance has come to my ears, I will put my hook in your nose and my bit in your mouth. (2 Kings 19:22, 25–28)[14]

ASSYRIAN ZENITH

Less than a century after Sennacherib's death, parts of the empire did indeed rise up and strike back against their overlords in the northern

Mesopotamian palace-capitals. Before that happened, the empire shot to its apogee under Sennacherib's grandson, Ashurbanipal, the last of the truly great, and well-documented, Assyrian emperors. Upon becoming king of Assyria in 668 BCE, Ashurbanipal inherited a vast realm stretching from western Iran to the Mediterranean shores of what are now Syria, Lebanon, and Israel/Palestine. Three years before, Ashurbanipal's father, Esarhaddon, had invaded the Nile delta, initiating a millennia-long confrontation between Iraq and the powerful kingdom whose rulers had rivaled those of Mesopotamia since the dawn of civilization and would continue to do so in the centuries to come. Esarhaddon had succeeded in taking Egypt's northern capital, Memphis, only to lose it to rebellion soon after his departure. In 667 BCE, Ashurbanipal's armies returned to Egypt to retake Memphis, and by 664 they had taken the ancient temple-capital at Thebes as well.

With Ashurbanipal's conquest of Egypt, the Assyrian empire had become by far the largest empire in history up to that time. Now, at its zenith, that empire was not only vast but exceptionally organized, divided into provinces ruled directly by Assyrian governors and vassal states overseen more indirectly by local client-rulers who swore to support the Assyrian king with their loyalty, tribute, and manpower. Many of the administrative tools the Assyrians developed to rule their realm were adopted by later Middle Eastern empires. These included a road system with stages, upon which the Persians later elaborated and for which Herodotus caused them to get most of the credit, and paid inspectors and spies to provide intelligence. Precisely because it served as a model for even larger empires to come – many of them with their capitals in Iraq – the Assyrians' system for managing their empire and the concept of universal dominion it was designed to sustain were their most enduring and consequential contributions to the history of the Middle East.

Although Ashurbanipal ruled this empire at its zenith, his greatest achievement, from the standpoint of posterity, stems not from his military conquests but from his decision to send royal agents across his empire to collect and bring to Nineveh thousands of cuneiform tablets. Together, these contained the accumulated tradition of centuries of ancient Mesopotamian science, literature, and scholarship. Comprising the palace archive he inherited from his grandfather and father, the archive he established in his own new palace, and the archive in the temple of the god Nabu (patron of writing and learning), the library that Ashurbanipal created was the world's largest and most comprehensive up to that time.[15] Discovered by the pioneering nineteenth-century archaeologists, the remains of Ashurbanipal's library are now housed mainly in the British Museum in London. They remain our single most important source for the scholarly and literary tradition of ancient Mesopotamia, and especially for the science of divination – that is, the interpretation of omens, which over centuries of ancient Mesopotamian kingship had been thought of as vital to the kings' success and well-being. The tablets in Ashurbanipal's library further testify to the longevity and deep traditions underlying this scholarship: a large proportion of them are written in the Sumerian language, which had ceased to function as a spoken language well over a thousand years earlier. Many of the tablets provide the Akkadian (the language of Babylonia and Assyria) equivalents of Sumerian terms, but among the scholars who consulted the knowledge preserved in these tablets the Sumerian language possessed an almost sacred status – very like the status of Latin in medieval European religion and scholarship.

By the end of Ashurbanipal's reign the seeds of Assyria's demise had begun to sprout. Although scholars now estimate Assyrian rule to have been considerably less exploitative and more cooperative than they did even twenty years ago, conquered peoples tended then – as they do today – to resent foreign control. It ought not to surprise us then that even by the early seventh century BCE, when the empire was still at its height, some of them were beginning to throw off the Assyrian yoke. Among them was a recently arrived Iranian people, the Medes, who were later to contribute to the destruction of Assyria.

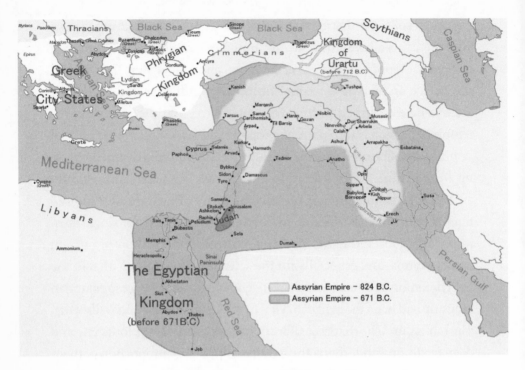

MAP 3. *Assyrian conquests (Wikimedia Commons)*

But nowhere does Assyrian rule seem to have been resented more than in the south, the traditional urban heartland of Babylonia.[16] It was here that, by the late eighth century BCE, yet another group of outsiders who were to become a major element in Iraq's history began to rise to leadership: the Chaldeans. Today, we know the Chaldeans as Iraqi Christians, many of whom have in recent years left the country. To Greek and Roman authors, the term "Chaldean" was associated with the Babylonian astronomers, astrologers, and scholars who had contributed so greatly to scientific knowledge – a debt to which those authors freely admitted. But when the Chaldeans first appear in cuneiform records (in 878 BCE) they are "tribal" people, perhaps of semi-nomadic origin and perhaps ethnically related to the Arameans and, like the Arameans, probably arrivals from the west. In contrast to the Arameans, they seem to have settled down quickly in both cities and villages, mostly in enclaves along the southern Euphrates, and to have readily adopted the culture of their Babylonian neighbors. Their chieftains soon assumed significant political and economic power in southern Mesopotamia, owing in large part to their geographical situation astride the major routes that connected the Mesopotamian cities located farther upstream with both the long-thriving Persian Gulf trade and trade partners in the Levant, northern Arabia, and Egypt.[17] Among those partners in the caravan trade were Arabs, groups of whom are in evidence in the lower Tigris–Euphrates floodplain by this time, profiting from that new engine of overland commerce that they had first domesticated: the camel.

With their economic resources, the Chaldean chieftains could muster sizeable armies, with which they sustained a political culture of resistance to Assyrian rule in what is now Iraq's deep south. The later Arab population of that region – down to the present – has traditionally manifested similar propensity to resist outsiders' attempts to dominate them.[18] By far the most celebrated of the early Chaldean rebels was Marduk-apla-iddina II (known as Merodach-baladan in the Bible), who usurped rule over Babylonia for about twelve years during the reign of the Assyrian emperor Sargon II. Sargon's successor, Sennacherib, was forced to send his armies into Babylonia on at least four different occasions to deal with the Chaldean rebels and their Elamite allies. In a harbinger of events to come more than 2,500 years later, Sennacherib's forces had to root out the rebels from the southern marshes, where they were often able to hole up beyond easy reach. In early 1991, after the Shi'ites of southern Iraq rose up against him following his defeat by U.S.-led forces, Saddam Hussein was forced to send troops into the region and, to deprive the rebels of a haven, to drain the marshes.[19]

Fed up with the Chaldeans' resistance, Sennacherib finally ordered his armies to sack and destroy the sacred city of Babylon, by then more than a thousand years old. This, which Babylonians and Assyrians alike regarded as sacrilegious, probably contributed to Sennacherib's later assassination. Aware how badly his father's actions had damaged Assyrian royal authority and prestige, Sennacherib's son and successor, Esarhaddon, began to rebuild Babylon. But Esarhaddon also contributed to the continuation of Babylonian resistance to Assyrian domination by assigning rule over Babylonia to his elder son, Shamash-shuma-ukkin, while allocating to a younger son, Ashurbanipal, rule over the remainder of Assyria's empire. In 652, seventeen years after their father's death, Shamash-shuma-ukkin rose against his brother in rebellion, aided and abetted by the Chaldean chieftains as well as by the King of Elam, Assyria's pernicious rival to the east. It took Ashurbanipal four years to quash his rebellious brother, who reportedly died in the conflagration of his torched palace. This event was remembered by Diodorus Siculus, as well as in later Western European art and literature, in the story of King Sardanapalus, who, faced with military defeat, killed himself by setting his own palace afire. Ashurbanipal then turned his attention to Elam, defeating and capturing the last of its kings in 640 BCE.

Almost as soon as he vanquished these threats, Ashurbanipal vanishes from our historical radar screen, leaving us precious little information with which to reconstruct the last fifteen years or so of his reign, which ended in 626 BCE. Upon his death, Babylonia broke away from Assyrian control once and for all, now to be ruled by the Chaldean prince Nabopolassar. Only seventeen years later, the mighty Assyrian empire was laid low, never to be revived, its great palace-capitals captured and smashed by the combined efforts of the new Chaldean rulers of Babylonia and the rulers of the Medes, those former Assyrian subjects in Iran who had risen up against their overlords and then sent their armies to destroy them.

Within a few centuries, the region of Assyria would begin to revive, though now under the tutelage of outsiders – this time, new Arab and Iranian overlords. By that time, the Bible's authors had compiled and edited the historical accounts and prophets' sayings that spawned the enduring image of Assyrian arrogance, and Greek and Latin authors had seized upon garbled memories of Assyrian might to construct tales of great figures like Semiramis, Ninus, Nimrod, and Sardanapalus. Many centuries later, after Layard, Botta, and their successors had brought to light the ruins of ancient Kalhu and Nineveh, the Christians of Iraq's north would claim the ancient Assyrians as their own ancestors, and the Iraqi Arab dictator Saddam Hussein would resurrect images of ancient Assyrian grandeur and frightfulness on murals, posters, currency, and postage stamps, appropriating them to advertise his own rise to power in the land of Sennacherib and Ashurbanipal.

BABYLON: THE CURSE OF AN ANCIENT IMAGE

The 2009 version of the *Merriam–Webster Online Dictionary* defines Babylon, very succinctly, as "a city devoted to materialism and sensual pleasure." [20] And a basic Google image search for "Babylon" will produce images ranging from fanciful depictions of the ancient city to covers of books bearing titles such as *Hollywood Babylon*, *Country Music Babylon*, and *Westminster Babylon* – not to mention a London escort agency named Babylon Girls.

Babylon was the nucleus of the lawgiver Hammurabi's kingdom and, after 610 BCE, became the capital of the Middle Eastern empire that the Chaldean king Nabopolassar inherited after the Chaldean–Median destruction of Assyria. Like the Assyrian capitals, Babylon was rediscovered and excavated only in modern times – in this instance, by a German expedition led by the archaeologist Walter Andrae, whose excavations of the site spanned the period 1899–1917. The architectural remains and cuneiform tablets those excavations produced demonstrated that Babylon was a huge city with a large, densely settled population, a myriad of temples and palaces, and an already ancient culture possessed of great learning and sophistication. But again, and even more than in the case of the Assyrians, the impact of scientific excavation and the translation of Babylon's clay tablets was largely preempted by the impressions that ancient literature had imprinted onto Western sensibilities over the centuries. The authors of the Bible and the historians of Greco-Roman antiquity had created an enduring, twisted image of the great city, only to have that image warped even further by medieval Christian European authors, for many of whom the idea of Babylon became bound up with their own bête noire, the Muslim evil in the East.

The perception of Babylon by Greek and Roman authors reflects a mixture of admiration of its wealth and stupendous construction and its learned scholars (especially its astronomers and astrologers) and revulsion from the strangeness of its customs.[21] The most famous aspect of Babylon's architecture was the so-called Hanging Gardens along with the city's walls, which were accounted one of the Seven Wonders of the World.[22] Reputedly built by a king for his Iranian queen who was homesick for the upland vegetation of her homeland, the Hanging Gardens were described as irrigated gardens constructed in terraces atop columns or arched vaults. These would have had to support tons of soil and vegetation. According to one account, the gardens included "broad-leaved trees of the kind that are commonly found in gardens, a wide variety of flowers of all species, and, in brief, everything that is most agreeable to the eye and conducive to the enjoyment of pleasure."[23] Modern archaeological excavation has found no trace of the Hanging Gardens. Recent re-examination of the evidence suggests that the Greeks and Romans may have got it wrong and these "gardens" were actually built at Nineveh by Sennacherib, under whom Assyrian engineers did rack up some outstanding achievements in hydraulic engineering.[24]

As early as Herodotus, classical authors also marveled at the size of the city and, especially, its walls. According to Herodotus, the walls of Babylon formed a perfect square, 120 Greek *stades* (more than twenty-one kilometers) on each side, with each wall 110 meters high and twenty-eight meters thick, all built of kiln-fired mud brick. Atop the wall were opposing single-room houses, with enough space between them for a four-horse chariot to be driven through. Another account claims that two four-horse chariots could pass each other in opposite directions. Set in the wall were a hundred gates, all of bronze. Within this great wall was another, so the city was protected with a double ring of fortifications. Babylon, says Herodotus, was divided into two halves by the Euphrates, one half dominated by the king's palace and the other by the great temple square, within which stood a great tower of eight stages (a ziggurat of classic type) topped by a great temple. In that temple was a great bed, upon which the god (whom Herodotus calls Zeus) would sometimes lie with a woman chosen by the Chaldean priests.

Although Herodotus refused to believe the priests' stories about the god visiting the woman in his temple, he was more credulous about another custom involving the women of Babylon – one about which historians have been arguing almost ever since. Herodotus relates that every Babylonian woman, whatever her social station, was required to prostitute herself in the temple of the goddess (Ishtar) whom he calls Aphrodite, by going to her temple, sitting in the sacred precinct with a string garland in her hair, and there having sex with the first man who tossed a coin into her lap. Good-looking women, he notes, needed little time to fulfill this requirement, but those less comely might have to stick around as long as three or four years. Most scholars today put little stock in Herodotus' account of Babylonian temple prostitution. One recent assessment calls it "rubbish" but notes that it has stimulated years of scholarly discussion; another suggests that it may preserve some memory of women who, more than a thousand years earlier, perhaps performed sexual acts as "priestesses" (not prostitutes) in rituals serving the cult of Ishtar.[25]

Whatever the impact of Herodotus' account of temple prostitutes, the modern perception of Babylon as a den of sexual license and depravity owes even more to the Bible's allegations. No biblical condemnation of Babylon is more famous than that in the New Testament's book of Revelation, where Babylon is a metaphor for the fallen Rome, which had long persecuted the early Christians. The author of Revelation conjures an apocalyptic vision of a woman sitting on a scarlet beast with seven heads and ten horns, "clothed in purple and scarlet, and adorned with gold and jewels and pearls, holding in her hand a golden cup full of abominations and the impurities of her fornication; and on her forehead was written a name, a mystery: 'Babylon the Great, mother of whores and of earth's abominations.'" Later an angel proclaims, "Fallen, fallen is Babylon the great! It has become a dwelling place of demons, a haunt of every foul spirit, a haunt of every foul bird, a haunt of every foul and hateful beast. For all the nations have drunk of the wine of the wrath of her fornication, and the kings of the earth have committed fornication with her, and the merchants of the earth have grown rich from the power of her luxury" (Revelation 17:3–18:3).[26] Over the centuries, during which many Western Christians adopted a literalist interpretation of what they believed to be God's word, Babylon was thus pinned with a reputation of evil, fornication, and depravity.

The Old Testament likewise hardly treats Babylonia and Babylonians kindly, although Genesis does claim that Abraham came originally from "Ur of the Chaldeans." Genesis also relates a famous story of how the descendants of Noah had migrated to a plain in the land of Shinar (Mesopotamia), where they found bitumen for mortar and material for making and firing bricks and thereupon decided to build a city and a great tower so as to "make a name for ourselves." At that time, Genesis notes, all peoples spoke the same language. When God saw these people raising this tower to the heavens, he feared that "nothing that they propose to do will now be impossible for them" and thereupon decided to confuse their language so they would not be able to understand each other. Consequently, these people scattered all over the earth, and the abandoned tower became known as Babel. The biblical author indicates that "Babel" is meant to convey the idea of confusion ("babble"), and the lesson here is to dissuade humans from such arrogance. In fact, the Tower of Babel quite obviously alludes to the building of a ziggurat, which required both fired brick and bitumen, the traditional temple-tower of Babylon ("Babel").

But the Hebrew Bible's perception of Babylon is shaped most strongly by one of the most searing, collectively traumatic, and historically consequential events in the history of the Jewish people. Before the modern recovery of cuneiform tablets that provided some evidence from the Babylonian perspective, the biblical accounts in the books of Kings and Chronicles and the books of several of the Hebrew prophets were our sole source of information about the Babylonian conquest of the kingdom of Judah and the events that followed. Today, with the benefit of that cuneiform evidence, we can assign exact dates to various events and corroborate elements of the biblical chronicle as well as other biblical stories relating to this event. For the Babylonians, these were relatively minor happenings – small-time compared with the events surrounding their overthrow and defeat of the Assyrians. For the Jews, however, Iraq now became a central part of their history.

With the fall of Assyria by 610 BCE, the Chaldean king Nabopolassar at Babylon inherited much of their empire, but Egypt – which had been under Assyrian dominion during the reign of Ashurbanipal – also re-emerged and tried to impose its sway along the Mediterranean, including in Judah. The Egyptians' hopes of entrenching their control there were smashed when the Babylonian army, led by Nabopolassar's son Nebuchadnezzar, defeated them. Soon afterward, Judah rose in rebellion against Nebuchadnezzar. In 597 BCE Nebuchadnezzar captured Jerusalem and deported the King, his family, and many of the upper class of Judah's society and carried off much of the wealth stored in the royal palace and the temple. Ten years later (587/586 BCE), after Zedekiah, the new king whom Nebuchadnezzar had installed to rule Judah, also rebelled, the Babylonians returned to inflict on Judah a horrible retribution. The Babylonian army once again conquered Jerusalem and laid waste to the city and its people. The Book of Lamentations describes them as vanquished and degraded, starved and suffering a humiliating punishment that God, using Nebuchadnezzar as his instrument, had decided to inflict upon his people because of their many transgressions. To complete their humiliation, the Babylonians looted and destroyed the cultic and spiritual centerpiece of early Judaism, the great temple Solomon had built. Finally, after killing the sons of King Zedekiah before him and then putting his eyes out, they deported him and thousands more of the people of Judah into exile in Babylonia. To be specific, cuneiform sources inform us, they were sent to the banks of the Kebar canal.[27]

There thus began the episode known in Jewish history as the Babylonian Captivity, as well as the even longer episode that came to be known as the Diaspora, or the dispersion of the Jewish people outside Palestine to eventually the four corners of the planet. The captivity was not to last all that long. Less than fifty years later, in 539 BCE, Cyrus the Great of Persia captured Babylon, brought an end to the line of Chaldean kings, and granted the exiles from Judah permission to return there, where they re-established themselves and soon began to build a new temple (the Second Temple) in Jerusalem. Yet, during that period of exile in Babylonia, many of the priests, scribes, and scholars who had been affiliated with the temple and the royal court in Jerusalem set to work collecting and editing manuscripts they had brought with them – manuscripts containing accounts and stories of their ancestors, kings, and laws. Thus began the process of assembling that body of literature that we know today as the Hebrew Bible, or Old Testament.

We now know that when Cyrus the Great offered the exiles from Judah the opportunity to return to Palestine, many – perhaps most – of them decided to stay put in Babylonia, where there soon arose several major centers of Jewish population, commerce, and learning, at Babylon itself as well as other cities in what are now Iraq and Iran. Those communities endured and prospered there for centuries. Before the events that led to the creation of the modern state of Israel in 1948, Iraq had the largest population of Jews anywhere in the Middle East. Life in Babylonia seems to have agreed with many of the exiled Jews. Those portions of the Bible that are set in the Babylonia of Nebuchadnezzar and his successors sometimes reflect how much they were awed by Babylon's size and splendor. But the biblical accounts also left an enduring image of the desolation and hatefulness of exile and subjugation at the hands of foreign rulers whose arrogance blinded them to the superiority of the Jewish God. The biblical prophets, none more powerfully than Jeremiah, promise a terrifying retribution against Babylon at the hands of a wrathful, avenging God. These themes are expressed in more biblical passages than I can begin to detail here, but some of those passages have been particularly well remembered and often cited, including in music. The heart-rending lament for Jerusalem with which Psalm 137 begins – "By the rivers of Babylon – there we sat down and there we wept when we remembered Zion" – was set to music by William Billings in his American revolution period allegorical choral work, "The Lamentation over Boston."[28] It also became the opening lyric of a popular reggae song during the 1970s.

Perhaps none of these tales has had more impact in this regard than the book of Daniel, which tells the story of a young Jewish man who with his friends was exiled from Jerusalem to Babylon. There he was able to parlay his skills as an interpreter of dreams into a career at the court of Kings Nebuchadnezzar and Belshazzar and eventually into the era of the Persian takeover, for Daniel also served the Persian king Darius – which from the standpoint of human longevity would have been quite impossible. Episodes from the book of Daniel reflect the biblical sense of the dangers that exile posed for the Jews, yet also the helplessness and futility of their royal captors before the power of the Israelite God. They also became for later medieval and modern European artists the inspiration for numerous works of art and music.[29] Thus, the story of the Fiery Furnace tells how Nebuchadnezzar condemned three young Jews to burn to death in a furnace because they refused to worship a golden idol, only to get his comeuppance when the flames refused to touch them and a fourth figure, presumably divine, appeared in the furnace with them. In another episode, the Persian King, at the behest of his jealous Babylonian courtiers, has Daniel thrown into a den of lions, only to find the next morning that the lions have not touched him – which causes the King to issue a proclamation commanding that the Israelite God be feared and revered throughout his kingdom. Finally, the book of Daniel relates the story of how King Belshazzar threw a great banquet and, evidently well in his cups, commanded that the gold and silver goblets that Nebuchadnezzar had looted from the temple in Jerusalem be brought in for all the party-goers to drink from. Suddenly, during the merriment, the fingers of a human hand appeared and wrote on the wall mysterious words that only Daniel could interpret. They foretold the destruction of the Babylonian empire and implicitly condemned its rulers for their hubris and their disrespect for the one true God. "Belshazzar's Feast" later became the subject of a famous painting by the seventeenth-century Dutch artist Rembrandt van Rijn, as well as the theme of a musical composition by the English composer William Walton. We still commonly use the expression "the writing's on the wall" when defeat or misfortune seems to be inevitable.

So the biblical authors were anything but glowing in their assessment of Babylon. Because the biblical version of Babylon became the template for later Christian assessments, Babylon was cursed to be remembered as a symbol of luxury, decadence, and virtually every possible kind of evil-doing, as well as a dangerous and powerful nemesis. The book of Revelation, as we have seen, perpetuated this stereotype. By the early Middle Ages, Babylon had been melded with the evils perceived in new existential threats to Christianity, be they barbarous pagans or the newest über-threat to Christian Europe: Islam. Although the early medieval epic *The Song of Roland* is about a supposed battle between the Christian Frankish warriors of Charlemagne and the Muslim Moors of Spain, it also tells of the "Amireil" of Babylon, "older than Virgil or Homer... [who] leads an army recruited from the entire non-Christian world, from pagan eastern Europe to Persia to Africa, under the banner of their triad of pagan gods. His recruits include monstrous subhumans" – including some with spines on their back, or that shine like armor.[30] In the late eighth-century Spanish *Chronicle of Alfonso III*, the Muslim rulers who then controlled much of Spain are characterized as "Chaldeans" who forced Christian Spaniards to pay tribute to the "King of Babylon" – for, by that time, Spanish chroniclers saw "their own struggles through the magnifying lens of the Old Testament prophets. The Muslims were the Chaldeans, who ruled from Babylon, and whose oppressive reign was ordained by God to punish the sins of the chosen people."[31]

The apocalyptic vision associated with Babylon in the book of Daniel, as well as in Revelation, even today influences political affairs. Those biblical books were among the sources used by the nineteenth-century Christian evangelist J. N. Darby, who formulated the version of Christian apocalypticism known as Dispensationalism, according to which the End of Days and the return of Christ hinge upon the restoration of Israel and the construction of the Third – and final – Temple at Jerusalem.[32]

"THE GREATNESS THAT [REALLY] WAS BABYLON"

The same H. W. F. Saggs who wrote a fine book on *The Might that Was Assyria* had earlier penned an equally fine book, *The Greatness that Was Babylon*, which was one of the first authoritative popular treatments that acquainted English-speaking audiences with the "real" Babylon as rediscovered by nineteenth- and twentieth-century scholars following the early excavations of the Assyrian capitals and Babylon. Since Saggs' book appeared, countless more cuneiform tablets have been translated and analyzed and more archaeological discoveries have been made at Babylon.

Between 610 and 539 BCE, Babylon was an imperial capital from where the Chaldean emperors ruled a vast realm that, though smaller than the Assyrian empire at its height, encompassed much of the Middle East. During its heyday in the sixth century BCE, Babylon was probably the greatest city on the planet. With the possible exception of Xian in China, it had no rival as an exemplar of monumental architecture or as a cradle and repository of high culture – religious, literary, and scientific. It was a cosmopolitan hub of commerce – as one scholar has described it, "a great harbor in a vast sea of resources, extending from Africa to Inner Asia, and from the borders of Europe to South Asia," a place where "a multitude of peoples, goods, and ideas mixed on a daily basis…gold from Africa, lapis from Afghanistan, amber from the Baltic, and carnelian from India."[33]

By the time of the Chaldean kings, Babylon was already an ancient city. Modern excavators have found practically nothing of Hammurabi's Babylon, which lies inaccessible beneath the underground water table. The remains that we know about today date to later periods, especially from the seventh century BCE, when the Assyrian king Esarhaddon began to rebuild the city after his father had destroyed it, down to the era of Alexander the Great's successors, during whose reigns some of Babylon's greatest buildings were degraded as their bricks began to be reused in new construction projects. Perhaps the most famous part of those remains, the Ishtar Gate, is no longer at the site of Babylon, having been removed by its German excavators and partially restored at the Pergamon Museum in Berlin. Other portions of the Ishtar Gate are housed in museums in cities across the West, including Istanbul, Detroit, Toronto, Paris, Philadelphia, New York, Chicago, Boston, and New Haven. None of it is in Iraq's possession, although Saddam Hussein did erect a replica at the site. In recent years, the site has been altered even more by politically motivated interventions. Saddam Hussein authorized a major "reconstruction" of portions of the site, and had a palace built there for himself, in order to tie his own political legitimacy to Babylon's greatness. During the post-2003 Anglo-American occupation, a military base was built atop the site, doing much damage to archaeological materials that military traffic churned up from beneath the surface.

Nonetheless, enough archaeological and textual information has been recovered and documented to enable us to reconstruct a magnificent city. Its greater area covered about 850 hectares, with an inner city of about four hundred hectares that could have sustained a population of around eighty thousand.[34] Both the greater city and its inner core were fortified with mud-brick walls. According to modern excavators, the outer fortifications formed a circuit of perhaps eighteen kilometers. Ancient sources claim a circuit several times longer, as well as wall heights anywhere from twenty-three to 102 meters.[35] Running along much of the western side of the outer walls was the Euphrates River, which thus served as an important component of the city's outer defense.

Within the outer fortifications wall lived a teeming, industrious population comprising people of various social stations and ethnicities: Babylonians, Chaldeans, Assyrians, Egyptians, Arameans, Iranians, and Jews. They occupied mud-brick houses that could be quite large, of two or three stories with a central courtyard. These dwellings were distributed across ten city districts that were served by a grid of straight streets. For some of these we even have street names, such as "Ishtar, Intercessor for Her People," or "Pray and He Will Hear You," or, more simply, "Narrow Street."[36] Interspersed among those city districts as well as within the city's inner core were forty-three temples and hundreds of shrines (fifty-five of them for Marduk, chief god of the Babylonian pantheon) and road-side chapels. [37]

Babylon's centerpiece was the magnificent monumental buildings of the inner, sacred city. This inner core was also the nerve center from where Nebuchadnezzar II, the conqueror of Judah, ruled an empire extending from the Mediterranean and the borders of Egypt in the west to what is now Iraq in the east. In that eastern region, besides the capital, were other cities of great antiquity and prestige. Although these too were under Nebuchadnezzar's sway, he was compelled to respect the status and prerogatives they had amassed over their long histories, some of which – as at Uruk, for example – extended more than two thousand years into the past. Nebuchadnezzar's dominions delivered to his royal treasury immense taxes and tribute. From the thousands of acres of irrigated floodplain owned by the King, the income the royal court received from thousands of cultivated acres managed by the great temple estates, and the cut taken by the crown from commerce that came through Babylonia, Nebuchadnezzar had a huge resource base with which to fund a variety of royal prerogatives.

None was more important than to build in the inner, sacred city great temples and palaces to shelter and serve the god Marduk and display the power and prestige of the King of Babylon, Marduk's earthly viceroy. Starting from north of the inner city was a great processional way along which images of Marduk and other gods were carried during the New Year Festival, in March or April, the most important of the ritual holidays in the Babylonian calendar. As it led south toward the inner walls that surrounded the sacred temple precinct, the processional way featured a colored stone-slab floor and was decorated along about 180 meters of the wall on both sides with blue-glazed brick bearing white images of lions, symbolic of Ishtar. It then crossed the inner walls through the Ishtar Gate, forty-eight meters long, originally more than twenty-three meters high, its bricks bearing 575 images of dragons and bulls, symbolic of the gods Marduk and Adad, respectively.[38] Past the Ishtar Gate, on the right-hand side of the processional way, stood the Southern Palace, the largest and most impressive of Nebuchadnezzar's three main palaces at Babylon. Its five courtyards and dozens of public and private rooms encompassed an area 325 by 220 meters. At the end of the central courtyard was a large throne room whose exterior façade was decorated with panels of glazed bricks bearing images of geometric patterns, trees, and animals.[39]

Farther down the processional way lay the holiest part of Babylon's sacred geography: the sacred precinct of Marduk. This included what was for Babylonians the holiest place in the world, Marduk's temple, Esagil (Sumerian: "House Whose Top Is High"). By Nebuchadnezzar's time Esagil was more than twelve hundred years old and had achieved huge dimensions, eighty-six by seventy-nine meters. It had always been the traditional responsibility of the king of Babylon to take good care of the god and his dwelling. Nebuchadnezzar had the resources to amply show his gratitude to Marduk as well as to ensure Marduk's continuing good favor. Thus, "there were gold, silver, and gemstones everywhere, and great doors and beams of Lebanese cedar. Throughout the temple were images of strange monsters – serpents and dragons, lion-demons and scorpion-men, bison and mermen; statues of dragons and goat-fish and sphinxes stood guard at its entrances." To top it off, rather than use the customary bitumen and gypsum to decorate interior walls, Nebuchadnezzar achieved the desired effect with much more luxurious materials: alabaster and lapis lazuli.[40] Esagil played a central role in the New Year Festival, for in a courtyard attached to the temple the festival culminated as the statues of Marduk and his son Nabu sat on a platform and determined the fate of the cosmos in the coming year. The platform was named the Dais of Destinies. It was sheathed in gold.

As one approached Esagil from the Ishtar Gate, one's field of vision would have been overwhelmed by the other component of the sacred precinct: the massive temple-tower, or ziggurat, known as Etemenanki (Sumerian: "Foundation Platform of Heaven and Underworld"), the basis for the Tower of Babel story in Genesis. Today it is simply a gaping hole, its bricks robbed away over the centuries, its demolition having started not many decades after Nebuchadnezzar's time. It is difficult to imagine how, in its time, it was never accorded the status of "Wonder of the World." As was noted earlier, Herodotus was hugely impressed by it. As was also noted before, archaeological findings cannot corroborate all that he says about it. But those findings, combined with evidence from a cuneiform tablet (the "Esagil tablet") that preserves an idealized description of its construction, make plain that this structure was one of the marvels of its time. The Assyrian kings Esarhaddon and Ashurbanipal worked on its restoration after Sennacherib had trashed it. Nebuchadnezzar's father Nabopolassar resumed the restoration. As completed by Nebuchadnezzar, Etemenanki measured ninety-one meters square and was of solid brick, with dried mud brick in the core and kiln-fired bricks for the outer casing. We cannot be certain of the height of the tower – the Esagil tablet says ninety-one meters whereas other estimates are as low as sixty-nine meters[41] – but we know that it consisted of seven stages of steadily decreasing size, with a triple stair-case on the south side that gave access to the top of the first stage. Atop the tower was a separate temple, covered in blue-glazed brick, with a courtyard, and in the temple Marduk sat enthroned, accompanied by Nabu and other gods. Of the rituals that were carried out in that temple, we know nothing.[42]

Etemenanki did not serve the same function as the pyramids of Old Kingdom Egypt – which were, after all, royal tombs – but in some ways its purpose was similar: to magnify royal glory and impress the onlooker. Etemenanki dominated the skyline of Babylon. Its looming presence must have awed residents inside the city as well as people approaching from outside the city walls – much in the way that someone approaching Chartres in France may be awed as the cathedral's spire rises on the horizon from several miles away.

Etemenanki also epitomized something else similarly to the Giza pyramids: that the king of Babylon, like the Old Kingdom pharaohs, possessed immense economic resources as well as the administrative apparatus and political clout to make effective use of them. To build such a massive temple-tower required both sophisticated engineering and the application of manpower almost unimaginable in a pre-industrial era. Nebuchadnezzar says he brought in workers from all over his empire and set them to work on the tower. Perhaps the babble of competing tongues contributed to the Tower of Babel story. The work would have been strenuous and the tasks diverse. None of the tasks would have been more important than making the bricks: mixing straw with mud, molding the bricks, setting them aside to dry, baking others hard in kilns, and procuring the fuel to keep the kilns fired up. Then would come the back-breaking work of stacking bricks, carrying bricks to the building site, laying the bricks, applying mortar to the fired bricks that made up the external casing. The laborers required water, food, clothing, shelter, all of which had to be organized by the royal administration. We can get a stronger sense of the immensity of the project by noting that the estimates of how many bricks were required range from thirty-two to forty-five million, with a total weight of several hundred thousand tons.[43]

With its temples, palaces, and commerce, Nebuchadnezzar's Babylon was *the* megalopolis of its era, surely a source of pride to its ruler and people then, just as it is a source of pride to Iraqis today. Yet one can argue that this urban bigness of Babylon obscures an even more significant, more enduring aspect of its greatness: its legacy as an engine of scientific learning and scholarship. Much of that scholarship was undertaken in the service of Marduk and other gods, as well as the king. As we will explore later, Babylonians and Assyrians believed that their destinies were in the hands of the gods, who controlled everything that happened in the human world, from weather to warfare. It was the gods who determined success or failure for human enterprises. Therefore, the most prudent course of action for humans was to honor and fear the gods and to serve and propitiate them properly. The king was especially responsible for ensuring that the god's house (the temple) was built sturdily, decorated sumptuously, and well served by priests and servants whose job was, as one Assyriologist once termed it, to ensure the god's "care and feeding" by performing sacrifices and other rituals at prescribed times throughout the year.

Keeping the gods happy was thought to be essential to alleviate one's sense of human powerlessness before them. A particularly effective safeguard against the potentially ill effects of divine decisions was the ritual taking of omens. Babylonians believed that the gods signified their decisions via natural phenomena and that experts properly trained in reading those signs could help the king avert disaster by ensuring that his actions accorded with divine intentions. Even before 2000 BCE, there had developed in royal courts a class of what we might call scholar-priests who had developed omen techniques based on the ritual sacrifice of a sheep and ensuing inspection and interpretation of its liver for signs of the god's intentions. Centuries later, Ashurbanipal collected his great library at Nineveh largely to ensure that his own scholar-priests had the best possible collection of reference works for the accurate interpretation of such omens.[44] We have evidence of other means of taking omens as well, including the interpretation of the appearance of celestial bodies: the moon, the planets, and the stars. By the time of Nebuchadnezzar, the science of divination was based increasingly on the observation and interpretation of the skies. We know that by 1600 BCE Mesopotamian observers were already recording movements of heavenly bodies and had devised a lunar calendar consisting of alternating months of twenty-nine and thirty days, adding a month every three years to keep up with the solar year. Even a century before Nebuchadnezzar's time, Babylonian astronomers had structured the day into twelve double-hours of sixty double-minutes, which later Greek astronomers converted to twenty-four single hours of sixty single minutes. The Babylonians had also calculated the exact length of the solar year and created a calendar that added an extra lunar month every two or three years. In time, the Jews exiled to Babylonia adopted this calendar. It eventually became the basis of the Jewish and Christian religious calendars.

Combining the work of their earlier counterparts with that achieved under Nebuchadnezzar and his successors, and still using much of the scientific vocabulary of the Sumerians, Babylonian astronomers compiled a record of systematic, detailed observations of the heavens that extends over eight hundred years – as one recent assessment puts it, "the longest sustained research project in world history."[45] The work of these "Chaldean" star-gazers became the foundation for the advances later made by Greek astronomers, whose legacy in turn became the foundation of Western astronomy. The Babylonian astronomers compiled this information in the service of divination, in the belief that the gods literally inscribed their decisions in the heavens. This became the foundation of astrology. It was Babylonian astronomers who first devised the zodiac of twelve divisions and then later used the zodiac along with the position of certain stars at birth to chart horoscopes. The "magi" famous to the Greeks and Romans, and in the New Testament, learned their astronomy and astrology from the Babylonians. Greek astronomers picked up this knowledge from them and came to refer to astronomers and astrologers, and wise men in general, as *magoi* – the origin of our "magic."[46]

Yet it is only recently that the Babylonian contribution to the history of Western science has come to be properly recognized as such.[47] A similar lack of recognition has undervalued the work of Babylonian mathematicians, whose sexagesimal system, based on the number 60, led them to order things in units of 6, 12, or 60, or in numbers evenly divisible by 60. Their use of place notation was adopted by Indian mathematicians, who converted it to a base-10 system and added the concept of zero – all of which was adopted in turn by Arab mathematicians, who bestowed it upon Western science.[48] As one scholar notes, the Babylonian scientific legacy:

> permeates the divination, astrology, and astronomy of Eurasia from the beginning of the last millennium BC, and was the basis for much of what was done in Greece, in India, in Sasanian Iran, in Byzantium, in Syria, in Islam, in Central Asia, and in Western Europe. Even when local cultures imposed changes and improvements, the Babylonian identification of significant phenomena,

and the parameters and structures of their mathematical models, provide continuing evidence of their presence.[49]

THE LONG TWILIGHT OF IRAQ'S ANCIENT IMPERIAL ERA

The reign of Nebuchadnezzar, despite its harsh treatment in the Bible, marked the zenith of the Babylonian empire, but it is also safe to say that by the time his reign ended (in 561 BCE) the writing really was on the wall. The succession after him was troubled and his successors for the most part were undistinguished. Their policies were dictated largely by the need to maintain trade, and hence wealth, but Babylonia's trade routes were becoming increasingly blocked to the east (by the Medes), north (by the newly emerged kingdom of Lydia in what is now western Turkey), and south, where the all-important harbors at the head of the Persian Gulf may have been becoming unusable because of the build-up of alluvial silt from the Tigris and Euphrates. Therefore, the Babylonian kings had to look west, but they faced problems there as well. Nebuchadnezzar's defeat of the Egyptians in 605 BCE had thwarted the Pharaoh's designs on the Mediterranean ports of Syria and Palestine, and his conquest of Judah by 586 had forestalled problems from that quarter. But by the sixth century BCE a new power was arising in the west: the Greek city-states of both the Greek mainland and Ionia (the western coastal region of modern Turkey), which were beginning to dominate trade in the eastern Mediterranean.

This may explain some of the unusual actions taken by the last of the major Chaldean kings, Nabonidus, one of Nebuchadnezzar's generals, who ascended the throne in 555 BCE. Nabonidus seems to have revered the ancient past of Babylonia, going to some lengths to excavate and restore ancient temples and to emulate practices of his ancient predecessors. For example, like the great Sargon of Akkad almost two thousand years earlier, he set up his daughter as high priestess of the moon-god, Sin, at the ancient city of Ur.[50] He himself hailed from a long-time center of moon worship, the city of Haran in northwestern Mesopotamia, where his long-lived mother, Adad-guppi, had served as the moon-god's chief priestess. As it turned out, it was probably his own devotion to the moon-god that troubled his reign and besmirched his later reputation. One ancient source describes Nabonidus as the "king who did not revere [Marduk]," though other sources show that he contributed dutifully to the upkeep of Marduk's temple precinct in Babylon.

Nabonidus abruptly left Babylon to set himself up for ten years at the Arabian oasis town of Taima, where he built a palace and served the moon-god, who already had a sanctuary there. To the Marduk priesthood this smacked of madness, especially because, although he did leave his son Belshazzar at Babylon to handle things in his absence, Nabonidus was ten years absent from the annual New Year Festival, the king's participation in which was considered indispensable for both his and the city's well-being. There may have been a method in Nabonidus' alleged madness, however. Worship of the moon-god was widespread among the peoples of his empire, especially among Arameans and Arabs. It is possible that with his sojourn at Taima Nabonidus was trying to promote such worship as a means of unifying his empire in the face of new threats.[51] Moreover, Taima was an important station along the camel-caravan route that now connected Mesopotamia and the Levant with the southwestern Arabian Peninsula (modern Yemen) – the region that produced the frankincense and myrrh of the booming incense trade. Nabonidus may have established himself at Taima in hopes of controlling this trade and thereby gaining much-needed revenue for Babylon.

Whatever his intentions, the ancient sources remember Nabonidus as despised by his subjects and rejected by the offended Marduk. Although he did eventually return to Babylon, it was too late to forestall his fall at the hands of a new conqueror, one of those few in world history who have rightfully been accorded the epithet "the Great."

Kurush of Parsua was looming on the imperial horizon. Parsua, or Persia, corresponds to the modern region of Fars in southern Iran. Kurush is more recognizable to us by the name by which the West came to know him: Cyrus. Because the Greeks believed he descended from a notable ancestor whom they knew as Achaemenes, we know his dynasty – perhaps the most celebrated in the history of ancient Iran – as the Achaemenids. Starting around 550 BCE, Cyrus had won a vast realm that stretched from the Indus westward into the region of modern Turkey. It included the realm of the Medes, who had been instrumental in felling Assyria, and – fatefully for Western civilization – the kingdom of Lydia and the Greek city-states along its western coast. Now it was to be Mesopotamia's turn. Cyrus' army fought its way down the Tigris and, in 539 BCE, marched into Babylon, where Cyrus dethroned the hapless Nabonidus. According to the (hardly unbiased) cuneiform text known as the Cyrus Cylinder,

> All the people of Babylon, the entire land of Sumer and Akkad, rulers and princes, bowed down to him, kissed his feet, and rejoiced at his rule, filled with delight. They happily greeted him as the lord, by means of whose trust those who were as dead were revived and saved from all trial and hardship; they praised his name.[52]

Thus ended the last dynasty of ancient rulers of Iraq who could claim to be, to some extent, natives of the region. Cyrus claims to have protected Babylon, its temples, and its people, as well as the other cities of Babylonia. Babylon continued to be a great city, but the great ceremonial city of Persepolis, in modern Iran, became the real showplace of Persian grandeur. Babylonia was incorporated as a province into the Persian empire, with Babylon now a center of Persian rule. The Persian overlords undertook new irrigation projects to generate even more of the great wealth that for centuries had been tapped from the

Mesopotamian floodplain; according to Herodotus, Babylonia was the wealthiest province in the Persian empire. Assyria and its once great capitals, meanwhile, were reduced to a backwater, evidently not recovered from their devastation at the hands of the Medes less than a century before. As had been the case with Elamites and Gutians in the past, and would be with Safavids and Shi'ite revolutionaries in the future, the people of southern Mesopotamia resisted domination by Iranian outsiders, rallying behind local insurgents against the Persians.[53] Two of the insurgent leaders adopted the nom de guerre "Nebuchadnezzar." The Persians responded, of course. In suppressing a Babylonian revolt, the Emperor Darius began to dismantle the outer core of Babylon's ziggurat of Etemenanki; in the decades to come, his Achaemenid successors – and the successors of Alexander the Great – would complete the destruction.

Among those residents of Babylonia who prospered with the coming of the Persians were the Jews whose ancestors had been deported there by Nebuchadnezzar. The prophet Jeremiah had exhorted them to make good lives for themselves in their new surroundings. If the evidence from a fifth-century BCE archive from the Babylonian city of Nippur is any indication, they seem to have taken that advice to heart.[54] Jews appear frequently in these texts operating as entrepreneurs unburdened by discrimination, freely participating in a range of commercial activities and fully assimilated into the local community, even giving their children Babylonian names. But, as we shall see, the Jews of Babylonia also engaged in an energetic spiritual life that would be enriched by new influences from Babylonia's cosmopolitan culture. Indeed, Babylonia was to become a cradle of Judaism itself.

On the other hand, those Jews of Babylonia who desired to return to Judah, now also a province in the Persian empire, had been freed to do so by Cyrus. Consequently, the biblical authors treat Cyrus the Great as a hero – something that by its contrast with the actions of Nebuchadnezzar and Belshazzar reinforces the Bible's negative view of the Chaldean rulers of Babylon. Yet it was under those Chaldean rulers that Jewish assimilation and acculturation in Mesopotamia began. As we shall see, as a by-product of that Chaldean-era assimilation the Jews of Babylonia may have contributed to a variant strain of monotheism, one that a few centuries later emerged from the oases and deserts of the Arabian Peninsula.

4

CRADLE OF RELIGIONS,
CRUCIBLE OF CONFLICTS

I N THE WEST, most discussions about religion are grounded in the
presumption that religion is a separate and distinct aspect of life –
belonging to a spiritual, supernatural realm that we take great pains
to keep separate from the secular aspects of existence. In much of the
ancient world – and especially in ancient Mesopotamia – we find little
evidence of such a distinction. There is no specific word in the Akkadian
language of ancient Assyria and Babylonia to which we can assign the
meaning "religion." As one scholar has noted, "the corollary was that the
whole range of experience that is distinguished and described as religion
in the modern world was taken for granted in ancient Mesopotamia."[1]
Moreover, Westerners have presumed that monotheism – especially the
Judeo-Christian tradition – is inherently superior to polytheism and
thus the proper foundation of the religions of civilized societies. We also
tend to think of that tradition of monotheism as essentially belonging
to the West. And no wonder. The preponderance of political, military,
and economic power in modern times has been situated in Europe
and the Americas, where Christianity has long dominated. And after
centuries of often virulent anti-Semitism the West has largely embraced
Judaism, especially in its political support of the modern state of Israel.

But neither Judaism nor Christianity was in its origins a "Western" monotheism. Both of these religions are deeply rooted in the soil of the Middle East, beginning in Palestine but then blossoming across the entire region, from North Africa to Iran.

Nowhere in this region were those early monotheisms nurtured and sustained more than in Iraq. Jews had come to Iraq by the eighth century BCE. Christians were likely there by the late first century CE. These two spiritually related communities coexisted and interacted there from then on, and interacted with other religious communities there as well, down to the late twentieth century. Those other communities helped to shape and enrich Judaism and Christianity, both of which in turn contributed to what became the predominant strain of monotheism in the region: Islam.

When monotheism first took root in Iraq, it did so in a spiritual soil already well watered and fertilized by millennia of religious belief and ritual. Among very traditional Muslims, the pre-monotheistic world is often regarded as the age of *jahiliyya*, or ignorance – specifically, of knowledge of the one God. For Jews and Christians, it was a world of "pagans" and "idolaters" in thrall to false belief, superstition, and evil. As we have seen, the Bible has nothing but scorn for them. Yet it was from the beliefs and stories of these people of ancient Iraq that there emerged some of the more enduring stories and doctrines preserved in "Western" monotheisms.

RELIGION IN ANCIENT MESOPOTAMIA/IRAQ

The connections of the early Jewish people with the history of ancient Mesopotamia are numerous, as we have seen, and are evident from the beginning of the Bible. Adam and Eve dwelled in the lush Garden of Eden, says Genesis, and historians today agree that the Garden of Eden story is set somewhere in the south of Mesopotamia. Indeed the word "Eden" is derived from the Sumerian word for "grasslands," *edin*. Genesis also claims that Abraham came from "Ur of the Chaldeans." For all the scorn that the biblical authors heaped upon the Assyrians and Babylonians, they show no awareness that some of their most enduring stories and religious attitudes parallel those of the people of ancient Mesopotamia and, quite often, were borrowed directly from them. Recent scholarship has discovered that the ancient Greeks owed them a great debt as well.

One of the most central concepts in the earliest religions of Mesopotamia was also embraced by the ancient Greeks but came to be rejected in the Bible: polytheism, or the idea that the supernatural world was dominated, not by one God, but by many gods. It is worth noting here that scholars believe that the early Hebrews likewise worshiped more than one god, perhaps even as late as the exile to Babylon. The exclusivist monotheism of the Jews perhaps did not really take hold until then. The Assyrian supreme god, Ashur, and the supreme god of the Babylonians, Marduk, were two of the more prominent of the hundreds of deities, major and minor, who inhabited the ancient Mesopotamians' world of the divine. Some of their names appear in the earliest administrative records of temple households at Sumerian cities like Uruk. The gods' origins are associated with natural forces and elements, but over time these divine forces of nature took on human attributes that often seem to be linked to the corresponding natural phenomena. Thus, among the early Sumerians, the gods An ("sky" or "heaven"), Enlil ("lord storm" or "lord wind"), Enki ("lord earth," but with reference to the fresh water underground), and Ninhursag ("lady mountain," also known as Nintu, or "lady birth") held special prominence. The scholar Thorkild Jacobsen identified these four deities as personifications of specific social–cultural forces: An, of authority; Enlil, of force; and Enki and Ninhursag, of creativity and fertility.[2] Among the other major Sumerian gods were Utu, the god of the sun (also associated with justice and divination); Nanna, the god of the moon; and Inanna (later known as her Semitic counterpart, Ishtar), the goddess of sex and feminine beauty. The late scholar Tikva Frymer-Kensky labeled Inanna/Ishtar earthily but accurately as the "cosmic cunt."[3] An early second-millennium BCE mythological tale about this goddess says, "sixty then sixty satisfy themselves in turn upon her nakedness. Young men have tired, Ishtar will not tire."[4]

Like Ashur at his city of Ashur and Marduk at his Babylon, these earliest Sumerian deities had their own temples at their own special cities in Mesopotamia – none more famously than Enlil, the most powerful of the Sumerian gods, with his temple Ekur ("house mountain") at the city of Nippur. They also had the company of their own "holy family" (spouse and children), just as some Bible scholars now believe that the Hebrew god Yahweh had his own divine consort, Asherah, whom the early Israelites also worshiped. A hierarchy of minor deities, all with their assigned roles and responsibilities, staffed the divine household of the major gods and goddesses.

As was also often the case for the Israelites of the Bible, the people of ancient Iraq believed themselves utterly dependent on the gods' good favor, which they could hope to curry only by treating them with the utmost respect. For that reason they built the temples that were the gods' domiciles, as Solomon did for Yahweh in Jerusalem, and provided them offerings, including animal sacrifices, as the Israelite priesthood did for Yahweh at the Jerusalem temple.

To neglect the gods and their temples, to fail to keep the gods content, was to invite catastrophe. The Bible's book of Lamentations bewails the destruction of Solomon's temple and attributes it to the disobedience of the people of Judah. More than a thousand years earlier, Sumerian authors composed lamentations that depicted with graphic eloquence how great cities like Ur and Nippur and their temples had been sacked and reduced to rubble because the gods had abandoned them. Their only recourse was to grovel before the gods, to beg them to return to their cities and restore their prosperity and happiness.[5] We have seen that ancient Iraq was blessed with the enormous agricultural productivity of the Tigris–Euphrates floodplain, but with that blessing came curses: spring floods that wiped out harvests and settlements alike, as well as misery and destruction inflicted by invaders intent on seizing their cities and overthrowing their rulers. Thereby was spawned in the Mesopotamian mindset a hard-bitten pessimism and fatalism, as well as a resilience, which are discernible in their religious beliefs and rituals, and in their literature, and that, some argue, still characterize the people of Iraq today, after decades of war, occupation, and chaos.

Nowhere in Mesopotamian literature are those qualities – or the biblical debt to that literature – more evident than in the *Epic of Gilgamesh*. We encountered Gilgamesh as a fabled ruler of the Sumerian city of Uruk during the mid-third millennium BCE, whose feats and fame were celebrated for millennia afterwards. Stories about him were written down in Sumerian as early as 2100 BCE, and they probably evolved from oral storytelling dating centuries earlier. The so-called "standard" version of the epic weaves together many elements from the earlier stories and was set down in writing by the late second millennium BCE.

The *Epic of Gilgamesh* is the story of one man's quest for immortality – a reflection of the universal human yearning to escape death. As the story begins, Gilgamesh, two-thirds god and one-third human, is ruling at Uruk as a mighty hero-king, but also as a tyrant prone to abusing his subjects, even going so far as to force himself sexually on new brides. To rein him in, the gods create Enkidu, a powerful man of the wild who, after a long and exhausting session of copulation with a prostitute whom the gods sent to "civilize" him, comes to the city to challenge Gilgamesh. The two have a knockdown-drag-out fight, which makes them fast friends. They then set out from Uruk on a series of heroic he-man adventures in which they defeat and dismember ferocious monsters: first Humbaba, the terrifying creature who guards the great cedar forest in the mountains of the west, and then the mighty Bull of Heaven, whom the gods sent in hopes of whittling them down to size, but to no avail. Smitten with Gilgamesh, the sex-goddess Ishtar proposes marriage, only to have both young worthies rudely reject and insult her. Deciding that such hubris shall not go unpunished, the gods decide that one of the two men must die. Enkidu soon falls ill, and Gilgamesh tends to his dying buddy, staying with Enkidu's corpse until maggots begin to fall from its nose.

Now terrified by the prospect of his own death, Gilgamesh resolves to travel to the ends of the earth to find Utnapishtim, the only human to whom the gods have ever granted immortality. After a long and perilous journey, Gilgamesh finds Utnapishtim, who tells him that his quest is impossible but nonetheless offers him a chance at immortality if he can stay awake for six days and seven nights. When Gilgamesh fails this test, the irritated Utnapishtim decides to send him away, but Utnapishtim's wife intercedes on Gilgamesh's behalf and persuades her husband to offer Gilgamesh a kind of consolation prize: a plant that, if Gilgamesh is able to retrieve it from the bottom of the sea, will restore his youth. Gilgamesh retrieves the plant, only to lose it when a snake eats it while he is sleeping. Foiled in his quest, a dejected Gilgamesh returns to Uruk. But there, at story's end, he gazes upon the great walls that he has built around his city, and he takes comfort in such earthly achievement, recognizing that, after all, death and dust are the destiny of all humans. One can find no more poignant a literary illustration of Mesopotamian fatalism.

It is during Gilgamesh's visit with Utnapishtim that we find a remarkable parallel with one of the Bible's most popular stories. Gilgamesh asks Utnapishtim why the gods bestowed the gift of immortality upon him. Utnapishtim recounts for him a story of how the gods long ago decided to send a great flood to wipe out humankind. According to an earlier version of the flood story, in which the hero is named Atrahasis, the gods, having created humankind to do their labor for them, became irritated with their noise and therefore decided to destroy them. In Utnapishtim's narrative, one of the gods, Ea (the Akkadian counterpart of the Sumerian god Enki), takes pity on Utnapishtim and instructs him to build a huge boat and bring aboard it all kinds of living things. Utnapishtim follows Ea's instructions, builds the boat according to a detailed description of its construction and dimensions, and brings his family and the beasts of the field on board. The gods then send a huge storm that lasts six days and seven nights and produces a flood that covers the earth and drowns all its people. Having ridden out the storm, Utnapishtim's great boat runs aground on a mountain-top. He sends out a series of birds – first a dove, then a swallow, neither of which finds a place to perch, and then a raven, which does. When the flood recedes and dry land emerges, Utnapishtim leaves the boat and makes a sacrifice, over which the gods gather "like flies." And no wonder; they're starving after having wiped out the labor force that produced their food. The supreme god, Enlil, is at first angry at Ea for tipping off Utnapishtim and allowing him to escape, but after the other gods shame Enlil, he relents and bestows upon Utnapishtim and his wife the gift of immortality.

Anyone familiar with Genesis will recognize this story immediately. In its main elements, and even in many of its details, like the release of the birds from the grounded boat, it and the earlier flood story about Atrahasis directly parallel the famous story of Noah and the Ark. But the *Epic of Gilgamesh* dates to the late second millennium BCE, and the Atrahasis story is known from tablets dating as early as 1700 BCE. Both are much earlier than any known version of the biblical account. They obviously are the source of the story of Noah's Ark.

The parallels between early Jewish belief and practice and those of ancient Mesopotamia, and the likely biblical borrowings from Mesopotamia, hardly end with the story of a great flood.[6] A number of parallels have been drawn between the laws recorded in the Bible – including the Ten Commandments and the so-called Covenant Code in Exodus as well as the laws in Deuteronomy – and the Laws of Hammurabi as well as an earlier, less well-preserved set of laws from the kingdom of Eshnunna, which was located on the Diyala river northeast of Babylon. In both the Hammurabi and Eshnunna laws as well as in Exodus, we find specific legal provisions for cases of a "goring ox." The provisions in Hammurabi's laws deal with restitution when an ox has gored a man, but in the Exodus and Eshnunna laws, which govern a situation when one ox gores and kills another man's ox, the phrasing as well as the restitution are essentially identical: share the carcass of the dead ox and split the sale price of the gorer.[7] Equally striking is how the laws in the Covenant Code (Exodus 21) and in Hammurabi's laws evidence the same formulation – "If X happens, then Y must be done" – and, along with monetary compensation, the same principle of restitution for death or injury: talionic law, which entails restitution based on a strict equivalence: an eye for an eye, a tooth for a tooth, a life for a life.

A final example of a legal parallel consists of the Israelite practice (prescribed in Leviticus 25:10) of the jubilee year, which stipulated, among other prescriptions, that every fifty years debtors be released from their debts. We find a similar practice in early Mesopotamia in which a king might issue an edict releasing debtors from their debts. In all of these instances, we cannot be sure how early these practices were incorporated into the life of the early Israelites, but because the provisions from Mesopotamian laws date much earlier than any known biblical manuscript, most scholars believe that the biblical laws were highly influenced by Mesopotamian precursors.

These few examples by no means exhaust the religious and literary parallels between the Bible and ancient Mesopotamian literature. In both we find evidence of prophets and prophecy, as well as texts that describe heaven and hell; the genres of psalms and lamentations; and the concept of the New Year celebration, the Day of Atonement, and rituals involving a scapegoat.

We also find in both biblical and Mesopotamian literature examples of what scholars call wisdom literature: fables, proverbs, instructions from sages, words of the wise. One Babylonian work commonly known as *The Poem of the Righteous Sufferer* shows distinct parallels to the book of Job in its enumeration of one man's sufferings and helplessness before a god who seems unsympathetic but with whom the unfortunate sufferer keeps faith as he patiently endures. Adrift in such helplessness, ancient Mesopotamians, like their biblical counterparts, also resorted to prayer. The literature of the Babylonians and Assyrians is full of eloquent examples of both royalty and commoners beseeching a god to intervene on their behalf.

On the other hand, ancient Mesopotamians also believed they might alleviate their helplessness if they could discover the gods' intentions ahead of time and thereby take steps to mitigate the worst effects of their decisions. From that quest emerged the practice of divination – the deciphering and interpretation of omens, as signified on the liver of a sacrificed sheep or the movements of celestial bodies as ascertained by astronomical observation – a practice that led to the development of astrology.

Also to be reckoned with were malevolent forces: supernatural ones such as witches, demons, and evil spirits – akin to the jinn ("genies") that traditional Arabs still believe lurk in their houses and villages – as well as more mundane evils ranging from angry people, snarling dogs, and poisonous scorpions to fever, headache, and flatulence. To deal with such threats and misfortunes, ancient Mesopotamians could resort to ritual specialists equipped with a panoply of magical spells and incantations.[8] The Bible would have us believe that the early Jews rejected such superstitions; but we would be wrong to do so. As early as the third century CE, centuries after the exile from Judah, members of the thriving Jewish community in Babylonia had adopted from their neighbors some very similar magical practices. We see this most notably in the practice by which Jewish home-owners would commission sorcerer-scribes to inscribe, in Aramaic script, the interior of ceramic bowls (or sometimes the exterior of a human skull) with a spell to prevent ghosts and demons from harming the members of their household. The inscribed bowl, which sometimes was embellished with an image of the shackled demon, was then buried beneath the floor of the house, upside down, to keep the demon trapped inside the bowl.

These Jewish folk-religion traditions that arose in Mesopotamia were to continue for centuries, often side by side with the strict monotheism that the religious elite in the Jewish community were at the same time laboring to refine and enforce.[9] Even today, elements of the kind of thinking from which these traditions arose may be detected in the folk customs of modern Shi'ites of Iraq, who continue to believe that "the human body is subject to all kinds of satanic onslaughts and must be constantly guarded against the enemy's insidious plots."[10] Such customs thus provide further evidence of the long history during which the traditions of Jewish monotheism were nurtured in the soil of Iraq's long religious tradition of polytheism. The greatest flowering of that Jewish tradition, the creation of the Babylonian Talmud, would take place in Iraq in the era of late antiquity, the early centuries CE.

By that time, other great traditions had been taking root there as well. To explain how that happened, we need to turn back to Iraq's history after its incorporation into the Persian empire and then into the series of empires that followed – empires that often were ruled from what is now Iraq, but not by people with much claim to being ancient Iraqis.

THE ACHAEMENID PERSIANS AND THE
RELIGION OF THE WISE LORD

Among those non-Iraqi rulers are the Achaemenid Persians, beginning with Cyrus the Great and continuing for more than two centuries under his successors. When they deemed it necessary, Persian emperors could act harshly against their Babylonian subjects. For example, Darius (ruled 522–486 BCE) had to put down a major rebellion there. Nonetheless, the Persians used Babylon as one of their capitals, along with four other capitals, all located in modern Iran: the ancient Elamite capital at Susa, the former Median capital at Ecbatana, the Achaemenids' own traditional seat at Pasargadae, and, beginning with Darius, a new capital and ceremonial complex at Persepolis.

Despite the brutal measures Darius took at Babylon, by and large the Achaemenid kings claim to have treated with respect the temples and religious traditions of their Babylonian and other subjects. This is nowhere more evident than in the remarkable document known as the Cyrus Cylinder.[11] Discovered at Babylon in 1879, this twenty-three-centimeter barrel-shaped clay cylinder bears a cuneiform inscription that testifies how Marduk, the supreme Babylonian god, had literally taken Cyrus by the hand and commanded him to liberate Babylon from the evil-doer Nabonidus, whom Marduk delivered over to him. The text goes on to extol Cyrus' magnanimity to the gods and people of Babylonia and indeed to all the peoples of his empire. Cyrus claims, "I have enabled all the lands to live in peace."

The Bible tells us that Cyrus specifically extended respect and toleration to the exiles from Judah whom Nebuchadnezzar had deported to Babylonia. Cyrus proclaimed that those Judahites who chose to do so could return to Jerusalem. Cyrus' magnanimity so impressed the Bible's authors that they referred to him with a title that soon would assume even greater significance in the history of world religions: in Hebrew, *mashiya*, or messiah – meaning "anointed" – which would be translated in the Greek-speaking Middle East as *christos*, or Christ. Jews who elected to remain in Babylonia prospered for the most part, under no significant burden of religious or social discrimination.

Our perception of Achaemenid rule has perhaps been unduly biased by the Bible's praise for Cyrus, but many scholars have noted that across their empire the Persians ruled with considerable toleration for the customs and religious practices of their subjects. Why? What benefits might the Persians have hoped to gain from such tolerance?

Although scholars have by no means reached a consensus about this, the answer may lie in the Persians' adoption by that time of what was likely an already ancient, yet revolutionary, system of religious belief centered on a great god named Ahura-Mazda. It had originated more than a thousand years earlier in the region of what is now eastern Iran and Afghanistan, among mainly nomadic, livestock-rearing peoples belonging to an ethno-linguistic group that linguists refer to as Indo-Iranians, or Aryans – a subgroup of the larger Indo-European family. One group of them migrated to the region of what is now India, another to the region of eastern Iran. Both groups were polytheists, worshiping a number of deities who were often associated with forces in nature but who in that capacity became associated by extension with important social and cultural forces.

Two of those gods were to have an immense impact on the history of Middle Eastern – and Western – religion. One of them, Mithra, was the lord of fire and was linked therefore to the sun, but also came to be associated with the bonds of legal covenants (the word *mithra* means "covenant"). This association evidently stemmed from the sun's presence overhead, looking down on humankind and able to detect any breaking of a covenant's bonds. It is manifested in at least one other ancient religious system of Iraq. The top of the stele upon which is inscribed the Code of Hammurabi features a depiction of Hammurabi being invested with the insignia of rulership from the sun-god, Shamash, who likewise was associated with the principle of justice. In time, Mithra became the personification of Truth.[12] More than a thousand years later, around the time of Christ – and having morphed considerably – he would be adopted farther west, to become the focus of a religion that competed with early Christianity across the Roman empire.

For the Achaemenids, however, the more important of these two early Iranian gods was Ahura-Mazda, or Ahuramazda, later Ohrmazd ("lord wisdom"). Ahura-Mazda became the focus of a revolutionary religious teaching. According to tradition – as with Moses, we have no other evidence of his existence – the religion of Ahura-Mazda was first taught by an Iranian priest and prophet named Zarathustra. Some would call him the First Prophet.[13] In the West, he is known by the name by which the ancient Greeks knew him: Zoroaster. The dates of his life are extremely uncertain. Some would place him as early as sometime around 1700–1500 BCE; others believe that he lived centuries later and died around 550 BCE. His principal teachings are to be found in seventeen hymns called the Gathas, which are part of the larger, incompletely preserved compendium of doctrine known as the Avesta. The Gathas are composed in a very ancient Iranian language that is unattested outside these texts. According to tradition, they were composed by Zoroaster himself. For centuries, they were handed down only orally within the community he had established. They were not set down in writing until centuries after the Achaemenids, during the era of a later Iranian dynasty, the Sassanids, who ruled Iran and Mesopotamia/Iraq from the third to the seventh century CE.

Because this new religious system is based on the teachings of Zoroaster, it is commonly referred to as Zoroastrianism. Some, however, who distinguish a period during which the early Achaemenid kings expressed devotion to Ahura-Mazda but made no mention of Zoroaster, use the term "Mazdaism" for that period. And there are some who prefer the term "Mazdaism" in recognition that Ahura-Mazda, not Zoroaster, is the focus of Zoroaster's teaching. Finally, because this religion's teachings were propagated and its rituals performed by priests known as "magi," some refer to the religion as Magianism. Over the centuries since its origin, as with most of the world's religions, Zoroastrian doctrine expanded and evolved. Modern scholars see it as a religious system that pulls together aspects of monotheism, polytheism, and dualism. Historically, the evolution of Zoroastrianism sometimes led to conflict and fragmentation within the Zoroastrian community, and to actions that Zoroaster might not have found in keeping with his teachings, such as the persecution of non-believers during the fourth century CE. But in its essence Zoroastrianism is one of the world's more humane religions. Its influence on the later monotheisms of Judaism, Christianity, and Islam, as well as on other religious movements that emerged in ancient Iraq, is difficult to dispute.

In traditional belief, Zoroaster's teachings are based on divine revelations that he first received around the age of thirty. Their major innovation was his declaration that Ahura-Mazda is the one supreme, eternal, uncreated God and the creator of all that is good in the universe. In the Zoroastrian system, Ahura-Mazda is also the creator of a number of lesser divine beings who represent aspects or manifestations of his power.

Also central to Zoroastrian belief is what scholars refer to as "dualism." Zoroaster declared that there coexists with Ahura-Mazda an adversary, Aingra Mainyu (later Ahriman), also uncreated, who is the source of evil in the universe and has his own entourage of lesser divine beings. Good (epitomized by Ahura-Mazda) and Evil (epitomized by Aingra Mainyu) are in perpetual, universal conflict. All of what Ahura-Mazda created was created to defeat evil. Human beings are sacred creations of Ahura-Mazda, and their role is to strive throughout their lives to defeat evil so that in time the world may be restored to the original perfect state in which Ahura-Mazda created it. It is the personal responsibility of all human beings to care for themselves and their fellow creatures and to lead their life in a way that will produce good thoughts, good words, and good deeds, which will thereby contribute to the ultimate defeat of evil. This doctrine also signifies a stupendous change in the nature of the relationship between humans and the divine. From passive, subservient dependants on the fickle, even whimsical divinities of earlier Mesopotamian polytheisms, humans have become active supporters, even partners, of a Supreme Being in his ongoing cosmic war against the forces of evil.

Furthermore, beyond this life, one will receive an eternal reward based on one's effort to help good defeat evil. Upon death, each person's spirit will undergo a moral judgment, with the scales of justice weighing good versus evil. Those found good will pass on to a heavenly paradise; those found evil will be consigned to a place of pain and suffering, where Aingra Mainyu presides. These individual post-mortem judgments are but precursors of the Final Judgment, which will take place at the end of time, after evil has been completely and finally defeated in this world. At that point, history will come to an end, the earth will give up the bones of the dead, and the Final Judgment will completely and finally separate the good from the evil. All evil will be destroyed, including Aingra Mainyu, as will the abode of suffering where he dwells. All good humans will become immortal and live forever with Ahura-Mazda in complete peace and happiness in this world.

To any practicing Jew, Christian, or Muslim, much of this will sound extremely familiar, for what we find here are concepts that are central to some of those faiths' major beliefs: a Supreme Deity, associated with Good, with whom are also associated lesser supernatural beings (angels); a counterpart, or adversary, who is the epitome of Evil (Satan); the injunction to lead a moral life that emphasizes charity to one's fellows and commands good thoughts, words, and deeds; an individual last judgment and eternal reward, with the good going to a place of peace and beauty (heaven) and the wicked condemned to a place of sorrow and suffering (hell); and an End of Time when the kingdom of God will come to the earth, and the good will be gathered and saved, to be with God forever in paradise (a concept that derives from the Persian word for "garden").[14]

Zoroaster seems to have believed that the End of Days and Final Judgment were imminent, to come in his own lifetime. But as he grew old and that possibility seemed less likely, he appears to have developed a belief that at some future time there would emerge a heroic figure, the *saoshyant*, who would lead humankind in the final battle against the forces of evil and pave the way for the restoration of the kingdom of Ahura-Mazda. Over time, Zoroastrians came to believe that the *saoshyant* would be a descendant of Zoroaster, whose seed was believed to be preserved in the depths of a lake where a virgin would bathe and thereby be impregnated.[15] Here, once again, we see a parallel, perhaps even the progenitor, of the concept of the messiah that became so central to Judaism and Christianity, and later to Islam in the concept of the Mahdi.

Zoroaster's teachings became the victim of a certain irony: whereas Zoroaster's cosmic vision for humanity would seem to be universally applicable, his teachings became increasingly tightly linked to, and almost the exclusive possession of, Iranian peoples – among them the Achaemenid Persian conquerors of Mesopotamia. We do not know if Cyrus and his successors were practicing Zoroastrians, although Darius' inscriptions do assert that he worshiped Ahura-Mazda. But most experts agree that by the time of Cyrus' conquest of Babylonia Zoroastrian teachings had spread quite far west from their geographical origin in eastern Iran, perhaps as far as modern Turkey, which Cyrus conquered in 546 BCE, well before his conquest of Babylonia. Those teachings had been widely adopted and were being practiced throughout the Persian priesthood. They also were being practiced among the Achaemenid ruling class – the same ruling class that, after Cyrus' conquest of Babylonia, ruled over the Jewish community there.

It should come as no surprise, then, that there took root in the Babylonian Jewish community some concepts that the Jewish and Zoroastrian communities could share. Among them was the idea of one Supreme God. In the view of many experts, it was only during this time that the Jewish scholars who were engaged in studying and editing the scrolls they had brought from Jerusalem began to elaborate fully the concept of Yahweh, not as the patron god of the people of Israel, but as the one Supreme God, the God of all creation – very much like the conceptualization of Ahura-Mazda in the Zoroastrian system. When one adds to this the concepts of the messiah, of a spiritually and morally directed way of life, and of a code of behavior that entailed strict laws involving ritual and bodily purity and framing unbelievers as presenting a threat of pollution, the debt that Judaism may owe to Zoroastrianism is evident.[16] For the Zoroastrian concepts of a resurrection of the body, Final Judgment, and eternal reward (in heaven or hell) to enter Jewish religious thought would require more time, but the later Christian and Muslim embrace of these concepts brought them squarely into the mainstream of the monotheistic traditions that were to dominate religious belief and practice in the Middle East and beyond.

The historian Garth Fowden has written that although the Fertile Crescent, with Iraq at its heart, has frequently suffered from its geographic vulnerability, it has also been "a vortex that pulls inward and fuses what lies around it."[17] Ancient Iraq, arguably, was a crucible for one of those East-meets-West episodes that have had such a huge impact on global history: from the west, the exiled Jewish community, with its roots in Palestine; from the east, Zoroastrian teachings, with their roots in eastern Iran/Afghanistan.

Iraq was the meeting ground for a spiritual and moral synergy that energized some of the earliest monotheistic religions. Within a few centuries, and with the coming of new influences into Iraq from both east and west, even further manifestations of monotheism were to emerge there and, from there, spread across the world. But those new influences often arrived in the company of other, dark forces that would leave Iraq and its people damaged and dazed.

ALEXANDER THE GREAT AND THE COMING OF HELLENISM

When the armies of the Macedonian king Alexander arrived in Babylon in 331 BCE, Greeks and Macedonians were no strangers to the people of ancient Iraq. As early as the eighth century BCE, the Assyrian kings at

Nineveh knew of the city-states that colonizers from the Greek mainland had founded in Ionia. When Cyrus conquered the kingdom of Lydia in 546 BCE, he claimed those city-states as part of his empire. It was the revolt of one of them, Miletus, at the start of the fifth century BCE, followed by Athens' support of the rebels, that motivated the Persian king Darius I to launch his invasion of the Greek mainland in 490 BCE. That adventure ended disastrously when the outnumbered Athenian hoplite infantry defeated the Persians on the plain of Marathon. Ten years later, Darius' son and successor Xerxes launched a second, even more formidable invasion during which the Persians, after initial opposition, rolled through the celebrated holding action of the "300 Spartans" at Thermopylae and then proceeded to Athens, where they sacked and burned the Acropolis. But that invasion, too, was turned back, in 479 BCE, by the Athenian navy at Salamis and the combined Greek armies at Plataea.

These events in many ways marked a watershed in the process whereby people in the West ("we") came to differentiate themselves from "them" in the East. By the end of the fifth century BCE, the writers of Greece's golden age had established to their own satisfaction that the Greeks were the standard-bearers of freedom and democracy, contrasted with what they denigrated as enslaved, inferior societies dominated by the Persian kings, whom they condemned as arrogant tyrants. In the eyes of the Greeks, the peoples of the East – including the peoples of the region to which the Greeks had given the name Mesopotamia – were of an inferior breed. The peoples of the East have labored under that Western stereotype down to the present.

After the Greek victories, the Achaemenid kings contented themselves to meddle in the Greeks' affairs as and when such meddling suited their own geopolitical agenda. Meanwhile, Greek warriors sold their now highly valued services as mercenaries to the Persian kings, or to rivals who hoped to usurp those kings' rule. In one instance of the latter, a pretender to the throne of the newly ascended Persian king

Artaxerxes II was able to bring to his side a force of more than ten thousand Greek warriors, who evidently acquitted themselves magnificently in battle in 401 BCE at a place called Cunaxa, on the Euphrates about forty-five miles north of Babylon. But when the pretender was killed during that battle the Greeks found themselves without a patron and, owing to betrayal by an erstwhile ally, even without their own generals. Yet, remarkably, the mercenaries were able to make their escape cross-country through what is now Iraqi Kurdistan and Armenia to the Black Sea. The mercenaries' newly elected general, Xenophon, commanded their retreat and later wrote what became a famous account of it, *Anabasis* ("March up Country").

By the time of Xenophon's adventure, the powerful Greek city-states of Athens and Sparta, with their allies, had suffered a disastrous, immensely destructive war among themselves. This set the stage for the rise of an outsider, Philip II, the king of a region north of Greece proper called Macedon. By 338 BCE, Philip was able to assert his control over all the Greek city-states. Philip then decided, for reasons historians continue to debate, to invade the Persian empire. When he was assassinated in his royal capital in 336 BCE, his dream fell to his young son, Alexander. Within two years, Alexander had assembled and led an army of forty-two thousand soldiers across the Hellespont into Turkey. In 333 BCE, he took on the Persian forces at Issus in southern Anatolia, forcing Darius III, the last of the Achaemenid Persian kings, to flee, leaving behind his wife and other members of his family. Alexander soon conquered the rest of Syria, Palestine, and then Egypt.

By 331 BCE, Alexander was ready to thrust his forces into the Mesopotamian heartland, crossing the Euphrates and Tigris and taking on the forces of Darius III for the decisive battle at a place usually identified as Gaugamela, not far from the city of Irbil, today the capital of Iraqi Kurdistan. Once again, Alexander was victorious, for a second time driving Darius III from the battlefield. Darius fled far to the east, into Iran, where he was eventually killed by one of his nobles. With the way to Babylonia and Persia now open, Alexander's armies marched on to Babylon, where he was received with pomp, flowers, and incense. Over the eight momentous years that remained to him, Alexander drove his armies to conquer all that had once been the Persian empire, and beyond – even into India. Along the way he won brilliant victories, even while antagonizing and sometimes killing his generals, and planted garrison-colonies whose long-term impact even he probably could not have imagined.

There is every indication that Alexander intended to make Babylon the capital of his empire. He had good reason to. Babylon was still the most magnificent city on earth, a crossroads of commerce, and possessed of immense history and unmatched prestige. In a continuation of Achaemenid policies, Alexander showed great respect for the gods, cities, traditions, and royal rituals of the Babylonians, including the New Year Festival. He evidently intended to restore the ruined temple of Marduk. And to boost his own claims to divine status as ruler of Mesopotamia and beyond, Alexander – and some of his successors – resorted to having himself depicted on coins and statues as having a head with horns, an attribute with which the gods of Mesopotamia had been depicted as far back as Sumerian times.[18]

By the time of his untimely death at Babylon in 323 BCE, his conquests embraced an area larger than any empire up to that time. The legend of Alexander "the Great" was secure. It remains secure today, even in Iraq. In January 2009, the governments of Greece and Iraq agreed to erect a statue of Alexander near the site of the Battle of Gaugamela. But that legend might have been tarnished had Alexander lived longer, for, as his successors soon discovered, it is one thing to bring such a huge region under one's sway by military conquest, but something quite different to hold it together. Upon their commander's death, Alexander's generals launched a bitter and complicated succession struggle with huge stakes: control of his empire. By the early third century BCE, several of them and certain local rulers had carved out of his empire a number of successor kingdoms, all of which historians label "Hellenistic," in recognition of the impact of Greek culture and rule throughout the Middle East.

One of those generals, Ptolemy, established himself fairly quickly in Egypt, founding a Macedonian dynasty and kingdom – the Ptolemid, or Ptolemaic – that was ruled from the most famous of the new cities Alexander founded: Alexandria. Over the next several centuries, Alexandria rose to become not only a political capital but the foremost cultural center of the Middle Eastern and Mediterranean world. Another of Alexander's generals, Seleucus, was able to establish himself at Babylon by 312 BCE, but his rule there became secure only after he had fended off the invading forces of his rival, Antigonus. Between 310 and 307 BCE, the two contenders' armies ravaged the Babylonian cities and countryside. Their war established a pattern that was to scourge the people of Iraq for many centuries to come, even into the early modern era, as rising powers to the east and the west confronted and tested each other in battle, hoping to claim the rich Mesopotamian heartland as their prize, but leaving death and desolation in their wake.

The policies of Seleucus and his successors in the Seleucid dynasty would continue to draw their attention away from the Babylonian heartland of their empire.[19] Over the next 250 years, as they began to deal with new threats from the west (the rising power of Rome) and the east (the Iranian Parthians) – who together would eventually swallow up their empire – the Seleucids moved the seat of their political power westward from Iraq into Syria. Seleucus' son and successor, Antiochus I, established his principal capital at the city of Antioch, one of a number of colonies Seleucus had founded and then named for a member of his family. The Seleucids also founded as many as twelve colonies in Mesopotamia, possibly including one where the modern city of Kirkuk is located.[20]

For a capital from which to govern their eastern domains they founded a new city, Seleucia-on-the-Tigris, about sixty-five kilometers northwest of Babylon. With a population of 600,000, the largest of any city in their kingdom,[21] Seleucia sat astride caravan routes from India and Arabia as well as the sea-and-river route from India. Continuing the policies of their Assyrian and Achaemenid predecessors, the Seleucids strived to control those routes so that the great wealth of that commerce passed through their hands on its way to destinations farther west.[22] Like many of the new Greek colonies across the Hellenistic world, Seleucia and the other Greek colonies in Mesopotamia attracted many colonists, including men steeped in the new philosophical, scientific, and religious ideas then surging through the Mediterranean and Middle Eastern world. We may also assume that the merchants who came to Seleucia from India and Arabia brought, along with commodities for trade, new ideas about technology, commerce, science – and the gods. Scientists, scholars, and spiritual teachers would feed off the intellectual and spiritual stew concocted in Mesopotamia during the Seleucid era for centuries to come.

Given the lasting fame of Alexander and his successors, it may seem ironic that we know so little today about the Seleucid administration of Iraq or how much of a role native Babylonians played in it. Historians also remain divided about how wide or deep an impact Greek culture had in ancient Iraq.[23] But as long as the Seleucids held sway in Babylonia, they continued to respect its ancient customs and its traditions of kingship.[24] Antiochus I seems to have been curious enough about Babylonian history that a Greek-speaking Babylonian priest named Berossus wrote a book about it for him, which we know only from a few surviving but interesting fragments. The city of Babylon likely suffered from the founding of Seleucia nearby, since part of Babylon's population moved from the old city to the new one, the center of Seleucid authority and therefore the new place to be. Nonetheless, the Seleucid kings restored Babylonian temples and had sacrifices performed in them on their behalf, and some Greeks did settle at Babylon, hence the construction of a Greek-style theater, gymnasium, and agora there. Uruk, now more than 3,500 years old, prospered under the Seleucids, with new temples built and their administrators continuing to manage their estates and keep records on clay tablets, many of which we still have. But much of the agricultural wealth from the irrigated floodplain was now going into the coffers of the Seleucid royal authorities. Unfortunately for later historians, they preferred to keep their records using Greek or Aramaic script on parchment.

Fortunately indeed for modern historians of science, and for the future of astronomy and astrology, the priest-scholars of the Uruk and Babylon temples continued to record their celestial observations in their now arcane Sumerian-Babylonian scholarly language, using the time-hallowed cuneiform script on clay tablets. The temples were where the prestigious tradition of cuneiform scholarship had begun at the dawn of the third millennium BCE. Now they were its last bastions. Their dwindling band of scholars pressed on even after their Seleucid overlords had been pushed out by yet another wave of invaders.

But not much longer. The last datable cuneiform record – an astronomical diary – was written in 75 CE. By that time, a new era – of both political rule and spiritual vitality – had dawned in Iraq.

IRAQ UNDER PARTHIAN RULE: RELIGIOUS
TOLERATION AND VITALITY

The downfall of the Seleucid empire came at the hands of two new imperial powers that sandwiched the Seleucids from west and east. Having made themselves master of the Italian peninsula, honing their war machine in the process, the Romans achieved domination of the western Mediterranean by 200 BCE by defeating the great general Hannibal and thereby obliterating the threat from their rival Carthage in North Africa. Now focused eastward, they forced the Seleucid king Antiochus III to hand over Asia Minor (modern Turkey) to them after they hammered his army at the Battle of Magnesia in 188 BCE. BY 146 BCE they had conquered Greece and Macedonia and were poised to establish themselves on the eastern Mediterranean seaboard. Less than ninety years later, in 64 BCE, the Roman general Pompey conquered Syria and brought an end to the Seleucid dynasty. The following year witnessed an event whose consequences have resonated for centuries, for in that year Pompey conquered Jerusalem. In so doing he brought into Rome's orbit the kingdom of Judea (the former Judah), which had asserted its independence from the Seleucids in 140 BCE. When the Roman general Octavian (later Augustus Caesar, the first Roman emperor) captured Egypt after the Battle of Actium in 31 BCE, the last Ptolemid ruler of Egypt, the celebrated Cleopatra, met her end and the last of the Hellenistic successor kingdoms of Alexander's great empire had fallen.

To the east, long before Pompey finished them off, the Seleucids had lost Mesopotamia to the next invading force from the east. The Parthians were originally a horse-riding, nomadic Iranian people, an early example of what became a series of warrior nomads – Huns, Turks, Mongols – who emerged from the Eurasian steppes to threaten, and sometimes dominate, the cities and civilization of Central and Western Asia, as well as Europe. The Parthians' origins remain obscure. Even though they dominated the Middle East for several centuries, our historical sources for them are very limited. And, since many of those sources were written by Roman authors who both feared and reviled the Parthians, they tend to be biased and untrustworthy. When the Parthians first appear in the historical record, they are a nomadic people known as the Parni who have crossed into the Seleucid province known as Parthia, in what is now northeastern Iran. Once established there, they assumed the name of the province for themselves.[25] In the years after 250 BCE, led by their first great king, Arsaces – hence the Arsacid dynasty – they established an independent state just beyond the reach of the Seleucids. According to the Parthians' own dating system,

Arsaces' reign began in 228 BCE. By the end of the Arsacid dynasty in 227 CE, the Parthian empire stretched across nearly all of the Middle East, and Mesopotamia was its heartland.

Their ability to expand their domain at the Seleucids' expense largely owed to their military prowess, especially as mounted archers and lancers. Parthian archers were known for their lightning speed and unmatched skill on horseback, and especially for the tactic that came to be known as the "Parthian shot," in which a Parthian archer would ride toward the enemy line, then wheel his horse about and ride quickly away, controlling his mount with his knees while facing backward to fire arrows at his foe. The "Parthian shot" became so legendary that a corrupted remembrance of it is preserved in the expression "parting shot." It required not only great balance and strength in the rider's knees and legs, but also great arm and shoulder strength, because the Parthian archers used what is known as the compound bow. Fashioned from wood, bone, and sinew bound with strong adhesive, the compound bow requires considerable time to make and great strength to bend and shoot. It can send an arrow a great distance (up to two hundred meters) at a deadly velocity that can pierce shields and armor.[26] The other, equally formidable arm of Parthian mounted military might consisted of heavier cavalry, known as "cataphracts," sheathed in helmet and chain-mail armor and equipped with a lance. This style of heavily armed, heavily armored cavalry likewise became legendary. The Parthians' successors, the Persian Sassanids, adopted it from them. In turn, the Byzantine (Eastern Roman) imperial armies who fought the Sassanids in Iraq and elsewhere in the Middle East learned of it from them and adopted it as well. Over time, it passed from them westward, to be adopted by the warriors of the Germanic kingdoms that emerged with the decline of Roman power in Europe. Thus was the pedigree of the medieval European knight in shining armor.

One might judge that over the course of their history the Parthians' military power was not consistently well served by their political power.

Kingship was a concept alien to the Parthians, as it has been to most nomadic peoples, whose societies and political organization tend to be based on blood and clan ties. Consequently, even as early as the reign of Arsaces I, Parthian kings needed to maintain a delicate balancing act between their own prerogatives as king and those of the leaders of the noble clans upon whose political and military support they relied.[27] As the Parthian empire grew, the Parthian kings had to recognize and respect sub-kingdoms whose rulers professed loyalty to the king but were permitted significant autonomy. Among those vassal kingdoms were several in Mesopotamia, including Osrhoene in the northwest, in the region of Edessa (modern Urfa, in Turkey); Adiabene in the northeast, corresponding to part of the core region of ancient Assyria; Characene along the Persian Gulf; and Araba, also in the area of Assyria and largely populated by Arabs, who had already begun to establish themselves in Iraq – although historians debate what exactly "Arab" referred to at this time and in this setting.

Because they had no established tradition of kingship, the Parthian kings looked elsewhere for exemplars. From the start, they seized upon those familiar from their experience: the Hellenistic Seleucid and Achaemenid Persian models. For example, the coins of Arsaces I feature elements that reflect earlier Persian iconography, but the inscriptions on them use the Greek word for "king."[28] Later Parthian kings used on their coins the epithet *philhellene* – or "lover of the Greeks." Until recently, many historians disparaged the Parthians as little better than Greek wannabes who had no significant culture of their own. According to less biased assessments, the Parthians picked and chose Greek themes and motifs as they suited their needs and tastes, rather than as slavish imitators.[29]

Whatever the drawbacks of their decentralized monarchy, by the mid-second century BCE, led by the great warrior king Mithridates I (171–138 BCE), the Parthians were able to expel the Seleucids from Mesopotamia and become the masters there. With a vast empire to govern, Parthian kings – like their Achaemenid predecessors – circulated from capital to capital across their empire as a means of keeping in touch with their realm. Besides their traditional capital at Hecatompylos (in the province of Hyrcania, now northeastern Iran and Turkmenistan), they adopted the ancient Median and Achaemenid capital at Ecbatana (modern Hamadan) in Iran as a summer residence. Although the capital the Seleucids had established at Seleucia continued to flourish – Mithridates even staged his coronation there – the Parthians founded a new winter capital on the Tigris upstream from Seleucia. Its name was Ctesiphon.

Ctesiphon was only a short distance from Babylon. Competition from Seleucia and Ctesiphon may have sealed that ancient metropolis' decline. Although some of the ancient cities of Babylonia were able to carry on several centuries longer, by 200 CE Babylon was deserted. It would not rise again.

Nor would the world of cuneiform writing and scholarship that had flourished there so long. Cuneiform had been steadily losing ground to the much more easily learned and used alphabetic scripts of first Aramaic and then Greek. The secrets of cuneiform vanished with the ancient cities of Sumer and Babylonia, beneath the brownish-gray mounds that now dotted Iraq's landscape and became the grist for local myths and legends for centuries to come.

Located in the western extension of their empire, and containing perhaps their most important capital, Iraq became a crucial component of the Parthians' regime. But as the Romans cemented their domination of Syria and Palestine, and their lucrative port cities, they began to see the Parthians as a rival and threat. Although most Roman authors knew little about the Parthians or their history and customs, they began to write about them in the same disparaging tone with which the Greeks had depicted the Achaemenid Persians only a few centuries earlier. For a Roman politico seeking to boost his political prospects through military victory and the generous application of largesse gained from booty, the

Parthian enemy was also an opportunity. In the most famous such quest, in 53 BCE, the wealthy Roman aristocrat Marcus Licinius Crassus – who with Pompey and Julius Caesar was one of Rome's "First Triumvirate" – invaded Mesopotamia and took on a Parthian army commanded by Spahbod Surena near the town of Carrhae, not far from the ancient city of Harran. Withering fire from the Parthian archers followed by the shattering charge of the Parthian heavy cavalry devastated Crassus' army. The Romans lost twenty thousand dead and perhaps ten thousand captured. Their humiliation was compounded by the disgrace of losing seven of their legions' eagle standards, the recovery of which required several decades of persistent diplomacy by the Romans. Crassus was put to death, allegedly by pouring molten gold down his throat. According to the Roman author Plutarch's account in *Parallel Lives*, the Parthians sent Crassus' head to the royal court. There, as it happened, the Greek tragedian Euripides' play *The Bacchae* was being staged. Crassus' head arrived just in time to be tossed onto the stage to represent the head of the play's doomed protagonist, the Theban king Pentheus.[30]

The next three centuries brought the Romans some degree of success against the Parthians, but for the most part the boundary between the two empires stabilized along the Euphrates. On several occasions during the second century CE, the Romans penetrated Mesopotamia far enough to capture Ctesiphon. The emperor Trajan even achieved a short-lived conquest of Mesopotamia, although his successor handed it back as part of a peace deal. Nonetheless, the Romans were never able to subjugate Parthia. That failure stuck long in the Romans' craw.

The people of Iraq suffered under the curse of living so close to the mid-point of the brutal Roman–Parthian tug-of-war. Their countryside was ravaged and thousands were enslaved. The next centuries would see this devastation visited upon Iraq many more times, when empires based in Iran and in regions to the west crossed swords there.

Even with the military setbacks the Parthians sometimes suffered in Mesopotamia, retaining it was vital to them, and not only because their great capital was there. As had been the case for three thousand years before the Parthians ascended to power, the alluvium of southern Iraq yielded immense agricultural wealth, and lucrative trade routes still converged there. The cities of the south had long been important nodes along the sea and land routes that linked India with the eastern Mediterranean via the Persian Gulf and the Euphrates. They continued to be important as merchants from the great Syrian caravan-trade center at Palmyra traveled to the head of the Persian Gulf to purchase spices, cotton, and pearls from Arab, Indian, and Chinese traders and then shipped them up the Euphrates and then by land to their home city, from where caravaneers could bring them to Mediterranean ports. But by the time of the Parthians, more northerly caravan routes were thriving – and would be celebrated for centuries to come. Known collectively as the Great Silk Road, they brought silk and other exotic goods from China west across Central Asia, across Parthian territory in northern Iran and Iraq, to the Mediterranean port cities, from where they could be shipped west to Rome. Because clever Parthian diplomats were able to deceive Chinese representatives into believing that it would be dangerous for them to try to establish their own relations with Rome,[31] the Parthians were able to maintain a monopoly on the silk trade from China. Consequently, they remained vital middlemen in East–West trade, and they and their dependants reaped huge rewards.

Some of the rewards that were derived from that trade – as well as evidence of the cosmopolitan society it helped to nurture – are on display even today in Iraq, at the ancient site of Hatra. Founded by the Seleucids, Hatra lay not far from the ancient Assyrian capital at Ashur, which also emerged under the Parthians from the economic doldrums that had befallen the region of Assyria since its devastation by the Medes and Chaldeans in the late seventh century BCE. Hatra was an important node on the caravan route to the west, as well as the capital of a small Parthian vassal kingdom ruled by a local Arab dynasty. Its six kilometers of fortification walls, with more than 160 square towers, enclosed a ceremonial complex of several temples that were built in largely Greco-Roman style yet also featured a distinctive Parthian architectural feature known as an *iwan* – a vaulted hall, open at one end.[32] Especially impressive is the multicultural diversity of the pantheons represented. The temple complex at Hatra boasts a great temple to the Akkadian sun-god Shamash,[33] as well as temples dedicated to the Sumerian/Akkadian god Nergal, the Aramean god Atar'at/Atargatis, the Arab deities Allat and Shamiyya, and the Greek god Hermes.[34]

In this rich brew of polytheism, worshipers of deities of different origins coexisted and interacted in what seems to have been an atmosphere of tolerance. Although we know relatively little of Parthian religious practice, we do know that Parthian kings honored the Zoroastrian supreme deity, Ahura-Mazda, and other ancient Iranian deities, yet seem to have been quite accepting of other religious traditions in Mesopotamia, including those of the Jewish communities of Babylonia.

Areas of northwestern Mesopotamia that fell under the sway of Rome show similar religious diversity. This is nowhere more evident than at the site of Dura-Europus, which lies on the Euphrates just within the Syrian side of the modern Iraq–Syria border. Founded shortly before 300 BCE by the Seleucids, by the second and third centuries CE, Dura-Europus sheltered a remarkably rich polytheistic mix that included deities from the Greco-Roman pantheon and from the Semitic pantheons of the Arameans and Palmyrenes, as well as Mithra, a god of Iranian origin whose cult was popular among Roman soldiers. New evidence of Mithra worship has recently been discovered in Dahuk province in northern Iraq.[35]

By the time Dura-Europus was destroyed in 257 CE, it also harbored monotheists, as evidenced by archaeologists' discovery of a Jewish synagogue and a small Christian church – both of them with superbly executed wall paintings depicting biblical scenes.[36] By this time, both of these groups were also well represented farther south, in the region of Ctesiphon and the old Babylonian heartland. What had happened there, however, was hugely influenced by what had transpired to the west, in Roman Judea and Palestine, during the first three centuries CE.

FROM PALESTINE TO MESOPOTAMIA: IRAQ AS A CRADLE OF WORLD RELIGIONS

Our sources for this period of the history of the Babylonian Jewish community are meager, but when later sources do shed more light on this community its size and prosperity suggest the Jews must have thrived under the Parthians, who allowed them significant autonomy under their own leaders, the exilarchs. But to the west, in their Palestinian homeland, the Jews were beset both by internal divisions and by Roman oppression, especially after Rome assumed direct control of the region following the death of their client king, Herod the Great, in 4 BCE. As Rome's avatar, Herod was reviled by many of his subjects, but he did undertake some major building projects – most notably, the rebuilding of the Second Temple at Jerusalem. This huge structure was the focus of Jewish ritual, sacrifice, and learning. Its high priest and high council (the Great Sanhedrin) were the most powerful authorities of the Jewish community, members of an aristocratic elite known as the Sadducees.

The Sadducees' authority did not go uncontested. By the first century BCE Roman oppression and doctrinal disputes had spawned factions that opposed them. These included the Pharisees, a small sect, described by one authority as a "self-constituted moral elite,"[37] who were learned in the written works of the biblical Torah but, unlike the Sadducees, also believed in a valid tradition of oral scriptural interpretation – the oral Torah, as it were. Again unlike the Sadducees, the Pharisees had come to accept the possibility of an immortal soul, a Last Judgment, and a resurrection after death – beliefs already current in Zoroastrian teaching as well as in other religious movements spreading through the Middle Eastern and Mediterranean world. Meanwhile, resentment of Roman rule had also spawned groups who hoped for the appearance of a heroic figure, a messiah, who would lead the fight against Rome. Among them were the Zealots, who advocated violent overthrow of Roman authority.

Around 30 CE, an itinerant preacher from the city of Nazareth in Galilee, Yeshua Bar Yosef – better known to history as Jesus, son of Joseph – bubbled up from this political and spiritual cauldron. Over a three-year career, he traveled among the Jewish communities of Palestine, healing the sick and infirm and preaching the imminent coming of the kingdom of God. Because his disciples acclaimed him as the long-awaited messiah, the Sanhedrin captured, tried, and condemned Jesus in Jerusalem for blasphemy, after which he was crucified by the Roman authorities, led at that time by an especially brutal and corrupt official, Pontius Pilate. Soon after his death, Jesus became the focus of what was at first an exclusively Jewish cult. Its adherents, known at first as Nazarenes, claimed that Jesus was the awaited messiah and had risen from the dead, and that accepting his message brought the promise of resurrection and eternal life. Within a short time, and especially at the forceful insistence of Saul of Tarsus, a former Pharisee who came to be known as Paul, some Nazarenes began to reach out, beyond the local Jewish communities, to the Gentile Greek-speaking, Greek-cultured population. Some Gentiles had already begun to embrace Jewish ideas and customs; now they began to accept the teaching of Paul and his disciples that Jesus was the Son of God and therefore divine in his own right. Around 100 CE, at Antioch, we find the first recorded instance of Jesus' followers being referred to by the Greek term for the followers of the messiah (*christos*). They had become *christianoi* ("Christians"). Also by that time, accounts of Jesus' career that had been recounted orally had been set down in writing, in texts that Christians refer to as "gospels." Soon, only four of them – attributed to Matthew, Mark, Luke, and

John – were sanctioned as authoritative, but early Christianity featured many more gospels than those four. There also arose, likewise in a very short time, multiple, often conflicting and contradictory teachings about who exactly Jesus was. Those doctrinal conflicts were to have a huge impact on the development of Christianity, including the divergence between its Western and Eastern (including Iraqi and Persian) forms.[38]

The vast majority of the Jewish community of Palestine did not accept Jesus as the messiah. They also continued to chafe under the yoke of Roman rule. In 66, the Jews of Judea rose in a rebellion that brought down upon their heads Rome's overwhelming military might. By 70, Roman armies had crushed the Judean revolt and, in an act that irrevocably altered the course of Jewish existence, obliterated the Second Temple – the centerpiece of Jewish life and ritual.

Decades later, in 135, the emperor Hadrian decided to establish a new Roman city on the ruins of Jerusalem. Outraged, the great rabbi Akiba called for a holy war and proclaimed the leader of the ensuing revolt, Simon Bar Kosiba (later known as Simon Bar Kochba), a messiah. The Romans obliterated that uprising as well, slaying tens more thousands of Jews. In the aftermath, Hadrian bestowed upon Judea a new name, Syria Palestina. According to some sources, he also prohibited the teaching of the Jewish law as well as the Jewish practices of circumcision and Sabbath observance. He may have intended to eradicate Judaism from Palestine altogether.

The destruction of the Jerusalem temple rendered irrelevant the temple priestly caste of the Sadducees; they soon disappeared. Pharisee scholars – men whose learning and piety had earned them the title "Rabbi" – emerged as leaders within the Jewish community in Palestine. They emigrated from the devastated Judea and moved northward to the region of Galilee. Here they founded new schools – most notably, the great academy at Jamnia/Yavneh – where they continued to study, as well as to edit the texts of the Bible, by 150 producing the standardized text of the Hebrew Bible (the Tanak). They also continued to elaborate upon their oral tradition of legal interpretation with the aim of producing guides for Jewish life; a critical necessity following the dispersal of the Jewish community from Palestine and into populous regions.[39]

By around 200, the rabbis of Galilee had assembled a new text that became a seminal component of the Jewish legal tradition: the Mishnah ("Repetition"). The Mishnah lists all the laws from the Torah, but then adds to them the laws handed down through the oral tradition. It also names about 150 rabbis who had been the chief contributors to this long process.[40] Over the next four centuries, the Mishnah itself became the focus for even further, increasingly elaborate commentary by the rabbis of Galilee and elsewhere in Palestine. By about 400 this resulted in a new text, the Palestinian Talmud.

By then, Judaism in Palestine had come under vicious attack from the emperors of the Roman empire, after Constantine, in the fateful proclamation known as the Edict of Milan, legalized Christianity around 313. From this point on, Roman emperors – with one major exception, the polytheist Emperor Julian "the Apostate" – became fervent patrons of the ever more prosperous and powerful Christian Church.

By 400, Christianity had been proclaimed the state religion of the Roman empire. Roman emperors now ruled from the new capital that Constantine had built on the site of an ancient, strategically well-located Greek colony called Byzantion and had dedicated in 330 as "New Rome." That city became better known as Constantinople (the "city of Constantine") and later as the modern city of Istanbul. The emperors made it their sacred mission to promote and defend the emerging "Orthodox," imperially sanctioned version of Christianity against unbelievers. Many of the unbelievers who found themselves under attack from the imperial authorities were simply Christians who happened to be adherents of forms of Christianity different from that approved and enforced by the emperor. That made them "heretics," whether inside or outside the empire's borders.

Iraq's history was to be shaped significantly by that, both for good and for ill. The advent of the militantly intolerant Christian Byzantine empire in the eastern Mediterranean forced the epicenter of Jewish intellectual and legal life eastward, away from Palestine, to Babylonia. There, Jewish life and scholarship had continued, even thrived, under the Parthians. For the most part it would continue to do so under their successors, the Sassanids. Now the arrival of rabbis and other refugees fleeing Christian oppression in Palestine was to enrich it even more.

But beginning with the Parthians, and continuing under the Sassanids, the Jews of Iraq were joined by new religious communities. All of them would leave deep footprints in Iraq. And some would use Iraq as a springboard to establishing new communities across Asia, even as far away as China.

IRAQ UNDER THE SASSANIDS: RELIGIOUS MOSAIC AND HOLY WAR

Weakened by Roman incursions, and perhaps not well served by a decentralized monarchy, the last Arsacid Parthian king was ousted in 227 by Ardashir, a prince of a noble Iranian family from Fars. Centuries earlier, Fars had been the region from which had emerged Cyrus the Great and the Achaemenids – from whom, the Sassanids claimed, Ardashir's lineage could be traced via an ancestor named Sassan. Although they had little inkling of who the Achaemenids had actually been, the Sassanid dynasty of *shahanshahs* ("kings of kings," the royal title the Achaemenids and Arsacids had claimed) associated themselves with the Achaemenids by building many of their own monuments near theirs – for example, at the Achaemenid royal cemetery at Naqsh-i-Rustam, near Persepolis. They also laid claim to the Parthian realm, and to Ctesiphon, the Parthian capital in Iraq. But whereas the Parthian kings had circulated among several capitals and favored a decentralized mode of kingship, the Sassanids made Ctesiphon their principal political and ceremonial city. The ruins of Ctesiphon stand today as a majestic reminder of yet another episode of Iraq's great imperial past; especially the great *iwan*, the audience hall of the royal palace, unfortunately damaged by the recent wars in Iraq. Also in contrast to the Parthians, the Sassanid kings ruled a highly centralized realm. They kept a firm grip on absolute power. To strengthen that grip, they made the king's physical person the focus of elaborate ritual, luxury, and ceremony that accentuated his status. The Sassanid king sat above a highly organized bureaucracy that was headed by a chief official, the vizier. As we shall see, the Arab rulers who ousted the Sassanids in the seventh century were to perpetuate the Sassanid model of kingship from their own new capital, Baghdad.[41] And like Mesopotamian rulers going back to the Sumerians three thousand years before them, the Sassanids counted on the abundant harvests from the Tigris–Euphrates floodplain to fill their coffers and be the foundation of their power. To that end – again, as the Sumerians had done millennia before – they built extensive irrigation networks, always the lifeblood of Mesopotamian agriculture.[42] They got rich from the long-distance trade that linked China, India, and Southeast Asia, via overland routes through Iran and Iraq and sea routes through the Persian Gulf and the rivers of Mesopotamia, with the eastern Mediterranean and beyond.

Perhaps in part because of the absolutist, highly centralized nature of their authority, the Sassanids seem to have been an even more formidable adversary for the Roman/Byzantine emperors at Constantinople than the Parthians. Like the Parthians, they made effective use of both heavily armed and armored cataphract cavalry and highly mobile archers. Again as the Parthians had done, the Sassanids inflicted crushing defeats on the Romans. One of the greatest Sassanid shahs, Shapur I, even captured the Roman emperor Valerian on the battlefield – a glorious feat depicted on his monument at Naqsh-i-Rustam, where Valerian kneels in submission before the mounted Shahanshah. Between the third and seventh centuries, until the Arab conquest of the Middle East, the Romans/Byzantines and Sassanid Persians were the two superpowers of western Eurasia, not unlike the U.S.–Soviet superpower confrontation of 1945–91 except that the U.S. and Soviet militaries never engaged each other directly. Each side saw the other as its most serious existential threat. Each side cultivated rulers of small states along their frontier as buffers and surrogates to fight against and try to control the aspirations of the other.

As in the Cold War, each side prided itself the standard-bearer of an ideology to which its power was linked directly. The emperors at Constantinople were the defenders and enforcers of Orthodox Christianity, and in that capacity they allied themselves with a powerful clergy that included the bishops of the major cities of their realm as well as clergy who were more closely affiliated with the royal court. The Sassanid shahs, on the other hand, championed Zoroastrianism and used fellow Zoroastrians almost exclusively to help them govern. As protectors of that faith, the shahs allied themselves with a hierarchy of priests, led by the chief priest, who wielded great influence at the shah's court at Ctesiphon. The priests were the magi, so some refer to the religion during this period as "Magianism."[43]

Thus, the long military confrontation between the Sassanids and Romans was imbued with a new, highly destructive dimension that seems absent from the Parthian–Roman struggle but will reappear in Iraq's long history: holy war – as, for example, when the Romans/Byzantines sought to recover the "True Cross" of Jesus' crucifixion after the Sassanids had made off with it when they conquered and plundered Jerusalem in the early seventh century. The feverish intensity that so often accompanies holy war also led in the Roman–Sassanid confrontation to episodes of state-authorized – and priesthood-incited – persecution, especially for Christians in Sassanid Iraq, who quickly fell under suspicion of complicity with the Byzantine Christian enemy. During the fourth century, the Sassanid authorities subjected their empire's Christians to an especially brutal and sustained persecution; the early Christian literature of Iraq is full of "martyr stories."[44] The persecutions and purging of "heretics" by the Byzantine emperors likewise had a decisive influence on the shaping of Christianity in Iraq. It often happens in such holy wars that the people caught in-between the armies of the holy warriors pay a horrific price. The people of Sassanid Iraq were no exception. The battleground for much of the Byzantine–Sassanid confrontation was in Iraq, especially in the north, where the Romans were able to advance across the Euphrates as far as the Tigris, and at times even beyond, only to be thrown back eventually. The early Byzantine historian Procopius, who chronicled the reign of the sixth-century Byzantine emperor Justinian, tells us that during that time the region along the upper Euphrates became a no-man's-land.[45]

Nonetheless, Sassanid rule in Iraq was often marked by stability and consistent, though sometimes tenuous, toleration of non-Zoroastrian religious communities. In fact, during the Sassanid era, Iraq was one of the world's great crucibles of religious belief.

JEWS UNDER THE SASSANIDS

Our historical sources for the Jewish community of Iraq during the Parthian era are meager[46] – and modern political circumstances in both Iraq and Iran have hardly favored the archaeological recovery of additional evidence of early Jewish, or early Christian, life there. Under the Parthians, the Jews of Babylonia had begun to displace the previously pagan population, and much of the Aramean population had begun to adopt Judaism.[47] Jews were established not only in the Babylonian heartland – especially at Nehardea, north of Babylon, and at Seleucia and Ctesiphon – but also further north at Edessa, Nisibis, and Dura-Europus, where in 1932 archaeologists discovered a third-century synagogue with wall paintings of biblical scenes. As noted above, the Jewish population in the region swelled with the arrival of refugees from

Palestine following the failed revolts of 66–70 and 132–35 CE.[48] The second wave brought with it the first infusion of rabbis from Palestine. They were to play a crucial role in the years to come.

Under the Parthians, the Jews of Babylonia had largely been allowed to govern themselves under a series of Jewish officials, the exilarchs. There is no evidence that the Parthians restricted Jewish religious practice as long as it posed no threat to Parthian authority. According to the Jewish historian Josephus, a Jewish merchant from southern Iraq succeeded in converting to Judaism some members of the Parthian vassal kingdom of Adiabene (the region corresponding to ancient Assyria). Although a hostile frontier separated the Palestinian and Babylonian Jewish communities, there was regular communication between the two, and rabbis traveled from one to the other.

With the ascent of the Sassanids to power in the early third century and the Christianization of the Eastern Roman empire under Constantine and his successors in the fourth century, the situation in Iraq began to change. With Palestinian Judaism and its rabbinic schools now suppressed by the Christian imperial authorities, the rabbinic schools of Babylonia assumed an even more important role, especially since the rabbis there had come to believe that their teachings and traditions had not been subjected to the same degree of pollution by Greek influence as had those of the Palestinian Jews, and were therefore more authentic. On the other hand, the Zoroastrian primacy that underpinned Sassanid rule posed problems for the Jews, some of whose beliefs and practices – such as interment of corpses in the ground and the use of candles in ritual – were in flagrant conflict with Zoroastrian beliefs about the purity of flame and earth. As one scholar has noted, "For Magians, Jews were a source of impurity and corruption in the world."[49] Nonetheless, by about 500 the Jewish population may have grown to two million, most of them poor laborers, peasants, and slaves.[50]

During this time, and under these conditions, Iraq became the hearth for a way of life as well as a text that ever since have been central to

Judaism. The way of life is rabbinic Judaism; the text is the Babylonian Talmud. Although a Talmud ("learning") was compiled in Palestine around 400, the Babylonian Talmud is four times larger and is the one to which the term "Talmud" today customarily refers. Compiled around 500, and augmented with further editing over the next couple of centuries, the Babylonian Talmud is a massive, authoritative, complex – and, to the uninitiated, bewildering – compilation of commentaries by the rabbinic scholars of Babylonia on the legal rulings that around 200 had been codified in Galilee in the Mishnah. It is also largely the product of the great rabbinic academies that flourished under the Sassanids in Babylonia. Those at Pumbedita (modern Fallujah), Sura, and Nehardea (all of them along the Euphrates) were among the most prestigious. In the rulings compiled in the Talmud, rabbinic religious scholars known as the Amoraim – the "speakers" or "interpreters" – strived to establish for the Jewish communities of early Iraq a properly Jewish way of life, with rulings related to prayer, ritual purity, diet, clothing, and countless other aspects of daily life. All of it was based on strict observance of the system of religious law, which in turn was based on a long rabbinic tradition of oral interpretation that by then was centuries old. Yet, even while the rabbis were insisting that Jewish life be governed by the strict application of religious law, another manifestation of religious belief continued to flourish in the Jewish communities. From a number of sites in southern Iraq, archaeologists have recovered hundreds of pottery bowls inscribed with magical incantations to ward off various evils.[51] These were obviously in great favor in Jewish households of this time, and they surely reflect an ongoing connection between those Jewish communities and the pagan polytheistic religions and customs of the Babylonians who had dwelled there long before them.

During much of the Sassanid era, the rabbis also functioned under the government of the Jewish exilarch as judges, market inspectors, and tax collectors in the many local Jewish communities. Renewed Sassanid persecution toward the end of Sassanid rule interrupted this system, but it was largely restored when the Muslim Arab conquerors of Iraq and Iran ousted the Sassanids.[52] Many of the rabbinic academies persisted, and because of their prestige the Babylonian Talmud became accepted "as the most authoritative collection of teachings in Judaism next to the Bible itself, and its rules became the rules governing Jewish communities from Mesopotamia to Europe down to modern times."[53] Across the globe, the Babylonian Talmud remains one of the foundations of Jewish life and practice – and yet another example of Iraq's role as a cradle of religions.

CHRISTIANS UNDER THE SASSANIDS

The beginning of Christianity in Mesopotamia is shrouded in the mist of legends and apocryphal accounts. Taken at face value, one of them would place the earliest Iraqi contacts with Christianity with Jesus himself. Around 300, the early Christian historian Eusebius of Caesarea claimed to have seen at Edessa, in the archives of the kingdom of Osrhoene (in northern Mesopotamia), some documents containing a letter to Jesus from Osrhoene's king Abgar, who had heard of Jesus' miraculous powers to heal the sick and asked him to come to Edessa. Eusebius also claimed that he had seen Jesus' reply, in which Jesus told Abgar that he would be with his Father by then but that someone would come. The documents went on to record that after Jesus' crucifixion the apostle Thomas sent to Abgar the apostle Thaddeus (known to Iraqi Christians as Mar Addai), who preached the gospel and healed Abgar of his ailment.[54] Other legends claim that, en route to India, Thomas, one of the original apostles of Jesus, became the first to evangelize among the people of Iraq and that others – including Peter, Addai, Agai, and Mari – came in his wake.[55]

None of these accounts is trustworthy, but we can surmise that early preachers must have played an important role in bringing Christianity to

Iraq. It reached Edessa and northern Mesopotamia by 100, likely because of influence radiating outward from Antioch, by then an emerging center of Christianity and a hotbed of ideas that shaped early Christian doctrine throughout the Middle East. Edessa's special significance in the history of Iraqi – and Syrian – Christianity is also reflected in the fact that the dialect of Aramaic that was spoken there, Syriac, became the dominant language of Christian literature in northern Syria and east of the Euphrates. The spread of Christianity throughout Iraq was also facilitated by the trade routes that crossed the region and by Iraq's network of well-established Jewish communities, where news of the Jesus cult would have been filtering into the synagogues and debated or even preached there. By around 200, we even have evidence of Jewish and Christian communities coexisting in the region – specifically, at Dura-Europus, where archaeologists discovered, besides the aforementioned synagogue, a Christian house-church. This was the earliest Christian church ever discovered and contained the earliest-known indoor baptistery.[56] The Sassanid shahs' military campaigns into Byzantine territory may have played a role as well. On more than one occasion, a Sassanid king deported captives or conquered populations from Byzantine territory eastward into his own realm. It is possible those deportees included Christians – a possibility that brings to mind how Nebuchadnezzar's deportation of Jews from Judea brought Judaism to Iraq.

Undoubtedly among the most important factors in bringing Christianity to Iraq were the bitter controversies that plagued the Christian movement during its early centuries. Almost from the start, the world of Christianity was beset with problems that were often much more threatening than the intermittent persecutions launched by Roman emperors. These problems centered on questions at the very heart of evolving Christian doctrine. For a twenty-first-century Christian, many of the questions may seem long settled; for a twenty-first-century secularist, they seem hopelessly arcane and irrelevant. But for Christians of the first centuries of the Christian era, they could be literally matters of life and death, in both this world and the next. When they became linked to other religious and philosophical movements that were becoming widespread at that time, the result was a spiritual and social maelstrom from which new religious communities were spun out.

A detailed discussion of the origins and doctrines of all the Christian and related religious movements of this era in Iraq's history is well beyond what we can undertake here.[57] But to understand the impact of early Christianity in Iraq, none of them is more crucial than the sects known as the Nestorians and the Monophysites.

By the sixth century, the Nestorians had become by far the majority Christian community in Iraq and throughout the Sassanid empire. Nestorianism had received its impetus from the teachings of Nestorius, an early fourth-century patriarch of Constantinople who taught that Jesus had two separate natures, divine and human, and that Mary had been the mother of the human Jesus but could not have been the mother of God. That position, combined with a lot of imperial politics, caused him to run afoul of both the powerful Bishop of Alexandria in Egypt (another great power center of the early Church) and the emperor. A great Church council convened at Ephesus in 431 condemned him as a heretic, and Nestorius was subsequently deposed and exiled to Egypt, where he died in 450.[58] In the following year, another Church council, at Chalcedon (near Constantinople), likewise condemned his teachings. Byzantine emperors hounded Nestorius' followers, so they fled eastward, into Sassanid territory. There the Church of the East was already well established and making major strides, having survived horrible persecution at the hands of Shah Shapur II during the fourth century, an episode that spawned many Syriac stories about early Iraqi Christian martyrs. The newly arrived Nestorians became part of the Church of the East (or the Church of Persia), which adopted aspects of Nestorian doctrine.

The Church of the East was able to develop a partnership with the Sassanid monarchy, which, in exchange for the clergy's efforts to ensure their flock's loyalty to the Sassanids, now offered toleration and patronage – valuable commodities in a time when Christians in the Sassanid realm might come under suspicion of preferring the Sassanids' mortal enemy, the Christian emperors at Constantinople. In 424, a council at Ctesiphon declared the Church of the East to be fully independent of Constantinople and its Orthodox Christianity. A subsequent council in 498 completely severed the Church of the East's ties with the Church in the West.

By 600, the patriarch of the Church of the East, installed at the imperial capital at Ctesiphon, could claim that it was his Church, not Constantinople's or Rome's, that was the preserver of the true apostolic faith, and in a land that was free of the evils of heresy. He headed a well-organized institution that encompassed six ecclesiastical provinces in Iraq and northern Mesopotamia and two in Iran. Throughout these provinces the Church of the East had its own schools – most famously, the one at Nisibis in the north, which was a seminary for the teaching of Nestorian doctrine. It was also one of the great hospital and medical schools of the time and a major center for the translation and propagation of seminal Greek works dealing with science, religion, and philosophy, which later were passed on to Arab scholars in places like Baghdad. Those schools were also centers for the study of Church law, vital to the continued organization and functioning of the Nestorian communities. Finally, the Church of the East was enriched and fortified with Nestorian monasteries all across Iraq, themselves centers of learning that also embraced a distinctive piety and monastic discipline.

By the sixth century, however, Iraqi Christianity was both expanded and complicated by the Church of the East's bitter rivalry with the emerging church of the Monophysites, also known as the Jacobites, after one of the movement's sixth-century leaders from northern Mesopotamia. Monophysite doctrine had taken shape largely as a response to Nestorianism. Whereas Nestorian doctrine insisted on the strict separation of Christ's divine and human natures, the Monophysites ("one nature") insisted on the primacy of the divine nature of Christ, into which his human nature had been subsumed. Monophysite teaching spread across much of the Middle East, taking root in the Coptic Church in Egypt and also in Armenia, and with adherents spreading as far south as Ethiopia. Monophysite doctrine also became popular in Syria, but after it too was condemned by the imperial Church of Constantinople at the Council of Chalcedon, in 451, many Monophysites fled from Syria east into Sassanid Iraq. The Nestorians reviled them as heretics and waged an unrelenting war with them for doctrinal supremacy and the conversion of new souls. Although the Monophysites always remained the minority religious community among Iraq's Christians, they grew steadily throughout the sixth and seventh centuries, becoming especially well established in the central Iraqi city of Tikrit, famous in modern times as the home of Saddam Hussein. Like the Nestorians, the Monophysites developed their own schools and monasteries throughout Iraq. They also attracted many converts, especially among the Arab tribal pastoralists in the south.

The Nestorians waged the war for converts energetically, winning over many, especially among the Persian Zoroastrians and the remaining Aramean and Persian pagans. But their impact on the spread of Christianity soon extended well beyond the Middle East. We have reports of Christian missionaries reaching as far east as the city of Merv in Central Asia by 200, and a bishop was established at Samarkand by 415. By 615, Chinese sources tell us, a Nestorian missionary had established a church in Xinjiang (in the far west of modern China), and eventually Nestorian Christianity became popular among the Turkish Uighurs of that region. By the eighth century, Nestorian Christians had established missions in China proper; great cities like Xian were to boast substantial Christian populations. In the wake of the conquests of Jingiz Khan and his successors, Nestorian Christianity became widespread across the huge Mongol realm, where medieval European merchants and envoys sent to the Mongol court by the Pope encountered its adherents. It remained so until the later conqueror Timur (to become famous in the West as Tamerlane), having converted to Islam, launched a persecution of Christians.[59]

"GNOSTICS" AND THE APOSTLE OF LIGHT

Although Judaism and Christianity became deeply rooted in Iraq's spiritual landscape under the Zoroastrian Sassanids, they hardly exhaust the inventory of religious movements that took hold there during this time. Especially notable are some that experts have often lumped, perhaps too readily, under the rubric of "Gnosticism." One recent appraisal claims that "Gnosticism" became a term into which both ancient defenders of Christian orthodoxy and modern experts could pigeonhole the many non-Orthodox interpretations of Christianity that became widespread during the first few centuries CE. Also included under this label are related movements that were influenced by some combination of later Greco-Roman philosophical concepts of the opposition of matter and spirit with Iranian concepts of the cosmic struggle between good and evil, light and dark. In other words, there perhaps was no such thing as "Gnosticism."[60]

Use of the term masks the tremendous religious diversity expressed in a large variety of movements, most of which reflect some degree of amalgamation of Greek philosophy and popular Middle Eastern beliefs. These movements tended to share a belief that the material world, including human beings, was created evil when forces or demons from the world of darkness invaded the world of light, but that some individuals retained a spark of light from the God of goodness and light. Individual humans could liberate that spark – and themselves – from the evils of the material world of the flesh and darkness and return to the world of light and the spirit only by acquiring a secret knowledge (Greek *gnosis*), which had been brought by a divine messenger. In Christian adaptations of Gnosticism, this messenger was Jesus Christ.

When assimilated into Christian doctrine, this idea led to the belief that Christ, who was sent to redeem humankind from the evils of the flesh, could not himself have been of the flesh; his body was a phantom. Christ, then, was not fully human. Another ramification of such concepts was embodied in the doctrines taught by the second-century bishop Marcion (from the Turkish coast of the Black Sea), who reasoned that, because the created world of matter is evil, then the God who created it was an evil God of hate and could not, therefore, have been the Father of Christ. Marcion identified this evil God with the Yahweh of the Old Testament. Consequently, he and his followers believed, true Christians must completely reject the Old Testament.

In Iraq, "Gnostic" ideas were to be found in the doctrines of two groups. One is the sect known as the Mandaeans (from Aramaic *manda*, "knowledge") in the West, but to Muslims as the Sabians. That name may be related to a word for "baptize;" if so, it reflects the ritual for which they are perhaps best known: baptism. The Mandaeans still exist as a distinct religious community in Iraq and trace their origins to John the Baptist. Until the nineteenth century, Europeans referred to them as John-Christians – mistakenly, for in Mandaean belief Jesus was a fraud. Their origins and early history are not well understood, but the Mandaeans probably originated in Palestine as a Jewish sect, some of whose members left Palestine for Iraq in the early centuries CE. Like other "Gnostic" groups, they believe in opposed worlds of good and evil, light and darkness, and that the individual soul is a trapped particle of light that needs to be liberated.[61]

The Mandaeans were not the only baptizing sect of ancient Iraq. By the early second century there also existed in southern Iraq, near Ctesiphon, a community known as the Elchasaites, who likewise practiced baptism and whose beliefs seem to have embraced elements of both Judaism and Christianity. In 216 there was born into this community, to parents of Iranian ancestry, a boy who would grow up to become the first person in history to attempt to establish a universal religion. His name was Mani, and the religion he founded was called Manichaeism (from the Aramaic words for "Mani lives").[62]

Mani seems to have experienced two episodes of revelation. The first, when he was twelve, commanded him to leave his father's sect; the second, when he was twenty-four, commanded him to begin his mission of teaching. He made his way to the court of the newly ascendant Sassanids, where he won the patronage of Shapur I. He even accompanied the Shah on the military campaign that captured the Roman emperor Valerian at Edessa in northern Mesopotamia. With this patronage, Mani dispatched evangelizing missions both east and west, including one to Alexandria which, along the way, reportedly converted Zenobia, the famous queen of the wealthy caravan city of Palmyra in Syria.[63] After Shapur died, his successor put an end to Mani's royal patronage, and Mani eventually fell victim to the jealous machinations of the Zoroastrian chief priest and died in prison around 277.

Until the modern era, Mani's teachings were known mainly from the works of Christian writers who excoriated him as a heretic of the worst kind. Such screeds are not the most reliable of sources. Modern discoveries of manuscripts containing his prolific writings have revealed that Mani, the self-designated "Apostle of Light" and "Seal of the Prophets," devised a bewilderingly complex, sophisticated religious system that drew upon and melded the teachings of his predecessors – specifically, Jesus, the Buddha, and Zoroaster (but none of the major Jewish prophets). These, he asserted, were valid teachings, but they had been contaminated over time, a position that the Qur'an later takes toward the Old and New Testaments. His doctrines also included distinctive, "Gnostic"-type accounts of creation and the cosmic struggle of light/ spirit versus darkness/matter, which he lays out in a history encompassing three phases: Past Time, when good/light and evil/matter/darkness were separate; Present Time, including the period of human history, when these opposed principles mixed; and End Time, when all particles of light were to be saved and the world of material darkness destroyed.

The parallels with Zoroastrian eschatology are plain. Beyond doctrine, Mani also devised a social system and way of life that were designed to hasten the liberation of light particles and the eventual End of Time. This entailed setting up a bipartite social system comprising a lower tier of believers (Hearers, or Auditors) and an upper elite tier (the Elect), with the Hearers charged to provide food and other support for the Elect. The Elect led an extremely restricted lifestyle of strict purity, including personal poverty, sexual abstinence, and strict vegetarianism, which was designed to prevent them doing anything that might keep light particles imprisoned. Their lifestyle was also instrumental in liberating light particles. For example, Mani taught that light particles were contained in the plants the Elect ate as food. Their belches helped to release those particles to return to the world of light. The Elect were also the recruiting pool, as it were, for an elaborate Manichaean clerical hierarchy of "pope," twelve apostles, seventy-two bishops, and 360 elders. The Auditors, on the other hand, were not forced to adopt as restrictive a lifestyle – nor could they have, if the Elect were to be properly cared for – but they were enjoined to perform five main duties: to observe the major commandments of Manichaeism, to pray, to give alms to the poor, to fast, and to confess their sins. As we will see, these duties show some close parallels with the Five Pillars of Islam.[64]

Given the later attempts in both the Roman/Byzantine and Sassanid empires to extirpate Mani's religion, its eventual success and wide expansion are remarkable. It won many adherents in the West, including the Church Father St. Augustine of Hippo, who spent nine years as a Manichaean "Auditor." Roman Catholic popes, like Leo I in the fifth century, felt compelled to inveigh vigorously against it. In Western Europe, its influence was felt into the thirteenth century, when the Pope sent a crusade to slaughter French heretics – the Cathars or Albigensians – who had adopted elements of Manichaean doctrine and social engineering. To the east, Manichaean churches were established as far away as China, and the great Mongol khans permitted Manichaean missionaries to proselytize in their realm. But by around 1800 the religion had evidently died out in East Asia as well. Until quite recently, Manichaeism, one of the earliest ecumenical world religions, was consigned to the category of pernicious heresy, another of the wicked contaminants with which the "East" had threatened the civilized, Christian "West." When we refer to Manichaeism today, it is usually as an adjective, "Manichaean," to describe an individual's or group's worldview when it is characterized by a strictly delineated, black-and-white distinction between good and evil.

It is quite an impressive legacy for a child born in an Iraqi village in the early third century. In its own time, Manichaeism was but one more ingredient in the potpourri of religions that took root in Iraq in late antiquity. The strict monotheistic principles of Judaism and Christianity; the dualistic systems of Zorastrianism, Mandaeism, and Manichaeism; the millennia-deep traditions of ancient Mesopotamian "pagan" polytheism still practiced in the towns and villages of Mesopotamia and reflected in the magic of the incantation bowls coveted by Jewish households – all of these bear testimony to Iraq's legacy as a hearth of religions.

In the middle of the seventh century, Iraq's riches were to attract yet another wave of invaders – this time from the western reaches of the Arabian Peninsula. They would bring yet another ingredient into the mix of religions, one that was extremely potent and long enduring.

5

IRAQ, ISLAM, AND THE GOLDEN AGE OF THE ARAB EMPIRE

B Y THE YEAR 600, Europe was mired in what earlier historians called the "Dark Ages." Whereas the Eastern Roman (Byzantine) empire had thrived culturally and economically and helped foster a vibrant, if contentious, Christianity, the Western empire had gone under, brought down by economic decline and political fragmenta-tion, much of it exacerbated by the incursions of "barbarian" Germanic tribes. In 410, one of them had sacked Rome itself. In 476, the last Roman emperor in the West was deposed, with none to follow him until 800, when the chieftain of one of those tribes, Charlemagne of the Franks, was crowned at Rome by the Pope as the new "emperor of the Romans." During Charlemagne's reign, intellectual activity begins to stir in Europe once again, only to be smacked down by invaders from the Scandinavian north (the Norsemen, or Vikings) and other quarters, including the Middle East. Not until the eleventh and twelfth centuries, when Europe enters the High Middle Ages, does European civilization begin again to come into its own. The High Middle Ages transitioned into the Renaissance, as Europeans rediscovered what they claimed to be their roots in the great "Western" civilizations of Greece and Rome. European scholars now studied and tried to emulate the literary and philosophical works of Greek and Latin writers. European scientists seized upon the advances that Greek and Roman investigators had made in astronomy, mathematics, and medicine, and built upon them, and created the scaffolding upon which the West rose to its modern global dominance.

But without the contributions made in Iraq, mainly by Arab and Persian scholars who lived and worked there, the Renaissance and all that followed for Europe might never have happened.

This part of the legacy of Iraq is a story to which most people in the West are oblivious. The reasons are not hard to identify. For the era that we are about to examine – of Europeans enduring a long period in the doldrums before their sails slowly begin to refill while the Middle East powers ahead under a full head of steam – is also one during which the Middle East spawned what the West has long considered an existential threat. I do not refer to Communism, which people of my own Cold War generation in the United States feared and hated as the greatest threat to our way of life – one likely to bring the planet to a thermonuclear Armageddon of "mutually assured destruction," and a threat that none of us could be sure was ever going to vanish. The threat of which I speak is Islam, and especially Islam as it expanded from the Middle East. Under its aegis, the Middle East became the standard-bearer of global civilization, nowhere more so than in Iraq, which two centuries after its conquest was to go from being an embattled frontier zone between two great empires, to being once again the heartland of one of the great empires of world history and the home – again – of what was perhaps the greatest city in the world. Also under Islam's aegis, Christendom saw its dominion in the eastern Mediterranean terminated, its holy places there conquered, and even its hold on Europe imperiled. Arguably, Europe – and by extension the West as a whole – has never forgotten the existential threat posed by the Muslim Middle East. Any debt the West may owe Iraq therefore tends to remain unacknowledged, even forgotten.

As for Iraq, while it led the world under the banner of Islam, Islam's history has visited its own special sorrows upon Iraq's people. As recent events attest, it continues to do so. Those sorrows were intertwined from the beginning with both the glories and the conflicts that attended Islam's emergence.

PRELUDE TO THE COMING OF ISLAM AND THE ARAB CONQUEST OF IRAQ

The Arab Muslim conquest of the Middle East was an epochal event in history. It ushered in a new ethnic group as the ruling class there, and it also ushered in a new religion that was to dominate the region for centuries, down to the present day. For that reason historians have tended to treat the Muslim conquest of the Middle East as a watershed event – very similarly to how they have treated Alexander the Great's conquest a thousand years earlier. But the Muslim conquest is perceived as even more special, in that it is *the* event that separates ancient history from medieval history in the Middle East. Most general histories of the Middle East, in fact, begin with the Muslim conquest, after a perfunctory chapter or two about "geography and environment" and "ancient prelude."

As is so often true of historical watershed events, the fact of the matter is that in both the Middle East generally and Iraq specifically the two sides of the Muslim-conquest watershed are bridged by much continuity. In Iraq, the Tigris and Euphrates continued to serve as the region's life-lines and the crucial foundation of its resource base. With the network of trunk canals and small feeders criss-crossing the alluvium, the rivers provided Iraq's life's blood of irrigation water. As they had for their ancient predecessors, the rivers provided the Arab conquerors vital sustenance and great wealth derived from the fertility of the floodplain.

Notwithstanding the popular misperception that the Muslim Arab warriors suddenly swept out of the desert into a Middle East that was terra incognita to them, Arabs had in fact been living in the Middle East, and playing a major role in what was going on there, centuries before the Muslim conquest.[1] Modern political maps show borders running through the desert of Iraq's west and southwest, dividing it from Saudi Arabia, Syria, Jordan, and Kuwait. But until the early twentieth century there were no such lines. And they can be almost meaningless even now. Tribal pastoralists today move their flocks across the desert that extends into all of those countries, and pay little attention to such borders. Moreover, the desert has its own built-in thoroughfares, in the form of wadis (dried-up river-beds), which serve as lines of contact and communication. For example, the Wadi al-Rimmah connects Iraq's southern lowlands with western Arabia, and the Wadi Sirhan connects northern Arabia with Syria. As early as 1100 BCE, camel-mounted warriors, presumably Arabs from the Arabian peninsula but referred to in the Bible as Midianites and Ishmaelites, were wreaking havoc in Syria and Palestine. On the other hand, the Bible also records a more cordial visit by Arabs during the tenth century BCE: the visit to King Solomon from the queen of the land of Sheba, the region of Saba, in the far south of Arabia. From the mid-ninth century BCE on, the Assyrian emperors frequently had to deal with Arabs, sometimes as foes, sometimes as allies. Later, under Parthian overlordship, Arab rulers held sway in small kingdoms in both southern and northern Iraq, including the great temple-caravan center at Hatra, where such rulers were first known to history to call themselves "kings of the Arabs."[2] By the time of the Persian Sassanids, Arab states ringed the desert fringes of the Fertile Crescent in what are now Iraq, Syria, and Turkey. Among them were those controlled by the Ghassanid and the Lakhmid tribal confederations, which served as frontier-zone avatars of the two superpowers of the era: the Ghassanids for the Byzantines, the Lakhmids for the Sassanids. The Lakhmids' capital was at Hira, on the Euphrates in southern Iraq (near modern Kufa) and on a major caravan route linking Syria with lands to the east. In later tradition, Hira was remembered as a wealthy, cosmopolitan city whose citizens were famed for their literacy and whose rulers extended patronage to itinerant Arab poets who came to their court. There is reason to believe that the Arabic alphabetic script – which was derived from Aramaic – was perfected at Hira, from where traders took it back with them to Mecca and other northern Arabian towns.[3]

Finally, Hira was also a major center of Nestorian Christianity under the Lakhmids, in contrast to their Ghassanid rivals, who adopted the Monophysite version of Christianity. The larger underlying point here is that before the Muslim conquest Iraq was a mosaic of monotheisms, with a long history of pluralism and toleration among religious communities. By the early seventh century the Christians were the largest of them, but the region also supported perhaps two million Jews as well as thousands of others who adhered to Zoroastrianism, Manichaeism, and other teachings. Soon after the arrival of the Muslim Arabs, many of these would convert to Islam, some out of conviction, others motivated by expediency. Many others would continue in their own faith traditions. Iraq under Muslim rule included vibrant, prosperous Jewish and Christian communities. It is also worthy of note that all three of these faiths, as well as Zoroastrianism and Manichaeism, shared a similar religious orientation: toward a single all-powerful deity who was male and who was served by a predominantly male priesthood.[4] That orientation in turn reinforced a vision of society that has dominated Iraq – and much of the world beyond – ever since.

Just as Arabs had influenced Iraq's history and culture long before the Muslim conquest, influences from Iraq and neighboring regions had had an impact in the Arabian Peninsula. The Sassanid shahs in the sixth century had dominion over portions of southern and eastern Arabia, as well as flourishing economic ties with these regions.[5] Especially significant to the rise of Islam, there existed in Arabia by 600 a number of Jewish and Christian communities. Some of them were centuries old, some of the Jewish communities possibly dating back to the sixth century B C E, the time when the last Babylonian king, Nabonidus, left Babylon for the Arabian oasis town of Tayma. As two respected Bible scholars have noted, there is a "strong possibility that Jewish soldiers and families accompanied him to Arabia, because practically all the oases he claims to have visited were later strong centers of Jewish settlement."[6] One of them was Yathrib, which was to figure so prominently in the rise of Muhammad and Islam that it would be renamed the "city of the prophet" – Medina. Among the more significant opponents the Prophet Muhammad had to deal with early in his career were Jewish Arab tribes centered at Medina. Obviously, then, the concept of monotheism was well known to many in Arabia by the time of the birth of Muhammad around 570. But the distinctly Arab version of it that was to emerge in the western region of the Arabia Peninsula (the area known as the Hejaz) through his preaching and his charismatic leadership would supersede the Jewish and Christian versions and become an enduring foundation of civilization throughout the Middle East and beyond. Nowhere more so than in Iraq.

MUHAMMAD AND THE ORIGINS
OF THE COMMUNITY OF ISLAM

By the time he died, the full name of the man who would be known, like the prophet Mani, as the "Seal of the Prophets" was Abu al-Qasim Muhammad ibn Abdullah ibn Abd al-Muttalib ibn-Hashim. It is useful here to point out three features of the Prophet Muhammad's name. First, the name Muhammad (the spelling preferred in Western academic works) has also been spelled "Mohammed" or "Mahomet." All of these refer to the same man and represent different attempts to render a common Arab name in the Roman alphabet. Second, the

Arabic term *ibn* means "son of" or "descendant of" and reflects the strong emphasis on kinship ties in the traditional Arab society from which Islam emerged. Third, the last part of Muhammad's name, "ibn Hashim," denotes the clan to which he belonged: the descendants of Hashim, or the Hashemites. Ever since the time of Muhammad, membership in the Hashemite clan, with its implied blood ties to Muhammad, has conferred special status – something that was to have a major impact on the formation and history of modern Iraq, Syria, and Jordan.

The Hashemites were one of a number of clans comprising a powerful tribe known as the Quraish, which dominated the region around the trading town of Mecca (Makkah) where Muhammad was born around the year 570. Our uncertainty about his birth year reflects even greater uncertainty about the details of his life. What has become the traditionally accepted account of his life derives mainly from accounts written more than a century after his death. Most modern historians agree that they are not very reliable. Although Muslims traditionally have placed great stock in them, similarly questionable as historical sources are the accumulated traditions and reports about sayings or actions of Muhammad and his companions which are known as *hadith*.[7] Muhammad's teachings were set down after his death (in 632) in the scripture that all Muslims regard as sacred, the Qur'an (or Koran) ("recitation"). In Muslim belief, the Qur'an is the actual words of God – or "Allah," the Arabic term for the One Supreme Being, just as "God" is the English word. The Qur'an is the final, perfect revelation from God as given to Muhammad in the Arabic language.

Muhammad received this revelation in a series of episodes that, according to Muslim tradition, began around 610. By that time, the forty-year-old Muhammad had built a successful career as a caravan trader. He had made commercial trips to the eastern Mediterranean region, where he came into contact with Christian and perhaps Jewish monotheists. His business skills had earned him the hand of his first wife,

Khadijah, a widow who had employed him in the commercial venture she inherited upon the death of her first husband. Muhammad had also developed a reputation in Mecca as a man of integrity and a just and fair arbiter, as well as a man of spiritual depth who was inclined to spend time in solitary reflection. It was during one such solitary interlude in a cave outside Mecca that a terrified and awe-struck Muhammad received from God, via the angel Jibril (Gabriel), the first of the many revelations that would be communicated to him over the rest of his life. Muhammad soon began to preach these revelations in Mecca. As set down in the Qur'an, they remain the foundation of the religion of Islam ("submission" [to God's will]) and its adherents, Muslims ("those who submit" [to God's will]).

We can hardly attempt here a complete history of Islam and its doctrines, but it is important to be aware of its basic beliefs and obligations. The parallels and continuities with Judaism, Christianity, and Zoroastrianism, all of which were being practiced in Iraq on the eve of the Muslim conquest, will be evident.

The fundamental beliefs of Islam are:

1. Belief in one God and in the indivisible Oneness of God – that is, God cannot be divided into "persons" as in the Christian doctrine of the Trinity. Nor does God have a "Son;" in Islamic belief, Jesus (Isa) is a great prophet, not the Son of God.
2. Belief in angels as creatures made by God who perform tasks assigned by God, including the bearing of revelation.
3. Belief in the authenticity of the earlier books of God's revelations – the Hebrew Bible and the New Testament gospels. In Muslim belief, the revelations given to Muhammad (the Qur'an) are the final revelation. Consequently, the earlier scriptures, though authentic, are obsolete, superseded by the Qur'an. Traditionally, Jews and Christians living under Muslim rule were accorded a tolerated and protected, though

second-class, status (in Arabic, *dhimmi*) as "peoples of the Book."

4. Belief in Muhammad as the messenger of God, and in the prophets who were his forerunners – among them Abraham, Moses, David, and Jesus.

5. Belief in a final day of judgment and eternal reward in heaven or hell.

6. Belief in predestination – in other words, God has known for eternity the fate of all human beings.

Closely related to these beliefs are the basic obligations incumbent upon all Muslims – the Five Pillars of Islam:

1. The profession of faith ("shahada"): "I witness that there is no God but the God, and that Muhammad is the messenger of God."

2. Daily prayer: Muslims are enjoined to pray five times a day, at dawn, noon, mid-afternoon, sunset, and evening.

3. Charity to the poor and disadvantaged ("zakat," or "purifica-tion"), to be accomplished by contributing a portion of one's possessions (one-fortieth of one's capital), usually once a year. Muslims are also encouraged to give alms throughout the year, preferably secretly.

4. Fasting during the month of Ramadan. During this month, a Muslim may partake of no food, drink, or other activity that causes a change in the body's composition (including sex) from sunrise to sunset. Ramadan is the ninth month of the Muslim calendar, which is a lunar, rather than solar, calen-dar. This means that Ramadan migrates across the seasons, sometimes falling during winter, when the daylight hours are short, but sometimes in summer, when the days can be very long. This practice of fasting is paralleled in Judaism

by fasting on the day of Yom Kippur, and in Christianity by fasting during the season of Lent. Just as Christians mark the end of Lent with great celebration and feasting on Easter Sunday, Muslims mark the end of Ramadan with the feast known as Eid al-Fitr.

5. The pilgrimage ("hajj") to Mecca. Every able-bodied Muslim who can afford it must make this pilgrimage once in a lifetime. Upon doing so, the pilgrim receives the honorific title of "hajji" – a title of respect among Muslims, but in recent years transformed by U.S. soldiers in Iraq into a rude designation for Iraqi Arabs in general.

Some recognize as a sixth pillar, jihad ("struggle"). The primary sense of "jihad" in the view of many Muslims is the inner struggle in which one must constantly engage in order to be a good Muslim, but "jihad" also refers to the military defense of the faith of Islam.

Note the parallels between Islam and the earlier monotheisms. There was another parallel between the earliest Christians and the earliest Muslims: persecution. Although a number of Meccans accepted Muhammad's teachings early on, many of the more powerful elements in Mecca's society rejected them. Part of their reason for doing so likely had to do with Mecca's importance as a trading center, where different groups could come in peace and do very profitable business. Mecca's status as a sanctuary of sorts seems to have been linked to the presence there of the Ka'ba ("cube" – owing to its shape), a stone-built shrine, evidently ancient already in Muhammad's day, that housed idols of the many deities worshipped by the local tribes. Later, a tradition developed that the Ka'ba had been built by Abraham and his son Ismail (Ishmael). Muhammad's insistence that there was only one true God obviously threatened the status of the Ka'ba, and therefore the profits of the local elite, who began then to persecute Muhammad's followers.

Around that time there took place one of those fortuitous events that change the course of history. By this point in his career, Muhammad's reputation as a just and fair man had spread beyond Mecca northward to the oasis town of Yathrib, which along with its immediate environs was the home of several Arab tribes, including some that were Jewish. Beset with dissension among their various tribes, Yathrib's leaders invited Muhammad to come and dwell among them as an arbitrator to help them reconcile their differences. Muhammad accepted. Soon thereafter he and his followers departed from Mecca and made the trek to Yathrib – an event known to Muslims as the Hijra (or Hegira; literally, "migration," though some translate it as "flight"). In the Western calendar, the year was 622; for Muslims, it is the year 1 of their calendar, the point in time that separates the era of Islam from the preceding era of *jahiliyya*, or ignorance of God's revelations as expressed in the Qur'an. It is also the date that marks the start of the "umma" – the eventually worldwide community of Muslims, for upon taking up residence at Yathrib, Muhammad began to organize a community of believers that was based on the revelations he had received from God. According to tradition, his house became the first mosque ("masjid," or "place of prostration" [in prayer]). Yathrib's association with the life of the prophet became so strong that it became known simply as the "city of the prophet," later shortened to "the city" – in Arabic, Madinah, or Medina.

With Medina as his base, over the next eight years Muhammad acted not only as prophet but also as field general, waging a war of both words and combat with the leaders of Mecca, who still regarded him as a threat and were intent on wiping out him and his followers. By 630, despite at least one major setback, Muhammad had both defeated the Meccans in battle and attracted other tribes to his cause. Ultimately, he and his followers were able to march to Mecca, where they peacefully took possession of the city. The culmination was Muhammad's destroying the idols in the Ka'ba and proclaiming it to be the shrine of the one God. Early in his career he had instructed his followers to face toward the holy city of Jerusalem when they prayed. Later he instructed them instead to face Mecca, and the Ka'ba, which today remains the ultimate destination of the pilgrims who make the hajj to Mecca.[8]

Muhammad continued to live at Medina, however. By the end of his life he had married a total of twelve wives, some to secure useful political alliances, and they bore him several children. None of the boys survived to adulthood, but his daughters were married to men who became outstanding leaders. His daughter Fatima wound up marrying a man whose story is crucial to the history of Islam and Iraq's special place in it. That man, Ali ibn Abi Talib (hereafter, Ali), was also Muhammad's first cousin and therefore a blood relative of the prophet; his marriage to Fatima also made him the prophet's son-in-law.

Muhammad died in 632.[9] His death was peaceful, but it inaugurated for the fledgling Muslim community a tumultuous era that would see the rapid expansion of the umma by means of military conquest, but also tremendous turmoil and even violence within the community. Muhammad evidently never designated a successor, nor did he specify a process whereby one might be chosen. Traditional Arab society relies on two different mechanisms to reach a decision concerning leadership. One entails discussion among the elite and the reaching of consensus to select a new leader; the other involves the respect and preference accorded to male heirs within the dominant family, as for example in the recent history of the royal family of Saudi Arabia. In this instance, the consensus-building process prevailed, and Abu Bakr – a respected early friend and supporter of Muhammad, and the father of one of Muhammad's wives – was selected as the first "successor" to the prophet as leader of the Muslim community. The Arabic word for "successor" is usually rendered in English as "caliph." Over the next few centuries, the rapid expansion of Islam would transform the role of the caliph from simple "successor" to, essentially, "divinely sanctioned universal ruler."

However, many in the fledgling umma believed that the title of caliph ought rightfully to have gone to Ali, who as Muhammad's first cousin was Muhammad's closest male blood relative, and was also the prophet's son-in-law. From the beginning, these supporters constituted a faction backing Ali, and eventually Ali's descendants, as the more legitimate successors to the prophet's mantle. Some even claimed that Muhammad had personally designated Ali to succeed him. The Arabic word for such a faction is *shi'a*. In time, the members of the pro-Ali faction became known as the Shi'a, or, in common Western terminology, Shi'ites.

Such were the origins of the schism that has been central to Islam's history and politics – perhaps nowhere more so than in Iraq – to this day. The dominant, majority element became known as the Sunni – from Arabic *sunna*, the "path" or "way" of the Prophet Muhammad. Today they comprise more than ninety percent of Muslims. Across most of the "Muslim world," Shi'ites have remained a minority dominated by Sunni political leaders. But in those countries of the Middle East east of Egypt, Shi'ites often comprise a majority of the population – especially in the Islamic Republic of Iran, where they are roughly eighty-five percent of the population. Whereas Iran's predominantly Shi'ite population is governed by Shi'ite religious leaders, in other countries in this region large, even majority Shi'ite populations have been dominated, and often oppressed, by governments led by Sunnis or even Sunnis and Christians. Bahrain's population is 65–70 percent Shi'ite yet governed harshly by a Sunni monarchy. Lebanon, where in the last forty years the Shi'ite population has grown rapidly to become forty-five percent of the population, was until recently dominated by Sunni and Christian political leaders. Shi'ites also predominate in the oil-rich eastern coastal region of Saudi Arabia, where they are often treated harshly by the staunchly Sunni Saudi monarchy.

Iraq was the historical cradle of Shi'ism and is the location of Shi'ites' most revered shrines and pilgrimage sites. But until the overthrow of Saddam Hussein its Shi'ite population – sixty-five percent of Iraq's people – was dominated, often brutally, by Sunni overlords.

THE ARAB MUSLIM CONQUEST OF IRAQ:
THE EARLY FORGING OF ARAB (VERSUS PERSIAN) IDENTITY

The period 632–61 was dominated by two trends that demonstrate both the vigor and the conflict within the early Muslim community. One trend was rapid military conquest, which by 661 brought under Arab Muslim rule a vast territory stretching from Iran to what is today the coast of Libya. The other trend was internal dissension within the community, some of it over questions of leadership, some of it over questions of doctrine. The dissension often provoked violence, including violence against the leaders. Of the first four caliphs to succeed Muhammad, only one – the first caliph, Abu Bakr – died a peaceful death. The five-year reign of the last of the four caliphs – Ali himself – from 656 to 661 was marred by the first civil war (*fitna*) in the Islamic community, ending in Ali's assassination. That the Arab conquests were able to succeed despite these tensions is testament to the vigor of early Islam.

The mainly Arab accounts upon which we have to rely for these events are hardly unbiased or straightforward, which has led to much debate among historians as to how and why the Arabs were able to achieve these conquests so rapidly.[10] The warrior tradition of the hardy Arab tribesmen, with its emphasis on personal bravery and upholding the honor and reputation of the tribe, surely had something to do with it, as did the lure of the booty – both in riches and in slaves – there for the taking in the prosperous cities of the Middle East. Moreover, although intertribal raiding had been customary among the tribes, that avenue to wealth was no longer open, for now the tribes were in theory bonded by membership in the Muslim community. If they were to sustain the economic base that raiding had traditionally provided and at the same time preserve their unity as Muslims, they would need to turn their attention to regions outside the Arabian Peninsula. Put simply, the alternatives were expand or collapse.[11]

Although in our secular age we tend to play down such motives, there is good reason also to believe that the Muslim warriors, like their later Christian Crusader counterparts, believed themselves to be fighting in a holy cause and that to die in battle for that cause would bring instant entry into paradise. Their Byzantine and Sassanid foes, meanwhile, had been hammering each other for centuries, and especially vigorously in the decades just before the Muslim invasion. Between 613 and 618, the Sassanid armies of the great shah Khosrau II swept into Syria and Palestine, where they captured and looted Jerusalem and carried away Christendom's holiest relic, the True Cross. They then advanced into Egypt and almost to the gates of Constantinople, only to be forced into retreat when the Byzantine emperor Heraclius launched a brilliant counterstroke that struck deep into the Sassanid heartland in Iraq. The resulting depletion of both sides' resources left them vulnerable to the Muslim onslaught, which also seems to have caught them by surprise – although later Muslim tradition claims that Muhammad sent Khosrau a letter urging him to accept the one true God or else be doomed. That same tradition claims that an enraged Khosrau tore up the letter.

The populations of both empires suffered under these attacks. In the largely Christian realm of the Byzantine empire, the emperors had often oppressed their fellow-Christian subjects, both with taxation and with attempts to repress adherents to "heretical" forms of Christianity – including the Monophysite interpretation favored in Egypt and much of the Levant, as well as the Nestorian. Frequent persecution of native, non-Orthodox churches had undoubtedly softened up their loyalty to Constantinople. It also left them more willing to convert or accommodate themselves to the faith of their Muslim conquerors, which was remarkably similar to their own in some of its fundamental doctrines and practices.

When the Muslim Arab forces arrived, they often engaged in some initial looting and killing, but in general they did not compel conversion to Islam; they even discouraged it to an extent. Christians, Jews, and Zoroastrians were accepted and tolerated as fellow monotheists and were granted the legal status of *dhimmi*, which entailed toleration and official protection, though at the cost of having to pay a special tax and accepting a lower status than that of Muslims. No wonder, then, that many of them preferred their new overlords – and in time many of them did convert to Islam.

Led by the brilliant commander Khalid ibn al-Walid, only a year after Muhammad's death in 632, the Muslim Arabs began their conquest of the eastern Mediterranean seaboard. Khalid's forces also struck out from Syria, down the Euphrates and deep into Mesopotamia, where they defeated the Sassanids in a series of battles and captured the great Lakhmid Arab capital at Hira. When the new caliph, Umar, sent Khalid back to Syria to deal with the Byzantine armies that were massing there to expel the Muslim invaders, the Sassanids used the breathing spell to reassemble their forces in Iraq. In August 636, the Arabs decisively defeated the Byzantines in Syria at the Battle of the Yarmuk River. Their victory ensured their control of the cities of Jerusalem, Antioch, and Damascus. Damascus soon emerged as the center of Muslim rule in Syria and the west.

The stage was now set for what has become a legendary encounter, one that was to seal the fate of Iraq. Under their new commander, Saad ibn Abi Waqqas, in 636 Muslim forces of probably several thousand, their numbers augmented by the arrival of some of the victors at the Yarmuk River, prepared to take on the Sassanid forces near the town of Qadisiyyah in southern Iraq about fifty kilometers from the town of Kufa. The battle that took place there was described at great length by Arab historians writing a few centuries later. It is also noted in the celebrated Persian poet Ferdowsi's epic poem recounting early Iranian history, the *Shahnameh* ("Book of Kings"). The actual events are difficult to reconstruct. Lasting perhaps three or four days, the Battle of Qadisiyyah was remembered for the bravery and heroism, and horrific carnage, on both sides. By its end, the rugged, God-inspired Arab warriors of Islam had inflicted a decisive defeat upon the famed archers and heavy cavalry of their Persian foes.[12] According to the Arab sources, their victory largely owed to the hardiness and martial virtue of the Arab warriors, which are contrasted with the decadence and arrogance of the Persians, much as Greek authors like Isocrates in the fifth and fourth centuries BCE had contrasted their own superior virtue to the alleged decadence and arrogance of the Achaemenid Persian armies of Darius and Xerxes.

Within a few months after the victory at Qadisiyyah, the Muslims had captured the Sassanid capital at Ctesiphon. After a victory at Jalula in 637 assured control of the agricultural bounty of the Tigris–Euphrates alluvium and opened the routes to the east, the Muslim forces completed the conquest of Iran. The Sassanid dynasty came to an end in 653 with the death of its last shah. The Arab conquerors brought under their sway a vast territory stretching across Central Asia to the gates of India and China.

For the history of Iraq, the Battle of Qadisiyyah was a turning point. It ensured the Arab Muslim conquest of Iraq, and it laid the foundation for Arab – and Muslim – predominance in Iraq during the centuries to come, even under future conquerors – Turkish, British, and American. The Battle of Qadisiyyah also became one of the most potent symbols of Iraqi Arab nationalism and its enduring antagonism with the Persian "otherness" of Iran. During his ruinous war with Iran from 1980 to 1988, Saddam Hussein made egregious use of the Arab victory at Qadisiyyah as a propaganda tool against what he identified as Iraq's historic mortal enemy, the perfidious Persians of Iran. Yet, as we will see, Persians were to make immense contributions to what was to become Iraq's greatest period of empire and high culture. And Iraq's contribution to the evolution of the Shi'ism that later came to dominate Iran would likewise be crucial.

IRAQ AND THE EARLY FORGING OF SHI'ITE (VERSUS SUNNI) IDENTITY

Some popular perceptions of the Muslim conquest evoke images of barbarous Bedouin hordes swarming the countryside, raping and pillaging, and forcing the population to convert to Islam or be exterminated. In reality, the new rulers of Iraq at first kept themselves apart from those they ruled, segregating themselves from the locals in the garrisons they set up in what one historian has referred to as "camp-cities."[13] Especially important among these were Kufa and Basra, both in southern Iraq.[14] The Arab military leaders and appointed governors wielded ultimate authority, but they continued to rely on the tried-and-true administrative methods their Sassanid predecessors had practiced. As the American archaeologist McGuire Gibson noted shortly after the invasion of 2003, "Unlike the current American occupation of Iraq, the Arabs kept the Sasanian bureaucrats in place and were able to keep the country running with little disruption."[15]

Meanwhile, in 644, only a few years after the victory at Qadisiyyah, the position of caliph had passed from the pious Umar to Uthman ibn Affan, who was selected by a group Umar had appointed to select his successor. With Uthman's accession, tribal politics seem to have become even more tense. Uthman belonged to the Quraysh clan known as the Umayyads, late converts to Islam, but wealthy and prestigious enough to command respect. Soon, Uthman used his new position to promote the interests of his Umayyad kinsmen, appointing them to lucrative positions or otherwise enriching them from the proceeds of empire. And whereas Umar had permitted his governors at Kufa and Basra to retain much of the revenues they gathered, as well as much of their autonomy, Uthman now tried to exercise a stronger hold there.[16] That was to cost him much support.

Perhaps no one among Uthman's Umayyad relatives benefited from his policies more than his kinsman Muawiya ibn Abi Sufyan. Muawiya had been an enemy of the Prophet Muhammad early in his career, embracing his message only after Muhammad took control at Mecca. Umar had made him the governor of Syria. Uthman now enlarged Muawiya's governorate to include much of northern Iraq. When rebels assassinated Uthman in 656, Muawiya controlled from his capital, Damascus, a sizeable realm and commanded a large army. Almost immediately, he would use those resources to great effect.

The man selected to succeed Uthman as caliph was none other than Ali, cousin and son-in-law of the prophet, whom many had supported from the beginning as the most legitimate successor to Muhammad. His valor as a warrior and military leader before his accession had only increased his prestige. But, having established his caliphate at the camp-city of Kufa, Ali undercut his own support by failing to apprehend Uthman's assassins. Among the first to rally forces against Ali to avenge Uthman was Muhammad's young widow, Aisha, daughter of Abu Bakr, the first caliph. In 656, in a famous encounter fought near Basra which became known as the Battle of the Camel, reportedly because Aisha's forces rallied around the camel that bore the litter in which she rode, Aisha's forces were vanquished by Ali's. [17]

As the Umayyad standard-bearer, and intent on avenging his kinsman Uthman, Muawiya now rose up against Ali, launching what is regarded in Muslim history as the first *fitnah*, or civil war, in the Muslim community. In 657, their armies met at Siffin on the Euphrates, near what is now the Syrian city of Raqqa. According to a traditional account of the battle, when Ali's forces began to get the upper hand, Muawiya's decided to request arbitration of their dispute and signaled their intention by charging onto the field with pages of the Qur'an on the tips of their spears – a gesture that it seems Ali felt he had to honor.

That decision perhaps cost him his life. Some of his followers believed that by agreeing to arbitration Ali refused to accept the judgment of God as it was being determined on the battlefield, so in the aftermath of Siffin they left his army and turned against him. In 661, Ali was murdered by one of these men, who came to be known as the Kharijites, while he was at prayer in the mosque of his Iraqi capital, Kufa. Soon after, Muawiya proclaimed himself caliph.

The legends about the selection of Ali's burial place, and even its location, are contradictory. Some believe him to be buried in the city of Mazar-i-sharif in Afghanistan. But the majority of Muslims today believe that his body lies in the tomb-shrine in the great mosque dedicated to him in the southern Iraqi city of Najaf. It is impossible to overstate the significance that Ali's entombed presence has bestowed upon Najaf. With the possible exception of Qom in Iran, Najaf is unrivaled as a spiritual center for Shi'ites. Millions of pilgrims come to Najaf each year from around the world, and especially from Iran, to stand in Ali's presence, by his tomb, and pray in his mosque. The very soil of Najaf is special because of Ali's presence. Devout Shi'ites covet the clay tablets (known as *turba*) fashioned from the soil of Najaf, which they place in front of them during prayer so they can touch their foreheads to Najaf's holy ground as they bow forward in prostration. The burial ground associated with Ali's tomb is possibly the largest cemetery in the world, owing to the fact that for centuries Shi'ites across the globe have had their remains brought there in order to be buried near Ali. This cemetery is known as the Wadi as-Salam ("Valley of Peace"), an irony lost on most of the U.S. soldiers who in 2004 battled Iraqi Shi'ite resistance fighters of Muqtada al-Sadr's Jaish al-Mahdi among its thousands of headstones. Ali's proximity helped fuel the development of Najaf's famous *hawza*, the assembly of theological scholars who make Najaf the preeminent center of Shi'ite theological study in the world, rivaled only by the seminary at Qom. Currently, the most esteemed member of the Najaf *hawza* is the Ayatollah Ali al-Sistani, the spiritual teacher most emulated by Shi'ites across the world, including the millions of Shi'ites in Iraq. He played a crucial role in Iraqi politics in the years after the 2003 invasion.

Nor is it possible to overstate the charisma and magnetism that even today surround the story and person of Ali ibn Abi Talib. He is the last in the series of the four caliphs who presided over the formative period of the early Islamic community's development after Muhammad. That period was extremely volatile, in no small part because of these caliphs' failings and decisions, which sometimes were intended to further the interests of themselves and their kin. Nonetheless, they are traditionally designated the "rightly guided" (Arabic *rashidun*) caliphs in recognition of their inspired leadership, their diligence in advancing the faith and cause of Islam, and their personal association with the Prophet Muhammad. They are highly revered as embodiments of Islam's early purity and success. Among Shi'ites, Ali has an even more distinctive status, as a leader who insisted on equality and social justice and who aspired not only to lead as a political head and military commander but also to provide religious guidance to ensure properly Islamic government. Ali also came to be recognized as the first of the Twelve Imams, descendants of Ali who served as divinely inspired leaders and models for the Shi'ite community. In the centuries to come, what had originated as a minority view about the selection of a legitimate ruler for the Muslim community was to undergo a long, often tortuous and fragmented evolution into a distinctive expression of Muslim belief, practice, and outlook. Among its other characteristics, Shi'ism would be defined by its embrace of the concept of martyrdom, of a righteous minority's prerogative to fight in the cause of justice and, if necessary, its willingness to die for that cause – as Ali had, and as would so many who came after him.

Among them, none was more important to the history of Iraq, or to the future of Shi'ism, than Ali's second son, Husayn. Upon Ali's death, Muawiya had inaugurated a new caliphate, with the capital now situated in Damascus. Later historians named the new caliphate for his clan, the Umayyads, and appropriately so, for until its end, in 750, all of Muawiya's successors belonged to that family, thereby forming the first real dynasty to rule the Arab empire. But when Muawiya's son Yazid became caliph upon his father's death in 680, supporters of Ali's family in Kufa prevailed upon Husayn to bring a force from Medina to oppose him. On a day that tradition identifies as the tenth day of the month of Muharram in the Muslim calendar (correlating to 10 October 680), Husayn and his force of fewer than a hundred warriors met an overwhelmingly superior Umayyad force at Karbala on the Euphrates, about a hundred kilometers southwest of Baghdad. After valiant resistance against impossible odds, which were made longer when Yazid's general diverted Euphrates canal water away from his troops, Husayn, the grandson of the Prophet Muhammad, was slain along with all his companions. Among them were his infant son, Ali al-Asghar, and Husayn's brother Abbas. Husayn's severed head was sent to the court of Yazid in Damascus. His captured sisters were imprisoned there for a year, where, according to the traditional accounts, they reviled Yazid and proclaimed the righteousness of Husayn's cause.

The Battle of Karbala gave Shi'ism its greatest hero and focus for commemoration. Husayn stands at the apex of the hierarchy of blessed Shi'ite martyrs. Shi'ites around the world commemorate his martyrdom at Karbala every year during the Remembrance of Muharram, which culminates with the day of Ashura (the "tenth" day of Muharram). On that day, Shi'ite communities across the Middle East stage reenactments of the battle and Husayn's martyrdom in public performances that have often been compared to the "Passion plays" in which Christians have commemorated the crucifixion of Jesus. Some also find parallels between Mary, the suffering mother of Jesus, and Fatima, the mother of Husayn. On Ashura, men and boys march in processions in which they cry out their devotion to Husayn, drawing their own blood by cutting their scalps or flogging themselves with chains to signal their readiness to emulate Husayn's example of martyrdom. Karbala, like Najaf, became a focus of pilgrimage, where Shi'ites from around the world converge during Muharram to pray at the great tomb-mosque where, they believe, Husayn's remains are interred. And, like Najaf, Karbala is a major center of Shi'ite theological instruction.

The Caliph Yazid, at whose behest Husayn was slain and beheaded, remains the arch-villain for Shi'ites, an epitome of evil-doing. In recent years, the Najaf *hawza* ruled that the game of chess was to be shunned by Shi'ites because Yazid reportedly was playing chess at the moment that Husayn's head was brought to him. Nowhere more than in Iraq has Yazid been identified with tormentors of the Shi'ites. Thus, when the Shi'ite leader Muqtada al-Sadr was trapped in Kufa by U.S. forces in 2004, he openly referred to President George W. Bush as a modern Yazid.[18]

Iraq's centrality in the history of Shi'ism is not limited to the careers of Ali and Husayn, or to the reverence for the shrine-cities of Najaf and Karbala. For the time being, the defeat at Karbala beat down support for Ali's descendants as the leaders of the Muslim community and state, but as Shi'ite identity coalesced over the following decades many continued to look to Husayn's descendants as the most truly legitimate successors to the mantle of the Prophet. Ali, his sons Hasan and Husayn, and Husayn's descendants over the next nine generations came to be regarded by most Shi'ites as the Twelve Imams. As we will see, some minority Shi'ite groups that evolved later disputed that lineage; by their reckoning, the line of true Imams ended with the sixth or seventh. The last of the twelve, Muhammad al-Mahdi, died in 872. Traditional Shi'ite believers and some Sunnis claim, however, that he never died, but rather disappeared from the world, and that he will return near the final day of judgment as Imam Mahdi, a divinely guided redeemer who will rid the world of injustice. Indeed, many Shi'ites, including a recent president of Iran, Mahmoud Ahmadinejad, seem to expect his imminent return. The Imams after Husayn often faced persecution at the hands of Sunni caliphs, at whose orders, according to Shi'ite sources, eight of them may have been poisoned, but, like Najaf and Karbala, their burial places later became sites of important mosque-tombs. The eighth Imam was buried at Mashad, in Iran, but Iraq contains the final resting places of six of the Twelve Imams, more than any other country. Besides the first (Ali) and third (Husayn) Imams, the seventh Imam and his grandson, the ninth Imam, are buried in the double-domed mosque-shrine known as al-Kazimayn (or al-Kadhmiya), after the seventh Imam. Built at the end of the eighth century, this mosque was originally located in a town that was swallowed up by the expansion of Baghdad. Consequently, like Najaf and Karbala, Baghdad too became an important focus of Shiʻite pilgrimage, processions, and learning. The tenth and eleventh Imams, father and son, are buried in the city of Samarra, upstream from Baghdad on the Tigris, in a mosque named al-Askari, after the eleventh Imam. It was also from a spot now within the al-Askari mosque that, in traditional Shiʻite belief, the twelfth and last Imam disappeared. Like all the Shiʻite holy places in Iraq, the al-Askari mosque was for centuries little known in the West, but it gained attention in Western media after February 2006, when Sunni extremists bombed it and destroyed its dome. That event launched a two-year period of Sunni–Shiʻite sectarian bloodshed across much of Iraq's south, especially in Baghdad.

IRAQ UNDER UMAYYAD RULE

The events at Karbala in 680 certainly had raised the specter of political discord and fragmentation within the early Umayyad caliphate. But Umayyad supremacy also brought tremendous expansion of the Muslim empire, as well as important advances in shaping its internal organization and administration. To the west, the Muslim advance swept up the Berbers of North Africa, who joined the Arab armies to conquer what are now Tunisia, Algeria, and Morocco. In 711, they crossed the Straits of Gibraltar, which were named after the Berber general who helped lead that campaign. In Spain – al-Andalus, as they called it – the Arabs established a Muslim presence that was to last until 1492.

To consolidate their rule, the Umayyads made Arabic the official language of imperial administration and created a properly Muslim coinage, with surfaces bearing only inscriptions and no depictions of human or animal forms. In formerly Byzantine-ruled lands, they adopted and adapted many of the methods of Byzantine administration; some scholars prefer to think of the Umayyad empire in this region as a Byzantine "successor-state." The caliphs signified their dynasty's power, as well as the new ascendancy of Islam, by putting to effective use the Roman/Byzantine style of architecture – and nowhere more magnificently than on the Temple Mount in Jerusalem, where the Caliph Abd al-Malik built the first Muslim monumental structure, the Dome of the Rock. In the imperial capital of Damascus, his successor, al-Walid I, employed Byzantine craftsmen to build the other great monument to Islam in this era, the Great Umayyad Mosque. Built on the site of a Christian church of John the Baptist, which itself had been erected on the site of a Roman temple, the mosque featured interior and exterior walls decorated with superb mosaics depicting the world's great cities, all reportedly donated by the Byzantine Emperor. Whatever rapprochement such cooperation might have augured seems to have vanished two years after al-Walid's death in 715, when the Umayyad army and fleet went on the attack, in hopes of capturing the bastion of Christianity in the East, the Byzantine capital of Constantinople.

With its capital in Damascus and its rule enforced mainly by its forces in Syria, the heart of Umayyad rule beat strongest there. But that heartbeat required transfusions of resources from Iraq. Those were not gotten easily. When Yazid died in 683, only three years after the victory at Karbala, Iraq had gone over to a rebel usurper. It was not until 691 that Abd al-Malik's forces were able to regain Iraq for the Umayyads. If the man he selected in 694 as his new governor in Iraq was any indication, Abd al-Malik was extremely determined to keep it, and to keep its people under his heel. Entering the mosque at Kufa in disguise and then seizing the pulpit to address those assembled, Al-Hajjaj ibn Yusuf al-Thaqafi made it clear that he meant business:

I see heads before me that are ripe and ready for plucking, and I
am the one to pluck them, and I see blood glistening between the
turbans and the beards…For a long time you have been swift to
sedition; you have lain in the lairs of error and have made a rule
of transgression. By God, I shall strip you like bark, I shall truss
you like a bundle of twigs, I shall beat you like stray camels…
By God, what I promise, I fulfill; what I propose, I accomplish;
what I measure, I cut off.[19]

Harsh though his methods may have been, by the time of al-Hajjaj's
death in 714 effective administration had been re-established, often
using tried-and-true Sassanid methods. In fact, modern scholars often
describe the eastern Umayyad realm as a Persian successor-state.
Modeling it on the earlier Sassanid province, which the Sassanids called
Asoristan, the Umayyads created in central and southern Mesopotamia
(including Kufa and Basra) a new province.

They named it "Iraq."

Perhaps in a premonition of more recent Iraqi history, they deemed
it wise to detach from the new Iraq the northern city of Mosul.[20] In
702, al-Hajjaj also established in Iraq a new capital city, Wasit – a blow
to entrenched interests in Kufa and Basra. From his new capital, al-
Hajjaj was the master not only of Iraq but of all the eastern part of the
Umayyad empire, which now stretched across Iran and Central Asia
to the frontier of China.

For the Umayyads, locking down Iraq was crucial to their ability to
rule. The revenues from the agricultural wealth of the Sawad, the irrigated floodplain that had always been the cradle of power and wealth
for Middle Eastern empire-builders, were vital. By the eighth century,
owing in part to al-Hajjaj's canal-building and land reclamation projects,
the revenues from the Sawad were four times as much as those from
that other great bread-basket of Middle Eastern antiquity – Egypt – and
almost five times as much as those from the Umayyad core zone in Syria

190

and Palestine.[21] Iraq's wealth was further augmented by the flourishing Indian Ocean trade that linked Basra with China and India – a trade that also was to leave an indelible imprint on the world's literature, as it provides the backdrop for the famous stories about Sindbad the Sailor in *The Thousand and One Nights*.

Given such prosperity, one might assume that Umayyad times were good for the people of Iraq. But, by and large, they chafed under Umayyad rule, for many reasons. For one thing, Al-Hajjaj's often severe rule was reinforced by garrisons sent from Syria. Essentially, Iraq was under occupation, and, just as after the invasion of 2003, its people resisted it. Also, while agricultural revenue was indeed flowing in, the Umayyads made sure that most of it went to Damascus. Anti-Umayyad sentiment was ratcheted up further by the resentment felt among the descendants of the early Muslim warrior-immigrants to Iraq, many of whom the new Umayyad order had deprived of prerogatives and prestige that they had once enjoyed. Even more discord bubbled up when new, often Persian or Aramean converts to Islam were forced to accept "client" status, subservient to Arab patrons. This was intended to preserve both the dominance of the Arab Muslim conquerors and the tax base of the ruling elite, but the system provoked great resentment among these clients, or *mawali*. Besides contradicting the equality of believers as professed in the Qur'an, it also insulted converts who were themselves heirs to a long indigenous, and arguably superior, cultural tradition. Finally, although Husayn's defeat at Karbala had been a major setback, many who had supported the family of Ali still believed that the Muslim community needed to be restored to more principled and charismatic Islamic rulership, preferably from the Prophet's family.

Between 747 and 750, a movement that both wove together and played upon these strings of resentment came together to challenge the Umayyads. The distant region of Khurasan, in what is now northeastern Iran, had been added to al-Hajjaj's Iraq-based governorate in 698, but, given the realities of long-distance communication in the eighth century, Khurasan was simply too far away to be tightly controlled from Iraq. In the years after the Muslim conquest of Khurasan, a Muslim community significantly different from that in Iraq evolved there. In contrast to Iraq, where the Arabs had founded garrison-cities at Kufa and Basra, they had never established in Khurasan garrison-cities that kept them apart from the locals. Consequently, the Arab newcomers had integrated much more with the local Iranians – including through many marriages. Many of the locals had converted to Islam and had thereby become *mawali*, but owing to the greater degree of Arab–Iranian assimilation the Muslim community of Khurasan featured a much more egalitarian relationship between Arabs and *mawali*. This egalitarianism fit well with the emphasis on social justice among those who believed that a member of the Prophet's family ought to lead. Both trends ran counter to Umayyad interests. Meanwhile, by the mid-eighth century, though many of those who wanted to see a member of Muhammad's family assume leadership still preferred a descendant of Ali, another faction had emerged in support of a different lineage within the Hashemite clan, one descended from Abbas, the brother of Muhammad's father. This group, the Abbasids, was at first content to ally itself with the supporters of Ali's descendants (the Alids), and both factions linked their cause to that of the anti-Umayyad movement in Khurasan.

From the ranks of the latter now emerged one of the more mysterious and charismatic figures of the era, a saddle-maker of unknown name and obscure origin who, taking the nom de guerre "Abu Muslim," became the military standard-bearer of what came to be known as the Abbasid revolution. By 750, Abu Muslim had led the Abbasid forces to a series of victories against the Umayyads, taking Kufa in 750 and then, in the same year, inflicting on them a final, crushing defeat in a battle on the Zab River, a tributary of the Tigris. The bloody purge that ensued almost exterminated the Umayyad elite, but a scion of the family was able to escape and made his way to Spain. There he eventually established an independent kingdom with its capital at Cordoba, which soon became the leading city of Muslim Spain and, in its heyday, the greatest cultural and artistic center in Europe.

Before Abu Muslim's victory on the Zab, the Abbasids had peremptorily set aside the claims of the Alids and proclaimed one of their own, a man named Abu 'l-'Abbas – better known by his epithet, "al-Saffah" ("the Shedder of Blood") – as the new caliph at Kufa. In doing so, they created a new source of resentment among the Alids, who felt betrayed. In the years to come the latter would periodically resort to armed rebellion, and al-Saffah's successors would in turn resort to brutal measures to repress them. Al-Saffah's own reign was neither long (only five years) nor especially distinguished, but the era that it inaugurated, the Abbasid caliphate, would raise Iraq to a primacy even greater than it had enjoyed in antiquity. Before the Abbasid caliphate was extirpated by the Mongols more than five hundred years later, Iraq would become the unquestioned political center of the Muslim empire. And the new capital that al-Saffah's successor was to build on the Tigris would rise to become arguably the most eminent seat of science and learning in the world, as well as a fount of modern memory and perception of the medieval Muslim world.

THE ABBASID CALIPHATE: IRAQ AS THE CENTER OF ISLAMIC CIVILIZATION

Al-Saffah was succeeded by his older brother, Abu Jafar, who is better known to history by his epithet, "al-Mansur" ("the Victorious"). In the view of one modern expert, al-Mansur was "the most remarkable individual in the whole story of the Abbasids."[22] The first years after his accession were consumed with tightening the Abbasids' grip on the caliphate. To accomplish that, al-Mansur orchestrated the assassination of his one remaining military rival, the hero of the Abbasid revolution, the great general Abu Muslim, and also quelled revolts instigated by the Alids. From then on, he strived to concentrate ever greater power in the hands of the caliph. In the years to come, his successors would become absolute monarchs of almost unlimited, divinely sanctioned authority, in the style of the Sassanid Persian shahs who had ruled Iraq and most of the Middle East little more than a century before.

It was probably to further those goals, and to distance himself from the pro-Alid sentiments and Arab tribal politics that festered in the south, that in 762 Mansur founded a new capital. He chose its site very carefully, devoting much prayer to the decision and ultimately confirming the place and date of its foundation by resorting to a method that his ancient Mesopotamian predecessors had regularly called upon: divination – in this instance, calling upon the expertise of astrologers, including a Zoroastrian. And continuing, no doubt unknowingly, another Mesopotamian practice that dated back thousands of years, Mansur reportedly laid the first brick of his new city himself. He named his new capital Madinat as-Salam, or "City of Peace," but it became known throughout the world as Baghdad.[23] The original city (the so-called Round City) was about a mile and a half in diameter and protected by two concentric mud-brick walls and a moat. Four gates were spaced evenly around the wall's perimeter, each of them facing one of four major destinations (Kufa, Basra, Damascus, and Khurasan) within the far-flung empire. The gates were also the termini for two avenues that transected the city. Within the walls were buildings to house the caliph's family and officials as well as administrative offices and shops. At the very center of the complex was Mansur's palace, the Golden Gate, as well as the police station and the great congregational mosque. Perhaps the most celebrated aspect of the palace was its two domes, atop one of which was a weathervane shaped as a horseman bearing a lance. In later years, it was believed that the lance would point in the direction of any new threat to the caliph.

Contemporary reports say that much of Baghdad's construction was in marble, although mud brick was surely the material most used, as it

Figure 1. Medieval citadel of Erbil, in northern Iraq. The citadel was built atop a tell – a mound that contains settlement remains dating to as early as the fourth millennium BCE (Wikimedia Commons).

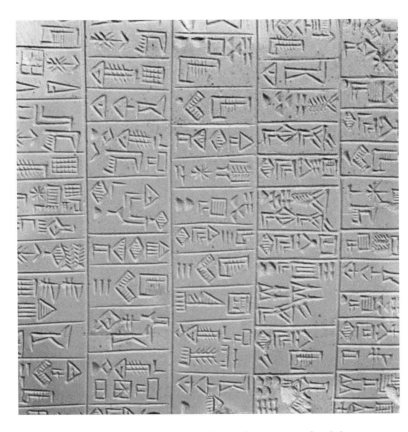

Figure 2. Detail of Sumerian cuneiform from site of Adab, twenty-sixth century BCE (Wikimedia Commons).

Figure 3. Detail of stele of Akkad king and conqueror Naram-Sin, grandson of Sargon; now in the Louvre. Naram-Sin is shown vanquishing the Lullubi, a Zagros Mountain people. The bull's horns on his headgear reflect his self-assigned divine status (Wikimedia Commons).

Figure 4a. Remains of ziggurat at Ur built by Ur-namma, Third Dynasty of Ur, ca. 2100 BCE (Wikimedia Commons).

Figure 4b. Reconstruction of ziggurat of Ur-namma (Wikimedia Commons).

Figure 5. Detail of stele of Hammurabi of Babylon (ruled 1792–1750 BCE). At top, Hammurabi (at left) is being invested with symbols of royal authority by Shamash, the Babylonian god of the sun and justice. Below this scene are inscribed the laws of the Code of Hammurabi (Wikimedia Commons).

Figure 6. Detail of an Assyrian attack on a town, from the Northwest Palace of Ashurnasirpal II at Nimrud (room B, panel 18), 865–860 BCE (Wikimedia Commons).

Figure 7. Mongol conquest of Baghdad under Hulegu Khan, 1258. From Rashid-ad-Din's Gami' at-tawarih, early fourteenth century (Wikimedia Commons).

Figure 8. European portrait of Ottoman Sultan Suleiman the Magnificent, the conqueror of Iraq (Wikimedia Commons).

Figure 9. Emir Faisal ibn Hussein (center) and entourage at the Paris Peace Conference, 1919. T. E. Lawrence stands above and to the right of Faisal. Nuri al-Said, future prime minister of Iraq, stands above and to the left (Wikimedia Commons).

Figure 10. Coronation of Faisal ibn Hussein as King Faisal I of Iraq, Baghdad, 23 August 1921 (Wikimedia Commons).

had been for millennia. Nothing remains of any of the physical structures of the palaces of the caliphs; the many conquests of Baghdad – fifteen in a history spanning 1,250 years – have seen to that. Nor does much of anything remain of the teeming slums and sprawling suburbs that quickly sprouted around the Round City. But from its founding by Mansur to its devastation by the invading Mongol horde of Hulegu Khan in 1258, Baghdad remained – with one major interlude – the capital of the Abbasid empire. During its heyday perhaps as many as 1.5 million people lived and toiled there, at a time when the population of Iraq may have reached twenty million. Contemporary descriptions – along with a wealth of later popular accounts and tall tales about the city, and the reams of poetry singing its praises – provide a cornucopia of vivid images and almost surreal impressions that have spawned different images of Baghdad, both complementary and contradictory. Like the biblical and classical accounts of ancient Babylon, some of those images are more enchantment than reality.[24]

The enchantment still delights us today. Over decades of lurid, lush literary and cinematic fantasies, we have been steeped in an image of Baghdad as a fairy-tale or even comic-book city chock-full of fabulous wealth, harem girls galore, genies in bottles, and magic carpets. Some of that can be justified by the accounts from Arab historians of the Abbasid era, who regale their readers with the splendor, intrigue, and conspicuous consumption of palace life in Baghdad. The writer al-Yaʿqubi piles on the hyperbole in stating his opinion of the city. After describing Iraq as "the center of this world, the navel of the earth," he tells us that Baghdad is "the center of Iraq, the greatest city, which has no peer in the east or west of the world in extent, size, prosperity, abundance of water, or health of climate."[25] He and others also make plain that great wealth was amassed in Baghdad. Surely, if Caliph al-Mansur's intent in building a new capital was to maximize his access to wealth, he chose an excellent location for his capital. Just to the south lay the agricultural bounty of the Sawad. Baghdad was also a nexus of both camel-caravan routes and water-borne commerce along the Tigris and Euphrates, and the canals that connected them, as well as the seafaring trade that came through Basra near the head of the Persian Gulf. Hear again al-Ya'qubi marveling at Baghdad's wealth:

> goods and foodstuffs come to it by land and water with the greatest ease, so that every kind of merchandise is completely available, from east and west, from Muslim and non-Muslim lands. Goods are brought from India, Sind, China, Tibet, the lands of the Turks, the Daylam, the Khazars, the Ethiopians, and others to such an extent that the products of the countries are more plentiful in Baghdad than in the countries from which they come. They can be procured so readily and so certainly that it is as if all the good things of the world are sent there, all the treasures of the world assembled there, and all the blessings of creation perfected there.[26]

And nowhere were all the wealth and luxury of Baghdad more evident than in the caliph's palace – or, for that matter, in the palace of the vizier, his chief administrative official. In 917, two envoys from the Byzantine Emperor paid an official visit to the Caliph in Baghdad. To judge from later accounts handed down from supposed eyewitnesses, they were treated to an ostentatious exercise in public relations that took two months to prepare and surely was designed to impress the ambassadors with the wealth and sophistication of Abbasid court life. Among the highlights as they were walked through twenty-three palaces were: more than fifty thousand carpets either hung from the walls or laid on the floor, many with gold brocade and images of birds and animals; horses with saddles of gold and silver; a royal zoo with lions and elephants; marvelous gardens and courtyards, including one with an artificial tree; and walls hung with thousands of suits of armor. Finally, overwhelmed – and exhausted – by all the grandeur they had seen, the envoys were brought before the Caliph himself, who, dressed

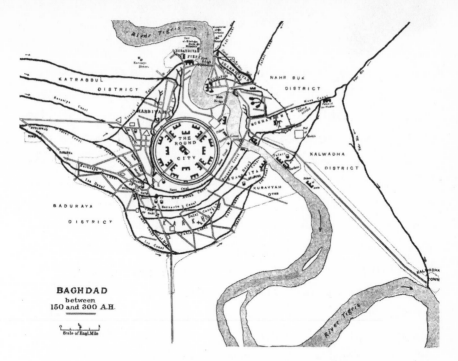

MAP 4. *The Round City of Baghdad, ca. 900* CE
Source: William Muir, The Caliphate: Its Rise, Decline, and Fall from
Original Sources, *revised by T. H. Weir (Edinburgh, John Grant, 1883,
revised 1915, reprinted 1924), facing p. 464. (Wikimedia Commons).*

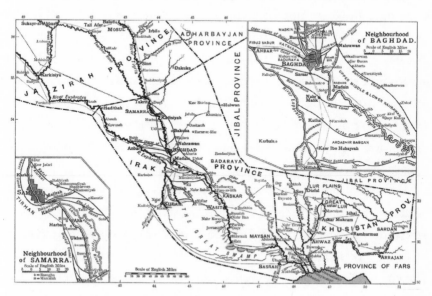

MAP 5. *Abbasid Baghdad and Iraq.*
Source: Guy Le Strange, The Lands of the Eastern Caliphate: Mesopotamia,
Persia, and Central Asia, from the Moslem Conquest to the Time of Timur
(New York: Barnes & Noble, 1905) (Wikimedia Commons).

in brocade with a cap embroidered with gold, sat on a throne of ebony and brocade, with strings of precious stones to either side.[27]

Most of Baghdad's residents did not enjoy such an elevated standard of living. Among our sources for the seamier side of life in medieval Baghdad, none is better known today than *The Thousand and One Nights*, also known as *The Arabian Nights*. The name of its heroine, the storyteller princess Scheherezade, has become famous in Western culture as almost a synonym for the sensuous allure of the "Orient" – and as the title of a famous orchestral work by the Russian composer Nikolai Rimsky-Korsakov. Some of its stories have been favorites of children and movie-makers for decades – among them, "Ali Baba and the Forty Thieves," "Aladdin and the Magic Lamp," and the tales of Sindbad the Sailor. *The Arabian Nights* is, in fact, a hodge-podge of stories, some elements dating back to Sassanid Persian times, and some of surprisingly recent vintage. The earliest-known version of "Aladdin and the Magic Lamp," for example, dates from 1709. *The Arabian Nights* brings together genres ranging from heroic epic to pornography and scatological jokes.[28] Indeed, owing to its often bawdy content, it was never enshrined in the corpus of "classical" Arabic literature. Many of its tales are set in Baghdad as well as in Cairo and Damascus. When we study them judiciously, and supplement them with accounts from other sources, we discover a city that, beyond the palace walls, teemed with squalor but offered possibilities of adventure, both rollicking and dangerous. It was studded with taverns, some of the best of them inside Christian convents.[29] If one left one of those taverns too conspicuously incapacitated, one might be waylaid by some of the thieves and con-men (and con-women) who infested the city's slums. Gangs of young thugs demanded protection money from local establishments in their quarter of the city and fought with gangs from other quarters to defend their turf. The city's elite despised the slums' denizens, many of whom practiced occupations they looked down upon: "blacksmiths, butchers, conjurors, policemen, night-watchmen, tanners, makers of women's shoes, dung collectors, well diggers, bath stokers, masseurs, pigeon racers, and chess players."[30] Some of our more colorful glimpses of Baghdad's urban life come from *Arabian Nights* tales of the nocturnal escapades of the most celebrated of the Abbasid caliphs, Harun ar-Rashid, who would sneak out of the palace, often with his boon companion Jafar the Barmakid, to wander the streets and see for himself how his people lived.

Yet life at Harun's luxurious court could be full of its own rollicking fun, featuring wine-soaked parties with lots of women, and song, and poets to write about it all. Much of the culture that surrounded the court of the early Abbasids was a robust celebration of poetry and song, lavishly patronized by the caliphs themselves. Arguably the greatest of the classical Arabic poets, Abu Nuwas,[31] composed superb poems to praise Harun – with whom Abu Nuwas appears in some of the *Arabian Nights* tales – and to celebrate both the joys brought by the wine that flowed so freely at court and the beauty of the young women and boys who served as singers and wine-bearers at the caliph's court.[32] Poets whose verse pleased the caliph might receive stupendous rewards – like the poet whose sonnet Harun himself rewarded with five hundred pieces of gold, a robe of honor, ten slave-girls, and a horse from the Caliph's own stables.[33]

Even though he composed his poems in Arabic, Abu Nuwas, like many other celebrated poets of the era, was Persian. Persian officials, scholars, and writers made huge contributions to Abbasid culture and administration. In turning to them now, we can redirect our gaze from the enchanted Baghdad to contemplate another image of the city, one that has been given little play in the West's perception. It is the Baghdad about which one ninth-century observer was to write,

No one is better educated than their scholars, better informed than their authorities in tradition, more solid in syntax than their grammarians, more supple than their singers, more certain than their Koran readers, more expert than their physicians, more competent than their calligraphers, more clear than their logicians, more zealous than their ascetics, better jurists than their magistrates, more eloquent than their preachers.[34]

The Abbasid caliphs owed much of their success to the expertise and efficiency of their top officials, especially the vizier, whose responsibilities essentially combined those of a prime minister and a C.E.O. From the time of Harun's predecessor, the Caliph al-Mahdi, the office of vizier was the preserve of a Persian family, the Barmakids. By all accounts, they did a magnificent job of managing the affairs of state, including the collection of revenues from across the empire, and promoting the prestige of the caliph. The latter task required the skillful use of court protocol. The fact that Baghdad was located close to the ancient Sassanid court at Ctesiphon meant they did not need to look far for a model. Originally Arab tribal-warrior sheikhs, the caliphs were now transformed into almost divine rulers, assuming titles such as "Shadow of God on Earth" and requiring that those appearing before them prostrate themselves before the imperial throne – near which was rolled out the executioner's carpet, signifying the caliph's absolute power over life and death.

The success of the Abbasid administration owed in no small part to their introduction of a new technology of literacy and record-keeping: paper, the making of which the Arabs had learned during their eastward expansion toward China, where the technology was pioneered. The use of paper was soon applied to purposes far beyond the mundane work of administration – specifically, in the quest for useful knowledge with which to manage the vast realm that Allah had assigned them. The Umayyad caliphs at Damascus had begun the gathering and translating of Greek manuscripts from the formerly Byzantine realm, although they had focused largely on materials relating to Islamic law and the practice of medicine. Now the Abbasids were able to cast an even larger net. Starting in the reign of Mansur, gaining momentum under Harun ar-Rashid and his successors, and with the support and inspiration of their Barmakid viziers and their successors, their efforts would make Baghdad both a repository of learning and an engine of progress in the natural sciences and philosophy. At first, they focused on collecting and translating into Arabic works of Persian learning, readily accessible in Iraq.[35] But Mansur was also determined to make use of the legacy of Greek science and learning that had blossomed in the colonies founded across the Middle East and Central Asia a millennium earlier by Alexander the Great and his Seleucid and Ptolemid successors.

To facilitate the translation and study of the burgeoning collection of Persian, Greek, and Sanskrit manuscripts that were being gathered at his behest, Mansur established a royal library in Baghdad. In this endeavor he consciously emulated his Sassanid predecessors. Decades later, under al-Mamun, the library evolved into the celebrated Bayt al-Hikma, or House of Wisdom; a translation and study center that was "the collective institutional and imperial expression of early Abbasid intellectual ambition and state policy."[36] Later caliphs sponsored even more scholar-translators, to whom were made available manuscripts in Greek, Latin, Syriac, Coptic, and Sanskrit, as well as Persian, gathered from all over the empire – and even from the court of the Byzantine Emperor, from whom they might be requested, or sometimes demanded as part of a peace treaty. During al-Mansur's reign, manuscripts arrived from even farther afield when a delegation from India brought a number of Hindu scientific texts, including works on mathematics and on astrology.[37] Many of the astrological texts were heavily influenced by the legacy of ancient Babylonian science that had been brought to India and was now returning to its source. The translation and study of the Hindu works of mathematics led the Abbasid scholars to adopt the system of numerals that we still refer to as "Arabic" numerals, though they originated in India, as well as the concept of zero. It is from the work of Abbasid scholars, building on Indian and Greek foundations, that we derive the apparatus of "algebra" (from Arabic *al-jabr*).

Modern civilization owes an even greater debt to those Abbasid-era scholars who, between the eighth and tenth centuries, translated, expanded upon, and preserved the works of seminal figures of ancient Greek mathematics, natural philosophy, science, and medicine – among them Plato, Aristotle, Euclid, and the astronomer Ptolemy. Not among them, you may notice, are the historians Herodotus and Thucydides, or playwrights such as Aeschylus, Sophocles, Euripides, and Aristophanes. The caliphs were interested in what they considered to be *useful* knowledge. The men who undertook this work were almost as diverse in background as the manuscripts they worked with. They serve as a microcosm of the cosmopolitan society that was Abbasid Baghdad. Among them were Arabs and Persians, some from Iraq, some transplanted to Baghdad from places many hundreds of miles distant. Most were Muslim, but some were Jews and Christians, like Hunayn ibn Ishaq, a Nestorian Christian who translated works of Plato and Aristotle but was especially celebrated for his translations of the works of the ancient physicians Hippocrates and Galen as well as for his own research on eye diseases. We might single out the Iraqi Arab al-Kindi and the probable Persian al-Farabi, polymaths who worked in Baghdad during the ninth and tenth centuries, respectively. Their broad erudition spawned many achievements, including translations of and commentary on the works of Plato and Aristotle, whose ideas they began to incorporate into an Islamic framework.

Al-Kindi, al-Farabi, and others were also crucial to the intellectual development of two later Muslim scholars whose contributions were seminal in the reawakening of science and philosophy in Western Europe after early medieval Europe's "Dark Ages." As the historian Philip Hitti once wrote, the caliphs ar-Rashid and al-Mamun were delving into Greek philosophy at the time that Charlemagne and his lords "were reportedly dabbling in the art of writing their names."[38] The Persian scholar Ibn Sina (ca. 980–1037) was, like his intellectual forebear al-Kindi, a polymath, with contributions in many fields of learning to his credit, but his special contribution to European civilization lay in his medical research. His *The Canon of Medicine* was translated into Latin well after his death. After it reached Western Europe, via Muslim Spain, Avicenna (to use Ibn Sina's Latinized name) became a founding father of Western European medicine. His *Canon* remained a standard medical text there as late as the seventeenth century. Likewise building on the foundations laid by Baghdad's scholars, the Andalusian Muslim polymath Ibn Rushd (1126–98) produced Arabic commentaries on the work of Aristotle. After their translation into Latin and introduction into Europe, these commentaries by Ibn Rushd (known as Averroes or simply "the Commentator") nurtured the development of the medieval scholastic theologians Albertus Magnus and his student, Thomas Aquinas, whose works are to a great extent a response to those of Averroes. With the help of the kick-start that Muslim scholars such as Ibn Sina and Ibn Rushd provided, European culture began its slow turn to secular rationalism as the foundation of knowledge – a development that, ironically, would eventually enable Western Europe to leap-frog and then dominate the Muslim world. That later Europeans recognized the debt their intellectual progress owed to Ibn Rushd is evident in the Italian Renaissance painting *The School of Athens*, completed by Raphael in 1511. Plato and Aristotle feature most prominently, standing side by side, top and center in the painting, but below and to the left one espies a crouched Ibn Rushd – an exceptional tribute to a Muslim during a period when Europeans generally reviled them.[39]

Lest we think, however, that Abbasid Baghdad's scholars left their mark primarily on European civilization,[40] we should note that in the eyes of at least one eminent scholar the most important contribution of the Abbasids lies in the development of Islamic law, or "shariah."[41] In the broad historical context of Islamic civilization, the study of Islamic law has always held a place higher than that of theology or philosophy. The Abbasid caliphs' patronage of the study of Islamic law, like their patronage of the study of Greek science, stemmed largely from their interest in effective government, as well as in self-preservation. In the eyes of many, the Umayyad caliphs had failed to construct a properly Muslim rule and commonwealth. Later commentators often condemned them for succumbing to the lure of luxury and foreign customs. The consequent loss of legitimacy and support had led to their demise. The Abbasids had no intention of following them down that path. So they lavished their patronage upon the emerging class of scholars of Islamic law, the "ulema." This term is often translated as "clergy" – but unlike, say, Roman Catholic clergy, the ulema have no priestly power to bless or sanctify, nor do they officiate over liturgical celebrations.

The need to develop a body of properly Islamic law had become apparent almost from the beginning of the Muslim conquest, for two principal reasons. First, the Qur'an itself includes no "code" of laws – in contrast to the Hebrew Bible, with, for example, the Ten Commandments in Exodus and the detailed laws listed in Deuteronomy. Second, as the Muslim Arab conquests expanded beyond the Arabian Peninsula, they brought under Muslim control a vast realm that included diverse societies with their own often ancient and deeply enshrined traditions and legal customs, most of which needed to be accommodated or regulated somehow within a legal framework that remained true to God's words in the Qur'an and to the example the Prophet Muhammad had set during his own lifetime.

By the mid-ninth century, four distinct legal "schools" – frameworks for the formulation, interpretation, and enforcement of Islamic law – had begun to take shape in the Sunni Muslim world. The Shi'ites developed their own jurisprudence, which the Abbasids tended not to recognize as legitimate. Of the four founders of the Sunni schools, one (ibn Anas) lived in Medina, but the other three (Abu Hanifa, Muhammad al-Shafi'i, and Ahmad ibn Hanbal) all lived and taught in Baghdad. Adherents of these schools competed for the caliphs' attention, and with each other. The writer Ibn al-Athir tells how, in 935, some puritanical, over-zealous adherents of the Hanbali school raided Baghdad's houses to confiscate wine and beat up singing girls, and even enlisted the blind men who took shelter in the mosques to beat with their canes any members of the Shafi'i school who passed by.[42] In general, the Abbasids accorded legitimacy to all four Sunni legal schools. They all survive to this day, with followers worldwide. But the caliphs were not uniformly ambivalent on matters of legal interpretation. One of the more controversial developments of the Abbasid era centered upon the emergence of a rationalist school of interpretation, known as the Mu'tazila. Influenced by the tremendous influx of Greek philosophical learning, its adherents emphasized the applicability of human intellect and rational deduction in interpreting the Qur'an. At their point of greatest influence, the Caliph al-Mamun gave the Mu'tazila position the sanction of imperial authority, and ulema of other schools were imprisoned or even killed – which was the fate of ibn Hanbal. [43]

But Abbasid Iraq's contributions to the elaboration of Muslim belief and practice went well beyond the realm of Islamic law, to embrace another movement, one that appealed more to the heart and soul than to the quest for a legal order. Among the early Christians in Iraq and elsewhere had appeared men and women who felt compelled to seek a more personal, emotional, mystical closeness to God. In Christianity, this movement later evolved into monasticism, in which such individuals came together in monasteries/convents, under the supervision of an acknowledged leader, to practice a common lifestyle devoted to this quest. In Abbasid Iraq, a movement that was similarly focused on mysticism emerged: Sufism. Nurtured in Iraq's fertile spiritual soil, it eventually branched out to implant itself in western Iran, Arabia, Khurasan, Central Asia, and perhaps as far as Spain. Today, Sufism is "the most pluralistic incarnation of Islam – accessible to the learned and the ignorant, the faithful and nonbelievers – and is thus a uniquely valuable bridge between East and West."[44] Baghdad played an especially important role in its development.[45]

This movement centered at first on individuals who chose to withdraw from mainstream social life, often committing themselves to a life of poverty and asceticism. Around the same time, many of them began to focus on cultivating the interior life, an "inward turn" to the world within themselves, in order to achieve a state of intimate, ecstatic closeness and love of God. A number of these mystics are said to have worn garments of wool, and it is from the Arabic word for "wool" that Sufism gets its name.

One of the more famous early Sufis of Iraq was a woman, Rabi'a of Basra. One of the sayings attributed to her epitomizes eloquently the melding of asceticism and selfless devotion that began to characterize the movement as a whole:

O my Lord, if I worship thee from fear of Hell, burn me in hell, and if I worship thee in hope of Paradise, exclude me thence, but if I worship thee for Thine own sake, then withhold not from me Thine Eternal Beauty.[46]

As the Sufi movement took hold in Baghdad, it abandoned its earlier emphasis on renunciation and withdrawal from mainstream society. Instead, Sufis now embraced the urban life of Baghdad, all the while still striving to practice a lifestyle marked by daily piety and a continuing effort to become closer to God. The Sufis did not reject the legalistic approach of the legal schools of Baghdad, but because they preferred a mystical, intensely personal approach to God, and even saw themselves as a special elect chosen by God, they often ran afoul of the legal scholars. And because the scholars and their legal schools had the official support and patronage of the caliph, it was not unusual for the Sufis to find themselves out of favor with the powers that be. Sufis also began to group themselves around leaders who were recognized as exemplars of piety and mystic devotion. In that process, they formed brotherhoods (or "convents") that became focal points of local religious and social organization, including the providing of social services.

ABBASID DECLINE: IRAQ DRIFTS AWAY FROM CENTER STAGE

Islamic civilization is fortunate that the Sufi brotherhoods emerged to anchor local social organization, and nowhere more so than in Iraq. During the ninth century, the Abbasids' fortunes began to dip and by the mid-tenth century the caliphs were reduced to mere figureheads. As their power and patronage waned and then vanished, and new conquerors burst onto the scene, Baghdad became a shadow of its former self, and Iraq lost its starring role at center stage of the Muslim world.

Even while prolific translators, high-minded legal scholars, and pious Sufis were brightening the world of culture and religion at Baghdad, the Abbasids' political fortunes were becoming cloudy. For reasons that are still debated, but must have involved tensions at the heart of the royal court, Harun ar-Rashid had found it expedient in 803 to eliminate the Barmakids, to whom the Abbasids owed so much of their success. After Harun died, two of his sons vied for control of the Abbasid throne. The resulting civil war left much of the floodplain and its irrigation systems damaged, and ended only after a long, destructive siege of Baghdad that saw street gangs taking on trained soldiers in defense of the capital. The agriculture of the floodplain (and its crucial revenues) sustained further damage when thousands of African slaves who had been brought to southern Iraq and set to work draining the marshes for agricultural production rose in rebellion against the Abbasids in 869. Just as Chaldean rebels centuries earlier had found refuge in the marshes while they rose against the Assyrians, these rebels, known as the Zanj, used them as a base from which to launch military campaigns against the Abbasids. By 883, Abbasid forces had smashed the rebellion, but not before it had devastated the agricultural infrastructure of the south. To compensate, the Abbasids overworked the land still left to them – an expedient, repeated throughout Iraq's history, that has invariably resulted in the salinization of the over-irrigated farmland, reducing yields even further. The Arab chroniclers of the era as well as the findings of twentieth-century archaeology make plain that the countryside of Baghdad and the Sawad was in decline.[47] Smaller harvests meant less revenue, depriving the Abbasids of resources they needed to maintain their power, especially the military forces upon which they depended.

The ensuing weakness cost the Abbasid caliphs dearly. During the later ninth and early tenth century, the caliphs handed over control of large regions of their realm to local dynasties that, though professing allegiance to them, in reality governed those regions more or less independently. One of these dynasties gained rule over Mosul near the start of the tenth century, which both diminished the Abbasids' direct control of Iraq and strengthened Mosul's ties with Aleppo and Syria to the west – an orientation that was long to persist and leave Mosul often beyond Baghdad's sphere of influence. In 969 a local dynasty that had gained control in Egypt was ousted and replaced by a new group professing a new, activist Shi'ite ideology. Calling themselves the Fatimids (from the name of Muhammad's daughter who had married Ali), they categorically rejected the hegemony of the Abbasids, who from this point regarded them as blasphemers worthy only of destruction. The Fatimids founded a new capital that soon came to surpass Baghdad as a center of political and cultural power: Cairo.

By that time, the caliphs of Baghdad had been losing power even closer to home, to new forces that they themselves had helped introduce. In the wake of the civil war that followed upon Harun's death, the caliphs had sought to stiffen their authority with a new military backbone whose loyalty might be more reliable than that of the Arab tribesmen who had traditionally enforced Abbasid rule. They turned to an expedient that would be emulated by Middle Eastern rulers for centuries to come: the recruitment of mercenaries and slave soldiers – denoted as *mamluk* ("owned") or *ghulam* ("young man") – who came to form a professional military class whose loyalty to the caliph was not compromised by any competing loyalties of tribal kinship. The Abbasids filled their ranks largely from a people the Arabs had first encountered at the far eastern reaches of their empire, but who eventually supplanted the Arabs as the most politically and militarily dominant group in the Middle East: the Turks. Like the Parthians who more than a thousand years earlier had confronted Alexander's Seleucid successors on the eastern frontiers of their empire, the Turks were rough, hardy nomads with a tradition as horse-riding warriors whose proficiency with the compound bow made them a formidable military force. One ninth-century Arab commentator remarked that for the Turks riding and fighting were "their only pleasure, their glory, and the subject of all their conversation. Thus, they have become in warfare what the Greeks are in philosophy."

But the mamluk bolstering of Abbasid rule exacted a price from the caliphs. The established residents of Baghdad began to resent these alien warriors who, besides rough-housing in their city, also threatened their own status. For this reason and others, in 836 the Caliph moved his mamluks away from Baghdad to a newly built capital at Samarra, about 130 kilometers upstream along the Tigris. By 892, when the caliphs left Samarra to return to Baghdad, Samarra boasted fabulous palaces and mosques – its ruins are today a World Heritage Site – but it had also witnessed great turmoil as Turkish mamluk military commanders began to impose their will on the caliphs. One of the caliphs bestowed upon one of those commanders a title whose prestige would surpass even that of the caliph in the centuries ahead: "sultan," from an Arabic word associated with power and authority. The move back to Baghdad did little to reverse that trend. The caliphs became the puppets of military commanders and even their own viziers. Some were deposed and, if not slain, might be brutally blinded or tossed into the street as beggars.

In the mid-tenth century, Abbasid fortunes sank to their lowest point yet. In 945, the Caliph was forced to recognize the ascendancy of an Iranian warlord family from what is now Azerbaijan, the Buyids (or Buwayhids), by granting one of their leaders the title of commander-in-chief and ceding to him all actual rulership, even if the Buyids nominally recognized the caliph's authority. Compounding the ignominy, the Buyids were Shi'ite. The following year, the Abbasid agricultural base in the Sawad suffered a shattering blow. Since Sassanid times, the great Nahrawan canal had been a vital component in the imperial agricultural regime, conveying water from the Tigris into the farmland around the Diyala, a major tributary of the Tigris. In 946 the Nahrawan canal was cut. The Sawad never recovered.[48]

The demise of Abbasid rule at Baghdad marks the end of an epoch in human history. The Abbasids were the last great political power in a long, unbroken chain of great, even world powers that had produced great states and civilizations, and had ruled vast empires, based on the agricultural bounty of the southern Mesopotamian floodplain. From the Sumerians, Assyrians, and Babylonians, to the Persians of Cyrus and Darius, to Alexander and his Seleucid successors, to the Parthians and Persian Sassanids at Ctesiphon, to finally the Muslim Arab Abbasids of Baghdad – all had built their power, and helped to shape our world, on the back of the black earth of the Sawad and the waters of the Tigris and Euphrates.

6

INTERLUDE:
FROM CRADLE TO BACKWATER

FOR THREE HUNDRED YEARS after the Buyid takeover, the caliphs still clung to their traditional seat at Baghdad, but Baghdad was never again to be a center of real imperial power. Less than a quarter-century after the Buyids took control, the Fatimids came to power in Egypt. Around the same time, the seafaring trade route through the Red Sea began to draw much of the trade from India and the East, to the great benefit of the Fatimids – as well as Pisa and Venice, the rising merchant cities of northern Italy, which cultivated trade ties with the Fatimids. As Baghdad's wealth and fortunes declined, the focus of Arabic culture shifted inexorably westward, to Egypt and Cairo.

IRAQ UNDER THE BUYIDS, SELJUKS, AND MONGOLS

The Buyids dispersed their rule across a decentralized realm that encompassed most of Iraq and Iran, since different members of the family held power in different cities. Shiraz and Isfahan in Iran began to emerge as major cultural centers. Although the Buyids continued to assert their loyalty to the caliph at Baghdad, whom they accepted as the supreme religious authority for the Sunnis who were the majority population, as Shi'ites they encouraged Shi'ite religious celebrations and supported the construction of Shi'ite shrines. Most notable among these is the al-Askari mosque at Samarra, which shelters the tombs of the tenth and eleventh Imams. Most Westerners knew nothing of this mosque till February 2006, when Sunni extremists exploded a bomb that damaged it severely, launching a sectarian civil war in Iraq that killed tens of thousands.

The Buyids were unable to sustain control everywhere. In Iraq local Arab dynasties assumed control at Mosul and in the south at Hilla, while in the northeast Kurdish tribes began to assert themselves in their mountain strongholds. Nor were relations between Sunni and Shi'ite in Iraq entirely peaceable. The militant Hanbali Sunni school centered at Baghdad was repulsed by such Shi'ite customs as visiting the shrines of the sainted Imams. When Hanbalis attacked and burned down the shrine of the Imam Husayn at Karbala in 971, Baghdad was rocked by riots involving clashes between gangs defending neighborhoods that had become defined by sectarian affiliation.[1] Again, it was a precursor of clashes a thousand years later.

THE COMING OF THE SELJUKS AND TURKISH AUTHORITY

The restoration of Sunni primacy, however, was right around the corner, for new conquerors were about to arrive onto the scene. The Seljuks were a component of a larger Turkish tribal confederation known as the Oghuz. Their arrival in northern Iran during the late tenth century marks yet another in the long series of migrations of nomadic horse-riding, bow-wielding tribes from Central Asia into the Middle East which stretches back to the Parthians in the fourth century BCE. It also marks the first major migration and conquest by a Turkish tribal group in the Middle East. It was not to be the last. Originally practicing a religion based on the worship of a sky-god and deities representing other elements in nature, the Seljuks converted to Islam shortly before 1000. Their chieftains ("khans") soon asserted themselves as champions of Sunni Islam against infidel religions, including Shi'ism. As the leaders of horse-riding warrior nomads who were continually in search of new pastures for their herds, they possessed the military might with which to back up their beliefs. Having conquered Afghanistan and Iran by 1050, the Seljuks continued to expand westward, hoping ultimately to unseat the reviled Shi'ite Fatimids of Cairo. This led to a collision in 1071 with the forces of the Byzantine Emperor, including mercenary knights from faraway France, at Manzikert in eastern Anatolia. There the Seljuks inflicted on the Christians a devastating defeat that opened Anatolia to further Turkish Muslim conquest and settlement.

Before then, the Seljuks had also brought Iraq under their control. In the process they partially resurrected the prestige of Baghdad and the Abbasid caliphs. In 1055, the Seljuk khan Tughrul entered Baghdad, bringing an end to Buyid rule and the perceived abomination of Shi'ite political hegemony, and proclaimed the primacy of Sunni Islam and his own fealty to the Caliph – whom Tughrul evidently did not bother to actually meet. The grateful Caliph rewarded Tughrul with the title of sultan, which Tughrul's successors would bear proudly for years to come. As with the Buyids, it was the sultans who were to have the real political clout, while the caliphs' authority was restricted to matters of religion. By and large, Sunni authority dominated during this era. In the wake of a short-lived Shi'ite resurgence in 1058 and 1059, Sunnis at Baghdad launched drastic reprisals; and in the ensuing decades Christians and Jews were subjected to persecution as well.[2]

At their height under the Sultan Malikshah (ruled 1072–92), the Seljuks dominated a vast realm stretching from Central Asia to the Mediterranean and Red Seas, their overlordship recognized as far away as Mecca and Medina. Malikshah's name – which he apparently took upon his accession – is testimony to the continuing influence of the Arab–Persian imperial culture that Abbasid Baghdad had nurtured. Although the Sultan was of Turkish descent, he assumed a throne name that combines the Arabic word for "ruler" – *malik* – with the corresponding Persian term – *shah*). The sultans also demonstrated their staunch support for Sunni Islam by establishing across their realm schools for religious teaching ("madrasahs"). The most celebrated of them were the "nizamiyyas," named for their founder, Nizam al-Mulk, the illustrious Persian vizier who served Malikshah. By far the most celebrated of the nizamiyyas was the Nizamiyya of Baghdad, established in the late eleventh century – which would make it, in the estimation of some, the world's first university. Its prestige was elevated right from the start with Nizam's decision to hire as its director the scholar al-Ghazali, arguably the most seminal figure in the history of medieval Islamic religious scholarship. With his presence a magnet, Baghdad continued to attract the cream of religious scholars and students, as well as poets. But none of the Seljuk sultans made Baghdad their capital; they preferred Iranian cities like Isfahan and, later, Hamadan. Culturally, Baghdad was a major center; politically, it remained a backwater.

Nizam was assassinated in 1092; Sultan Malikshah passed away shortly after. Nizam's death came at the hands of members of an extremist Shi'ite sect spawned at least indirectly by the doctrines of the Fatimids at Cairo – the same doctrines whose pernicious influence Nizam had sought to counter by founding madrasahs. The sect that killed him later became famous for its alleged practice of plying its devotees and would-be agents with hashish to help them imagine the beauties of heaven after martyrdom. They thus became known as the *hashishin* – those who use hashish – which is the origin of the word "assassin."

Upon the death of Sultan Malikshah internal dissensions caused the Seljuk empire to fragment. In Iraq, local Arab, Turk, and Kurdish rulers vied for power during the twelfth and early thirteenth centuries. A Bedouin Arab dynasty briefly asserted its autonomy in the south, a

Turkish dynasty known as the Zangids ruled in the north at Mosul, and for a while the Abbasid caliphs at Baghdad took advantage of the Seljuk weakness to re-establish themselves as the rulers of much of central and southern Iraq, even fending off a siege of Baghdad by one of the Seljuk sultans in 1157. Over the longer term, perhaps the most significant events pertinent to Iraq's history during this time did not actually occur in Iraq. Rather, they were influenced by a man born in Iraq, in Tikrit, on the Tigris north of Baghdad. To understand his significance, both in his own time and for Iraq's later history, we need first to set the stage upon which he became famous.

THE CRUSADES AND SALADIN

In 1095, Pope Urban II received a letter that changed the course of history and set a tone for relations between the Middle East and the West which has endured to this day.

With the Seljuks' unraveling already underway, the Byzantine emperor Alexius I Comnenus believed that he might be able to regain from the Turks some of the territory his predecessors had lost to them in the fifteen years after the defeat at Manzikert. But he needed help to accomplish that. Although the Roman Catholic Church had long been at odds with the Eastern Church at Constantinople, of which the emperor was officially the head, Alexius wrote to the Pope to ask his help in rallying support for an expeditionary force of Christian European mercenary knights to trek eastward and take on the Turks. Undoubtedly sensing his own opportunities in the Emperor's letter, Urban took the request to heart. Only months later, at a church council at Clermont in France, he issued an impassioned appeal to the lords and knights there assembled to take up arms in the cause of Christ and reconquer Jerusalem and the "Holy Land" from the barbarian, iniquitous Turks, whom Urban accused of nearly every horror and sacrilege one might imagine.

As it turned out, his audience – and those across Europe to whom news of his appeal quickly spread – were eager to embrace the task the Pope had set them. An initial wave of tens of thousands of warrior-pilgrims – only later would they come to be known as "Crusaders" – set out from France and Germany, where, in a horrific foreshadowing of the Holocaust of the 1940s, they massacred hundreds of Jews in the towns of the German Rhineland. When they arrived at the gates of Constantinople in 1096, the Emperor welcomed them but quickly had them ferried across the straits into Anatolia. Soon they were slaughtered by the forces of the Seljuk Sultan of Rum ("Rome"), who controlled most of Anatolia. A subsequent wave comprising thousands of (mostly French) knights and soldiers crossed into Anatolia in 1097 and began fighting their way across the peninsula. One group, splitting from the main body, moved eastward into northern Mesopotamia and took control of Edessa on the upper Euphrates, a heartland of ancient Syriac Christianity. The main body proceeded southward into Syria, which had become badly disunited after Malikshah's death five years earlier – a serendipitous circumstance that now played nicely into the European invaders' hands. Reaching the ancient Seleucid capital of Antioch, they besieged the fortified city for several months and at great cost, only to take the city but then be besieged themselves by a relief army dispatched from Mosul. They were able to break that siege, inspired, according to traditional accounts, by miraculous visions and the discovery, buried beneath the floor of the ancient church there, of what was alleged to be the lance used to pierce the side of Jesus during his crucifixion. They then resumed their rampage southward, advancing upon the ultimate prize, Jerusalem, and capturing it on 15 July 1099. If we accept the accounts at face value, the conquest was accompanied by slaughter that was perhaps unrivaled in its indiscriminate shedding of blood, Muslim and Christian alike.

Thus ended the First Crusade, with Jerusalem in Christian hands and newly installed European lords ruling four "Crusader states" that consisted mostly of a narrow strip of territory along the eastern Mediterranean seaboard. If we are to believe the Iraqi chronicler Ibn al-Jawzi, the people of Baghdad, including the Caliph, were not stirred to action when they received news of the catastrophe. Ibn al-Jawzi tells how a delegation arrived from Damascus with the terrible news during the Ramadan fast. Its leader went to Baghdad's great mosque, took out some food, and began to eat. Spotting the disgust on the faces of his onlookers, he turned on them and accused them of gross hypocrisy to be so disgusted when much greater sacrileges were taking place in Syria and Jerusalem. Some of the onlookers were moved to tears and demanded action.[3] The fact of the matter was that the physical impact of the First Crusade was limited to the eastern Mediterranean seaboard and immediate hinterlands. The enfeebled Caliph, with no significant military arm of his own, was hardly in a position to do much about it. Baghdad was still revered as the caliph's seat and a center of scholarship, but its military and political irrelevance was clear. The Caliph's impotence to do much to improve his situation was even more evident in the fact that in thirty months between 1099 and 1101 the city changed hands between competing Seljuk lords as many as eight times.[4] Nor did the Seljuk princes themselves deign to respond effectively to the outcry in 1099, or to subsequent reports. Over the next twenty years, the Sultan dispatched several military expeditions westward to Syria, including some led from Mosul, to fight the Crusaders, but they had little impact on the Crusader occupation. Nor did the Sultan ever personally lead any of these expeditions. Iraq and Iran were more important to him, and the situation there was too precarious.[5]

In a little more than fifty years after the Crusader conquest of Jerusalem, a Muslim response began to gather momentum under the leadership of Zengi, a Turkish commander who had become the governor of Mosul in 1127 and then added Aleppo to his realm the following year. This gave him enough of a power base, extending across much of northern Iraq and Syria, to launch a jihad to expel the Christian invaders.

With various ebbs and surges, it lasted for almost 150 years. In 1144, Zengi took Edessa, thus regaining the first of the four Crusader states. The European response was to summon a Second Crusade, but it met failure at the gates of Damascus in 1148.

One of its leaders, the French king Louis VII, brought with him on crusade his beautiful and indomitable queen, Eleanor of Aquitaine. In 1152, after her marriage to Louis had been annulled, she married the ambitious Henry Plantagenet, Count of Anjou and Duke of Normandy. Less than three years later, he became King Henry II of England. The third of the five sons Eleanor bore Henry, Richard, succeeded Henry as king in 1189. As Richard the Lionheart, he was to become the most famous – and most romanticized – of all the Crusader kings.

Richard's fame as a Crusader required a suitably formidable foe. Such a man had begun to come into his own a few decades after the defeat of the Second Crusade. Following Zengi's death, his son Nur ad-Din, who gained fame among Muslims as a thorn in the Crusaders' side, moved to unify all of Syria under his rule. He also succeeded in extending his influence into Fatimid Egypt when one of his commanders, Shirkuh, managed to compel the Fatimid caliph to appoint him as his vizier. Upon Shirkuh's death in 1169, his nephew, who had accompanied him to Egypt, moved swiftly to secure for himself his uncle's position. This upstart, a thirty-year-old Kurd who had been born in the Iraqi town of Tikrit, north of Baghdad, had already distinguished himself as a military leader. Over the next two decades, his exploits were to garner him great power and fame, and earn him a reputation that would spread beyond the Middle East to Europe, where he would later be remembered as a heroic figure unrivalled by other Muslims. His full name was Salah ad-Din Yusuf ibn Ayyub. Among his Egyptian subjects, he would be regarded as the second Joseph (Yusuf), hearkening back to the figure revered by Jews in the Hebrew Bible and by Muslims in the Qur'an. In the West, he would be remembered, and feared, as Saladin.

Not long after becoming vizier, Saladin repudiated his Fatimid overlord and abolished the Shi'ite Fatimid caliphate of Egypt. (This, by the way, also marked the last time that a Shi'ite-dominated political authority was to hold sway over a major Arab region until the advent of a Shi'ite-dominated government of Iraq after the 2003 invasion.) Although Saladin officially restored Egypt to the suzerainty of the Sunni Abbasid caliph in Baghdad, he in fact now ruled Egypt in his own right. Saladin's meteoric ascent had not gone unnoticed by the increasingly wary Nur ad-Din, but when the latter died a few years later Saladin was able to bring Nur ad-Din's Syrian realm under his control as well – despite the opposition of Nur ad-Din's son, whose supporters for decades would tar Saladin as a usurper. Recognized by the Caliph in Baghdad as sultan of Egypt and Syria, Saladin had become the most powerful Muslim ruler in the Middle East.

But it was the brilliant success of his jihad against the Crusaders that was to earn him fame and the respect of Christian Europe, as well as his iconic status as a stalwart opponent of the West. By 1182, Crusader commanders were harassing Muslim traders and pilgrims and were even threatening Saladin's control of the Red Sea, loss of which would expose Mecca and Medina to attack. Saladin now launched a concerted military effort to eliminate that threat, focusing on the forces of the Crusader kingdom of Jerusalem. On 4 July 1187, Saladin's forces annihilated the army of the King of Jerusalem at the Horns of Hattin, near Tiberias in present-day Israel, claiming as a prize the relic of the True Cross which the Crusaders had brought with them to inspire their campaign. Its defenders decimated, Jerusalem fell to Saladin's army on 2 October. In contrast to the treatment the Crusaders had meted out to Jerusalem's inhabitants when they conquered the city in 1099, Saladin graciously permitted many of its Christian residents to leave the city unharmed, and then invited the Jews of the region to resettle there.

The response of an infuriated Christendom was not long in coming. The Third Crusade was led at first by a triumvirate of powerful monarchs, but, owing to the Holy Roman Emperor's death en route and the King of France's defection, they were soon winnowed down to one, the aforementioned Richard the Lionheart, who had succeeded his father as king of England in 1189, and whose army's expenses were funded by a "Saladin tithe" specially levied in his realm. Between 1189 and 1192, Richard's forces battled Saladin's on several occasions and achieved some success, but by the time Richard departed from Palestine with his army the holy city of Jerusalem and most of what had been the kingdom of Jerusalem lay firmly in Saladin's grasp. The truce that for the time being ended the fighting granted Christian pilgrims unhindered access to the city and its holy places.

Less than a year later, Saladin was dead, his body laid to rest in Damascus, near the great mosque of the Umayyad caliphs. According to a contemporary, "Men grieved for him as they grieve for prophets. I have seen no other ruler for whose death the people mourned, for he was loved by good and bad, Muslim and unbeliever alike."[6] His descendants, a dynasty known as the Ayyubids, ruled Egypt only until 1250, when they were ousted by their own corps of Turkish mamluk slave-soldiers. Ruling until 1517, the Mamluk sultans of Egypt would finally expel the Crusaders from the Levant, one of them actually taking the name "Saladin" as a title.[7]

Although some Muslim sources castigate Saladin as a usurper, they generally ascribe great personal virtue and piety to him. On the other hand, some European Christians of his time regarded Saladin, victor of Hattin and conqueror of Jerusalem, as a treacherous if formidable enemy who, as a Muslim, was in league with Satan and capable of horrifying sacrilegious acts. In one medieval depiction of Saladin jousting with Richard – which never happened; they never met face to face – Saladin has the blue skin and horned head of Satan. One Crusader is reported to have written to the Pope with an allegation that Saladin had thrown the holiest relic in all of Christendom, the True Cross, into a fire, only for it to jump out of the flames.[8] Another source alleged that Saladin was accustomed to tying the Cross to the tail of his horse and then riding through Jerusalem's streets, dragging it behind in the dirt. Contemporary European sources also depict him as a scourge sent by God to punish the Crusaders for their wickedness[9] – much as the biblical prophets had interpreted the conquering armies of the Assyrians and Babylonians as divine scourges sent to punish the people of Israel for their evil-doing.

Yet Saladin was also reported to have treated Richard, and other Christian commanders, with great generosity and chivalry. For example, when Richard fell ill with a fever during his campaign, Saladin is said to have sent him fruit chilled with ice; on another occasion, Saladin sent Richard horses to replace a mount he had lost. Such reports of Saladin's gallantry helped remold his reputation in European Christian imagination into that of a pure and gallant warrior-prince, the epitome of knightly virtue.[10] In the early fourteenth century, the Italian poet Dante Alighieri, in the tour of Hell, Purgatory, and Heaven that he relates in his famous work, the *Divine Comedy*, felt justified in assigning Saladin to the outermost ring of Hell, which in Dante's imagining was a place, not of perpetual suffering, but of eternal rest for those virtuous men who had been deprived of the grace of Christian baptism during their lifetime. Other inhabitants of that blissful realm included many of the great authors of Greco-Roman antiquity, the heroes of Troy and ancient Rome, and the great Muslim philosophers Avicenna (Ibn Sina) and Averroes (Ibn Rushd).[11]

Saladin's fame in the Muslim world began to fade in the centuries after his death, when he was often viewed as a usurper who had unseated the heirs of Nur ad-Din, who tended to receive more credit for his role in the anti-Crusader jihad, or as relatively lackluster compared with the thirteenth-century Egyptian Mamluk sultan Baybars, who all but eliminated the Crusaders from the Levant.[12] But as European interests – and interventions – in the Middle East began to increase in the nineteenth century, episodes like the German Kaiser Wilhelm II's highly respectful speech during his visit to Saladin's tomb in 1898 helped Muslims become aware of the reverence with which Europeans had come to regard Saladin.[13] As European interest blossomed into European domination after World War I, Saladin was rehabilitated among Middle Eastern Muslims as a warrior-leader who had defended the region during an earlier era of European intrusion, and his zeal in standing up against European invaders was elevated as an example for emulation. As one scholar has noted, Saladin was "well placed to become a hero to many groups" – ethnically a Kurd, raised in a Turkish military milieu, ruler over Arab lands, and lionized by the Sunni majority as a hero of Sunni jihad against the Crusaders and a vassal who strove to have his conquests recognized as legitimate by the Sunni Caliph in Baghdad.[14] On the other hand, many Shi'ites regard Saladin as a villain, if for no other reason than his role in bringing an end to the Shi'ite Fatimid caliphate in Egypt. After World War I, Arab Palestinians saw his victory over the Crusaders at Hattin in 1187 as a model for their resistance to the onslaught of Zionist settlement.[15] His potency as a symbol of resistance undoubtedly contributed to the report about the French general Henri Gouraud, who, after the French takeover in Syria in 1919, went to Saladin's tomb in Damascus and there allegedly kicked his coffin and proclaimed that the Crusades were finally over, the Christian Europeans the victors. Several decades later, after France had relinquished its control of Syria in the wake of World War II, the new Arab regime erected in Damascus a monumental statue of Saladin, majestic on horseback and with two Crusaders trailing behind.

In his homeland of Iraq, Saladin's image was appropriated by Saddam Hussein, who happened to share with him a common birthplace, Tikrit.[16] (Indeed, early in his career he was known as Saddam Hussein al-Tikriti.) In his propaganda during the 1980–88 war with Iran, Saddam would have himself depicted shoulder to shoulder with Saladin, his fellow stalwart against the enemies of Iraq. In doing so, perhaps Saddam was mindful that Saladin was a Kurd, and was associating himself with the great Kurdish war leader in order to reach out to the Kurdish component of Iraq's population. One can only wonder, though, whether Saladin could have stood side by side with a man who eventually numbered Iraq's Kurds among his enemies and exterminated tens of thousands of them.

THE MONGOL INVASION AND ITS AFTERMATH

The Crusades were waged mainly in the coastal plain of Syria and Palestine and, later, in the Nile delta in Egypt. They posed scant danger to Iraq, except the northern city of Mosul, which was threatened by the short-lived Crusader state of Edessa before Nur ad-Din reconquered it. During Saladin's time the Caliph an-Nasir even succeeded in getting out from under Seljuk authority and revived Baghdad's fortunes somewhat, patronizing the still prestigious Sunni law schools as well as providing funds for the city's Shi'ite shrines. In 1233 his successor, al Mustansir, founded one of Baghdad's greatest institutions of higher learning, the Mustansiriya, where scholars of all four of the major Sunni legal schools taught. But contemporary observers felt that the city's greatest glory had come and gone. The traveler Ibn Jubayr, visiting from Andalusia, noted in 1184 that although Baghdad still served as the Abbasids' capital, and "is greater than can be described…most of its substance is gone. Only the name remains. Compared to what it once was – before it fell victim to recurrent misfortunes and repeated calamities – the city resembles a vanished encampment, a shadow of a passing ghost."[17]

Meanwhile, far to the east, in the Mongolian steppes of Central Asia, the nucleus of what would soon metastasize into a vast new empire was taking shape under the military genius of an ambitious, dynamic, and ruthless warrior-chieftain named Temujin. By 1206, he had united under his leadership many of the tribes of the nomadic Mongol people. That achievement enabled him to claim the title that most now think of as his name: Jingiz (Genghis) Khan ("Universal Ruler"). As Jingiz turned his attention to further conquests, he attracted to his banners many tribes of the Turks as well, in quest of plunder and new pastures. Like their nomadic precursors who had swept across the steppe to conquer large empires, Jingiz's Mongol–Turkic armies relied first and foremost on skilled, swift horsemen wielding compound bows; but Jingiz's commanders also adopted the more sophisticated technologies of catapults and siege engines that were needed to besiege walled towns and cities.

Like the Assyrians two thousand years before, the Mongols made brutally effective use of the scare tactics of massacre and devastation to intimidate populations into submission. During the early thirteenth century, the armies of Jingiz (who died in 1227) and his descendants rampaged from China in the east to the Caucasus, Russia, Poland, and Hungary in the west, leaving a wake of destruction on a scale seldom seen before. They massacred armies sent against them, demolished cities and towns, and annihilated their inhabitants. Jingiz's descendants continued the Mongol expansion. By 1255, the Mongols had devastated much of Khurasan, Azerbaijan, and parts of Iraq. According to one inflated yet indicative contemporary reckoning, they left 700,000 dead at the city of Merv and reduced the population of these regions by as much as ninety percent.[18]

That expansion left the glory of Abbasid Baghdad forever shattered.

In 1255, a huge Mongol force under the leadership of Jingiz's grandson Hulegu set out westward from Mongolia, having been commanded by the Great Khan Mongke to subdue the lands of Southwest Asia. After campaigning across Iran, in January 1258 three of Hulegu's armies converged upon and surrounded Baghdad. The arrogant Caliph rejected Hulegu's demand that he submit; the Mongols promptly defeated the Abbasid army that was sent against them, and on 5 and 6 February they took the city's walls. Hulegu reportedly commanded the population to exit the city, only to have them killed. He then ordered his troops into Baghdad, where they tracked down and killed those who had chosen to remain.[19]

The ensuing orgy of looting, rape, and destruction wreaked incalculable devastation to the city the Caliph al-Mamun had founded almost five hundred years before. It is difficult to quantify the extent of the damage; the surviving reports vary. Fires that lasted forty days consumed many of the city's mosques and palaces – among them, the great mosque of the caliph, the caliphs' tombs, and the shrine of the Shi'ite Imam Musa al-Kazim.[20] The devastation of 1258 is a major reason why virtually none of Abbasid Baghdad's architecture survives. The library that the caliphs had so long patronized was also destroyed, its books burned or else thrown into the Tigris, whose waters reportedly ran black from their ink. The people who had remained in the city resorted to hiding in wells, sewers, and latrines to try to escape the Mongols' swords, but mostly in vain. Estimates of the toll in human lives range from 90,000 to an unlikely one million; Hulegu himself believed it to have been around 200,000. Whatever the number, the stench of decaying corpses left from the carnage forced Hulegu to move his armies upwind and lingered over the city for months; the decaying flesh reportedly caused an epidemic to break out in Syria. Hulegu spared most of Baghdad's Christians, perhaps because his mother and two of his wives were Nestorian Christians; a decision that fostered lingering resentment among the Muslim population. Such reports of Mongol magnanimity helped nurture among European Christians the hope that the Mongols could be enlisted as allies in a crusade to exterminate Islam. Subsequent Mongol actions rapidly disabused them of that notion.

In the aftermath of Baghdad's conquest, it was reported that the Caliph had been betrayed by some of his officials, including his vizier, who had reduced the Abbasid army defending Baghdad to a mere ten thousand, no match for Hulegu's hordes. The vizier, al-Alqawsi, was a Shi'ite. Although modern historians doubt the veracity of that report, it was remembered and put to propaganda use centuries later. After the invasion of Iraq in March 2003, Saddam Hussein broadcast an appeal to Iraqis to remain steadfast, and compared those Iraqis who helped the Americans to the Shi'ite vizier who had betrayed Baghdad to Hulegu.[21]

Baghdad's destruction was remembered in a poem by Taqiaddin ibn Abil-Yusr, a lament that mirrors those written by Sumerian scribes for ancient Sumer's great cities after other marauders from the east devastated them more than three thousand years before:[22]

How many an inviolate household has the Turk taken
    captive with violent hands, though before that
    curtain were many protecting bastions…
How many treasures have become scattered abroad through
    plundering, and passed into the possession of infidels;
How many punishments have been inflicted by their swords
    upon men's necks, how many burdens of sin there laid down;
…as the captives were dishonored and licentious men
    of the enemy dragged them to ravishment –
And they were driven like cattle to the death that they beheld,
    "The Fire, O my Lord, rather than this – not the shame…"
After the capture of all the house of Al-Abbas, may no
    brightening illumine the face of the dawn…
There remains for neither the Faith nor the world,
    now that they are gone, any market of glory,
    for they have passed away and perished.
Truly the Day of Judgment has been held in Baghdad, and
    her term, when to prosperity succeeds adversity.
The family of the Prophet and the household of
    learning have been taken captive, and whom,
    think you, after their loss, will cities contain?

The Caliph al-Mustasim, last of the line of the Abbasid caliphs at Baghdad, was indeed taken captive, and killed – probably in a manner that assuaged the Mongols' taboo about shedding the blood of royalty:

by wrapping him in a carpet and then either kicking him to death or else trampling him under the hooves of their horses.

After conquering Baghdad, Hulegu's armies headed west into Syria, but their advance was stopped in Palestine in 1260 in the Battle of Ayn Jalut ("The Springs of Goliath"), where the forces of the Mamluk sultans of Egypt defeated them. The rest of Iraq did not escape the Mongol rampage unscathed. In 1262 both Mosul in the north and Wasit, the former Umayyad imperial center in the south, were attacked and their populations massacred. Other cities and towns opted to submit to Mongol rule, and Iraq now became part of the Ilkhanate, the kingdom of the Ilkhans, Hulegu's successors. At its zenith, the Ilkhanate extended across most of Southwest Asia, from the Aegean coast of Turkey, across Iraq and Iran, to Central Asia and the borders of India. It was one of the four Mongol kingdoms, ruled by descendants of Jingiz Khan, that made up the vast Mongol empire, the largest contiguous empire in history. By the time that the Ming dynasty regained control of China and brought down the Mongol empire in 1368, Mongol rule, though beset by fallings-out between the Mongol kingdoms, had brought prosperity to much of Eurasia, thanks to the flourishing trade routes that criss-crossed the empire. And as has happened so often in history, the once savage conquerors were soon "conquered" by the civilized, urbane cultures that became part of their realm. Just as their Umayyad and Abbasid Arab predecessors had done centuries before, the Ilkhans rapidly assimilated into the long-established Persian culture of Iran. When the Ilkhan ruler Ghazan Khan converted to Islam in 1295 the Ilkhans also became patrons of that faith – and occasional persecutors of others, especially Buddhists but also, for a while, Christians. Ghazan's successor, Uljeitu, erected at his capital a mausoleum that is regarded as one of the architectural jewels of the period.

Uljeitu's capital, Soltaniyeh, was in northern Iran, and his predecessor Ghazan and other Ilkhans ruled from either Tabriz or Maragheh, in northwestern Iran. None of the Ilkhanids ruled from Iraq. For the next five centuries, until the late nineteenth century, the once great metropolis of Baghdad became a backwater – one provincial capital of one of the frontier zones to which Iraq was reduced; Mosul served more and more as the chief political center of northern Iraq. Although Hulegu began to rebuild Baghdad not long after he had destroyed much of it, it never regained anything approaching its previous size or status. Baghdad was never again the capital of an empire, nor did it, or Iraq, ever reclaim the central position they had held for so long in the Sunni Muslim world.[23] More and more, that status now came to be claimed by the other hearth of civilization in the Middle East, Egypt, and Cairo assumed the mantle that Baghdad had so long and proudly worn. Egypt's Mamluk rulers were of Turkish or Circassian (Caucasian) origin, but from the late thirteenth century on they defended the Arab world from further Mongol inroads and sponsored the construction of mosques and other religious buildings in Cairo to assert their primacy as defenders of Islam. Under Mamluk patronage, Cairo's great mosque of al-Azhar, which Saladin had converted from a Shi'ite Fatimid to a Sunni institution of worship and religious learning in the twelfth century, became the single most prestigious institution of Sunni scholarship, its prestige enhanced by the arrival of scholars who had fled before the Mongol onslaught in Iraq and elsewhere. The handing over of leadership of the Muslim community from Baghdad to Cairo was signaled by the Mamluks' decision to recognize a surviving relative of the Abbasid line as caliph and thus restore the caliphate, but at Cairo, not Baghdad. He was purely a figurehead, exercising no real authority, but he served as a symbol of the Mamluk ascendancy.

Finally, besides ending the glory days of Baghdad, the Mongol invasion also resulted in further degradation of the irrigation infrastructure on the Mesopotamian floodplain. Combined with the ongoing effects of salinization, this spelled the doom of the agricultural bounty that since the mid-fourth millennium BCE had made Iraq the cradle of cities and civilization, religions and empires. The Ilkhanids' favoring of Iran over

Iraq also meant that Baghdad and the Tigris–Euphrates Valley lost their preeminence in the great East–West trade network that criss-crossed Eurasia. The previously favored route had run from India, through the Persian Gulf to Basra and Baghdad and on to the Mediterranean; it was now superseded by an overland route through Iran and Anatolia as well as a sea route that ran through the Indian Ocean and up the Red Sea to Egypt and the Mediterranean and contributed greatly to the prosperity of Mamluk Cairo.

Iraq's infrastructure was ruined, its cities diminished, its countryside increasingly in the hands of rural tribal confederations more interested in gaining more pasturage for their flocks than in promoting an expansion of agriculture or a rejuvenation of urban life. The fourteenth and fifteenth centuries saw Iraq afflicted by raiding, epidemics, starvation, and depopulation. They also inflicted on Baghdad one more cataclysm, at the hands of the last of the Mongol–Turkic "world conquerors": Timur-leng (Timur the Lame), celebrated in European literature and song as "Tamerlane." Timur claimed descent from Jingiz, whom he held up as his role model. Between 1369 and his death in 1405, from his capital of Samarkand in what is now Uzbekistan, Timur led his armies as far east as Delhi in India and as far west as Ankara in Turkey, in "a series of plundering expeditions on a massive scale" in which he "indulged in destruction and wanton cruelty to an extent that Chingiz would have found pointless,"[24] since they were "imbued with no purpose other than the agglomeration of sheer power built on the corpses of millions."[25] Although the impact of his campaigns in Iraq was not limited to Baghdad – he raided Hilla and Basra as well – Timur's treatment of Baghdad and its remaining population provides a case study of his cruelty. Because the local tribal confederation (known as the Jalayirids) that controlled the region refused to cooperate, Timur had to take Baghdad twice. The first conquest, in 1393, was relatively bloodless. The second, in 1401, may have exceeded Hulegu's conquest of 1258 in its savagery. His armies had to besiege the city for six weeks, in the terrible heat of summer, before they breached the city's walls. Many of the inhabitants reportedly jumped into the Tigris to try to escape, only to be cut down by Timur's archers. Timur ordered that each soldier bring the head of one man of the city. Some of his soldiers, afraid of his wrath, resorted to decapitating women. The heads were then fashioned into 120 towers that were set up around the city. In total, ninety thousand inhabitants of Baghdad were killed, and many of the city's buildings were razed.[26] The city's remaining scholars were spared and brought back to Samarkand.

Not long after Timur's armies departed, the Jalayirids returned to power in a now even more enfeebled Baghdad. They were soon supplanted, by a succession of Turkmen nomad groups, the lyrically named "Black Sheep" and "White Sheep" confederations. Under their rule, Baghdad and Iraq slid yet deeper into decline as rural tribes assumed more and more control of the countryside and, like modern-day Mafiosi, compelled cities to pay protection money. With tribes coming to wield such power as the enforcers of what little security could be had, it ought not be surprising that "well into the 19th century, about three-quarters of the people of Iraq still had strong rural tribal affiliations."[27] Even in the twentieth and twenty-first centuries, tribal affiliations have continued to exert major influence in Iraq, especially under Saddam Hussein's regime but also in the aftermath of the 2003 invasion.

IRAQ IN THE ERA OF THE "GUNPOWDER EMPIRES"

In world history, the sixteenth and seventeenth centuries are often characterized as the era of the "gunpowder empires," for they witnessed the introduction and increasingly sophisticated use of new military technology based on gunpowder, the knowledge of which had been brought from China. By the fifteenth century, new dynasties had begun to equip their armies with cannon, firearms, and mining techniques in order to impose their rule over large territories. Shortly after 1500, two of these dynasties, both of Turkic origin, had emerged in the Middle East: the Ottomans, with their capital at Constantinople, and the Safavids, whose capital was at Isfahan during their heyday. If we define the Middle East extremely broadly, we may also include a third dynasty: the Mughals – "Mongols" – of India, a dynasty descended from Timur. By the end of the sixteenth century, the frontier zone between the Ottoman and Safavid empires included Iraq. The region and its inhabitants bore the cost of that location, in destruction and bloodshed.

The Ottomans began their rise to power in the late thirteenth century, when much of the Middle East had been destabilized by the Mongol onslaught and the ensuing jockeying for power between the Ilkhanids and the Mamluks. A Turkish chieftain named Osman and his nomadic tribal followers (the men of Osman, or Osmanli; hence "Ottomans") established themselves in the northwestern corner of what is now Turkey, where they set themselves up as *ghazi* (frontier warriors) against the Christian Byzantines, who were still hanging onto their ancient capital of Constantinople. Over the next hundred years, the Ottomans expanded their realm farther east across Anatolia and westward into southeastern Europe, portions of which the Ottomans were to control for many centuries. The Ottoman ascent was briefly stymied in 1401, when Timur smashed the armies of the Ottoman sultan Bayezid at Ankara and carried off Bayezid into humiliating captivity. According to some accounts, Timur kept him in a cage and forced him to watch while Bayezid's favorite wife, stripped naked, served him. But by the time Mehmet II acceded to the sultanate in 1451, the Ottomans were poised to reassert their dominance.

Mehmet did so, spectacularly, in 1453, by accomplishing what neither the Arab caliphs nor the Seljuk sultans before him had been able to: the conquest of Constantinople, which thereafter served as the capital of the Ottoman empire until its end after World War I. Mehmet's conquest of Constantinople signaled the advent of the "gunpowder empires," since his armies used huge cannons to blast the city's fortifications as well as to sink the ships that tried to run the blockade of the city. Even before Mehmet's time, the Ottomans had adopted a practice that by then already had a long and distinguished history in the Middle East: the recruitment of slave soldiers to create an elite fighting force with unquestioned loyalty to the ruler. The Ottomans obtained the raw material for this force by periodically rounding up boys from the Christian villages of their southeastern European possessions – a process called the *devshirme* – and taking them to the capital. There, they were made into Muslims and educated in palace schools for service either as royal officials in the burgeoning imperial bureaucracy or as soldiers in the disciplined, firearms-wielding infantry corps that Europeans knew and feared as the "janissaries."

Only between 1512 and 1520, with the reign of Sultan Selim I ("the Grim"), did the Ottoman empire truly become a Middle Eastern as well as European empire. By the time he died, Selim had conquered Syria and Palestine and reached the pinnacle of an extraordinary career with the conquest of Egypt in 1517, thus bringing to an end the Mamluk sultanate at Cairo, if not their influence there. Selim and his Ottoman successors were now recognized as guardians of the holy cities of Mecca and Medina. The moral and spiritual authority that that entailed helped to legitimize Ottoman sovereignty across the Muslim Middle East.

However, Selim needed to attend to a formidable new threat to his realm's eastern borders. It had emerged with the ascendancy in Iran of a dynasty that was to rival the Ottomans for power and prestige in Iraq and eastern Anatolia. Its rise is linked to the career of a man named Ismail, who, starting at a very young age, was able to build on his inherited status as grand master of a militant Sufi order to achieve a rapid ascent to power and in 1501 proclaim himself the shah. As Shah Ismail, he was the first ruler of a dynasty that took the name of that Sufi order: the Safawiyyah, or Safavids. Among the members of this order were Shi'ite Turkmen tribesmen of Iran and eastern Anatolia, the Qizilbash (named for the red caps they wore), who flocked to Ismail's banner and served his cause devotedly.

With their military support, Ismail launched a series of conquests that reached into Iraq, where in 1508 he took Baghdad and Mosul, and eastward across Iran into Afghanistan. Important for the future of Iraq, Ismail militantly championed Twelver Shi'ism (albeit in rather heterodox fashion; Ismail claimed for himself special status owing to his alleged descent from the lineage of Ali, the First Imam). He and his successors compelled the mostly Sunni population of Iran to convert to Shi'ism or else face persecution. Ismail's decision set the course of Iran's history, and of Iran's relations with the rest of the Middle East, ever after, since Iran became the predominantly Shi'ite country that it remains today.[28]

By declaring his rule to be partisanly Shi'ite, Shah Ismail spawned an additional dimension of what was to become an enduring rivalry, and animosity, between the Safavids and the Ottomans. The Ottomans' origins in Anatolia were linked to their role as warriors for Islam, but the Safavids' declaration of their Shi'ite partisanship seems to have sharpened the Ottomans' sense of themselves as staunch champions of Sunni orthodoxy, which they now felt the duty to defend against Shi'ite heresy. Thus, the Ottoman–Safavid rivalry became about much more than control of territory and trade routes;[29] it took on the nature of a religious war. The first major military encounter in that war came in 1514, at Chaldiran, in eastern Anatolia, not far southwest of Ismail's capital, Tabriz. Selim I's larger Ottoman forces, equipped with artillery, crushed Ismail's Qizilbash cavalry, forcing him to abandon Tabriz to the Ottomans. Although the Ottomans did not tarry long in Tabriz, they soon laid claim to Mosul and also to the mountainous region of northern and northeastern Iraq, which they later attempted to rule as the province of Shahrazor. Ottoman authority in that province, like the authority of Iraq's central government more than four hundred years later, would almost always be contested, for Shahrazor was home to the hardy – and independent-minded – Kurdish tribes.

Central Iraq and Baghdad remained in Safavid hands until ten years after Ismail's death in 1524, when they were targeted by the most celebrated of all the Ottoman sultans, Suleiman I, who came to be known as "the Magnificent" and, especially among his subjects, "the Lawgiver." Historians identify his reign (1520–66) as the zenith of Ottoman military power and diplomatic prestige. Under Suleiman, the Ottoman empire stretched from Iraq to almost the gates of Vienna (which Suleiman besieged, unsuccessfully, in 1529), and the coast of Algeria. Between 1532 and 1555, Suleiman launched three campaigns against the Safavids in Iraq. His armies conquered Baghdad in 1534, and in 1546 the Ottoman navy took control of Basra. In 1555, a treaty with the Safavids left Iraq in Suleiman's hands. But even during Suleiman's reign Ottoman control of Iraq could be tenuous, with the Safavids still coveting the region, especially the holy Shi'ite shrine-cities of Najaf and Karbala, and local rulers occasionally rebelling against Ottoman rule.

The most celebrated of the Safavid shahs, Abbas the Great (ruled 1587 to 1629) is known not only for his military conquests and diplomatic prowess, including his outreach to European rulers such as Elizabeth I of England, but also for moving his capital to Isfahan, which he recreated as one of the most beautiful cities of the Middle East. Abbas also forcefully reasserted Safavid designs on Iraq, again turning it into a battleground with the Ottomans. After Abbas' forces took Baghdad from the Ottomans in 1623, they exacted a horrible retribution, killing many Sunnis in southern Iraq and also destroying two of Baghdad's great Sunni mosques. When the Ottomans retook Baghdad fifteen years later, they took vengeance in turn, putting thousands of Shi'ite Persians to death. In 1639, however, the two sides agreed to a treaty that established what later became the modern boundary between Iran and Iraq. By the mid-eighteenth century, the Safavids had gone into eclipse. Although the dynasties that succeeded them in Iran often continued to fight for control in Iraq, especially in Baghdad and the south, it is the Safavids who have continued to hold a special place in the collective memory of modern Iraqis: the Sunni Arabs of the region of Baghdad and central and western Iraq even today sometimes refer to Iranians – and even Iraq's Shiʿite Arabs – as "Safavids." It is not a term of endearment.

The Ottoman hold in Iraq meanwhile loosened, devolving onto local governors at Baghdad, Mosul, and Basra whose allegiance to the sultan at Constantinople was often quite weak. Similarly weak was these governors' ability to control the surrounding countryside, where grinding poverty and disease were exacerbated by the threat of raids by Arab tribes in the south and Kurdish tribes in the north. By the late eighteenth century, the outlook for Iraq was uncertain and precarious. Just as the Roman/Byzantine wars against the Parthians and Sassanids more than a thousand years earlier had ravaged much of Mesopotamia, the wars between the Ottomans and Safavids left the region in bleak circumstances, its cities and towns in decay, its countryside imperiled by pestilence and banditry.

EUROPEAN INROADS

By the early sixteenth century, the situation had been complicated even more by the return of European Christians onto the scene. They brought with them their own agendas, deeply imbued with self-interest: expanding their trade and markets, creating and protecting new colonies and empires, and digging for the riches of ancient Assyria and Babylon.

The beginning of the European intrusion onto the Iraqi stage is linked to the imperative that drove Christopher Columbus and his three ships westward from Spain in 1492: the quest for a direct route to the spices, silks, and other fabulous goods of "the Orient," bypassing Mamluk and Ottoman middlemen. After Columbus' voyages, Spain and other European countries focused their attention westward, upon the "New World" of the Americas. The Portuguese, on the other hand, had initiated European exploration down the western coast of

Africa decades before Columbus' voyage of 1492. This exploration culminated in 1497 when Vasco Da Gama sailed around the Cape of Good Hope and on to India, where the Portuguese quickly established a commercial and naval presence. To protect the new sea route that they had pioneered, they tried to establish themselves in the Persian Gulf as well, even gaining control of Basra in 1529, only to lose it to a counterstrike by Sultan Suleiman's Ottoman navy in 1546. Meanwhile the British and the Dutch were hardly content to sit back and let the Portuguese dominate the Persian Gulf and Indian Ocean. By 1600, the British had established trade ties with Shah Abbas the Great's Persia and were helping the Safavids to expel the Portuguese from the bases they had established in the Persian Gulf.

Having pushed the Portuguese out of the Persian Gulf, the British now proceeded to push themselves in. The former Portuguese bases were taken over by the premier agent of British commercial and colonial expansion at this time, the British East India Company. By 1763, the Company had made Basra its headquarters – a move that gave the British government even more leverage with which to influence both local and Ottoman imperial politics in Iraq and the Persian Gulf.

By the early nineteenth century, the British were well on their way to making the Persian Gulf a British lake. Their reasons for doing so were driven by one over-riding concern: to protect their access to India, which had become the single most prized possession in the British empire after the loss of Britain's North American colonies through its defeat in the American War of Independence. Although threats to British influence in the region from the Portuguese and the Dutch had long receded, France had posed a threat to British access to India when Napoleon Bonaparte launched his invasion and brief occupation of Ottoman Egypt in 1798. Although the Royal Navy under Admiral Horatio Nelson forced Napoleon to abandon that enterprise, the French initiative was sobering enough for the British to take charge of the western shores of the Gulf.[30] By dint of diplomatic treaties and military intimidation via the chief enforcer of its worldwide will – the Royal Navy – throughout the nineteenth and into the early twentieth century, Great Britain secured its domination of the petty sheikhdoms that later became the United Arab Emirates (formerly the "Trucial States" because of the truces governing their relations with Britain) and Bahrain. This process of creeping British hegemony in the Gulf culminated in agreements with Kuwait in 1899 and Qatar in 1916.[31]

THE SEEDS OF IRAQ'S REVIVAL

By the eighteenth century, as European (mainly British) commercial interests identified profits to be made from Iraq's produce (like dates), and markets, trade within Iraq and between Iraq and India was rejuvenated, and the populations of Baghdad, Basra, and Mosul began to revive.[32] As British interests dragged Iraq into the globalizing economic system, irrigation systems were improved, as was transport infrastructure, especially with the establishing of steamship travel on Iraq's great rivers. This set the stage for a significant expansion of grain production, which was now transformed from largely a subsistence venture to a major cash crop.

The rejuvenation of trade also benefited many of the Jews and Christians of Iraq's cities. By the early 1800s Jews comprised perhaps twenty percent of the population of Baghdad, where they played an important role as merchants and financiers. Iraq's indigenous Christians had been predominantly Nestorians, but after the sixteenth century many switched their spiritual allegiance to the Pope. This latter group came to be referred to as Chaldean Christians, although they were completely unrelated to the Chaldeans who ruled the Babylonian empire under Nebuchadnezzar, and over time they gravitated to Baghdad and Basra. Those who continued to adhere to Nestorian doctrine became known as Assyrian Christians, as they were associated mainly with the northern region around Mosul, the core region of ancient Assyria.[33] Moreover, a new element was introduced among Iraq's Christian communities during the era of Safavid control when Shah Abbas, hoping to boost trade and diplomatic links with Christian Europe, transplanted merchants from the Safavid territories in Armenia to his new capital at Isfahan. With a foothold and royal patronage there, Armenian merchants branched into Iraq, where their mercantile success soon rivalled that of their long-established Jewish counterparts. For the most part, all of these groups – Jews, Armenians, Chaldeans, and Assyrians – prospered during the era of Ottoman suzerainty, and they continued to play significant roles in Iraq well into the twentieth century.

During the nineteenth century, after many years of lapsed imperial authority and the rise of local power centers across much of the empire, as well as inroads by their European rivals, the Ottomans launched a sustained reform program, the Tanzimat, that aimed to modernize their administration and reassert the sultan's authority across the empire.[34] This resurgence of imperial authority in Iraq coincided with, and had huge impact on, developments that were to further enrich, and further complicate, Iraq's sectarian diversity. The consequences were so momentous that the modern nation-state of Iraq has yet to come completely to terms with them.

These changes were set into motion in the late eighteenth century, when thousands of Arab tribesmen migrated into Iraq from the Arabian Peninsula. Most of the new arrivals established themselves in southern and central Iraq, including the countryside around Baghdad as well as the Shi'ite shrine-cities of Najaf and Karbala. When they entered the region, their numbers were overwhelmingly Sunni. But the Ottomans' efforts to strengthen their hand in Iraq soon changed this.[35] The Ottomans hoped to induce these nomad tribesmen to settle down as farmers and livestock-raisers, so they sponsored the construction of a major new canal, the Hindiyya, in the south, in order to provide irrigation water. The Sunni tribesmen did indeed begin to settle. However, they also began to interact with the towns of Najaf and Karbala, which served them as granaries and markets.

Unforeseen by the Sunni Ottoman authorities, Najaf and Karbala also served the tribesmen as sources of Shi'ite proselytizing. By the early twentieth century, most of these now sedentarized tribes had been converted to Shi'ism. Because of those conversions, the majority of Iraq's population was by then Shi'ite: fifty-three percent by 1919, and fifty-six percent by 1932.[36] On the other hand, those tribes that opted not to settle down tended to remain Sunni – as the tribes of Iraq's large western province, Anbar, remain today.

The implications of this development for Iraq's later history were enormous. Previously, Iraq's Shi'ites had been a minority, lorded over and occasionally persecuted by a series of mainly Sunni states from the time of the Umayyads down to the later stage of Ottoman dominion. By the advent of the twentieth century, only twenty years before European intervention created the new state of "Iraq," Shi'ite Arabs had probably become the single largest sectarian group in the country. Nonetheless, they were to remain under the domination of a Sunni minority for more than another century.

As was the other of the three largest components of Iraq's ethnic mix: the Kurdish tribesmen who for centuries had dominated the rugged mountainous regions of Iraq's north and northeast. The vast majority of the Kurds were Sunni Muslims. As the Ottoman sultan in Istanbul began to claim more assertively the title of caliph and leadership of the Muslim community worldwide, many of them could feel some affinity with him as fellow Sunnis. But for many the tradition of autonomy and resistance to city-based political control – a tradition that stretched back to Abbasid times and earlier – pulled stronger.

By the end of the nineteenth century, the Ottoman authorities had made significant strides in reasserting their hold over Iraq, which they now governed as three provinces administered from the three major cities: Mosul in the north, Basra in the south, and Baghdad in the center. But, in a foreshadowing of the later state of Iraq, authority was increasingly centralized in Baghdad.

Since the late eighteenth century, the Ottoman imperial administration had also been engaged in major reforms to modernize its military, transportation, and administrative infrastructure, and to introduce more liberal, secular notions of citizenship – all in the hope of resisting the continued ascendance and encroachment of the West. In hindsight, many historians have judged these reforms as "too little, too late" – although the modernized Ottoman military was to prove its mettle against better equipped British forces during World War I. In Iraq, one of the more important results of Ottoman reform was the creation of new schools to train Arab officers in the Ottoman military in modern science and technology. Some of those officers were to play a major role in the birthing of modern Iraq, not only as a modern nation-state but also as a cradle of a new assertion of Arab identity – and resistance to European domination – throughout the Middle East.

7

THE CREATION AND ZENITH
OF MODERN IRAQ

U P TO THIS POINT, this book has emphasized Iraq as a birth-place of ideas and institutions – cities and civilizations, empires, religions, seminal contributions to culture, science, and technology – that have had huge impact on societies across the planet and so have made Iraq's history important to all of us as well as a source of pride to the Iraqi people. We have seen how Iraq's great wealth was a magnet for migrants, invaders, and raiders, who often brought turmoil and devastation. Iraq was also cursed for long periods by its location on the frontier between rival empires to the east (Parthians, Sassanids, Mongols, Safavids) and west (Romans/Byzantines, Mamluks, Ottomans), which at times reduced the country to an embattled and ravaged no-man's-land.

It is useful to keep this historical dynamic in mind as we come to the modern era, defined here as the period from the mid-nineteenth to early twenty-first century. Over the last twenty years, a legion of academic experts, journalists, and think-tank pundits have published a cornucopia of studies detailing Iraq's modern history, with "surges" around the time of Operation *Desert Storm* in 1991 and in the wake of Operation *Iraqi Freedom*, later renamed Operation *New Dawn*, from 2003. I rely on several of them here and encourage the reader to consult them for more detail on specific developments and issues that we can treat here only in outline.

Although by the late nineteenth century Iraq had been revived by increased trade and the Ottoman program of centralization and reform, the country had long ceased to be a great center of wealth production. For the ascendant European powers, Iraq was a backwater. Nonetheless, Iraq's location on the approaches to India made it a place to and through which Great Britain needed to ensure it had access. With the discovery of oil next door in Iran in the early twentieth century, Iraq's geostrategic importance to the British empire – and the inevitability of Western intrusion – increased exponentially. That intrusion culminated in 1921 when, under the auspices of the newly formed League of Nations, Britain midwifed a new birth and jerry-rigged a new cradle: the new kingdom of "Iraq."

As history so abundantly attests, unbidden intrusions into a people's homeland tend to elicit hostile responses. Iraq was to be no different. During the high point of British interference, Iraq became a center of long-standing resistance to Western intrusion in the Middle East – first by Britain and France, then by the United States, and also by what many people of the region perceived as yet another colonial creation of the West: the Zionist movement and its offspring, the new state of Israel.

SETTING THE STAGE

By the dawn of the twentieth century, Britain had taken crucial steps in the Middle East to ensure access to its imperial possessions in India. Its treaties with the local sheikhdoms, enforced by naval intimidation, had cemented its hold over the Persian Gulf. The British had also established a colony in Aden (in modern Yemen).

But it was in Egypt that the British presence in the Middle East was strongest, its attention focused there because of the construction of the

Suez Canal to link the Mediterranean Sea and the Red Sea via the western edge of the Sinai Peninsula. Opened in 1869 to great fanfare, the Suez Canal eliminated the need for ships from the West to sail around Africa in order to reach India. It thereby dramatically reduced the length and time of the passage. In 1875, the British took advantage of the financial woes of the Ottoman empire's viceroy in Egypt (the Khedive Ismail "the Magnificent") to purchase the Egyptian government's share of the canal at a bargain price of only £4 million. Seven years later, in 1882, Colonel Ahmad Urabi, an Egyptian army officer, led a proto-nationalist uprising against the encroachment on Egyptian sovereignty by Britain and France, whose "Dual Control" had hijacked Egypt's economy to force the repayment of the massive debt Egypt owed them. Britain dispatched a Royal Navy flotilla to bombard Alexandria and seize the canal. In the aftermath of the revolt, the British stationed troops at the canal. The ensuing howls of protest – both European and Egyptian – led the British government to offer assurances that it would soon withdraw those troops, which they finally did seventy years later in 1956.

Before long, the British established a protectorate over Egypt, installing their own officials in key ministries in its government. This proved an invaluable military asset when World War I broke out in 1914 and the British went to war against the Ottomans. It also spurred a growing Egyptian resentment of the British that was to play out in the mid-twentieth century, with a lasting impact on Iraq.

The opening of the Suez Canal also had an almost immediate impact on Iraq's economy – and on Britain's burgeoning share of it. Between 1870 and 1914, Iraq's exports increased markedly. Iraq's dates had long been one of its most sought-after products, but with the opening of the Suez Canal and the advent of steamship transport along the Tigris and Euphrates, grain too could now be exported at a profit. Grain thus became a cash crop in Iraq, much to the profit of British merchants.[1] At the same time, the import of British-made goods – mostly textiles, brought in through Basra – skyrocketed. Between 1868 and 1909, the value of those imports went from £51,000 to more than £3 million. When war broke out between Britain and the Ottoman empire in 1914, Britain's share of the trade with Iraq and the Gulf region had grown to become 75 percent of the total.[2] This economic upswing also had some impact on Ottoman policy in Iraq. Whereas before the 1870s Ottoman control had been split among the three centers of Mosul, Baghdad, and Basra, in the late nineteenth century the Ottomans began to make Baghdad their chief administrative center in Mesopotamia.[3] Much of the earlier insecurity had stemmed from their inability to control the rural tribesmen of Kurdistan and the Arab south. Now, the Ottoman authorities began to take steps to rein them in.

Meanwhile, a new threat to British India had emerged: the Russia of the Romanovs, Russia's final dynasty of czars. By 1800, Russia had become a threat not only to British interests in the Middle East but also to the Ottoman empire and to Persia, where a new dynasty, the Qajar shahs, had taken control in 1794. As the Russians extended their influence south into Iran, the British, alarmed about their intentions toward India, took diplomatic and military action to counter them. The ensuing Anglo-Russian rivalry for influence in Iran and Central Asia, including Afghanistan – the "Great Game" – came to a formal end in 1907 when the two sides agreed to divide Iran into spheres of influence. Russia was to control the north, Britain was to control Iran's southeastern approaches to India, and a rump central area was to serve as a buffer between them and be ruled by the now enfeebled Qajar shahs, who were readily cowed by intimidation from either side. By the 1870s the Shah also needed to refill his treasury, dissipated by his expensive tastes and travels, among other things. To do that, he began to make deals (referred to as "concessions") to sell off – to both sides – the rights to build infrastructure, such as dams and railroads, or to harvest and market Iran's natural resources. In 1891, however, the increasingly powerful Shi'ite religious leaders, allied with the urban merchants, thwarted the Shah's proposed sale of Iran's tobacco harvest to a British entrepreneur. This turn of events was a harbinger of the rise of a new power bloc in Iran's domestic affairs.

One resource the Shah did succeed in selling off was Iran's oil. Evidently clueless as to how precious a commodity petroleum would become, in 1901 he sold to a British entrepreneur, William Knox D'Arcy, the concession to explore for oil in southwestern Iran. After several years of financial struggle that nearly drove D'Arcy out of the field, his drillers struck oil there in 1908. The following year, the Anglo-Persian Oil Company (A.P.O.C., the ancestor of British Petroleum) was formed, with an agreement that left the majority of control – and the profits – in British hands. In 1914, A.P.O.C. exported from its new refinery at Abadan in southwestern Iran a quarter of a million tons of petroleum.[4] In that same year, the British government, in an act entirely unprecedented, purchased a controlling interest (fifty-one percent) of the company. Nothing was to prove more important in determining the tenor of British–Iranian relations for the next several decades. The impact on Iraq was to prove enormous as well.

Before the early twentieth century, oil had been used principally as fuel to produce heat and light. As the technology of the oil-fueled internal combustion engine advanced during the late 1800s and early 1900s, securing access to oil acquired strategic importance for the European powers – and none more so than Great Britain. In 1911, Britain's First Sea Lord, Admiral John Fisher, with the support of the young and supremely ambitious First Lord of the Admiralty, Winston Churchill, launched a wholesale modernization of the Royal Navy. It was predicated upon the conversion of the British fleet from coal- to oil-fired propulsion, which would enable British ships to achieve faster speeds and acceleration.[5] By far the greatest producer of oil at this time – and the most important supplier to the Royal Navy – was the United States, which in 1913 produced 140 times as much oil as A.P.O.C.'s fields in Iran. Britain's objective now was to secure a source of oil that was closer at hand and could not be withheld or threatened by a foreign power. To British thinking, Iran's oil served that end nicely – provided that British diplomatic and military leverage could ensure control of the oilfields and of Abadan, the location of the refinery from which the oil was shipped. This was why the British government purchased a controlling share of A.P.O.C. However, Abadan was located perilously near Ottoman-ruled southern Iraq. This became a major concern to the British once World War I began.

Meanwhile, in 1911, British, Dutch–British (Royal Dutch Shell), and German interests had teamed up to form a consortium – named the Turkish Petroleum Company (T.P.C.) a year later – to exploit oilfields that had been discovered in northern Iraq, near Mosul. In 1913, the T.P.C. merged with A.P.O.C. Consequently, when the British government purchased control of A.P.O.C. in 1914, it gained control of the T.P.C. as well – and with it the rights to exploit the oil of northern Iraq.[6]

In 1914 Iraq still lay within the boundaries of the Ottoman empire. But it was only a matter of time before Iraq's curse was to be compounded: by yet another invader and by the West's quest for Iraq's oil.

WORLD WAR I AND ITS AFTERMATH: THE HASHEMITE
MONARCHY, THE BRITISH, AND OIL

You may have just noticed the mention of a country heretofore unmentioned in this narrative: Germany. Once Germany came into being as a nation-state, in 1871, it quickly established itself as a major player in Europe and the Middle East. After decades of increasing indebtedness to and unrelenting encroachment by Great Britain (in Egypt and the Persian Gulf), France (in Lebanon and North Africa), and Russia (in the Black Sea and Caucasus region), the Ottoman sultan Abdul-Hamid II must have found the German Kaiser Wilhelm II a refreshing change. Wilhelm offered the Sultan much assistance in modernizing his military as well as his industry and transport infrastructure. This included an agreement in 1903 to build a railway linking Baghdad with Berlin; a project that quickly focused British attention on German intentions, perhaps in part because it also granted Germany the mineral rights – in other words, oil rights – twenty kilometers either side of the track.[7] Germany's trade with the Ottomans burgeoned, its rank as a commercial partner leaping from fifteenth place in 1886 to second by 1910.

To the Sultan's eye, these benefits from Germany came with seemingly no territorial strings attached. But as the Kaiser began to expand his military and flex his muscles in other arenas, rival European powers grew increasingly wary and, soon, hostile. By 1914, the European nations had coalesced around two poles: the Triple Entente, comprising Great Britain, France, and their erstwhile enemy Russia; and the Central Powers, comprising Germany, the Hapsburg empire of Austria–Hungary, and the Ottoman empire. Bulgaria joined the Central Powers in 1915.[8]

When World War I broke out in Europe in July and August 1914, Britain's chief concerns in the Middle East were obvious: to protect its control of the Suez Canal, its access to India, and A.P.O.C.'s vital oilfields in Persia. Ottoman domination of Iraq was an obvious threat to all of that, and the British wasted little time before trying to counter it. By November 1914, they had seized control of Basra. In the following year, British forces (comprising mainly Indian troops) under the command of General Charles Townshend advanced up the Tigris. By September 1915, they had captured the town of Kut (south of Baghdad) and seemed poised to move on to Baghdad. But they had moved well ahead of their logistical supply, and by December they were surrounded and besieged by Ottoman forces, who were then able to stymie British attempts to send a relief force, which were slowed by British reluctance to shift troops away from the battlefields of France. On 29 April 1916, the thirteen thousand sick and starving survivors of the British force at Kut surrendered – the largest mass surrender of British forces since General Cornwallis' surrender in 1781 at Yorktown during the American War of Independence.[9] In the aftermath, four thousand died as captives after being forced to march hundreds of miles to internment. Within a year, however, the British, intent on restoring their prestige among the locals – a recurring theme in British accounts of the time – had bounced back from this humiliating nadir of their "Mesopotamian Campaign." They regained Kut and then moved upriver to enter Baghdad, unopposed, on 11 March 1917. But much of northern Mesopotamia – including the oil-rich region around Mosul – remained in Ottoman hands until just before the war ended in November 1918.

By the time the British took Baghdad, events had transpired farther to the west – both on the battlefield and in the meeting-rooms of European diplomats – that were eventually to create the modern state of Iraq; shape its history, and that of the broader Middle East, down to the present day; and sear Arabs across the Middle East with an enduring sense of betrayal by the European powers, along with lingering wonder about what might have been.

As they prepared to move their armies north from Egypt, where troops from across the empire assembled and trained, into Ottoman Palestine, the British recognized that their chances of success would be much improved if they could attract local Arab support to their side. They pinned their hopes on Sharif Husayn ibn Ali, an Arab notable ("sharif") whom the Ottomans had established in 1908 as their governor of the Hejaz – the region of the western Arabian Peninsula, bordering the Red Sea, that includes the holy cities of Mecca and Medina. Husayn ibn Ali was a member of the Hashemite clan, to which the Prophet Muhammad had belonged. This invested him with an added prestige well suited to British designs both for him and for two of his sons, Abdullah and Faisal. In 1915, the British High Commissioner in Egypt, Sir Henry McMahon, initiated a correspondence with Husayn that remains a matter of controversy to this day, in terms both of the promises Britain made to Husayn and of Husayn's motives in acting upon them. What is certain is that the British promised Husayn that, if he took their side and provided military support against the Ottomans, then, in the event of victory, Husayn would be granted some form of rule over most of the Arab-populated region from the Mediterranean to the borders of Persia. Some of the British leadership evidently intended to set up Husayn as a new caliph who would be beholden to them.

In 1916, proceeding on the basis of this offer, Husayn launched what came to be known as the Arab Revolt (or the "Revolt in the Desert"), a campaign of mostly hit-and-run attacks on Ottoman troops and railways. Husayn's son Faisal was its nominal field commander, but the tactics and field leadership were largely entrusted to a young British archaeologist-turned-army officer, T. E. Lawrence, who came to be celebrated in newsreels of the time – and, decades later, in a much acclaimed film – as "Lawrence of Arabia." By December 1917, the combined successes of the British regular forces and the Arab Revolt enabled the British commander, General Sir Edmund Allenby, to enter Jerusalem as its conqueror – and thereby, in the eyes of a contemporary British caricaturist, to complete the task that Richard the Lionheart had left unfinished 725 years before, at the end of the Third Crusade. Before the war's end, British and Arab forces had advanced to Damascus. There, in 1920, the newly established Syrian Arab Congress proclaimed Faisal king.

Faisal's reign was to be very short-lived. Unbeknownst, at least at first,[10] to Husayn and his sons, since 1915 Britain, France, and Russia had been making plans that took scant notice of theirs. In that year, a British government commission had recommended that, once the Ottomans had been defeated, a new Middle East would be created, comprising five autonomous provinces: Syria, Palestine, Armenia, Anatolia, and Jazirah-Iraq.[11] In 1916, the British and the French, with Russia's blessing, concocted in secret a deal that many Arabs regarded then, and today, as a monumental act of European betrayal of Arab aspirations, even if Husayn's aspirations were more about Husayn than about "the Arabs." The Sykes–Picot Agreement, named for the British and French diplomats who finalized it, made no provision for a truly independent kingdom under Hashemite rule. Instead, it divided most of the Ottoman Arab Middle East into areas of British and French control, apportioning most of what later became Iraq (as well as Jordan and Palestine) to Britain and what later became Syria and Lebanon, as well as the region of northern Iraq around Mosul, to France. Although T. E. Lawrence, who was sympathetic to the cause of Arab self-rule, had already tipped him off, Husayn was overtly confronted with this deal only after the Bolshevik revolution took Russia out of the war in 1917 and the new Soviet government apprised him of how his British and French allies had double-crossed him.

On the same day the Bolshevik revolution began – 2 November 1917 – the British did something that compounded the Arabs' sense of grievance and betrayal. On that fateful day, Great Britain's Foreign Secretary, Arthur Balfour, sent to a prominent British Jewish financier, Lord Rothschild, a formal letter officially declaring Britain's intention to establish in Palestine a homeland for the Jewish people. Britain's motives in promulgating the infamous Balfour Declaration have been debated ever since. To some extent they were rooted in a feeling of religious and historical obligation to Britain's Jewish population[12] – even if anti-Semitism was rampant within the British government. But the Balfour Declaration sprang mostly from British considerations of political and strategic expediency, including the expectation that grateful Jewish immigrant settler-colonists in Palestine would serve as a proxy British garrison that would help to protect Britain's control of the all-important Suez Canal as well as access to Iraq and Iran.[13]

The Balfour Declaration signaled a monumental victory for the proponents of Zionism, the Jewish nationalist movement that since the late 1800s had pushed for the creation of such a Jewish homeland. That that homeland should be in Palestine had not been a foregone conclusion; at one point before World War I, the British had offered Uganda to the Zionist leadership. Many came to rue the day that the British government issued this declaration, for it boosted the momentum of the Jewish colonization in Palestine that had already begun in the later nineteenth century. The colonization, almost entirely European in origin, gathered yet more steam in the 1930s and 1940s before and after the catastrophe of Adolf Hitler's "Final Solution." In May 1948, it resulted in the creation of the modern state of Israel – an event that has brought the Middle East untold recrimination and devastating violence and has structured the region's politics and international relations ever since.

Although the British and their Arab allies had vanquished the Ottoman armies by the time the war ended in November 1918, the British, French, and Arab leaders were no longer quite on the same page on the postwar disposition of the Ottomans' Middle Eastern possessions. The boundaries delineated by the Sykes–Picot deal had been tweaked a bit to accommodate their respective interests. For the British, a chief concern was to stake its claim to the oilfields of the Mosul region. They accomplished that by rushing forces northward to seize them in early November, just as the war was ending. Presented with a fait accompli, the French premier Georges Clemenceau effectively ceded Mosul to Britain. He was confronted by an inescapable reality: France had been so drained by the war that he had no troops to send to the Mosul region.[14]

A new complication for the postwar settlement was the coming of age of the United States as a Great Power. In 1917, President Woodrow Wilson had guided the United States into the war, infusing American men and materiel into a British–French effort that had been bled nearly to death by the trench warfare of France's battlefields. But Wilson also infused Great Power relations with a new diplomatic wrinkle: his "Fourteen Points," a visionary blueprint for the postwar era that looked dreamily ahead to a new international order of open diplomacy and mutual cooperation, to be promoted and enforced by a new international body that he proposed but that, fatally for its long-term prospects, the United States Senate rejected: the League of Nations. Wilson's plan also

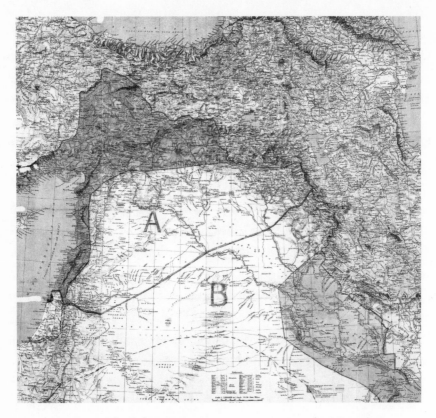

MAP 6. *The Sykes–Picot Agreement was signed 8 May 1916. Area A plus shaded area to northwest was apportioned to France; Area B plus shaded area to southeast, to Great Britain (Wikimedia Commons).*

proposed that the non-Turkish nationalities of the Ottoman empire "be assured an undoubted security of life and an absolutely unmolested opportunity of autonomous development." These words were sweet and stirring music to many across the region – among them, the Kurds of Iraq, Iran, and Anatolia, and the Hashemite would-be kingpins, Husayn ibn Ali and his sons.

FBut Wilson's dream hardly jibed with British and French intentions. They paid lip service to the noble intentions of the American ally whose armies had bailed them out: in the last week of the war they issued a joint declaration that the peoples of the Ottoman empire would be allowed to establish "indigenous Governments and Administrations."[15] In reality, though, they were not about to hand over to "autonomous development" the valuable Arab and Kurdish lands they had reserved for themselves during the preceding years. When in 1920 Faisal proclaimed an independent Arab kingdom at Damascus, where he had established himself since October 1918, the French brutally booted him out and took possession of what soon became the new states of Syria and Lebanon.[16]

Faisal would not sit forlorn off-stage for long. Nor would the Ottoman Arab military officers who had helped him establish and govern his short-lived kingdom. Many of them were of Iraqi origin, products of the modernizing schools the Ottomans had established at Baghdad and elsewhere. Seasoned by war, but thwarted in their initial attempts to create an independent Arab state, many of them returned to their homeland. They were men with a mission.

By early 1918, the British were on the way to establishing an administration over southern and central Iraq, where they controlled what had been the Ottoman provinces centered on Basra and Baghdad.[17] They opted to follow in the Ottomans' footsteps by centralizing their regime at Baghdad. Because the British officials now installed in Iraq had won their spurs governing Britain's possessions in India, they now intended to govern Iraq as they had governed there – directly, as overlords, and tolerating neither meaningful input nor opposition from the locals. The man installed in April 1918 as the acting civil commissioner, Colonel Arnold T. Wilson, went about his job in a manner so heavy-handed as to earn the British authorities in Iraq the enmity of the local Arab leadership. Their relationship worsened in 1920 when European diplomats meeting at San Remo in Italy decided that Britain and France were to take charge of the Ottoman Arab lands as "mandates" – an arrangement the League of Nations formalized in 1922 – bestowed as "sacred trusts of civilization" through which the "civilized" European states were to usher the peoples of the region into the modern nation-state system. France received the mandate for what became the new state of Syria, from which it quickly carved out the new state of Lebanon in order to promote the interests of its long-time clients there, the Maronite Christians. Great Britain received the mandate for Palestine and, with it, a simmering Arab–Jewish conflict that boiled over as Zionist colonization expanded. Partly to restrict that colonization, as well as to assuage Arab concerns and perhaps soothe their own guilt about their shabby treatment of the Hashemites, in 1921 the British carved off the eastern portion of the Palestine mandate as a separate entity, Transjordan, which they placed under the rule of Husayn ibn Ali's son Abdullah. The following year, they informed the League of Nations that Transjordan would not be open to Jewish colonization – an act that many Zionists even today regard as a betrayal. After World War II, Transjordan became the independent Hashemite Kingdom of Jordan. To this day, it has been ruled by Abdullah's descendants. The current king, Abdullah II, is his great-grandson.

In June 1920, Iraqis from almost all sects, ethnicities, and back-grounds – Sunni and Shia, Arab and Kurd – rose up in armed insur-rection against the British mandate. Today, in the aftermath of the 2003 Anglo-American invasion and occupation, Iraqis look back upon the Great Revolt of 1920 with pride, as one of those few times in their history when they came together with a sense of common, national purpose. In fact, however, that resistance had no truly national basis or coordination. Kurdish insurgents worked independently of Arabs, and for their own reasons; some Arab sheikhs sided with the British because they hoped that British control would improve their own prospects, as we shall see it often did. A major center of resistance emerged around the Shi'ite shrine-cities of Najaf and Karbala, where local tribes put up stout opposition and were among the last insurgents to knuckle under to the British. The Shi'ite religious leaders in those holy towns had been opposed to Husayn's Revolt in the Desert, as it had allied the Hashemites with the infidel British.[18] Their persistence was to cost them dearly. When the British re-established control – and later orchestrated the creation of a Sunni monarchy – they regarded the Shiʻites as untrustworthy. This was the same position in which the Shiʻites had found themselves during Sunni Ottoman rule. It was to persist under the British and worsen in the decades to come.

In the end, the Great Revolt of 1920 was brutally quelled by British troops (many of them Indian), who were authorized to resort to scorched-earth tactics and summary arrests and executions. As many as nine thousand Iraqis were killed or wounded, at a cost of two thousand casualties – including around 450 killed – to the empire. Instrumental to the British success was a terrifying new kind of coercion – aerial bombing by the Royal Air Force. Well into the 1920s and 1930s, the British frequently dispatched the R.A.F. to strafe and bomb recalcitrant tribes into terrified submission, especially when they refused to pay taxes.[19] Winston Churchill even authorized in 1920 the use of chemical weapons, although there is no proof the R.A.F. actually used them.

A major incentive for such heavy use of the R.A.F. was to try to achieve success as cheaply as possible. Expense had become by then a huge consideration in British thinking about Mesopotamia. The Iraq revolt was a wake-up call for the British government and the British public. The cost in British lives in 1920 was compounded by the growing sense that direct British rule would never work there and by the escalating clamor in Britain that the "Mesopotamian mess" was becoming prohibitively expensive. It tied down tens of thousands of troops and burned through millions of pounds, at a time when Britain was reeling from the horrific toll that the Great War had exacted. The British still fully intended to control the region – their interests in India, and in Iraq's oil, dictated that – but they now recognized that British control had to be masked with an Arab face and a veneer of Arab self-determination if Iraqis were ever to buy into it enough to make the arrangement work for Britain.

A useful and willing Arab face was readily at hand: that of Faisal ibn Husayn, whom the French had evicted from his fledgling Arab kingdom at Damascus. In 1921, after conferring in Cairo with Middle

East officials and experts – among them Gertrude Bell, an intrepid traveler and writer who was to play an influential role in shaping the new Iraq – British Colonial Secretary Winston Churchill jump-started a process to install Faisal as king of Iraq. On the ground in Iraq, that process was carefully stage-managed by Percy Cox, who had arrived in Iraq in 1920 to serve as the British high commissioner, replacing Arnold Wilson, whose installation in 1918 had been as a replacement for Cox, who had been temporarily reassigned to negotiating a new treaty between Britain and Persia. The elaborate charade that Cox crafted to grease Faisal's progress to the kingship featured a "referendum" – Faisal garnered an improbable ninety-six percent of the vote, most of the north not participating – and the elimination of Faisal's only potentially significant rival, a respected local notable from Basra. Cox invited the man to tea, but then had him arrested and eventually deported to Ceylon.[20]

Thus, on 23 August 1921, with High Commissioner Percy Cox and a British honor guard on hand while the notes of "God Save the King" wafted over the blistering summer heat, Faisal, son of the Hashemite Husayn ibn Ali of the Hejaz and brother of the soon-to-be emir of Transjordan, was crowned king of the newly named Kingdom of Iraq.

By itself, a coronation could not rescue Faisal from the precarious situation he was in. Given his efforts to establish an independent Arab state in Syria, he obviously sympathized with the cause of Iraq's self-determination, like many of his new subjects. Yet the only natural constituency he could claim among those subjects consisted of the Sunni city-dwellers of Baghdad, for whom he represented the continuation of the Ottoman-era rule by a Sunni minority over a growing Shi'ite majority, and those Arab officers who had signed on with the Hashemite cause during the war and then accompanied him to Iraq. So, to hang onto his kingship, Faisal needed to keep British support but at the same time signal to his new subjects that he rejected Britain's mandate as an insult to Iraqi sovereignty.

Securing approval of the resulting Anglo-Iraqi Treaty of 1922 required some British high-handedness and strong-arming of local Iraqi opponents.[21] From the standpoint of Faisal and the British, it was a win–win outcome. Only a year after his coronation, and after dogged insistence, Faisal succeeded in wresting from Britain an agreement that incorporated at least a pretense of sovereignty for Iraq and a bilateral relationship with Britain. For the British government, the treaty signaled to a restive British public that it was moving toward divesting itself of the expenses of the mandate, but at the same time it included various stipulations to ensure that they, and not Faisal, would be calling the shots in Iraq. Faisal had no choice but to go along with it.

By the terms of the treaty, the British reserved the right to station the R.A.F. at bases in Iraq. Well into the 1930s, they used that airpower to quell uprisings (especially among the Kurdish tribes of the north), maintain civil order, enforce the payment of taxes to Faisal's government, and thereby keep Faisal's kingdom whole. In a precursor of the "shock and awe" air tactics that the U.S. military unleashed against Saddam Hussein's regime in 2003, Iraq provided the British military a handy laboratory for testing newly developed theories about the application of fearsome air-strikes that could terrorize and thereby pacify villagers with incendiary bombs and night raids. Relying on the R.A.F. also enabled the British to avoid the costs of maintaining a large garrison of imperial troops. All the while, they rejected Faisal's ambitions of creating a large Iraqi army, based on mass conscription. Such an army, Faisal hoped, might help foster a new sense of Iraqi national identity.[22]

The treaty also gave the British ultimate control over Iraq's foreign relations. They used that control to further British interests in the region, including securing Faisal's kingdom. But some of their actions stored trouble for later Iraqi rulers and the wider Middle East. In 1922, Percy Cox steamrolled Iraq, Kuwait, and the fast-emerging, aggressive new power in the Arabian Peninsula, the al-Saud family and its sheikh Abdul Aziz ibn Saud, into an agreement that has defined these countries' boundaries ever since. Cox wanted to buffer Faisal and the new Iraq against ibn Saud, even though for years the British had been providing the latter a hefty stipend that he could use to build his influence and diminish that of the Hashemites. The solution that Cox insisted on – reportedly by drawing the new boundaries onto the map with his own pen – accomplished that, but it also left Iraq with a very short coastline on the Persian Gulf. Sixty-eight years later, in 1990, when Saddam Hussein sent Iraqi forces to occupy Kuwait, he cited this slight as part of his rationale. And Saddam was not the first of Iraq's rulers to try to forcibly rectify Cox's solution. On the other hand, Faisal's father, Husayn ibn Ali – who by now had proclaimed himself the caliph – was not lucky enough to retain Britain's favor. A few years later, in 1924, ibn Saud expelled Husayn from the Hejaz and into exile; he died in 1931, in Amman, the capital of his son Abdullah's emirate of Transjordan. It did not take ibn Saud long to establish himself as ruler of a new kingdom, formally named in 1932 the Kingdom of Hejaz, Najd, and Dependencies. We know it today as the Kingdom of Saudi Arabia – and Ibn Saud and his sons have ruled it ever since.

The ability of Britain's policies in the 1920s to store up trouble for the future of Iraq was not limited to foreign policy. As we have seen, when the Ottomans attempted to secure their control of Iraq in the late nineteenth century, one of their policy imperatives was to undercut the power of Iraq's myriad Arab and Kurdish tribes.[23] The British largely turned that policy on its head – by means of what one scholar has termed the "rational imposition of a romantic figure":[24] they elevated the sheikhs' status by treating them as mini-autocrats who spoke authoritatively for their tribes. This approach was motivated in part by the British tendency to romanticize the tribesmen as the more trustworthy, nobler element in Arab society, in contrast to the supposed deviousness and decadence of the "town Arabs," who had been tainted by too many years' association with the "pathological degeneracy" of their city-based Ottoman overlords.[25] Mark Sykes – co-author of the Sykes–Picot Agreement – once characterized them as "cowardly," "insolent yet despicable," "vicious as far as their feeble bodies will permit."[26] Ironically, these town Arabs included many of the same Sunni Arab elite who were Faisal's chief backers. The British also seemed to assume that ultimate control over tribal lands also lay in the sheikhs' hands. The reality was more complex. Traditionally, tribal members had exercised a largely communal ownership of land. The British authorities were oblivious of that tradition, or else they simply felt that it needed modernizing according to their more rational, "civilized" assumption that land ownership was the prerogative of individuals, not communities.[27] They bestowed upon the sheikhs the legal authority to register thousands of acres of tribal lands as their own personal property.

Seldom has such cultural cluelessness birthed greater misery, or had such a massive long-term effect. The sheikhs – as well as enterprising townsmen whose ranks would come to include Baghdad's government officials and politicians – soon carved out for themselves huge personal estates, especially in the largely Shi'ite regions of the south. With the possibility of irrigating thousands more acres with newly developed motorized pumps, these new landowners were positioned for a bonanza. The statistics tell the story plainly. Whereas in 1913 only 937,000 acres were under cultivation, in thirty years that acreage had mushroomed to 4,242,000; and by 1958 one percent of the country's landowners held fifty-five percent of all its private land. As they grew wealthy, many of the sheikhs headed for the attractions of city life, leaving behind thousands of tenants, sharecroppers, and landless laborers upon whom the absentee landlords set hired managers who sucked mercilessly from them the profits of their labor. Those who worked the land struggled perpetually with poverty (often the product of inescapable debt) and poor health. Later, many fled to the cities, only to find opportunities limited and continued poverty awaiting them. The need to address their misery has played an immense role in shaping Iraq's politics and social tensions ever since.[28]

The British decision to empower the sheikhs was the product of what by the 1920s was an entrenched sense of their own mastery of the subject peoples of their empire, whose thinking, they believed, they had an innate ability to penetrate.[29] In the case of Iraq, it was also the product of an ignorance rooted in romanticized, quasi-racist views of Arab social and moral values which are reminiscent of the long history of Western antipathy toward the Middle Eastern "Orient" of Babylon and Islam. Those views extended even to their opinion of their man in Iraq, King Faisal, whom Percy Cox once characterized as a man immoral and over-sexed, beneath whose skin lurked his "racial weakness."[30] British attitudes toward Faisal also reflected an underlying belief that the Arabs in general were incapable of self-government. Even as sympathetic a figure as Gertrude Bell, who by the end of her life in 1926 had become Faisal's most influential British counselor, once declared that "the oriental is like a very old child,"[31] characterizing Iraqis as mute and passive beings who aspired to benign British rule, since an independent Iraq would be a disaster.[32] Passive, mute, weak, over-sexed, essentially incompetent – all of these are traits that "orientalizing" Europeans since Herodotus had defined as characteristic of Middle Eastern people.[33]

ENTER OIL

In their minds, then, the British had good reason to be wary of Faisal's motives and dependability and to put little stock in his ability, or willingness, to protect their interests in the kingdom they had created for him. But when an exasperated Winston Churchill, fed up with Faisal's demand for a treaty ending Britain's mandate, considered withdrawing the British presence from Iraq entirely, David Lloyd George counseled caution, for, "If we leave, we may find a year or two after we have that we have handed over to the French and Americans some of the richest oilfields in the world."[34]

Even before the war, as we have seen, the British had begun maneuvering to stake their claim on Iraq's oil wealth. The war had hardly ended when the American and European press began hinting that Britain's willingness to accept a mandate in Mesopotamia stemmed from its hopes of controlling Iraq's oil. [35] They had good reason to believe so, for by August 1918 the British Foreign Office had decided that because the only sources of oil that Britain controlled were those in Persia and Mesopotamia, Mesopotamia could not be allowed to remain under Turkish or Arab rule – a decision that contravened an earlier decision that the British empire was not to expand as a result of the war.[36] As early as 1919, the prospect of international tensions over access to Iraq's oil riches loomed when the British refused to allow geologists from the American oil giant Socony (Standard Oil Company of New York) to enter the country. American protests grew even louder in the wake of the 1920 San Remo Agreement, which, besides defining the French and British mandates in the Middle East, also divided the oil wealth of the region between those two powers. Nonetheless, the British and Americans soon decided to work together in exploiting Iraq's oil: the British knew they could not develop Iraq's fields on their own, and the Americans knew they needed the British to maintain a strong stabilizing presence in Iraq if the oil was to be exploited. In 1922, seven U.S. oil companies informed the U.S. State Department of their desire to work with the British oil concession in Iraq. Through a pact that has come to be known as the Red Line Agreement, this decision led in 1928 to the creation of a Euro-American cartel that for the next few decades monopolized oil production throughout much of the Middle East.[37]

Around the same time, the British decision in November 1918 to rush forces from Baghdad to occupy the Ottoman vilayet of Mosul in northern Iraq – where oil was known to lie – paid off in a big way. In the early 1920s, Iraq's claim on the Mosul region was briefly contested by Mustapha Kemal Ataturk, the founding father and first president of the new republic of Turkey, which declared its independence in

1923. Because the region had a substantial Turkish population, Kemal hoped to annex it to the new Turkish state. In 1925, however, the League of Nations apportioned Mosul to Iraq – a decision it might not have taken were British forces not already occupying it. Without Britain's help in securing Mosul from both Turkey's aggrandizement and local Kurdish resistance, the viability of Faisal's Iraq would have been crippled, perhaps fatally – and Faisal knew it. In that same year, the British were able to leverage their assistance to Faisal in retaining Mosul to coerce him into granting a seventy-five-year concession to the T.P.C. In 1929, the T.P.C. was renamed the Iraq Petroleum Company (I.P.C.). Each of its four major shareholders – the British-dominated A.P.O.C., Royal Dutch Shell, the French firm Compagnie Francaise des Petroles, and the Near East Development Corporation (comprising five U.S. oil companies including Standard Oil of New Jersey and Socony-Vacuum) – received a 23.75% share; the independent entrepreneur C. S. Gulbenkian held a smaller share. Thus American oil corporations acquired a major interest in Iraq's oil. Within a few years, the I.P.C.'s concession was expanded to include areas near Mosul and Baghdad. Moreover, U.S. interests in Middle Eastern oil in general were ratcheted up when in 1933 the new king of Saudi Arabia, Abdul-Aziz ibn Saud, awarded a sixty-year concession to Standard Oil of California, and in the following year U.S. and British oil firms received a joint conces-sion to form the Kuwait Oil Company. In 1938, major deposits were discovered in both countries.[38]

In 1927, the I.P.C.'s first oil well came in near Kirkuk, in that same Ottoman vilayet of Mosul the British had been so intent on occupy-ing.[39] The discovery of oil brought the promise of great wealth and, one might think, a great boon to the government and people of Iraq. But, although the Hashemite monarchy did receive some royalties, its share in the I.P.C. was zero. Faisal had at first insisted that his government be given twenty percent ownership of the Iraq Petroleum Company, but he was forced to agree to a deal that allowed his government no shares in the company. Britain's assistance to Faisal in hanging onto Mosul had come at a steep price indeed.

Thus, when the new treaty signed with Britain in 1930 declared Iraq a fully independent state – which, in reality, it certainly was not – and ushered it into membership in the League of Nations in 1932, the government of Iraq had no control over what was to become by far Iraq's most important natural resource.[40] As had happened so many times during Mesopotamia's millennia-long history, its natural bounty had become its curse.

THE BIRTH OF IRAQI AND ARAB NATIONALISMS

History abounds with states that, after centuries of gestation, have spawned within themselves what Benedict Anderson calls the "imagined community" of "nationhood."[41] Some states (like Germany) have achieved this largely on the basis of ethnic, cultural, and linguistic unity; others (like Great Britain and France) have achieved it on the basis of a shared experience of political development and unification.

When Britain midwifed its birth in 1921, the new state of Iraq could claim as its birthright none of these unifiers. Its people had gone from being subjects of an empire that encompassed a huge and diverse region, to citizens thrust into the modern, Western structure of the nation-state. Even when Iraq achieved formal independence with the Anglo-Iraqi Treaty of 1930, the possibility of its achieving "nationhood" still seemed far off. Iraq's peoples were divided by a plethora of conflicting identities. Relations among them were often plagued by mutual distrust and antagonism born from long historical experience. Iraq's Arabs, Kurds, Persians, and Turkmen were all proud of their distinctive identities. They professed a variety of religious affiliations: Sunni and Shi'ite Muslim, Assyrian and Chaldean Christian, Jew, Yazidi, Mandaean, and others. Compounding this were deep-seated rivalries among the dozens of tribes, as well as the distrust that for millennia had characterized urban–rural/nomadic relations. This was hardly a good starting point for constructing a nation.

Moreover, in 1932 these people were ruled by outsiders whom the British had ensconced in Baghdad. The Hashemites who ruled Iraq were "a small clique, imposed on the country from the outside, which had few claims to the acceptance, approbation or trust of the rest of the population," while "the British authorities retained supreme power, and the vast majority of the population continued to be excluded from any meaningful participation in government."[42] If Iraq's history since 1932 is any guide, it remains uncertain whether a cohesive, sustainable, truly inclusive "Iraqi" identity that all of the people of Iraq can buy into can be built to last over the long haul.

The story of modern Iraq has been dominated by the struggle to create such an identity, or to impose it. In the twentieth century, Iraq became a cradle of new, sometimes competing national identities. It became a crucible in which they were forged, and from which they were asserted in response to Western intrusion and domination.

Before he ascended the throne of Iraq at Baghdad in 1921, Faisal had attempted to create at Damascus, the other great capital of Arab past political greatness, a new kingdom in which he might bring together under one rule the Arabic-speaking peoples of much of the former Ottoman empire. The concept of an overarching unity of the Arab-speaking peoples – their identity as a nation – had begun to take root years earlier. During the nineteenth century, the idea of the nation and nationalism led ethnic groups in the Ottomans' Balkan territories to proclaim their nationhood and assert their right to political autonomy by rebelling against the rule of the sultan. By the late nineteenth century, Arab intellectuals in Syria (many of them Christians) had begun to reflect upon, and write about, the distinctive history and contributions of the Arabs, their past greatness, as well as their essential unity as a "nation;" a development that has since been labeled the "Arab

Awakening."[43] By the time the British made Faisal the king of Iraq, he and his cadre of former Ottoman military officers were steeped in the emerging ideology of Arab nationalism. Faisal and his officials now seized upon it as a promising means of crosscutting the sectarian and tribal divides of Iraq's people to create a new basis for citizenship in the Iraqi state – that is, for "Iraqiness." Unfortunately for Iraq's future, there was no real place for the Kurds or the Turkmen in an Iraqi identity founded mostly on "Arabness."

Over time, Arab nationalism found a welcoming home in the Iraqi army. But the effort to develop a sense of Iraqi Arab nationalism was spearheaded in Iraq's schools. It was led by Sati al-Husri,[44] a former Ottoman education official who had served Faisal first as director of education in his aborted Syrian kingdom and was then appointed by him in 1921 as Iraq's director of general education. Under his leadership, Iraq became the cradle of the earliest "coherent theory of Arab nationalism."[45] Over the next four decades the ideology of Arab nationalism – or "pan-Arabism" – was to dominate political discourse across the Arab world and provide a new focus of both identity and response in the face of Western domination. Although it was an Egyptian leader, Gamal Abdul Nasser, who, from the early 1950s until his death in 1970, became the most recognized and celebrated face of Arab nationalism, it was in Iraq that Arab nationalism as a viable political ideology first took shape.

Sati al-Husri's most significant method of fashioning and inculcating Arab nationalism in Iraq was through a national education program that used new textbooks to target Iraq's young people in the schools. Seizing on the German model of nationalism, Husri designed the textbooks to imbue in young students a strong sense of the past glories of the great Arab people, as well as the conviction that the great Arab people had been artificially and forcibly divided, first under the Ottomans, then by the Europeans' mandate system. Only by reuniting those disparate parts could the Arab people regenerate that greatness and become a nation.

Sati al-Husri's efforts were not limited to textbooks and schoolrooms. In 1934, he was appointed director of antiquities in Iraq, a position that he used both to assert Iraq's claims to its ancient heritage – major portions of which had been grabbed by British and French archaeologists – and to focus attention on the Arabness of ancient Iraq, in an attempt to "integrate the pre-Islamic heritage with the pan-Arab ideology."[46]

By the same time, however, there had also emerged in Iraq a competing, more localized Iraqi nationalism that focused on the ancient greatness of Iraq as a homeland and of Iraqis themselves – whatever their religion or sect – as the descendants and heirs of the civilizations of ancient Sumer and Babylon. Even before World War I, during the last years of Ottoman rule, several authors – among them Shiʻites and Christians as well as Sunni Arabs – writing in the journal *Lughat al-Arab* had referred to the land of Iraq as a "homeland" (*watan*). During the mandate era of the 1920s, Shiʻite intellectuals contributed to Iraq's newspapers numerous essays celebrating Iraqi nationalism as well as Sunni–Shiʻite cooperation against the British.[47] Perhaps ironically, a significant contributor to this development was one of Faisal's chief British advisors, and one of the architects of the new Iraq, Gertrude Bell, who before her untimely death in 1926 helped found the Iraq National Museum in Baghdad. Despite damage and looting suffered in the wake of the 2003 invasion, it remains a leading repository of Sumerian and Babylonian antiquities, including those discovered by the Anglo-American expedition led by Leonard Woolley at Ur from 1922.

Thus, by the 1930s, two related but distinct versions of nationalism had begun to develop in Iraq. Although they shared an emphasis on the cultural and political unity of the Arabs, one version reserved a special place for patriotism that focused specifically on Iraq and asserted both its special identity within the larger Arab framework and its special right to serve as the natural leader of the Arab people. Iraq-centrist Arab nationalism competed with the other, more pan-Arab nationalism that was spreading across the Arab Middle East – with, as we will

266

see, major consequences for Iraq's later history and its relations with the Arab world.

Left out of such visions of Arab-centered Iraqiness, of course, were the Kurds of northern Iraq. During the Ottoman era they had often been outside the realm of effective Ottoman authority. In the new Iraq, from early on, the Kurds were again marginalized, and they have remained so to a greater or lesser extent up to the present. Although Arab nationalism emphasized a secular, non-religious basis, the reality was that the vast majority of Arabs across the Middle East who embraced it were Muslims and, to be specific, Sunni Muslims. In Iraq, then, Arab nationalism came to be identified increasingly with the Sunni Arab minority who ruled Iraq under the Hashemite region and indeed under all regimes until 2003, and Iraq's majority Arab Shi'ites came to distrust it as an ideology designed to keep them subjugated within a large Sunni-ruled state. That perception was reinforced in 1933 when a new book referred to Iraq's Shi'ites as "Sassanids," hearkening back to the seventh-century Arab conquest of Mesopotamia from the Sassanid Persians of Iran, and also accused them of being more loyal to Shi'ite-dominated Iran. The Shi'ites responded emphatically, attacking the government's security forces, whose new Iraqi flag they associated with the forces of the "evil" Caliph Yazid who had martyred Hussein and his followers at Karbala in 680.[48]

THE NATIONALIST RESPONSE TO BRITISH DOMINATION

Arab nationalism established especially strong roots in Iraq's new army. From the outset, Faisal hoped to nurture a sense of Iraqi Arab nationalism by developing a large army of mass conscripts, but, to his annoyance, his British overseers insisted on a less expensive, relatively small military to be bolstered by the power of the R.A.F. Nonetheless, as the Iraqi army grew throughout the 1930s, especially after conscription was introduced in 1934,[49] and into the 1940s, its officer corps became the most powerful institutional locus of Arab nationalism in the country. By 1936, it had also become politically powerful enough that, in a precursor of the decades ahead, its commander-in-chief, Bakr Sidqi, was able to overthrow the civilian government. This military coup was encouraged by King Faisal's son and successor, Ghazi I, an Arab nationalist whose brief reign ended only three years later when he was killed in an automobile accident. Because his son, Faisal II, was only four years old when his father died in 1939, Ghazi's cousin and brother-in-law, Abd' al-Ilah, stepped in as regent and remained head of state until 1953, when Faisal II assumed the throne. But the military assumed ever greater importance in Iraq's politics, removing and installing new governments almost at will until 1941.

Even as Arab nationalism took deep hold in the military, some of Iraq's civilian political leaders continued to believe that Iraq's fortunes – and their own – lay in continuing allegiance to Great Britain. Chief among them was Nuri al-Said, a native of Baghdad who had fought in Faisal's Revolt in the Desert and had been a prominent member of the King's entourage from the beginning. It is fair to say that from the creation of the Hashemite kingdom in 1921 until its demise in 1958, Nuri al-Said was the single most enduring and influential fixture in the Iraqi political firmament. Between 1930 and 1958 he served several stints as prime minister. Even when he was not prime minister, he excelled at manipulating the government and fashioning policies from the wings. His policies generally looked to preserve the interests of the traditional Sunni elite and the tribal landlords, often against what became increasingly louder calls for land reform and social justice on behalf of the rural poor and urban working classes. He also tended to enforce those policies with repression and brutality, when necessary calling upon the army and police to quell popular opposition.

Nuri tended to hew closely to British dictates. Among the military, on the other hand, Arab nationalism acquired an increasingly anti-British

flavor, born largely out of resentment at the continued British domination of Iraq, which the 1930 Anglo-Iraqi Treaty had cemented. Another
factor contributing to that resentment was the increasingly volatile situation emerging in Britain's mandate in Palestine, where Arab resistance
to burgeoning Zionist Jewish settlement – largely by emigrants fleeing
Nazi anti-Semitism in Europe – had led by 1936 to a general strike and
subsequent rebellion by an angry and fearful native population.

Resentment came to a boil in Iraq in 1941, after Nuri al-Said was
replaced as prime minister by an anti-British nationalist, Rashid Ali al-
Gailani. Rashid Ali soon antagonized the British by sympathizing with
both the anti-Zionist Palestinian Arab leader Hajj Amin al-Husseini,
who had fled British-controlled Palestine for Baghdad in 1939, and
Adolf Hitler's regime in Nazi Germany, with which the British had
been engaged in a desperate struggle since September 1939, when the
German invasion of Poland had launched World War II. When Rashid
Ali declared that his government would not allow Britain the military-
basing rights stipulated in the 1930 treaty, the British, with the support
of the Shi'ite tribes around Baghdad, forced Rashid Ali to step down.
When, in turn, the largely Arab-nationalist leadership of the Iraqi army
overthrew the new government and reinstalled Rashid Ali as prime
minister, the British landed troops at Basra, quickly overpowered the
Iraqi forces, and reoccupied the country. With Britain's acquiescence,
the monarchy was reinstated and Nuri al-Said once again installed
as prime minister. Immediately, he began to purge Arab nationalists
from the ranks of the military's officers, as well as close down clubs and
organizations whose members included pan-Arabists. Thus, when the
Arab nationalist tide began to rise in the early 1950s, Iraq's military had
no cadre of young Arab nationalists ready to sail with it. It would fall
to Egypt's young nationalist officers to lead the way.[50]

Nuri was not completely out of touch with concepts of Arab political
self-determination. He had been a fervent supporter of the Hashemite
cause during World War I, and as late as 1943 he advocated the formation

of an Arab "Fertile Crescent" league[51] comprising Transjordan, Syria, Palestine, Lebanon, and ultimately Iraq and Saudi Arabia (but excluding Egypt). Nuri continued to dominate Iraq's politics after World War II, but the British reoccupation of Iraq thoroughly discredited both him and other pro-British civilian politicians in the eyes of many of their countrymen, especially those who embraced pan-Arab nationalism.

It also sealed the doom of the Hashemite monarchy. Although it would survive for thirteen more years after the end of the war, it would eventually be drowned in the rising tide of Arab nationalist, anti-West anger that crested in the 1950s and 1960s across the Middle East.[52] The British presence would be expelled, only to be replaced by the West's new standard-bearers in the region: the United States and Israel. As their power emerged, Iraq's fortunes would hang in the balance.

ARAB AND IRAQI NATIONALISM, THE COLD WAR,
THE EMERGENCE OF ISRAEL, AND THE POISONED BLESSING OF OIL

Although they were among its victors, World War II weakened the status of both Britain and France as Great Powers. Buckling under their now straitened economic and military circumstances along with the demand from the peoples of their vast empires for freedom from foreign domination, they began to withdraw from their colonial possessions across the globe. No region was more affected by this development than the Middle East. Even before the war had ended, France's former mandates in Syria and Lebanon had achieved formal independence, and by 1962 France would also lose its grip on Morocco, Tunisia, and Algeria.

Britain's presence in the Middle East had been motivated by three imperatives: to protect access to India, which meant controlling the Suez Canal and Persian Gulf; to protect their mandate in Palestine, where they had pledged to establish a Jewish homeland; and to protect their access to oil in Iran and Iraq. But in 1947 Britain gave up its possessions in India, and the independent states of India and Pakistan came into being. This reduced somewhat the strategic necessity to control the Suez Canal. In the same year, having abandoned their mandate in Jordan in 1946, leaving Abdullah ibn Husayn, brother of Faisal I, to become the first king of the newly named Hashemite Kingdom of Jordan, Britain also decided to call it quits in Palestine, where British policies had alienated both Arabs and Zionists, who were now in violent conflict both with each other and with British occupying forces. In May 1948, the new state of Israel was proclaimed, one day after the last British troops left Palestine. As a harbinger of what has become a strong partnership, U.S. President Harry Truman immediately extended diplomatic recognition to the new state – against the advice of his secretary of state and much of the U.S. diplomatic establishment. The creation and rise of Israel to dominate the Middle East was to have immense impact on Iraq's history.

Although World War II had undercut the viability of European colonies and empire across much of the globe, Britain tried to cling to its position in Iraq. The British regarded Iraq as vital to their interests; it was a critical nexus of communication links within what remained of their empire. Moreover, as an ally of the United States in its postwar rivalry with the Soviet Union, Britain needed to be able to offer military support to the U.S., but it could launch a military strike against the Soviets only from the Middle East, which made hanging onto military prerogatives in Iraq yet more imperative.[53]

And the war had only accentuated the towering strategic significance of Britain's access to the oil of Iraq and Iran. Modern military defense, industrial production, and economic growth were now predicated on oil. It was because of the need to ensure access to a sufficient supply of oil that in 1945 U.S. President Franklin Roosevelt, recognizing that the United States' domestic petroleum deposits would not in the long run satisfy U.S. demand, met with Saudi King Abdul Aziz ibn Saud to shore up America's relations with his oil-rich country. Roosevelt promised him that the U.S. would take no actions in Palestine that might injure Arab interests.

Britain, meanwhile, relied on oil from elsewhere in the Middle East. In Iran, the Anglo-Iranian (formerly Anglo-Persian) Oil Company (A.I.O.C.) still controlled production, with the bulk of the profits going to Britain. In Iraq, the I.P.C.'s agreements with the Hashemite monarchy starting in the 1920s had cemented its control over oil production – and revenues – in the country. But because some of the partners in the I.P.C. consortium were already producing oil from deposits in other countries (e.g., the A.I.O.C., in Iran), the I.P.C. was slow to ramp up production in Iraq. In 1934 the I.P.C. completed two pipelines to link its Kirkuk fields to Mediterranean ports at Tripoli (in French-controlled Lebanon) and Haifa (in British-controlled Palestine), but none of the Kirkuk oil was shipped out until 1938. Moreover, during the war the Allies decided that their oil needs could be supplied less dangerously from American sources across the Atlantic, which further deterred the exploitation of Iraq's oil. As late as 1946, Iraq's oil production was only 4.6 million tons per annum, with revenues of 2.3 million Iraqi dinars – paltry amounts compared with what the I.P.C. would be extracting a few years later.[54] Because the I.P.C. was so closely tied to British influence in Iraq and because the fortunes of the Hashemite monarchy depended so much on British goodwill, the Iraqi government had brought little pressure to bear on the I.P.C. to increase production. But after 1945, with Britain's postwar global status diminishing and anti-colonial voices ever louder across the Middle East, control of Iraq's oil production and revenue became a rallying point for Iraq's increasingly outraged nationalist movements.

Another rallying point for Arab nationalists both in Iraq and across the Arab world was the anger provoked by the West's support for the creation of Israel. In 1947, the newly formed United Nations enraged many across the Middle East by voting to partition Palestine into separate Arab and Jewish states, Jewish settlers being apportioned land in which in some instances they were a tiny minority. Between 1947 and

1949, the military successes of Jewish/Israeli forces in Palestine dis-possessed and forced into exile hundreds of thousands of Palestinian Arabs. In the process, they also defeated decisively the armies that had been dispatched from several Arab states, including Iraq, to oppose them. The resulting anger and sense of humiliation were directed at Israel and its U.S. and European supporters, and, tragically, at Jewish communities across the Middle East.

Well into the 1920s, Iraq's Jews were accepted as citizens of the new state of Iraq. Especially those among the urban middle class could embrace an emerging Iraqi nationalism that they saw as inclusive, even if it centered on Iraq's Arabs.[55] Many Iraqi Jews identified strongly as Arabs in language and culture. When Jewish colonization in Palestine began to increase rapidly in the 1930s, many among the Iraqi Jewish intelligentsia sided with the Palestinian Arabs. Nonetheless, Jewish communities in Baghdad, whether pro-Zionist or not, were vilified, especially by pro-Arab nationalists, who identified them with the British occupiers of Arab Palestine and rejected Iraqi Jews' claims to Iraqi identity. When the British forced the anti-Zionist Rashid Ali from power in 1941, Baghdad's Jews were targeted for reprisal in a massacre that took two hundred Jewish lives and left the Jewish community doubting their future in Iraq.

In 1947, Iraq's Jews numbered around 117,000. Between 1948 and 1952, "Zionism, Arab nationalism, and Communism each played their part in making Iraqi Jewish identity into a 'question' or a 'problem.'"[56] Jews, along with Kurds and the southern Shi'ite tribes, were reviled as disloyal and dangerous to the state. Their vilification was further spurred by some young Iraqi Jews' embrace of Communism as a force for social justice and resistance to British influence. Using anti-Zionist sentiment as a cover, Nuri al-Said responded by spearheading the promulgation of laws that discriminated against Jews.

In the wake of the government's threats to expel them after Israel's defeat of Arab forces in Palestine in 1948–49, and with the encouragement of the new Israeli government, the vast majority of Iraq's Jews emigrated from the country. By 1952 only a few thousand remained. With the rise of Arab nationalist governments in Iraq starting in 1958, and Israel's further military victories against Arab countries and its continuing subjugation of the Arab Palestinian population, their numbers have dwindled further since then.[57] Thus came to an end the vibrant community of Babylonian Jewry, which for 2,500 years had been a vital component of both Iraq's history and culture and the development of Judaism.

Arab nationalist outrage in Iraq also peaked early in 1948 when Iraqis became aware that their government, at British insistence, had secretly negotiated a new treaty with Britain that would extend British influence in Iraq a further fifteen years beyond the date established in the 1930 treaty. Outrage against the Portsmouth Treaty combined with anger about the British involvement in the 1947–48 crisis in Palestine to spark violent protests, known as the Wathba ("Leap"), that forced the government to abandon the treaty.[58]

From 1950 to the end of the Hashemite monarchy in 1958, the history of Iraq was dominated by the struggle between the Iraq-centered, pro-West Hashemite regime and the eventually victorious tide of pan-Arabist Arab nationalism. To a great extent, that struggle can be seen as embodied in the careers of two men: the Iraqi kingpin Nuri al-Said, and the Egyptian officer Gamal Abdul Nasser, who by 1955 had become the most celebrated leader of the pan-Arabist form of Arab nationalism. Each was intent on making his country the leader of the Arab world. One may note the parallel with Egypt and Mesopotamia as the two great poles of power and civilization in the Middle East thousands of years before.

Although Iraq's actual heads of state were the Hashemite regent Abd' al-Ilah and (from 1953) King Faisal II, Nuri al-Said was throughout this period the real strongman of Iraqi politics. To carry out his policies, Nuri was increasingly able to rely on the financial clout provided by the oil revenues that by the mid-1950s were finally flowing into the state's treasury. In 1952, inspired by a model created by Venezuela to secure a more just share of oil profits, and by the example of Iraq's neighbor Iran, where the nationalist leader Muhammad Mossadeq had taken the popular but extreme step of nationalizing his country's oil, enraging Britain in the process, the Iraqi government secured a fifty–fifty split of oil profits with the I.P.C. Between 1951 and 1954, the contribution of oil revenues to the Iraqi government's budget shot up from thirty to sixty-five percent. Agriculture, for millennia the greatest source of Mesopotamia's wealth, contributed only three percent. Oil production skyrocketed from 4.6 million tons in 1946 to 35.8 million tons in 1958, revenues increasing from a little over two million Iraqi dinars to almost eighty million in that span.[59] Under Nuri, seventy percent of the oil money was allocated to a government-controlled Development Board for funding infrastructure projects. At a time when tens of thousands of Iraqis had woefully inadequate access to education, medical care, or even food, and the average life expectancy of an Iraqi peasant was only thirty-nine years,[60] Nuri decided to fund projects, like land reclamation and irrigation systems, designed to bolster the regime's political support among the elite landowner class. When groups protested against Nuri's policies, he could turn to a mostly compliant military to crush them. This was hardly a new wrinkle in Iraqi politics; he was following a precedent established in the earliest days of the Hashemite era, when Faisal I relied upon the British military, especially the R.A.F., to enforce his writ. But in the 1950s Nuri was also creating a broader template that future Iraqi regimes – from 1958 to the end of Saddam Hussein's regime in 2003 – would employ: using oil profits to purchase public support, and using the state's security apparatus to crush all opposition.[61]

Rising among the ranks of the opposition to both Nuri's regime and British influence by the 1950s was the increasingly popular Iraq Communist Party (I.C.P.), one of several groups clamoring for the government to improve the economy and living conditions for ordinary

Iraqis. The I.C.P. also developed a following among the restive Kurds of northern Iraq, where Kurdish ethnic nationalism had been emerging as a political and military force under Mustafa Barzani and the Kurdish Democratic Party (K.D.P.), a new force that was to play a major role in Kurdish and broader Iraqi politics for decades to come.

Meanwhile, resentment of the former colonial powers burgeoned across the postwar Middle East. Nuri al-Said remained convinced that Iraq's survival – and especially that of his own government – depended upon retaining the support of Great Britain and, increasingly, the U.S., upon whom he relied more and more for the weapons needed to modernize Iraq's army and thereby, he hoped, maintain the allegiance of its officer corps.[62] Although anti-Western Arab nationalists in Iraq resented the Anglo-American-controlled I.P.C., he generally went easy on it, despite growing complaints that the I.P.C. was under-exploiting its oil concessions, depriving the Iraqi government of badly needed revenue. When in 1955 Nuri brought Iraq into the Baghdad Pact, a military alliance engineered by the United States, he sailed the Iraqi ship of state squarely into a maelstrom of anti-imperialist anger swirling across the region.

That anger had been fired by the meteoric rise of a man who even today is widely regarded as the greatest superhero of pan-Arabist Arab nationalism: Gamal Abdul Nasser. He was one of the leaders of a revolutionary cadre of young Egyptian military officers (the "Free Officers") who in 1952 overthrew the British-dominated monarchy of King Farouk in Egypt and expelled the King into exile. By 1955, he had taken control of the government of the new republic of Egypt. Nasser was first and foremost an Egyptian patriot. According to one expert, he "slid into Arab nationalism through the back door of anti-imperialism."[63] But now his fiery appeal to pan-Arab unity against the West fired the ardor of anti-Western anti-imperialists across the Middle East. Nasser disseminated his message via stirring broadcasts over Voice of the Arabs radio, which the advent of the transistor radio had made accessible to thousands more listeners. His popularity approached its apogee in 1956 when, after the U.S. had reneged on its offer of a major loan to build the Aswan High Dam, a centerpiece of Nasser's plans for Egypt's modernization, he nationalized the Suez Canal. He stood defiantly in the face of the invasion that the combined forces of Great Britain, France, and Israel launched against Egypt in what became known as the Suez Crisis of 1956.

It was the U.S. President, Dwight Eisenhower, who bailed Nasser out of a nasty situation. Angered by their action, Eisenhower forced the aggressors to back down. In doing so, he closed the book on British ascendancy in the Middle East. He also won considerable Arab goodwill for the U.S., only to squander it the following year when he enunciated what became known as the Eisenhower Doctrine: hereafter, the U.S. would take the lead in providing military and economic assistance to any Middle Eastern country imperiled by the advance of Soviet-backed Communism. Only months later, in 1958, Eisenhower dispatched U.S. marines to the streets of Beirut in support of a Christian-dominated, pro-West government of Lebanon that was threatened by a rising tide of what the U.S. perceived as Communist-supported Arab nationalism.

Despite Eisenhower's role in saving him, it was Gamal Abdul Nasser who emerged as the hero of Arab nationalists and anti-imperialists. He was soon able to parlay his new clout into the high-water mark of pan-Arabism: the formation of the United Arab Republic (U.A.R.), the political union of Iraq and Syria, in 1958. Many of Iraq's Arab nationalists wanted their country to join it. Among them was a new political group that was eventually to evolve into the dominant party in Iraqi politics. Founded in Damascus in 1947, the Baath ("Renaissance") Party was based on the ideology of pan-Arabism – that an indivisible Arab nation had been wronged and arbitrarily divided by Western imperialists. They also emphasized a secular basis for governing the state, in which the interests of religion and state were to remain separate; one of the party's founders and intellectual godfathers, Michel Aflaq, was a Syrian

Christian. The Baath also demanded social justice. To that end they merged in 1953 with the Arab Socialist Party to form the Arab Socialist Baath Party. In the early 1950s, the Baath established themselves in Iraq, where they aligned themselves against the Hashemite monarchy's pro-West stance and as allies of Nasser's scheme for pan-Arab political unity. Their early success in Iraq owed in no small part to their appeal to both Sunni and Shi'ite Arabs, which by the late 1950s had helped to reduce sectarian tensions. In the decades to come, that would change.

Nuri al-Said was extremely wary of Nasser's pan-Arabism and resentful of Egypt's rise to rival Iraq as a leader of the Arab world. As always, he remained steadfast in his conviction that the Hashemite monarchy's survival depended on the support of the West. Therefore, when the Western powers came courting with an invitation to an alliance, he was ready to be wooed. In 1955, he signed on to the U.S.-engineered Baghdad Pact, thereby casting Iraq's lot with the imperialists and – in a further outrage to Arab nationalists – with their non-Arab Middle Eastern lackeys Turkey and Iran. In 1955, with the Cold War with the U.S.S.R. well underway, the U.S. hoped that this alliance, into which Nasser's Egypt was not invited, of a "northern tier" of Middle Eastern states would block Communist expansion into the Middle East.

Arab nationalists in Iraq – and Nasser – were infuriated by Nuri's decision. Iraqis were even more outraged when Britain joined Israel in attacking Nasser's Egypt during the Suez Crisis. When riots erupted in Basra, Baghdad, and Mosul, and even in the Shi'ite shrine-cities of Najaf and Karbala, the government was forced to declare martial law.[64]

Fatefully for the monarchy, the outrage now took hold in the Iraqi army, where a cadre of younger nationalist officers plotted to rid Iraq of the Hashemite regime. Striking swiftly on 14 July 1958, Iraq's Free Officers, led by Brigadier Abdul Karim Qasim and Colonel Abdulsalam al-'Arif, took control of Baghdad and the royal palace. The young Faisal II, Crown Prince Abd' al-Ilah, and most other members of the Hashemite family were taken into the palace courtyard and shot. Nuri al-Said evaded capture for a day, but on the next day he was found on the streets of Baghdad, trying to escape clad in a woman's over-garment, and shot. He was quickly buried, but an enraged mob dug up his body and dragged it through the streets. Reportedly, one of the Iraqi officers cut off one of Nuri's fingers and later presented it to Nasser in Cairo as a gift, but Nasser was disgusted.[65]

Thus ended the career and life of a man who had dominated Iraq's political life throughout the duration of the Hashemite monarchy and, perhaps more than any other, embodied Britain's domination of that country. Thus also ended the Hashemite monarchy of Iraq, never to be resurrected. It had been created in the image of a British model of constitutional government, and its leaders had hoped that it might become an independent, truly self-governing Arab nation-state. But it had been forced to keep itself propped up by its Western patrons, and its aspirations to parliamentary democracy had been kept in thrall to a narrow traditional elite of urban notables and landowners, most of them Sunni Arabs, who were motivated more by greed and the interests of their family or clan than by an impulse to serve the public good or build a nation.[66] In the process, they alienated most of their Shi'ite and Kurdish fellow citizens. The regime was terminated at the hands of what now became the dominant elements of Iraqi politics: the military, and Arab nationalism.

THE REPUBLIC: COMPETING NATIONALISMS,
RESISTANCE TO THE WEST, AND NEW WEALTH

As we noted near the beginning of our exploration of Iraq's history, historians have traditionally felt compelled to slice up history into neat, easily digested chunks, usually on the basis of major political change. Customarily, they have divided Iraq's twentieth-century history at July 1958, between the monarchy and the republic – and with good reason, for the upheaval that led from one to the other kicked off major changes, most notably the elimination of Britain's hated influence over Iraq's leadership. On the other hand, the republic showed several continuities from the monarchy, and it continued to do so right up to its overthrow by the U.S.-led invasion of 2003.

Throughout its history, the republic was based on the rule of a strongman able to call upon the state's security apparatus to repress opposition, stifle dissent, and forcibly keep the Iraqi state together. This was hardly a new pattern in Iraq's history. During the earliest days of the Hashemite monarchy, Faisal I relied on the British military, and then on his own, to enforce his government's writ. In the late 1940s and 1950s, when Nuri al-Said dominated the government, either as prime minister or from the wings, he had few compunctions about sending in the Iraqi military to quell political opposition. He was able to depend on it until almost the very end.

The revolution that ended the monarchy and installed a republic in 1958 brought the continuation of an authoritarian state, in the form of a de facto military dictatorship, under Brigadier General Abdul Karim Qasim, who was made prime minister of the new government and also commander-in-chief of the military. During the early years of Qasim's tenure, however, many Iraqis had high hopes for a more inclusive regime that would tend more to the needs of the rural and urban poor for education and health care. The new leadership included represen-tation of Sunni, Shi'ite, and Kurd alike, and Qasim at first reached out to the Kurdish leadership in the north. Qasim's regime also promoted leftist, secularist ideas and reached out to the I.C.P. But a new law that was enacted to redistribute land to help the rural poor earned Qasim the resentment of the traditional landlord class who had been stalwart supporters of the monarchy. Another new law designed to better the legal rights and status of women, combined with Qasim's secularist orientation and embrace of the Communists, brought him the resent-ment of religious conservatives – most notably, the Shi'ite clergy of Iraq's shrine-cities. There now emerged in Iraq a more activist expression of Shi'ism that featured an especially lasting development: the formation of a Shi'ite religious party known as al-Da'wa ("the Call"), under the spiritual guidance of a highly respected mullah, Muhammad Baqir al-Sadr. Over the following decades, al-Da'wa and other Shi'ite parties championed traditional Shi'ite values against the secularist values that dominated under the regimes of Qasim's republican successors; and scions of the al-Sadr lineage became – and remain today – heroes of Shi'ite resistance to the republic. The last two years of the Qasim regime were also plagued with civil war against the Kurds, who, it turned out, were supported by the Baath. Thus, on the eve of the Baath Party's overthrow of Qasim in 1963, Iraq's national unity was in shreds. Qasim had styled himself as the embodiment of the Iraqi state. By the end, he was referred to – not approvingly – as "Sole Leader."[67]

Subsequent regimes were similarly authoritarian in nature – and increasingly brutal in their use of intimidation, even torture, to quell dissent. When the Baath briefly assumed power in February 1963, they cracked down on the I.C.P., killing as many as three thousand members. By November they had been ousted, to be succeeded by five years of military dictatorship, first under Abdul-salam al-'Arif and then, after his death in a helicopter crash, under his brother, the ineffectual Abdul-rahman al-'Arif. Although he came to power ostensibly as an Arab nationalist, Abdul-salam al-'Arif soon turned to an Iraq-first brand of nationalism, underpinning his power with his kinship, tribal, and patronage ties within the officer corps.[68] In 1968, the Baath Party regained power and established a dictatorship that was at first headed by a Baathist military officer, Ahmad Hassan al-Bakr, but came increasingly under the control of his chief lieutenant, Saddam Hussein,[69] who forced out al-Bakr in 1979 and ruled Iraq as its president until ousted by the invasion of 2003.

Under Saddam, the authoritarian tendency in modern Iraq reached a level previously unseen. Saddam's rise to power was predicated in part on his development and control of a highly organized and diversified security and surveillance apparatus (the Mukhabarat), which one expert has described as "the best organized and most efficient secret service in the Arab world."[70] Its functions included "electronic surveillance, secret operations, counterintelligence, propaganda, surveillance, and military industrial security."[71] Employing secret police, torture, incarceration, and summary execution, as well as an enormous bureaucracy that was employed to keep files on suspected dissenters, Saddam consolidated his power by intimidating and eliminating rivals and dissenters both in the military and in Iraqi society as a whole.[72] He created what one commentator called a "republic of fear."

Especially during the 1980–88 war with Iran, Saddam also orchestrated a cult of personality that focused on himself as the embodiment of the Iraqi state. Its best modern parallels are the cults of personality that centered on Joseph Stalin in the Soviet Union and Adolf Hitler in Nazi Germany. But despite his gargantuan efforts to present himself as the champion of Iraq, hero of the Arab world, and leader of the Baath Party, Saddam's ability to rule Iraq depended on the loyalty of a tightly knit core of old friends and tribal relations largely from his home region of Tikrit and the surrounding Sunni Arab northwest of Iraq. Rather than ideology, the true basis of his power was the ties of kinship and patronage that had characterized much of Mesopotamian/Iraqi society for centuries. Saddam's ability to use those patronage ties was invigorated from the 1970s on by a massive infusion of oil wealth.

THE CONTINUING DEVELOPMENT AND IMPACT OF IRAQI AND ARAB NATIONALISM UNDER THE REPUBLIC

One of the most important features of the Hashemite era was Iraq's emergence as a cradle of Arab nationalism. Faisal's political rise during and just after World War I was tied to that. His reign was distinguished by the success of his education minister, Sati al-Husri, in disseminating the ideology of pan-Arabism in Iraq's schools. As we have seen, however, there also emerged in Hashemite Iraq a competing, more Iraq-focused form of Arab nationalism that likewise recognized the essential unity of the Arab people, but emphasized the ancient greatness of Iraq as a homeland and of the Iraqi people as the heirs of ancient Sumer and Babylon. Nuri al-Said's notion of nationalism was of this variety, but by the mid-1950s its incompatibility with pan-Arabism was accentuated by the surging popularity of Nasser.

Much of the history of the Iraqi republic revolves around the tension between these two aspects of Arab nationalism, and how it was eventually resolved. In the process, Iraq became perhaps the most potent embodiment of some of Arab nationalism's central tenets: resistance to the Western imperial powers and Israel, and the separation of politics from religion. But, as one commentator notes, the struggle between the rival versions of nationalism "left scars that remain today," including "a legacy of escalating violence and ruthlessness that worsened as time went on."[73]

From the outset, the road to republican Iraq's assumption of the mantle of Arab nationalist leadership had many twists and turns. The cadre of Free Officers who overthrew the monarchy in 1958 were inspired by Nasser's example, and professed their allegiance to the Nasserist principle of pan-Arab unity.[74] Some among them – notably, Abdulsalam al-'Arif – hoped that Iraq might be folded into Nasser's U.A.R.

But Qasim rejected any union of Iraq with the U.A.R. and temporarily removed al-'Arif from the local political scene. To widen the distance between his regime and Nasser, Qasim steered Iraq away from Nasser's pan-Arab nationalist ideal and toward a more Iraq-centered nationalism. He encouraged historians and archaeologists to focus on Iraq's ancient Mesopotamian ancestry and antiquities, with the purpose of promoting a Mesopotamian-Iraqi national identity that both crosscut the country's ethnic and sectarian divisions and separated Iraq from the pan-Arab mainstream. In the process, he alienated his pan-Arabist colleagues and provoked an assassination attempt by pan-Arabist dissidents – among them, the young Saddam Hussein.

Even as he dampened down the forces of pan-Arabism, Qasim took steps to assert Iraq's sovereignty over territories that, according to pan-Arabist doctrine, non-Arabs had separated from the Arab nation. He further strained his already tense relations with the Shah of Iran – who was already emerging as one of the U.S.'s chief proxies in the region – by asserting Iraq's rights over the predominantly Arab region of Khuzistan, in Iran's southwest, even going as far as to refer to it as "Arabistan." Foreshadowing Saddam Hussein's actions in 1990, Qasim also tried to assert Iraq's claim to the newly independent kingdom of Kuwait, on the grounds that before Britain had made Kuwait its protectorate via a treaty in 1899, Kuwait had been part of the Ottoman province of Basra, one of the constituent parts of Iraq when it was created after World War I.[75] He even appointed Kuwait's ruler as its "district governor." As in 1991, Qasim's actions were not allowed to stand; British and Arab League troops saw to that.

The installation of the al-'Arif regime after Qasim's overthrow in 1963 brought a brief resurgence of Nasser's style of pan-Arabism in Iraq. But within a few years the comet of pan-Arabism was flaming out. In June 1967, after years of steadily rising tensions with Nasser and his Arab allies, Israel launched a preemptive strike that, after six days, left the Egyptian military beaten and humiliated, more Arab lands (Jerusalem, West Bank, Gaza Strip, Golan Heights, and Sinai Peninsula) under Israeli occupation, and Nasser's pan-Arab ideal discredited. Nasser's defeat opened the door for Iraq to become the most powerful Arab nationalist state. But his passing from the scene may also have had a less fortunate impact on Iraq. His heyday instilled in many Iraqi Arabs a stronger sense of their "Arabness," one that paid little notice to Sunni and Shi'ite sectarian differences. The disillusionment that set in after 1967 – and the emergence of Islamism at the same time – may have contributed to a re-sharpening of the sectarian division that had previously beset Iraq.[76]

As the mantle of pan-Arab leadership slid off Nasser's shoulders, Iraq's leaders were positioning themselves to replace him. The coup that ousted Abdul-rahman al-'Arif in 1968 brought the installation of the Baath regime that ruled the country until 2003. The Baath had originally established itself as a pan-Arabist party that stood for the political union of the disparate Arab states. But from the 1970s onward the Baath leadership found it expedient to meld its pan-Arabism with an Iraq-first nationalism of a type that Qasim had favored more than a decade before.

These two ideals of nationalism played to divergent emphases in Arab and Iraqi history. Pan-Arabism focused on the ancient greatness of the Arab peoples, with allusions to the nobility, valor, and hardiness of the pre-Islamic Arabs as well as the imperial and cultural heights the Arabs had reached under the Abbasids of Baghdad. Iraq-centrist nationalism, although it by no means disregarded the greatness of the Arab past, plumbed Iraq's history more deeply, by emphasizing also the greatness of the pre-Arab civilizations of ancient Mesopotamia – knowledge of which, ironically, had been furnished largely by archaeologists of the colonial powers the Baath reviled.[77] In his formulation of Arab nationalist history, Sati al-Husri had disdained any summoning up of Iraq's pre-Arab greatness as tantamount to trying to restore flesh to a mummified corpse. But with the Baath's "Project for the Rewriting of History," "Iraqi national existence was given a breathtaking history of five thousand years – extending from the Dawn of the Dynasties, through Akkad, Babylon, Assur, and Chaldea, the Arab conquests, Harun ar-Rashid and his Abbasid Golden Age, and all the way to Saddam Husayn."[78] In the 1980s, when he faced the necessity of rallying an Iraqi collective identity to withstand the Iranian army, Saddam Hussein appealed to that past, making copious use not only of images of heroes from the Arab golden age but also images of the glory of ancient Mesopotamia, from featuring an Assyrian winged bull from Nineveh on Iraqi currency to having himself depicted in the warlike image of one of the all-conquering Assyrian kings, shooting arrows from the back of a chariot. Saddam also lavished funds on the exploration of Mesopotamian antiquity, including archaeological excavations and an international congress of Assyriologists that was slated to be held in Baghdad until the events that led to the 1991 Gulf War forced its cancellation. But the centerpiece of it all was Saddam's rebuilding of the ancient ruins of Babylon, where he authorized the use of bricks commemorating the work in cuneiform. He also had one of his royal palaces built at the site.

After Nasser succumbed to a heart attack in 1970, Egypt tossed away the torch of pan-Arab leadership. His successor, Anwar al-Sadat – another of the Free Officers who overthrew King Farouk in 1952 – tried to regain the Sinai from Israel by launching a surprise attack in October 1973, only to be beaten back after a stunned Israeli military, facing possible defeat, was resupplied by the U.S. In 1978, Sadat succeeded in regaining the Sinai, after negotiations at Camp David with U.S. President Jimmy Carter and Israeli Prime Minister Menachem Begin resulted in a peace treaty between Egypt and Israel. Sadat became a heroic peacemaker to many around the world, and received a Nobel Peace Prize, but in the Arab world, he – and Egypt – became a pariah. The country that had been the vanguard of pan-Arab unity against Israel and its Western patrons had become the first Arab country to break the Arabs' common front against Israel. Jordan would soon follow, under its Hashemite king Husayn, the grandson of Abdullah bin Husayn. The pan-Arab torch was picked up and held aloft by Iraq, which took the lead in organizing an Arab summit meeting from which emerged in 1980 an Arab Charter calling for solidarity against foreign aggressors. That call was directed principally against Israel, but also at a new threat to both Arab solidarity and Arab nationalism's secular orientation: the new Islamic Republic of Iran. By 1980, it was increasingly obvious that the Baath's push for leadership in the mostly Sunni Arab world would only shunt further to the margins of the regime's tender mercies the largest component of Iraq's population – the Shi'ite Arabs – as well as the non-Arab Kurds. [79]

IRAQ'S CONQUEST OF ITS OIL UNDER THE REPUBLIC

Without a doubt, the Baath's campaign during the 1970s and beyond to rewrite history was invigorated by the sudden, massive infusion of funds from Iraq's oil wealth. Throughout the history of the monarchy, oil had been a major point of contention between the Iraqi government and the foreign oil companies to whose interests Faisal I had so often been forced to accede. Nonetheless, by 1958 both production and revenue had increased almost exponentially from what they had been twenty years before. However, when Qasim's regime came to power, there was still considerable frustration with the I.P.C.'s failure to exploit its concessions more diligently. Its policy of delay was costing the Iraqi government millions of dollars of much needed revenue.

Whatever his failings as a pan-Arabist, some of Qasim's actions aimed to address one of pan-Arabism's most important goals: standing up against the Western colonial powers and their oil companies. Qasim set himself squarely against the United States by taking Iraq out of the Baghdad Pact and turning to the Soviet Union for military and economic aid (undoubtedly one of the reasons why the U.S. said nothing when the Baath removed and killed him – possibly with American encouragement). Iraq remained in the Soviet orbit for the next two decades. Qasim also took on the long-time instrument of foreign domination of Iraq's economy: the I.P.C. When the I.P.C. rejected his demands for increased government ownership, he promulgated a law in 1961 that dispossessed it of 99.5 percent of its concession, on the grounds that the I.P.C. was failing to exploit it. The Iraq National Oil Company (I.N.O.C.) was formed as the state's instrument for exploiting these fields. In reprisal, the I.P.C. cut back production to starve Qasim of revenue. This back and forth continued until 1967, when the al-'Arif regime decided that I.N.O.C. was to have exclusive rights to the vast Rumaila oilfield in the south. (To develop that field, al-'Arif turned to the Soviet Union.) By 1973, the Baath government had nationalized the I.P.C.'s and all other foreign oil concessions in the country.[80]

A decades-long struggle had finally been ended, in Iraq's favor. The foreigners had been booted out, and Iraq's oil finally belonged to Iraq. The money truly began to roll in during the 1970s when the oil-producing countries (especially the members of OPEC – the Organization of Petroleum Exporting Countries – which had been founded in 1960, and whose membership included the major Middle Eastern oil-producing states) took control of production and oil prices. The price of oil skyrocketed throughout the 1970s and again, when Iran's revolution caused a reduction in the oil supply from that country, in the early 1980s. The consequences were dramatic, both for global consumers and for oil-rich countries. The increased price of gasoline led automobile manufacturers to start building more fuel-efficient models.

Iraq profited immensely. Between 1972 and 1980, Iraq's oil revenues mushroomed from U.S.$575 million to U.S.$26 billion or more. As billions of dollars flowed into Iraq's treasury, the Baath government used the funds first and foremost to serve its own interests, but to that end it began to provide Iraqis with a standard of living that the population outside the elite had never seen. By 1980, Iraq's standards and availability of education, health services, electricity production, and large-scale industry were among the most advanced in the Arab world. On the other hand, using oil revenue to augment goods and services effectively bought the public's acquiescence in the rule of an authoritarian, one-party state – which could – and did – crush any dissent. Oil revenues also made taxation unnecessary. The regime could do what it wanted.[81]

A major portion of those revenues (U.S.$4.5 billion in 1975, com-
pared with U.S.$500 million only five years before) were also used to
build a powerful military along with an industrial complex that was
used to develop potent weaponry and munitions. Courtesy of a 1972
"Friendship Treaty" with the U.S.S.R., the Iraqi army and air force
acquired an up-to-date arsenal stocked with advanced Soviet weaponry and warplanes. Iraq also took steps to develop nuclear capability
by purchasing nuclear reactors from France. One of those reactors,
Osirak, was constructed within a few miles of Baghdad. Predictably,
this set off alarms among Israel's leadership, who had been eyeing
Iraq's military build-up with growing concern. The Israeli response
was devastating and provocative. In June 1981, the Israeli air force
launched a surprise attack that destroyed the Osirak reactor before it
became operational.[82]

The Israeli action was condemned by the U.S. and in the United
Nations, but Saddam had nonetheless been harshly confronted
with Iraq's vulnerability. His response sowed the seeds of his own
destruction and his country's devastation: he authorized the continued development of chemical and biological weapons at secret locations dispersed across Iraq, and he launched a program designed to
provide Iraq with nuclear-weapons capability. That step, more than
any other factor, was seized upon as reason for launching the U.S's
invasion in March 2003.

In the immediate wake of the Israeli raid, Iraq launched no military
reprisal. In 1981 Iraq was dealing with a more dire threat that an over-
confident, over-reaching Saddam had brought down upon his country.
He took a country that had begun to achieve both a First World standard
of living and a position of primacy in the Arab Middle East, and set it
on a path to catastrophe and ruin.

8

THE LONG DESCENT

MODERN IRAQ WAS CREATED by Great Britain, and the first three decades of its history were substantially driven by its relationship with that imperial nation. With the 1958 revolution, those who had favored a continued dependence on British, and American, favor lost out to Arab nationalists who wanted more or less to sever Iraq's links to those powers. Iraq's nationalization of its oil was another major step in this prolonged process.

After World War II, all of the Middle East's nations were caught up in the jet-wash of Israel's turbulent emergence as the dominant regional power. Global geopolitics were largely shaped by the West's need to ensure its access to Middle Eastern oil and by the Cold War between the U.S.-led "Free World" and the Communist Soviet Union and its bloc of allies. After 1979, simmering Cold War tensions were stoked further by a completely unforeseen development: the revolution that overthrew the Pahlavi Shah of Iran and gave birth to the Islamic republic that still governs Iran today. That development raised to a new level the tensions of what was already a strained relationship between Iran and Iraq – and added a new dynamic of hostility to Iran's relations with both the United States and Israel. The matches that lit many of the geopolitical fires of this era were all too often struck in what one writer has aptly named the "tinderbox" that is the Middle East.[1] All too often, Iraq lit the match – and caught fire.

A hundred years from now, when historians look back upon the history of Iraq and decide where and how to compartmentalize it into periods, they will surely point to 1980 as a watershed date, for that was the year when Saddam Hussein began to over-reach, both with the capabilities of his new military and with his self-assigned role as leader and hero of the Arab nation. In the process, he shattered whatever progress the regime might have claimed in bringing together Iraq's diverse communities into an Iraqi nation-state. He also set in motion a train of events that resulted first in the military defeat, then the economic blockade, and finally the invasion and occupation of his country by the Western powers against which he had pledged to defend it. Between the onset of Iraq's war with Iran in 1980 and the departure of the last American combat troops at the end of 2011, Iraq was devastated. Hundreds of thousands of Iraqis were killed or maimed, millions more were forced into external exile or refugee status inside their country, and most of those still living in the country were reduced to a Third World standard of living. As of 2010, to cite the British journalist Patrick Cockburn, Iraq was "recovering from 30 years of dictatorship, war and sanctions, and the recovery is grindingly slow and incomplete because the impact of the multiple disasters to strike Iraq after 1980 was so great…Iraq has never recovered from these catastrophes."[2]

REPUBLICAN IRAQ AND THE COLD WAR POWERS UNTIL 1980

Before 1980, Iraq's republican regimes had kept the U.S. and Britain at arm's length. Qasim even antagonized the British with his ill-fated push to reclaim Kuwait for Iraq in 1961. France came forward for a while as a significant military supplier. Then Qasim began to flirt with the Soviet Union, and in 1972 Saddam went to Moscow and negotiated a

Friendship Treaty that brought the Iraqi military an infusion of sophisticated weaponry.

Meanwhile, the U.S. had done a lot of courting of its own in the
region. From 1973, it supplanted France as Israel's most generous and
dependable military supplier; it has remained to this day Israel's most
reliable and powerful patron. Bolstered by that patronage, Israel inflicted
a major defeat on Egypt and its Arab allies in October 1973, intervened
militarily in Lebanon in the late 1970s during that country's devastating civil war, launched a massive invasion into Lebanon in 1982 and
occupied part of its south, and continued its occupation of Palestinian
Arab lands on the West Bank and Gaza, as well as the Golan Heights in
Syria. It also served as one of the U.S.'s chief proxies in the Middle East.

The other powerful U.S. proxy was the monarch of Iran, Shah
Muhammad Reza Pahlavi, whose power the U.S. had secured in 1953
courtesy of Operation *Ajax*, a coup engineered by the U.S.'s Central
Intelligence Agency, which ousted Iran's nationalist premier, Muhammad
Mossadeqh, who had antagonized Britain by nationalizing A.P.O.C. and
raised the suspicions of the U.S. by his tolerance of Iran's Communist
Party.[3] Throughout the 1960s and 1970s, as the Soviet Union lavished
assistance upon the Baathist regime in Iraq, the U.S. lavished assistance
upon the Shah – including some of the most sophisticated weaponry
in the U.S. arsenal and (ironically from the standpoint of 2015) the
go-ahead for Iran to develop a nuclear reactor.

Cold War tensions now played out along the Iran–Iraq border,
where the Kurdish nationalist-separatist movement played a featured
role. Under their stalwart leader Mustapha Barzani, Kurdish *peshmerga*
fighters rose again to thwart Baghdad's continuing efforts to dominate
Iraqi Kurdistan. In 1945, Barzani had taken refuge in the Soviet Union
after his attempt to establish a separatist Kurdish republic failed, but in
1971 the vicissitudes of Cold War politics enabled him to turn for help
to the U.S.S.R.'s foes: the Shah of Iran, Israel, and U.S. President Richard
Nixon, who authorized the C.I.A. to provide Barzani with U.S.$16

million of assistance. In 1974, full-scale war broke out between Barzani's fighters and the Baath's Iraqi forces. The Soviets rushed to Baghdad's aid, providing top-of-the-line fighter jets and Soviet pilots to fly them. But in 1975 Iraq came to terms with the Shah (in a treaty known as the Algiers Agreement, much reviled by Saddam Hussein, who would renege on it five years later). Sold out by the Shah and the U.S., both of whom now ended their assistance to him, Barzani was forced to flee. Saddam tried carrot-and-stick measures to win the Kurds' loyalty to the Arab-nationalist Iraqi state. He proffered the carrot by applying some of Iraq's oil revenue to the improvement of living conditions in the Kurdish north. At the same time, he wielded the stick with such brutal ferocity that the repercussions tear at Iraq's national fabric even today. He directed the military to demolish Kurdish villages along the Iranian and Turkish borders and tried to Arabize the region by forcing Kurds out and putting Arabs in.[4]

It was obvious, then, that just as the British had intended in setting up the monarchy, and the Ottomans had done before them, the Baath regime intended to rule Iraq as an elite Sunni minority over a marginalized majority comprising the Arab Shi'ites in the south and the Kurds in the north. The Baath predicated their legitimacy as rulers of the Iraqi state on melding Iraq-first nationalism with an ideological appeal to pan-Arabism. In so doing, they associated their own Sunni-ruled Iraqi state with the predominantly Sunni Arab political domination across the Middle East. When Anwar Sadat abdicated Egypt's position of pan-Arab leadership by making a separate peace with Israel in 1979, Saddam jumped to position Iraq as the new leader of the Arab world.

Although the Baath paid lip service to an Iraqi identity that crosscut sect and ethnicity, they refused to accommodate either the Kurds' sense of ethnic identity or their hope for the autonomy that had been promised them as early as World War I. The Arab Shi'ites, too, had felt welcomed by the Baath initially, and for a while during the 1970s the regime sought to buy their allegiance by devoting a substantial portion of Iraq's oil revenue to improving conditions in the Shi'ite south, and by recruiting more Shi'ites into the military and police.⁵ But in the 1970s the regime found itself increasingly confronted by a new Shi'ite political activism spearheaded by al-Da'wa, led by the Grand Ayatollah Muhammad Baqir al-Sadr, a leading member of Najaf's clerical establishment who commanded enormous respect among the Arab Shi'ite faithful. Al-Da'wa and al-Sadr reviled the Baath's secular and socialist policies. The regime responded with attempts to mollify Shi'ite sentiment, but also cracked down on Shi'ite political activism. Worse was to come.

In 1978 and 1979, after years of growing protests against the Shah's repression of popular dissent and his close ties to what many Iranians saw as the corrupting cultural influence – "Westoxication" – and overbearing political domination of the United States, Iran was convulsed by a violent revolution. The Shah was forced to flee into exile, where he soon died of cancer. Although the revolutionaries included figures of various political stripes, from Marxists and secular liberals to conservative Islamists, by far the most charismatic and energizing was the Ayatollah Ruhollah Khomeini. An Iranian Shi'ite scholar and spiritual leader, Khomeini had condemned the Shah's government in the early 1960s and then been forced to leave Iran. He eventually resided for thirteen years in Najaf, only to be hounded from there by Saddam and into exile in Paris in 1978. With the Shah's departure, Khomeini returned to Tehran in triumph. Several turbulent months later, Khomeini's supporters gained the upper hand and were able to proclaim Iran an Islamic republic, to be governed under the principle, espoused by Khomeini, of *velayat-i-faqih* – the primacy of Islamic religious leaders as appropriate leaders of the state. But Khomeini and the new Islamic republic incurred Americans' wrath when student supporters of Khomeini – initially without his approval – occupied the U.S. embassy in Tehran and then held hostage the American diplomatic contingent for 444 days before they were at last released.

Khomeini also condemned Saddam, who became Iraq's president in 1979, and the Baath regime as godless secularizers and persecutors of Islam. Caught in the middle were the mostly poor, often religiously conservative Arab Shi'ites of southern Iraq, whom Khomeini now called upon to rise up against Saddam. Among them were al-Da'wa and its leader, al-Sadr. Saddam quickly identified them as allies of the new threat on Iraq's eastern border.

It did not take Saddam long to strike. Al-Sadr was rounded up along with his sister and imprisoned, tortured, and on 9 April 1980 executed – according to one account, by having a nail driven into his head. Most of the other leaders of al-Da'wa fled into exile in Iran. Others fled to Syria – among them Nuri al-Maliki, who, thirty-six years later, was to become the prime minister of Iraq.

But, as far as Saddam was concerned, Iran and the Ayatollah Khomeini still had to be dealt with.

SADDAM'S QADISSIYA: THE IRAN–IRAQ WAR, 1980–88

In 1980, Saddam Hussein had both the motivation and the opportunity to attack Iran. The 1975 Algiers Agreement that he had signed with the Shah's government had fixed the boundary between Iraq and Iran much to the Shah's satisfaction. This boundary traversed the Shatt al-Arab waterway, where the agreement established the median (or thalweg) as the border between the two countries. Saddam, however, believed that Iraq was entitled to the entire waterway. And like Qasim before him, he also nursed the claim that Iraq was entitled to the predominantly Arab – and oil-rich – region of Khuzistan across Iran's southwestern border. Saddam assessed that, because of the purges that had eliminated many of Iran's officer corps, and the destabilization the revolution had spawned, and because the revolution had cost Iran the military support of the U.S., the time might be ripe to forcibly correct the 1975 treaty's provisions.

On 22 September 1980, Saddam sent six Iraqi divisions across the border into the southwestern Iranian regions of Khuzistan,

Khorramshahr, and Abadan – all of which contained major oilfields. He may have thought the affair would be over quickly: that Iran's leadership would knuckle under quickly to such a show of force and accept it as but one more episode in a long-running territorial dispute between fellow autocratic regimes, with, this time, Iraq coming out on top.[6] Instead, what Saddam got was fierce resistance and then a counter-attack from an implacable foe who demanded Saddam's removal and the termination of the Baath regime as the necessary conditions for Iran to lay down its arms.

From the Iranian leaders' viewpoint, the war was about much more than political rivalry and territory. They cast the hostilities as an existential conflict that pitted the forces of the divinely guided Islamic Republic of Iran against the godless secularism and socialism of the Baath regime. As late as the last year of the war, 1988, Iran's leaders insisted the conflict was about "a continuous confrontation between the righteous and the wicked." Khomeini declared the Islamic regime to be a "God-given absolute mandate" and "the most important of the divine commandments and [to have] priority over all other derivative commandments – even prayer, fasting and pilgrimage to Mecca."[7] Moreover, he deemed Saddam's aggression to be part of an international conspiracy, led by the United States, whose "hands…emerged from Saddam's sleeve."[8]

The result was total war – the most protracted war of the twentieth century. By its end, the Iran–Iraq War (known to some as the First Persian Gulf War) had devastated both sides, leaving scars that have yet to heal. It also gave the United States a pretext to intervene directly in the Persian Gulf – an ominous portent of what was to come. The Iran–Iraq War featured tactics and weaponry with which the West had become all too familiar in the two World Wars: ferocious tank and infantry battles, trench warfare, waves of foot soldiers mowed down by machine-gun fire, artillery shelling and aerial bombardment of major population centers, and attacks on merchant shipping. The

Iranians countered the Iraqi superiority in weaponry with human-wave attacks that involved unarmed adolescents, carrying keys that they were assured would unlock for them the gates of paradise, who marched into withering Iraqi gunfire, setting off Iraqi land mines and thus blazing a path for the Iranian infantry. In making martyrs of themselves they emulated the hallowed Shi'ite tradition of martyrdom that Imam Hussein, the Prophet's grandson, had modeled thirteen hundred years before at Karbala. Their sacrifice, coupled with the collective suffering of the Iranian people during the war and the propaganda of the Islamic regime, rallied the Iranian people to the regime's support.

To sustain public support in Iraq for the war, Saddam applied the state's resources to projects and propaganda designed to accentuate Iraqis' shared national identity, but simultaneously to focus on him personally as the heroic embodiment of the Iraqi nation. He summoned the ghosts of Iraq's illustrious history to create "a Mesopotamian national myth, designed to convince all Iraqis – Sunnis, Shi'a, Kurds, and Arabs – that they were all the genetic as well as cultural heirs of ancient Mesopotamia and its glories."[9] In 1982, to the dismay of archaeologists across the world, he reconstructed ancient Babylon, rebuilding the palace of Nebuchadnezzar with bricks stamped with the declaration, "In the era of Saddam Hussein, protector of Iraq, who rebuilt civilization and rebuilt Babylon." But as the war with Iran wore on, and as he strove to attract the political and financial support of his Arab neighbors, Saddam's conjuring of the shades of Iraq's past reached out increasingly to its legendary Arab heroes. The conflict with Iran was dubbed "Saddam's al-Qadissiyya," enabling Saddam to identify his coming victory over Iran with the celebrated victory of Arab warriors over the Sassanid Persians at Qadissiyya in 636. A twenty-five-dinar note of the time even featured Saddam's face juxtaposed with an imaginary scene of Arab horsemen charging into that battle. To attract the support of Iraqi Kurds, Saddam also associated his own image with that of one of the greatest of all Muslim heroes, Saladin, a Kurd who, like Saddam, was born in Tikrit. The Arab-Iraqi heroes who were thus celebrated were Sunni, serving both to reinforce Sunni Arab ascendancy in Baghdad and to celebrate Iraq's pan-Arab nationalist bonds with the Sunni-dominated Arab countries of the region, whose defender against the perfidious Persians and their "anti-Arab and reactionary, pseudo-Islamic contagion" Saddam styled himself.[10] Meanwhile, the authors whom Saddam entrusted with rewriting Iraq's history took pains to denigrate Shi'ite Arabs, whom they labeled as Persian sympathizers. Iran, Persians, and Persian culture were consistently reviled. Iranians were pilloried as "Magians" (i.e., Zoroastrians), and the Persian-inspired Shuubiya movement that centuries earlier had so enriched Baghdad's Abbasid era was demeaned as a Persian attempt to impose a culture that had falsely been regarded as superior to that of the Arab overlords.[11] In Saddam's telling, the Shuubiya's origins could be traced back to the era of Nebuchadnezzar, thereby broadening the anti-Arab conspiracy to include both the Persian Zoroastrians and the Jews whom Nebuchadnezzar had deported to Babylon – and thus implicate, by historical association, both modern Iranians and modern Israelis.[12] Saddam's effort to link Iranians and Israelis in a conspiracy against Iraq was not all that far-fetched. Three days after Iraq invaded Iran in 1980, Israeli Foreign Minister Moshe Dayan urged the U.S. to back Iran; and in 1982 Israeli Defense Minister Ariel Sharon announced that Israel, notwithstanding the ban announced by its U.S. patron, would sell arms to Iran.[13]

Yet, as much as eighty percent of the Iraqi infantry's ranks and twenty percent of its officers were, though Arabs, Shi'ite Muslims. From Saddam's perspective, their loyalties might be suspect. To try to dampen down any disloyalty, Saddam throttled down his repression of the Shi'ite clergy at Najaf; and perhaps to good effect, for although some of Iraq's Shi'ite soldiers did desert – and when apprehended were punished by having their ears and nose cut off – they never did mutiny en masse. As the war dragged on and the Iranian threat to Iraq grew more dire, Iraq's

Shi'ite soldiers by and large stood bravely against their Iranian fellow Shi'ites. When the war began they may have identified less as members of the larger Shi'ite community and more as members of local tribes and clans, but over the course of the war they came to perceive themselves more solidly as Iraqis.[14] However, among the Iraqi Arab Shi'ites who did support the Iranian side during the war were those exiles who in 1982 formed a pro-Khomeini group, the Supreme Council for the Islamic Revolution in Iraq (S.C.I.R.I.). Led by the Ayatollah Muhammad Baqir al-Hakim, who had fled to Iran in 1980, S.C.I.R.I. formed an armed wing to launch missions into Iraq. After returning to Iraq following the 2003 U.S.-led invasion, S.C.I.R.I. played a major role in establishing Shi'ite political domination in the wake of Saddam's fall.

By 1982, Iranian counter-attacks had reached into Iraq and put Saddam's army on the defensive. He found himself in a trap of his own making, knowing that surrender meant the end of his rule, but that the Iranians were vastly superior in manpower. So he opted for a brutal tactic: warfare by attrition, designed to inflict on Iran as heavy a cost as he could. Iraqi bombers devastated Iran's infrastructure. Saddam expanded their target list to include population centers, hammering the capital at Tehran but also symbolically potent centers such as the traditional Safavid capital at Isfahan and the Shi'ite seminary center at Qom. Khomeini reciprocated by blasting Baghdad and Basra with bombs and artillery. By 1988, Saddam's forces were also using cluster bombs against the Iranians. At least as early as the summer of 1983, Saddam unleashed his most horrific tactic: chemical weapons, starting with mustard gas but graduating in March 1984 to tabun – the world's first recorded battlefield use of a nerve gas.[15] Iraq may have used chemical weapons as many as 195 times, suffocating, burning, or blinding thousands of Iranian soldiers and civilians – according to Iranian sources, as many as fifty thousand.[16] Those not killed by suffocation were frequently left with chronic, often severe respiratory distress for the rest of their lives.

Such devastation was not reserved only for Iranians. Iraqi and Iranian forces battled for territory not only in the south but also along that part of their border that ran through the Kurdish region in the north. After 1986, the Iranians had the armed support of the two dominant Kurdish political parties – the K.D.P. and the Patriotic Union of Kurdistan (P.U.K.) – and their militias of *peshmerga* ("those who face death"). The K.D.P. even had a base inside Iran. Given the decades of Arab–Kurdish tensions that had characterized Iraq's history, it was to be expected that Saddam would crack down on the Kurdish insurgents, whom he saw as having sided with his enemy.

His actions went well beyond counterinsurgency. Between 1986 and 1989, his regime launched a campaign – named *al-Anfal* ("the Spoils") after a verse in the Qur'an – that arguably constituted an attempted genocide against Iraq's Kurds. [17] Saddam declared zones along the Kurdish border with Iran no-man's-lands and had two thousand Kurdish villages leveled. Although many of the dispossessed villagers fled into Turkey, Iran, or Syria, hundreds of thousands were collected into larger towns, where they could be monitored, and which also served as convenient points from which Kurdish men were transported to sites where they were executed en masse. An investigation by the human-rights N.G.O. Middle East Watch determined that, between February and September 1988, the Iraqi military killed at least fifty thousand – and possibly as many as 100,000 – Kurds, the vast majority of them non-combatants.

A significant number of those killed died in air attacks in which Iraqi forces used poison gas. World opinion was especially horrified by reports and photographs of the aftermath of the attack on Halabja, a Kurdish town whose population had mushroomed from forty thousand to eighty thousand in the course of Saddam's program of village demolitions and forced relocations. Located just inside the border with Iran, Halabja was in March 1988 fought over by Iraqi forces and the Iranians and their Kurdish allies. After the Iraqis had been driven out, they counter-attacked with poison gas. As many as five thousand towns-people were killed – most of them non-combatants, including women and children.[18] Halabja was not the only such incident. At least forty such attacks were launched, with Saddam's approval. Perhaps Saddam could not have anticipated the delayed impact of these atrocities, but in the run-up to the U.S.-led invasion of Iraq in 2003 his use of chemical weapons in the 1980s became part of the rationale for the invasion: he obviously possessed "weapons of mass destruction" (W.M.D.s) and, because he had used them to "gas his own people" (the Kurds), he would be willing to use them again.[19]

At the time, though, many people in the U.S. and Europe remained blissfully oblivious of these horrors. Their governments certainly were not. Before the start of the war, the U.S. had pretty much written off Saddam's Iraq as a Soviet client. Five years earlier, when Baghdad and the Kurds were engaged in civil war, the U.S.S.R. had rushed military aid to the Baghdad regime while the U.S. and Israel provided assistance to the Kurds. During the war with Iran, the Soviets for the most part remained on Iraq's side. But the overthrow of the Shah, the long imprisonment of American hostages in the U.S. embassy in Tehran, and the establishing of an Islamic regime that demonized the U.S. as "the great Satan" and proclaimed itself the vanguard of the coming worldwide Islamic revolution had turned both the U.S. political leadership in Washington and the American public in general squarely against Iran. Soviet client and brutal dictator that he undoubtedly was, Saddam received the blessing – and support – of the U.S. throughout the war that he had instigated.[20] As the New York Times journalist Thomas Friedman noted in an interview, "Yes, he was a thug – but he was *our* thug."

Thus, in 1984 – when it was already known that Saddam was using poison gas against Iran – the U.S. President Ronald Reagan graced Saddam with two cordial visits from his representative Donald Rumsfeld and then restored diplomatic ties with Iraq, which had been broken since the 1967 Arab–Israeli war. Perhaps just as central to U.S. interests in Iraq,

Rumsfeld was also tasked with lobbying Saddam for the building of a new oil pipeline to convey Iraq's oil to Jordan's port at Aqaba.[21] During the war, the U.S. provided Iraq with satellite-derived military intelligence, sold Iraq trucks and helicopters, and provided Iraq agricultural credits for food exports, thereby freeing up money to buy more weapons.[22] A British company built Saddam a chemicals-production plant, and the U.S. also provided Iraq with biological agents (including agents for anthrax and botulinum) that could be applied to weapons development. [23] By the later stages of the war, American officials in the State Department were quite aware that Saddam had used poison gas – illegal under the Geneva Conventions – against Iran's forces and Kurdish civilians, but they raised only a feeble protest, citing the need to maintain the U.S.'s now improved relations with Iraq. Some even claimed, on flimsy evidence, that it was Iranian forces, not the Iraqis, that had perpetrated the poison-gas attack on Halabja. Late in the war, the U.S. Congress passed a bill calling for weak economic sanctions against Iraq; but the bill never became law.[24] Some in Congress were appalled by the U.S.'s weak-kneed stance. Senator William Cohen of Maine declared, "It is the smell of oil and the color of money that corrodes our principles."[25]

In 1987, the U.S. military entered the fray openly, and on Iraq's side, after Reagan dispatched to the Persian Gulf a flotilla of some forty warships, including the aircraft carrier U.S.S. *Enterprise*. United States naval forces destroyed Iranian oil rigs and sank or crippled Iranian naval vessels. On 3 July 1988, in a tragic event that even today can rekindle Iranians' anger, the cruiser U.S.S. *Vincennes* shot down Iranair Flight 655 on a routine flight between Bandar 'Abbas and Dubai, having mistaken it for an Iranian fighter jet, killing all 290 people aboard. The year before, an Iraqi warplane had mistakenly fired two missiles at the destroyer U.S.S. *Stark*, killing thirty-seven American sailors. Although the incident heightened tensions with Iraq, the U.S. accepted the apology of Saddam's government. A U.S. Department of Defense official declared at the time, "We can't stand to see Iraq defeated."[26]

The entry of the U.S. military into the war was prompted not so much by fears of Iraq's defeat as by Iran's threat to the U.S.'s most important strategic interest in the region: the unobstructed transport of oil from Persian Gulf countries to global markets. The U.S. had asserted that interest unambiguously in January 1980, only nine months before the outbreak of the war, when Jimmy Carter enunciated in his State of the Union address what became known as the Carter Doctrine. In 1979, the U.S. and its allies had been alarmed by the Soviet Union's invasion of Afghanistan, which, in the U.S.'s reckoning, put the oil of the Gulf region into play. Carter now declared,

> The Soviet effort to dominate Afghanistan has brought Soviet military forces to within 300 miles of the Indian Ocean and close to the Straits of Hormuz, a waterway through which most of the world's oil must flow...Let our position be absolutely clear: An attempt by any outside force to gain control of the Persian Gulf region will be regarded as an assault on the vital interests of the United States of America, and such an assault will be repelled by any means necessary, including military force.

As noted by one prominent historian of the international oil industry, the Carter Doctrine hewed very closely to a declaration issued almost eighty years earlier (in 1903) by the previous Western oil hegemon in the region, Great Britain, warning Russia and Germany that Britain would "regard the establishment of a naval base or of a fortified port in the Persian Gulf by any other power as a very grave menace to British interests, and we should certainly resist it with all the means at our disposal."[27]

By 1987, provoked by Saddam's attacks on its oil infrastructure, Iran's reprisals were taking a significant toll on tankers shipping oil from Kuwait and the Gulf emirates, whose rulers had aligned themselves with Iraq, and the Iranian navy had also seeded portions of the Persian Gulf with anti-ship mines. Beyond the threat to oil transport in the Gulf, the U.S. also feared that an Iranian victory over Iraq might imperil even the oilfields and infrastructure of Kuwait and Saudi Arabia, which were major suppliers to the U.S. and Europe. Consequently, as well as engaging the Iranian navy and destroying Iranian oil rigs, the U.S. offered Kuwait the option of "reflagging" its oil tankers – that is, flying the U.S. flag from their masts – which would signal that they were sailing under the official protection of the U.S. Navy. Later, the U.S. extended the offer of reflagging to all neutral shipping in the gulf.[28] Meanwhile, Iran's military woes were compounded by a Saudi-led campaign by Iraq's Gulf allies to ramp up their oil production and thereby cripple Iran's economy by driving down the price of oil.[29]

Therefore, in July 1988, facing a resurgent Iraq bolstered by the military might and diplomatic muscle of the U.S., which effectively had entered the war on Saddam's side, the Ayatollah Khomeini announced that Iran would accede to United Nations Security Council Resolution 598, which almost exactly a year earlier had called upon Iran and Iraq to end the fighting. It was a decision, he said, "more deadly for me than taking poison."

Over eight years, the war had exacted an immense human cost, with more than a million people killed or wounded. According to conservative Western estimates, Iraq's dead numbered around 105,000, Iran's more than twice that number. Other estimates place the totals as high as 450,000 to 750,000 for Iran, and 150,000 to 340,000 for Iraq.[30] The scars left by that cost have marred relations between the two countries to the present day. Although relations warmed significantly after Saddam's downfall and the emergence of a Shi'ite-dominated government in Iraq, Iran's policies toward its neighbor have been governed since 1988 by a viscerally felt imperative to prevent Iraq ever again being in a position to wreak such horrific damage on Iran.

Throughout the war, Saddam styled himself as the embodiment of Iraq. It may well be, as one scholar has put it, that the Iran–Iraq War

marked the "high point of Iraqi identity."[31] Saddam elevated himself –
and Iraq – as the defender of the Arab nation against the perfidy of
Persia. But the Arab solidarity that Egypt had punctured with its separate
peace with Israel in 1979 was further deflated by the continuing hostility
of Hafez al-Assad, the President of Syria, toward Saddam. Ironically,
and tellingly, Assad, like Saddam, was the leader of an Arab-nationalist
state governed by the Baath Party.

THE CRISIS WITH KUWAIT

After eight years of war, Iraq could still boast a powerful military, with
a standing army of one million (out of a population of sixteen million)
and several hundred thousand more men under arms in local militias.
But the war had also thrust Iraq into massive debt. Saddam had been
able to sustain his war effort because the leading oil-producing Arab
countries of the gulf (the United Arab Emirates and especially Saudi
Arabia and Kuwait) had loaned his government billions of dollars. They
had little choice but to do so. All of them had weak militaries and thus
had to rely on Saddam to safeguard the passage of their oil through the
Gulf against the Iranian threat. With the war over, Saddam expected his
fellow-Arab creditors to demonstrate their gratitude by absolving Iraq
from repaying what they had loaned him. When they refused to do so,
Saddam focused his anger on Kuwait, accusing its leaders of producing more oil than the quota that O.P.E.C. allotted it – thereby driving
down the price of oil and crippling Iraq's own reconstruction – and of
stealing Iraq's oil by drilling diagonally from Kuwaiti soil into Iraq's
giant Rumaila oilfield.

Saddam also used his alleged grievance against Kuwait to resurrect
a territorial claim that previous Iraqi heads of state had advanced: that
Kuwait had been severed illegitimately from Iraq by British imperial
high-handedness and rightfully ought to be part of Iraq. When Qasim

had asserted Iraq's right to Kuwait in 1961, both Britain and the Arab League had sent military forces to compel him to back off. Now, in August 1990, after negotiations with Kuwait went nowhere, Saddam dared to go beyond simply reasserting that claim. He sent in troops, tanks, and helicopters that smashed Kuwait's forces and seized control of the country and forced its leaders into exile. Saddam proclaimed that Iraq had restored to itself what was rightfully one of its own provinces, and sent an Iraqi governor – his own cousin – to rule it.

Some still claim that when Saddam invaded Kuwait in the summer of 1990 he believed that the U.S. government would not oppose him and had given him the go-ahead to do so. That April, a visiting Congressional delegation had assured Saddam of the U.S.'s goodwill. Indeed, one senator blamed Saddam's public-relations troubles on the "spoiled and conceited" media in the West.[32] In late July, as his troops were massing at the border with Kuwait, Saddam met with the U.S. Ambassador to Iraq, April Glaspie, who assured him of President George H. W. Bush's friendship and informed him that the United States had no opinion concerning inter-Arab issues.[33] America had sided with him against Iran and professed a desire for closer relations with Iraq. Saddam may therefore have been convinced that the U.S. would readily acquiesce to his seizure of Kuwait.

Most members of the community of nations reacted with an outpouring of rage that Saddam truly seems not to have expected. Leading the chorus was his friend of only a few weeks before, U.S. President Bush, who declared to the world that Saddam's aggression "will not stand." From August through December 1990, the formidable military might of an international coalition massed in the Persian Gulf region. That effort was orchestrated by the leaders of a United States that had been invigorated by the break-up of its arch-nemesis, the Soviet Union, in 1989, an event that left the U.S. by far the planet's strongest military power and even inspired one notable scholar of international relations to trumpet the American ascendancy as the "end of history."[34]

The military build-up was hosted by Saudi Arabia, the country with the world's largest reserves of oil – and therefore a huge strategic concern for the U.S. – but also the land of Mecca and Medina, the two most sacred cities of Islam. King Fahd, their official protector, permitted hundreds of thousands of Christian and Jewish, American and European troops (many of them women) to mass in the land that Muslims worldwide revere as most holy to Islam. That perceived defilement was to later stoke the fury of the men – including Osama bin Laden – who perpetrated the terror attacks against the United States on 11 September 2001. At the insistence of the U.S., Israel did not join the coalition, which opened the door for contingents from most of the leading Arab nations to join up. Among them were Saddam's erstwhile benefactors Saudi Arabia and the United Arab Emirates, as well as Gulf Arab countries like Oman and Bahrain. Perhaps most notably, this huge coalition numbered among its ranks contingents from the two Arab countries that historically had been, with Iraq, the well-springs of pan-Arab nationalism: Egypt and Syria. Operation *Desert Shield* and its aftermath kneecapped the dream of pan-Arab nationalism as a viable political project.[35]

In August, the United Nations Security Council passed two resolutions to bring Saddam to heel. Resolution 660 demanded that Saddam's forces evacuate Kuwait. Resolution 661 would prove especially consequential in the years ahead, for it imposed stringent economic sanctions that forbade the U.N.'s member states from importing from Iraq any of the resource that was the life's blood of its economy: oil. Saddam refused to comply – and at one point, perhaps in a final play for Arab sympathy, made Iraqi withdrawal from Kuwait contingent upon an Israeli withdrawal from the West Bank and Gaza Strip. Israel's withdrawal was, of course, something that earlier U.N. resolutions had called for; and even the exiled Emir of Kuwait, in an address to the U.N. General Assembly, explicitly likened Iraq's occupation of his country to the Israeli occupation of Arab lands, including southern Lebanon. Efforts to avert war via a negotiated solution were to no avail.

On 15 January 1991, the coalition forces launched a ferocious campaign of aerial bombardment of Baghdad and elsewhere across Iraq. The name chosen for the attack – *Desert Storm* – was grandiose, even melodramatic, but it described its impact with brutal succinctness. Iraqi perceptions of its severity were reflected by Iraqi commentators' likening President Bush's onslaught to a second coming of Hulegu, the Mongol khan whose horde demolished much of Baghdad in 1258. By the time *Desert Storm* was over, it had devastated Iraq's infrastructure.

Saddam retaliated with missile attacks against coalition bases in Saudi Arabia, and a temporarily successful attack and occupation of the Saudi city of Khafji. In hopes of getting the Arab forces opposing him to withdraw, he made an unsuccessful attempt to lure Israel into the war by launching missiles against it. Evidently hoping to reduce the aerial pounding by limiting pilots' visibility, Saddam exacted yet another cost from Kuwait by ordering his forces to torch hundreds of Kuwait's oil wells. Many of them burned uncontrolled for months after the war was over, consuming five million barrels of oil, belching an enormous cloud of black smoke easily visible from satellites in orbit, and wreaking environmental damage on the Gulf's upper reaches. During this first phase of the war, Saddam also reached out to his erstwhile patron, the Soviet Union, in hopes that, as the Cold War was winding down in the U.S.'s favor, the Soviet premier Mikhail Gorbachev would intercede with Bush to persuade him not to send in ground forces.[36]

Gorbachev's intercession was fruitless. On 23 February the coalition's ground forces crossed into Kuwait and Iraq. Within five days they had completely expelled Iraqi forces from Kuwait. By the time that Bush declared a ceasefire on 28 February, *Desert Storm* had swept away more than three thousand Iraqi civilians – including more than two hundred obliterated in a Baghdad bomb shelter – and twenty thousand Iraqi soldiers, many of them while in headlong retreat from Kuwait on what became known as the "Highway of Death."

Wary of the potential costs and casualties, and the potential consequences of destabilizing the Middle East region further, Bush and his allies now made a fateful decision, which set the stage for catastrophic consequences for Iraq and its people more than twenty years later: they chose neither to pursue the Iraqi forces to the gates of Baghdad, nor to force Saddam Hussein and the Baath regime from power.

One week before the ground invasion began, President Bush had exhorted the Iraqi people and military via a Voice of America radio broadcast "to take matters into their own hands, to force Saddam Hussein the dictator to step aside." Long-suffering Kurds in the north and Shi'ite Arabs in the cities of the south took Bush's words to heart, many assuming that implicit in his exhortation was the promise of American military support if they rose up against Saddam. They did indeed rise up, and in the process fractured a sense of Iraqi identity that, only three years earlier, arguably had reached its zenith.[37]

Thousands among the defeated soldiers – most of whose ranks were Shi'ites – and local citizens struck against Saddam's regime, killing or expelling Baath officials and gaining control over most of the southern cities and much of the north. However, in the truce that had ended the military hostilities, despite having imposed restrictions on the Iraqi military, the U.S. negotiators permitted Saddam's army to keep their helicopter gunships. Saddam now directed those troops who remained loyal to him to unleash the power of the gunships to smash the uprisings. Although they were close by, the U.S. forces spurned the Shi'ite rebels' pleas for help. In one instance, they radioed rebels the response that because they were Shi'ites they must be collaborating with Iran, and so American forces would not help them.[38] Meanwhile, Iraq's Sunni Arab neighbors looked on as Saddam, brutally reasserting his control, exacted a horrible retribution upon Shi'ites and Kurds. His gunships, tanks, and artillery shelled and strafed the cities of the south, including the hallowed shrine-cities of Najaf and Karbala, killing thousands in their homes or in the streets. His security forces rounded up, tortured, and executed thousands more, dumping their mutilated corpses into mass graves that decades later continue to be discovered. His tanks rolled into the northern cities and reclaimed them as well, although the Kurdish *peshmerga* were able to retain a small foothold in the north. A month after the rebellions had erupted, Saddam's "summary executions…razing of cities, and massive deportations" had smashed them.[39]

As many as two million Iraqis, three-quarters of them Kurds, had fled into the countryside. In the south, where the ancient marshes had once nurtured the beginnings of Sumerian civilization, sheltered the Chaldeans who rebelled against the Assyrian kings of Nineveh, and sustained the Zanj African slaves in their uprising against the Abbasid overlords in Baghdad, Saddam built canals to divert the rivers' waters around the marshes, turning them into desert and making refugees of those Marsh Arabs his forces did not kill. Among those forced into homelessness were not only Arab Shi'ites, but also much of Iraq's remaining population of Mandaeans, the two-thousand-year-old Gnostic sect whose roots lay in the era of the earliest Christians.[40]

In the mountains of the north, tens of thousands of Kurds displaced by Saddam's reprisals languished without shelter or food. With a humanitarian disaster of epic proportions looming, in April the United Nations Security Council passed Resolution 688, condemning Saddam's treatment of the Kurds. In what it named Operation *Provide Comfort*, the U.S. military rushed food and tents to the refugees. Claiming that Resolution 688 had given them the legal authorization, the U.S. and Great Britain also established over much of the Kurdish region and southern Iraq "no-fly zones" patrolled by American warplanes whose pilots were tasked with preventing Iraqi warplanes from doing any more harm to those below.

By October 1990, Kurdish guerillas succeeded in driving out the Iraqi forces that remained in the north. In the years to come, their success, combined with the no-fly zone, was to have a significant impact on the unfolding relationship between the central government in Baghdad and the Kurds. As early as 1992 the Kurds established a new, supposedly unified Kurdish Regional Government (K.R.G.) at Irbil. Yet, even with their long-sought political autonomy just over the horizon, Iraq's Kurds remained divided. Between 1994 and 1996, their two dominant, fiercely contentious political parties (and leading clans) – the K.D.P. (led by Massoud Barzani) and the P.U.K. (led by Jalal Talabani) – pitted their respective militias against each other in a civil war. In 1998, with each still controlling its own portion of Kurdistan, from its own capital, the two sides quit fighting and reluctantly embraced a coexistence made more bearable by burgeoning economic prosperity after the U.N. eased the sanctions prohibiting the purchase of Iraq's oil. Revenues from both legitimate sales and illegal smuggling of oil re-energized Kurdistan's economic development. By the eve of the Anglo-American invasion of Iraq in 2003, Iraq's Kurds had achieved de facto political autonomy, as well as a level of prosperity that destitute, sanctions-plagued Iraqis in the south could only envy. Their envy may have been shared by the millions of Kurds who lived beyond Iraq's borders, in Turkey and Syria, and also in Iran.

Iran undoubtedly was one of the biggest beneficiaries of the 1991 war. Less than three years earlier, the Shi'ite Islamist regime in Tehran had been compelled to cave in to the military might of Saddam and his American backers. Now the Americans had crippled Saddam's military,[41] leaving Iran primed to re-emerge as a major power in the Persian Gulf.

The U.S. now perceived a dual threat to its strategic interests in the Gulf (its access to oil) and also a threat to its chief Middle Eastern ally and proxy, Israel, against which Saddam had launched long-range missiles during the war. The new U.S. president, Bill Clinton, adopted a new policy of "dual containment" of Iraq and Iran. To enforce this policy, the U.S. positioned military forces at bases in Kuwait and other

Gulf states – including the holy soil of the Arabian Peninsula, where their defiling presence became a new focus of resentment against both the Saudi monarchy and the United States.

1991–2003: THE SCOURGE OF SANCTIONS

Dual containment demanded that Iraq's capabilities be kept in check as long as Saddam was in power. The U.S. and its allies achieved this through a combination of tactics, including the continued patrolling of the no-fly zones the U.S. had established over Iraqi airspace just after the war and the intermittent launching of air attacks to "degrade" Iraq's defenses.[42] Between 1992 and 2000, U.S. warplanes averaged eight thousand sorties per year over the no-fly zones. In 1998, the U.S. Congress also passed the Iraq Liberation Act, which made the removal of Saddam's regime the official policy of the U.S. government. For all intents and purposes, the U.S. was still in a state of war with Saddam.[43]

By far its most devastating tactic was the continued rigorous enforcement of the economic sanctions the U.N. Security Council had authorized in the summer of 1990 and afterward. Besides prohibiting U.N. member states from buying and importing Iraq's oil, the sanctions prohibited Iraq from importing any materials that, in the judgment of the Security Council committee charged with managing the implementation of the sanctions (the "661 Committee," after Resolution 661), might be used to manufacture nuclear, chemical, or biological weapons (W.M.D.s). The U.N. also required Iraq to divulge information about chemical and biological weapons it still possessed and to submit to repeated visits by teams of inspectors tasked with locating those weapons and verifying their destruction. Only after Saddam had complied and the W.M.D.s had been verifiably destroyed were the sanctions against Iraq to be lifted. Unsurprisingly, Saddam's government did not welcome these intrusive inspections, nor was their credibility bolstered when it was discovered that the U.S. had planted C.I.A. agents in the inspection teams. Saddam had in fact decided to destroy these weapons stocks, as well as dismantle his embryonic nuclear weapons program, shortly after the war had ended. But, fearful that Iran's leaders might vengefully take advantage of Iraq's weakened state, he chose not to publicize this. Saddam's silence was to have almost apocalyptic consequences for his country eleven years later.

Compounding the economic decline that the war with Iran had set in motion, the massive aerial bombing of Iraq's cities during *Desert Storm* had demolished much of the country's infrastructure, in a matter of weeks reducing one of the Arab world's most prosperous countries to what U.N. observers reckoned a Third World, pre-industrial level. Now, although the war had ended, the U.N. sanctions compounded that devastation, crippling Iraq's economy – its oil production declined by more than twenty-five percent because Iraq was denied crucial equipment – and ruining what a few years before had ranked among the best educational and medical-care systems in the Middle East.[44] Between 1991 and 1996, when the U.N. permitted a limited resumption of oil sales, sanctions decimated Iraq's once-thriving middle class as well as its rural and urban poor.[45] With the U.S. often taking the lead in its deliberations, the 661 Committee blocked Iraq from importing any materials that, in its estimation, might be used to manufacture chemical or biological weapons – among them, electrical switches and sockets, water pipes, and chlorine. As Iraq's water, sanitation, power-generation, and medical systems became increasingly dilapidated and dysfunctional, disease and malnutrition felled thousands of Iraqis, including, by some estimates, 880,000 Iraqi children under five years of age.[46] An assessment of the impact of these sanctions that was published in 1999 spotlighted the irony that the number of Iraqi deaths they had caused exceeded the number "slain by all so-called weapons of mass destruction throughout history."[47]

Yet, even though his regime had been shaken by the uprisings of 1991, and even though the Kurds had carved out an autonomous existence in the north, and even though the sanctions weighed brutally upon his people, Saddam was able to sustain his authority throughout most of Iraq. It is plain that his top priority was the survival of himself and his most trusted, clan-based supporters rather than upholding the centrist and secular Baath ideology. Thus, he reached out to tribal leaders and celebrated Arab tribal values. He also reached out to the Sunni religious establishment via a Faith Campaign that fostered mosque construction and religious activism.

Mindful of the prestige of the ayatollahs of the Shi'ite *hawza* of Najaf – and worried about their links to Iran – he sought to curry favor among the Shi'ites by allocating funds for the maintenance of the hallowed mosque-shrines at Najaf and Karbala.[48] But Shi'ite opposition to Saddam had been reactivated by the emergence of the Ayatollah Muhammad Sadiq al-Sadr, a cousin of Muhammad Baqir al-Sadr who led al-Da'wa during the 1970s. Saddam resorted to brutal tactics. His security services rounded up and detained, often tortured, and executed or otherwise "disappeared" Shi'ites suspected of anti-regime activity. Sadiq al-Sadr was assassinated along with two of his sons in 1999.

Even as the lives of thousands of Iraqis were devastated by the U.N. sanctions, Saddam found ways to undermine those sanctions, enlisting both Iraqi (even Kurdish) and foreign officials – indeed anyone who might help his regime survive – in schemes to smuggle Iraqi oil into Turkey and Iran. As one scholar noted, during this period "Saddam was nothing if not brilliant in dispensing rewards or punishments to ensure his survival."[49]

Thus, when George W. Bush, son of George H. W. Bush, was inaugurated president of the United States in January 2001, a seemingly resilient Saddam Hussein continued to rule in Baghdad. The self-declared nemesis of the United States and Israel still possessed a substantial, though enfeebled, military. His enemies also feared that he possessed arsenals of chemical and biological W.M.D.s and even a program to develop nuclear weapons – or that he might already have them.[50] Although war and sanctions had damaged Iraq's oil production, Saddam still sat atop vast reserves of crude oil and natural gas – strategic resources crucial to an early twenty-first-century industrialized world that was dominated by the United States but also featured newcomers, like China and India, whose own modernization required access to such energy sources.

Like the Abbasid caliphate of the mid-thirteenth century, Saddam's Iraq, weakened but clad in a patina of perceived strength, was a prize ripe for picking. But in the context of twenty-first-century statesmanship a usable pretext needed to be found.

THE ANGLO-AMERICAN INVASION OF IRAQ

On the morning of 11 September 2001, four small bands of young men affiliated with a shadowy Islamist militant organization known as al-Qaeda hijacked four commercial jets, all of them packed with unsuspecting passengers, and succeeded in piloting three of them into the two most famous architectural icons of American military and commercial power: the twin towers of the World Trade Center in New York, which were destroyed, and the Pentagon in Washington, D.C., which suffered major damage.[51] These attacks killed in total almost three thousand people, most of them Americans. America and the world were stunned, horrified – and angry. A leading French daily newspaper proclaimed the next day that "we are all Americans." Americans were eager to exact retribution – none of them more so than U.S. President George W. Bush, after a lackluster first year in office.

Al-Qaeda's chief leaders were a Saudi Arab (Osama bin Laden) and an Egyptian Arab (Ayman al-Zawahiri); most of the men who carried out the attack were Saudi or Pakistani. For several years before the attacks, al-Qaeda had used Afghanistan as a base of training and planning operations. They were hosted by that country's Islamist Taliban regime, which had come to power after a devastating civil war that had erupted in 1989 – when the Soviet Union, which had occupied the country since 1979, had been forced out by Afghan resistance fighters who had been supplied funds and weapons by Saudi Arabia, Pakistan, and the U.S.[52] Consequently, it was Afghanistan that was targeted in the initial American response, to try to seek out and destroy the al-Qaeda leadership and remove the Taliban from power.

As became public knowledge soon after the attacks – and was verified in an U.S. government report published in July 2004 – not one of the men who planned or carried out the attacks was an Iraqi. Nor did that report document any evidence of a significant relationship between al-Qaeda and Saddam Hussein's regime.[53] Nonetheless, before the dust had settled on the ruins of the World Trade Center, Bush administration officials began to explore ways of pinning the blame on Saddam and using that as a springboard to act against him.[54] Their reasons for doing so have become – and likely will remain for years to come – the focus of controversy. Among them have been cited the opportunity to protect Israel and safeguard its military superiority in the region by removing Saddam,[55] the quest to promote American political ideals in the Middle East by bestowing democracy upon a conquered Iraq,[56] George W. Bush's alleged quest to punish Saddam's alleged attempt to have his father assassinated when the latter visited Kuwait after his presidency, and even some psychological need on the part of the younger Bush to outshine his famous father by sending American troops to take Baghdad, which his father had declined to do in 1991.[57]

Foremost in the minds of some of the invasion's planners, however, was the same consideration that had tantalized British planners like Winston Churchill and Admiral John Fisher during and after World War I – and, for that matter, would-be conquerors of Mesopotamia since the beginning of history: control of the country's natural wealth. One respected analyst noted in 2002 that, for several reasons, Iraq's oil was an especially attractive prize. Its oil reserves were the world's second largest (after Saudi Arabia's) and remained largely underdeveloped. Iraq's oil was also of high quality, relatively easy to extract (especially in the southern fields) – which made production costs relatively low – and located close to modern sea-lanes. These were distinct advantages when one considers the reserves then being discovered in Alaska, the North Sea, the Caspian Basin, Mexico, and Venezuela. The importance of such considerations surely resonates when one thinks of the catastrophic oil spill from a British Petroleum operation in the Gulf of Mexico in 2010. Moreover, as a country that relied so much on Saudi Arabia's oil, but was attacked on 9/11 by a group headed by a Saudi and numbering other Saudis among its operatives, the U.S. understandably might have wanted to diversify its sources of Middle Eastern oil. As Paul Rogers of Bradford University and the Oxford Research Group noted, "this could be seen, perhaps, as the real al-Qaeda link with the Iraq question."[58]

In May 2001, only a few months before the 9/11 attacks, the U.S. government's National Energy Policy Development Group, headed by Vice President Richard Cheney, reported that the petroleum of the Persian Gulf was a central strategic interest of the U.S.

> By 2020, Gulf oil producers are projected to supply between 54 and 67 percent of the world's oil. Thus, the global economy will almost certainly continue to depend on the supply of oil from Organization of Petroleum Exporting Countries (OPEC) members, particularly in the Gulf. This region will remain vital to U.S. interests. [59]

Predicting that U.S. oil consumption would double between 2001 and 2005, Cheney's task force recommended vigorous efforts to convince friendly Gulf nations to allow American oil companies to invest in their oil resources. Even before that report appeared, a National Security Council document dated 3 February 2001 had directed the council's staff to cooperate fully with the Energy Task Force as it considered the "melding" of two seemingly unrelated areas of policy: "the review of operational policies towards rogue states," such as Iraq, and "actions regarding the capture of new and existing oil and gas fields."[60] A little more than a year later, in a speech to the U.S. organization Veterans of Foreign Wars, Cheney noted among the reasons for removing Saddam the importance of retaining control of Gulf oil resources. Meanwhile, a U.S. State Department effort known as the Future of Iraq project recommended the privatization of Iraq's oil resources once Saddam was removed. Such a prospect was sure to quicken the pulses of oil executives – one of whom commented to the New York Times in February 2003 that "being in Iraq is like being a kid in F. A. O. Schwartz" (a well-known New York toy store).[61] That Iraq's oil bounty did indeed feature prominently in the plans of Bush administration officials became plain when, three months after the invasion, U.S. Undersecretary of Defense Paul Wolfowitz was asked why the U.S. had decided to attack Iraq rather than North Korea, which was known by then to have developed a nuclear weapon. He responded, "Let's look at it simply. The most important difference between North Korea and Iraq is that economically, we just had no choice in Iraq. The country swims on a sea of oil."[62]

Whatever his actual motives, in January 2002, only four months after the 9/11 attacks, President Bush used his State of the Union address to label Iraq – along with Iran and North Korea – as a member of an "Axis of Evil" that was imperiling global security. Thereafter, proceeding on the basis of flawed assumptions, relying on poor or even bogus intelligence, and assisted by largely compliant print and electronic media, Bush and his officials, along with British Prime Minister Tony Blair, convinced millions of citizens and many of their elected representatives that (1) Saddam, the leader of a secularist regime, had been conniving with al-Qaeda's Islamist terrorists, and (2) he had stockpiled chemical, biological, and nuclear "weapons of mass destruction" that he might use against the United States or Europe or even hand over to al-Qaeda. This latter claim flew in the face of the effects of years of U.N. sanctions, as well as U.N. inspections that, up to the eve of the invasion, had found no evidence of any such W.M.D.s.[63] Nonetheless, terrified by the threat Saddam appeared to pose, and angered by his alleged complicity in the 9/11 attacks, Americans and Britons alike were goaded into supporting an immensely destructive invasion of Iraq.

Although Saddam had played no role in the 9/11 attacks, then, they had a catastrophic impact on Iraq, for they became the foundation upon which, in March 2003, the U.S. and its allies launched a military operation of such "shock and awe" (to borrow the U.S. military's phrase) that it quickly defeated the overmatched Iraqi forces, brought down Saddam, and extinguished his regime. Saddam fled, was captured by U.S. troops, and executed at the end of 2006. The regime was replaced initially by the Coalition Provisional Authority, an occupation government headed by an American diplomat/viceroy (L. Paul "Jerry" Bremer) and staffed by officials who were hamstrung by the kind of cultural cluelessness that had plagued British-mandate administrators in Iraq after World War I. Unlike the British, the Americans had no prior experience in governing Middle Eastern peoples. All too often they were abysmally ignorant of Iraq's history and culture and had been recruited on the basis of partisan-political loyalty rather than useful expertise.[64]

The following August 2010 comments of one of the top U.S. commanders during the fighting, General Raymond Odierno, as quoted by the journalist Anthony Shadid, speak volumes about the U.S. military's preparedness:

> "We all came in very naïve about Iraq…We came in naïve about what the problems were in Iraq; I don't think we understood what I call the societal devastation that occurred," he said, citing the Iran–Iraq war, the Persian Gulf war and the international sanctions from 1990 to 2003 that wiped out the middle class. "And then we attacked to overthrow the government," he said.

The same went for the country's ethnic and sectarian divisions, he said: "We just didn't understand it."

Asked if the United States had made the country's divisions worse, General Odierno said, "I don't know."

"There's all these issues that we didn't understand and that we had to work our way through," he said. "And did maybe that cause it to get worse? Maybe."[65]

EPILOGUE

"TELL ME HOW THIS ENDS"

A S ONE MIGHT EXPECT, unpreparedness, ineptitude, and hubris on the part of the United States and its coalition allies in the invasion and occupation of Iraq exacted a steep price. It exacted a price from the U.S.: from the budget of the federal government, from American citizens (at least those from military families), and from the U.S.'s diplomatic and moral standing across the world, especially in the Middle East. Yet, unquestionably, Iraq and the Iraqi people paid the lion's share of the price, and will continue to do so for years to come. Within weeks after it had begun, Operation *Iraqi Freedom* had opened a Pandora's box of forces inside and outside Iraq that today still threaten to tear the country apart. As of early 2015, the possibility of closing that box is in serious doubt. For that reason, it is too early to write a comprehensive account of the U.S. occupation and its consequences. The consequences are still playing out. Because of them, although U.S. combat troops were withdrawn by the end of 2011, the U.S. has lately resumed air-strikes in Iraq.

Meanwhile, dozens of historians, journalists, and think-tank "experts" have analyzed the military operations of 2003–11, the resistance to them on the part of both Iraqis and those jihadists and others who came to Iraq to fight the U.S.-led coalition, and their effects on Iraqi politics and society. Overall, the fighting has wreaked colossal damage on Iraq. Although a detailed account and assessment of all of this are beyond the scope and purpose of this book, we can at least outline some of the most significant developments and consequences of this tragic, and still unfolding, episode of Iraq's history.

Except in the Kurdish region, where the U.S. had been perceived as a liberator as early as the 1990s, almost from the beginning the invasion spawned insurgency against the occupation across the country, especially in the so-called "Sunni Triangle" around Baghdad and in the Anbar region of western Iraq – notably in the city of Fallujah, which U.S. forces devastated in 2004 – and also in the Shi'ite south, where a militia (the "Mahdi Army") affiliated with the young mullah Muqtada al-Sadr (son of the Ayatollah Muhammad Sadiq al-Sadr) battled the Americans in and around Najaf. That insurgency was stoked by an ill-advised decision by L. Paul Bremer, the American proconsul installed after the coalition's takeover, to disband the Iraqi army and outlaw the Baath Party. Disbanding the army left thousands of Iraqi soldiers unemployed and Iraqi officials uprooted, with dim prospects of supporting themselves and their families, and correspondingly dim attitudes toward the occupation. After thirteen months, Bremer was replaced with a politician hand-picked by the U.S: Ayad Allawi, a long-time expatriate, secularist Shi'ite and former Baath Party member whom Saddam had once tried to assassinate. By 2005, political pushback by the Shi'ite clerical hierarchy in Najaf – most notably, the Grand Ayatollah Ali al-Sistani, Iraq's most revered Shi'ite religious leader – forced the U.S. to acquiesce to a series of elections, beginning in 2005, as well as the drafting of a new constitution to structure the new Iraqi republic. In sum, the initial round of elections, which were largely boycotted by Sunni Arabs, and the new constitution yielded a political landscape riven by the same ethnic and sectarian mistrust that had plagued Iraqis since well before Saddam's time: Arabs vs. Kurds vs. Turkmen; Sunni vs. Shi'ites, with Christians and Yazidis also in the mix. Because of the Shi'ites' demographic predominance, Shi'ite Arab political parties – including al-Da'wa and S.C.I.R.I., renamed the Islamic Supreme Council in Iraq (I.S.C.I.) – backed by their respective militias, came to dominate the government.

The elections of 2006 brought to power as prime minister a little-known and lightly regarded figure, the leader of al-Da'wa, Nuri al-Maliki, whose ascension was blatantly orchestrated by the U.S. In the years that followed, Maliki steadily concentrated both civil and military power in his own, increasingly authoritarian hands. His security agencies resorted to severe and widespread repression of Sunnis, whom Maliki suspected of working to thwart the new Shi'ite ascendancy. Thousands were imprisoned and intimidated, even tortured. The pace of executions by his government became a cause of concern to international human-rights organizations. Nonetheless, the U.S. government under George W. Bush as well as his successor, Barack Obama, continued to regard Maliki as Iraq's most dependable political leader, and intervened to ensure his continuation as Iraq's prime minister after the disputed Iraqi elections in 2010. Many across the Arab Middle East perceived Iraq's Shi'ite-dominated government as doubly flawed in having been brought to power and sustained by the United States and in being linked to Shi'ite Iran.[1]

Yet, in many ways, the dysfunction and failure that have plagued Iraq's politics since 2003 pale in comparison with the damage done to Iraq's people. The destabilization and harsh conditions caused by invasion and foreign occupation, the political ascent of the Shi'ites at the Sunnis' expense, and the provocations of foreign Sunni jihadists pried farther apart the ethnic and religious fault lines of Iraq's society. In February 2006, Sunni extremists bombed and partially destroyed the Shi'ite al-Askariya mosque in Samarra, which contained the tombs of the tenth and eleventh Shi'ite Imams and is revered as the place where the twelfth "Hidden" Imam is said to have disappeared. This kicked off a period of massive Shi'ite reprisals against Sunnis, and vice versa, which drastically reshaped the demography of Baghdad. Sunnis expelled Shi'ites from predominantly Sunni neighborhoods; Shi'ites expelled Sunnis from theirs. Both sides resorted to kidnapping and murder. By the time the worst of the blood-letting had abated in 2009, thousands

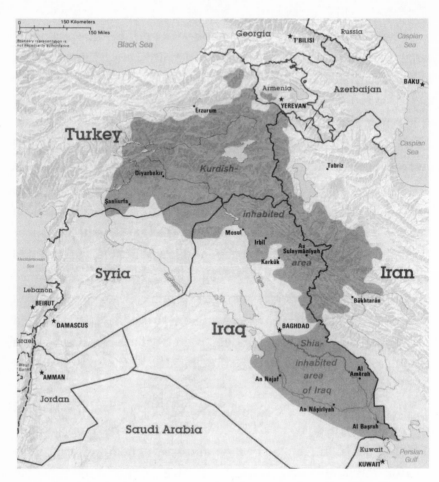

MAP 7. *Iraq and surrounding countries, with Shia-inhabited and Kurdish-inhabited regions (Central Intelligence Agency).*

had been killed, and the map of Baghdad had been dramatically altered not only by sectarian violence but also by the massive concrete blast walls the U.S. military erected to separate antagonistic groups and stifle the carnage. From being a mixed Sunni–Shi'ite city, Baghdad became eighty-five to ninety percent Shi'ite.

Iraq suffered an apocalyptic toll in destroyed or displaced humanity. Internal and external exiles, combined, number as many as 4.5 million. More than two million Iraqis, most of them Sunni, fled into exile in neighboring countries – mainly Syria, Lebanon, and Jordan, where they became an enormous burden for already taxed infrastructure. Another 2.4 million became "internal exiles" inside Iraq.[2] Most have chosen not to return home. The prospects that await them upon their eventual return are grim.

The number of Iraqis killed between March 2003 and the departure of U.S. forces at the end of 2011 has been estimated at between 100,000 and one million, with hundreds of thousands more maimed physically or devastated psychologically, perhaps irreparably. Tens of thousands of women were made widows – a horrific toll in a traditional society in which men are looked to as protectors and providers. Iraq's future has been made even grimmer with the millions of children who were orphaned, made homeless, or emotionally incapacitated by the death of family members, the destruction of their homes, their uprooting from their communities, or the interruption or termination of their education.[3]

Beyond the toll of lives lost or ruined, by the time of the U.S. withdrawal thousands of Iraqis were still contending with damaged infrastructure, shoddy or incomplete reconstruction of facilities, and other effects of war. Electricity, sanitation, and water supply remained woefully deficient. Sewage still flowed in the streets of many towns; water supplies remained polluted and unreliable; and electricity was, for too many, in short supply, with outages of sixteen hours per day common.

From once being a cradle of religions and exemplar of religious diversity, Iraq between 2003 and 2011 suffered the displacement, exile, and killing of thousands from its other religious minorities. Among them were hundreds of thousands of Iraqi Christians. Before the 2003 invasion, Iraq's Christians may have numbered as many as 1.5 million. By late 2010, their numbers across had declined to perhaps as few as 400,000; in Mosul alone, their numbers had dropped from 100,000 to maybe five thousand. Some have compared this exodus of

Iraq's Christians, descendants of some of the world's oldest Christian communities, to the near disappearance of Iraq's ancient Jewish community in 1948.⁴ One writer noted the irony that the decisions of two professedly devout Christians, George Bush and Tony Blair, "led to the destruction of Christianity in one of its ancient heartlands – something Arab, Mongol and Ottoman conquests all failed to pull off."⁵ Also among Iraq's displaced religious communities were hundreds of members of its ancient Mandaean and Yazidi sects.

Similarly devastated by the invasion and its aftermath was the cultural heritage of Iraq. Beginning with the looting of the National Museum of Iraq after the U.S. conquest of Baghdad in March 2003, the remains of ancient Mesopotamia – the cradle of civilizations and empires – suffered grave, even irreparable damage. Babylon was seriously damaged by coalition troops who established a military base atop the site. Many other sites – including ancient cities such as Isin and Umma – were looted, mostly by local Iraqis, but sometimes by coalition troops. Countless artifacts were illegally spirited out of the country and into the hands of antiquities dealers and their clients.⁶

Finally, one of the evils loosed by the invasion now threatens to destroy modern Iraq as a unitary state. Under Saddam Hussein's regime, al-Qaeda had no significant presence in Iraq. But the invasion caused Sunni jihadists to flock to Iraq. Under the banner of al-Qaeda in Iraq (A.Q.I.) they attacked U.S. forces, whom they labeled "Crusaders" as well as "Christian, Protestant, and Jewish Zionists." They were able to take control of some Sunni communities, especially in the western province of Anbar, but their brutal high-handedness soon led many to turn against them. In what became known as the Anbar or Sunni Awakening (or "Sahwa"), local Sunni Arab fighters, with assistance from U.S. forces and promises of future employment from the Shi'ite-dominated government in Baghdad, recovered their communities from the jihadists and largely succeeded in driving them out. But in the aftermath the Baghdad government reneged on its promises and imprisoned many of the Sahwa fighters. In late 2010, as the withdrawal of U.S. forces gathered steam and American news media decamped from Iraq, A.Q.I. began to re-emerge, notably in Mosul, Anbar, and Baghdad. It launched attacks to under-mine the Shiʻite-dominated government, assassinating security forces and members of the Sahwa militias, bombing government ministries and other buildings in Baghdad, and wreaking havoc with bombs in the poverty-ridden Shiʻite neighborhood of Sadr City in Baghdad and during Shiʻite religious observances there and in Karbala. After U.S. troops departed from Iraq at the end of 2011, these attacks escalated. The Maliki government made little effort to address the growing frustra-tion of Anbar's Sunni citizenry and instead intensified its repression of them. Thousands of Sunnis vented their anger in large protests, which Maliki's forces put down violently, killing many demonstrators and stoking Sunni mistrust in Maliki's government.

For much of the world outside the Middle East these events passed unnoticed. Many of the Western media had left Iraq before the U.S. troops completed their withdrawal. The Western public had turned the page and begun to consign Iraq to the dustbin of history. But they began to notice the Sunni jihadists when they emerged as highly motivated and effective front-line soldiers in the civil war that erupted in 2011 in neighboring Syria. In that year, Syria's President, Bashar al-Assad, deployed his military to smash the predominantly Sunni cities and towns where locals, inspired by the pro-democracy "Arab Spring" in Tunisia and Egypt and frustrated with the government's failure to provide eco-nomic relief, had risen in protest. Assad and much of his ruling cohort belong to the Alawites, a quasi-Shiʻite sect who, like Shiʻites, are reviled as heretics by Sunni jihadi groups. Al-Qaeda in Iraq thus joined the fight in a sectarian cause against a regime that it saw as dominated by heretics. In 2013, they broke with the al-Qaeda leadership and declared themselves a separate organization, which came to be known as the Islamic State of Iraq and al-Shams (I.S.I.S.) or, alternatively, the Islamic State of Iraq and the Levant (I.S.I.L.).[7]

By early 2014, the threat that I.S.I.S. also posed to Iraq's Shi'ite-led government could no longer be ignored. It had also become apparent that I.S.I.S. was working in conjunction with other Sunni groups in Iraq, including remnants of the Baath Party and Saddam-era Iraqi military. Given the burgeoning anti-Maliki animosity in the broader Sunni population, it perhaps was predictable that when I.S.I.S. forces attacked Fallujah and other cities in Anbar province, local Sunnis resisted Maliki's Shi'ite-dominated Iraqi army when it was dispatched ostensibly to defend them. I.S.I.S. gained control of Fallujah and much of Anbar. In June, alarms sounded in the Western political establishment when I.S.I.S. took control of Mosul, Iraq's second-largest city. They also attacked Saddam's home city of Tikrit and began to press southward into Iraq's Shi'ite heartland.

Ominously, I.S.I.S. renamed themselves as, simply, the Islamic State (I.S.) and proclaimed the re-establishment of the religious cum imperial institution that epitomized the apogee of Muslim rule centuries before: the caliphate. But this new caliphate's rule has manifested none of the religious toleration that characterized the rule of the Abbasid caliphs of Baghdad's golden age. It espouses a grotesque, often gruesome version of hyper-Sunni Wahhabist ideology – the same ideology that underpins the modern Saudi monarchy. Islamic State forces have perpetrated mass executions of "heretic" Shi'ite soldiers of the Iraqi army. They have beheaded Western journalists and publicized these acts by videotaping and broadcasting them. They also seem bent on eliminating what remains of Iraq's Christian and Yazidi minorities.

Finally, in their prohibitions, per their Wahhabi ideology, against buildings and art that they deem contravene strict monotheism because they encourage idolatry, I.S. has engaged in a wholesale assault on Iraq's cultural heritage. Ancient churches and mosques – including the shrine of the prophet Jonah in Mosul – have been demolished. The ruins of Hatra are in peril, as are the palaces of the Assyrian kings at Nineveh and Nimrud. And in a quest as cynical as it is destructive, archaeological mounds across I.S. territory are being pillaged for antiquities that can be sold to help finance their rule.

As of this writing, I.S. controls much of northern and northwestern Iraq as well as eastern and northern Syria. The U.S. and a host of partners European, Arab, and (unofficially) Iranian have brought air-strikes and other military power to bear on I.S. forces. But for the foreseeable future Iraq's predominantly Sunni west and northwest have been wrested from Baghdad's writ.

Meanwhile, the Kurdistan Regional Government (K.R.G.) continues to dominate northern Iraq's Kurdish provinces, even as I.S. forces threaten their borders. When the Iraqi army fled in disarray from the I.S. onslaught, Kurdish forces seized the opportunity to grab their long-coveted "Jerusalem": the city of Kirkuk, along with the oil beneath the surrounding earth. Few predict they will ever give it back to the government in Baghdad. More are predicting that before long – despite the opposition of the U.S., which wants to preserve Iraq as a unitary state – the K.R.G. will declare itself an independent Kurdish state.

As early as 2005, some American observers were touting the wisdom of partitioning Iraq into three separate regions – one Shi'ite, one Sunni, one Kurdish. Whether Iraq is to be a centralized state, a loose federation, or some melding of those two principles – or whether a state named Iraq will even exist in a few years – remains an open question.

At the end of 2011, Patrick Cockburn, one of the most informed and prescient journalists writing about Iraq, noted that "The most likely future for Iraq is fragile stability with a permanently high level of violence, presided over by a divided and dysfunctional government." In the same essay, he also wrote, "Iraq is unlikely to break apart because all communities have an interest in getting their share of the oil revenues. Most disputes are about how to cut up the cake of national wealth."[8]

Current events may be overtaking Cockburn's analysis.[9] Whatever political-geographical disposition of Iraq ensues, the fact remains that if the Iraqi people are ever to rebuild their economy and regain a standard of living akin to what was achieved in the 1970s, that recovery will need to be founded on what rulers of Iraq have relied on since the days of the Sumerians: its natural wealth. From the time of Gilgamesh to the Abbasid caliphate of Baghdad, that wealth was extracted, hard earned, from the rich floodplain soil that, when irrigated and properly cultivated, yielded the massive grain harvests that made Mesopotamia's great cities, kingdoms, empires, and civilizations possible. Today Iraqis are confronted by a terrible irony: what was a breadbasket of the pre-modern world must now import much of its food. More than thirty years of war and sanctions, persisting drought, and dam construction in neighboring Syria and Turkey, which has reduced the life-giving flow of the Tigris and Euphrates into Iraq, have dramatically reduced Iraq's water supply, causing farmland and villages to be abandoned. Compounding those challenges, the projected effects of global warming promise to rob Iraq of even more farmland as the level of the Persian Gulf rises and salt water encroaches upstream along the Tigris and Euphrates and into the floodplain soils.

In another glaring irony, Iraqi farmers are being forced off grain fields and date plantations – the pre-modern engine of Mesopotamia's wealth – by the imperatives of the modern engine: oil production.[10] It was the prospect of oil that attracted Europeans to Iraq after World War I; it was ramped-up oil production and a spike in oil prices that enabled Saddam to build Iraq into a regional power with a modern standard of living; it was oil supply and profits that helped motivate the U.S. to invade Iraq and remove Saddam Hussein in 2003. Future revenue from the sale of its oil could bring a new dawn to Iraqis, but that can happen only if political, sectarian, and ethnic fissures can somehow be soldered shut and the struggle to end inter-community violence be won. The prospects of greater oil revenue are also dimmed by the fact that, after so many years of war and sanctions, Iraq's oil-production infrastructure – its wells, pumping facilities, pipelines, port facilities, and general export capacity – is badly damaged and underdeveloped – and in some places on the brink of collapse. It cannot be repaired or replaced without massive investment from outsiders: according to Iraq's Deputy Prime Minister for Energy, at least U.S.$30 billion per year if Iraq is to meet production targets established in 2013.[11]

Outside investors can hardly be expected to inject new capital if the current security situation cannot be stabilized. Yet such investment could bring a huge payoff. As we noted, the geology of Iraq's oilfields makes its oil relatively easy to extract, and its southern fields are near a major Persian Gulf port at Umm Qasr. Iraq's proven oil reserves are 150 billion barrels (worth around U.S.$10 trillion), placing them fifth in the world and second in O.P.E.C., behind only Saudi Arabia; Iraq passed Iran into second place in 2012. Moreover, as a recent U.S. government report has noted, "just a fraction of Iraq's known fields are in development, and Iraq may be one of the few places left where much of its hydrocarbon resources has not been fully exploited." The undeveloped fields are thought to contain many billions of barrels more.[12] Iraq also has an abundance of another lucrative energy source: natural gas, with proven reserves of three trillion cubic meters. Like its oil, Iraq's natural gas is severely under-exploited; in fact, more than sixty percent of its current natural-gas production is flared – in other words, lost. Today, "Iraq's five natural-gas processing plants…sit mostly idle."[13]

By late 2013, oil companies from many nations – China, Russia, South Korea, Malaysia, and Turkey among the state-owned companies; the U.S., Italy, Britain, France, and Norway among the private ones – had signed deals to help Iraq develop its oilfields. If we choose to think of earlier outsiders, like the Mongol khan Hulegu and his horde, who came to grab a share of Iraq's wealth as "barbarians at the gate," we might think of their early twenty-first-century counterparts as suitors at the front door. Hulegu's onslaught cursed Iraq with devastation and ensuing centuries of decline caused by wrecking of the irrigation systems that sustained its primary resource – its agricultural bounty. But in their quest for Iraq's other great resource – its fossil-fuel energy sources – the newly arriving outsiders may bring a curse that has the potential to blight our entire planet. That curse is bound up with the ever-growing demand for oil to fuel the economies of emerging countries across the world. Perhaps ironically, two of those countries – India and China – are, like Iraq, countries where great civilizations arose in antiquity and gave birth to sophisticated cultures and long histories of empire followed by Western intrusion. But because they lack adequate domestic sources of oil, both China and India can sustain their rise only by ensuring access to foreign sources. It should come as no surprise then that China is heavily invested in Iraq's oil and natural gas – and it has also invested heavily in the oil of Iraq's now friendly neighbor, Iran. That both Iraq and Iran could become a locus of competition – even conflict – over access to the vast resources that lie beneath their soil is a possibility that we would be foolish to ignore.

But, of course, as climate scientists have been warning us for years, we are even more foolish to ignore the burgeoning impacts of man-made climate change and global warming. If we hope to head off those potentially catastrophic impacts, traditional industrial powers like the U.S. and Europe, and up-and-comers like China and India, need to transform their economies – and ways of life in general – by developing energy sources other than fossil fuels.

And that, of course, means leaving a huge portion of Iraq's fossil fuels in the ground. Iraq's current leaders are counting desperately on the wealth that harvesting those fuels will produce. Such wealth would dwarf the wildest imaginings of Gilgamesh and Nebuchadnezzar, or Harun ar-Rashid, or even Faisal ibn Husayn and Nuri al-Said. But what if producing it – and burning all those fuels – ultimately brings the entire planet to ruin?

In 2003, as "Mission Accomplished" in Iraq had begun to tail-spin into insurgency and civil war, General David Petraeus made during an interview an offhanded comment that arguably has come to epitomize Iraq's situation since then: "Tell me how this ends." As of this writing, the answer must be: "To be determined," although recent events inspire little optimism. Yet, whatever the ultimate fate of Iraq as a unitary state, we in the West ought to find in Mesopotamia/Iraq's long history much to admire, much to learn from, and even more to be grateful for. Surely the people of Iraq will continue to find in that history a source of well- and hard-earned pride – pride that might steady them along their path forward into an uncertain future.

Notes

INTRODUCTION: THE GLORY AND THE CURSE OF IRAQ'S PAST

1. See Daniel E. Fleming, *Democracy's Ancient Ancestors: Mari and Early Collective Governance* (Cambridge: Cambridge University Press, 2004).

CHAPTER 1: PLACES, PEOPLES, POTENTIALS: THE ENDURING FOUNDATIONS OF LIFE IN IRAQ

1. Kamal Salibi, *A House of Many Mansions: The History of Lebanon Reconsidered* (Berkeley: University of California Press, 1988), p. 61.

2. See McGuire Gibson, "Violation of Fallow and Engineered Disaster in Mesopotamian Civilization," in *Irrigation's Impact on Society*, ed. T. E. Downing and M. Gibson (Tucson: University of Arizona Press, 1974), pp. 7–19.

CHAPTER 2: CRADLE OF CIVILIZATION

1. See, for example, Samuel Noah Kramer, *History Begins at Sumer: Thirty-Nine Firsts in Recorded History* (3rd ed.) (Philadelphia: University of Pennsylvania Press, 1988).

2. In the 1920s and 1930s, historians and archaeologists in the new Turkish republic, with the encouragement of the republic's founder and first president, Mustapha Kemal Ataturk, tried to add luster to burgeoning Turkish ethnic nationalism by arguing that the Sumerian and Turkish languages were related. Today, no serious experts accept that claim.

3. See, for example, Jennifer R. Pournelle, "KLM to CORONA: A Bird's-Eye View of Cultural Ecology and Early Mesopotamian Urbanization," in *Settlement and Society: Essays Dedicated to Robert McCormick Adams*, ed. Elizabeth C. Stone (Los Angeles: Cotsen Institute of Archaeology, University of California, Los Angeles, 2007), pp. 29–62. See also Andrew Lawler, "Did the First Cities Grow from Marshes?" *Science* 331 (2011), p. 141. Aspects of Mesopotamian urbanism's evolution from settlements

in the Tigris–Euphrates marshes are also addressed by Guillermo Algaze, *Ancient Mesopotamia at the Dawn of Civilization: The Evolution of an Urban Landscape* (Chicago: University of Chicago Press, 2008).

4. See Pournelle "KLM to CORONA;" Robert M. Adams, *Heartland of Cities: Surveys of Ancient Settlement and Land Use on the Central Floodplain of the Euphrates* (Chicago: University of Chicago Press, 1981).

5. Andrew Lawler, "Murder in Mesopotamia?" *Science* 317 (2007), pp. 1164–1165.

6. See Hans J. Nissen, Peter Damerow, and Robert K. Englund, *Archaic Bookkeeping: Writing and Techniques of Economic Administration in the Ancient Near East*, trans. Peter Larsen (Chicago: University of Chicago Press, 1993).

7. Nir Rosen, "No Going Back," *Boston Review*, September–October 2007.

8. Translation by Maureen Gallery Kovacs, http://www.ancienttexts.org/library/mesopotamian/gilgamesh/tab1.htm

9. *Electronic Text Corpus of Sumerian Literature*, http://etcsl.orinst.ox.ac.uk/cgi-bin/etcsl.cgi?text=t.2.1.7#

10. John Noble Wilford, "At Ur, Ritual Deaths that Were Anything but Serene," *New York Times*, 27 October 2009.

11. http://www.museum.upenn.edu/new/exhibits/ur/about.shtml

12. For a detailed, comprehensive discussion of the Hurrians, see Gernot Wilhelm, *The Hurrians* (rev. ed.) (Warminster: Aris & Phillips, 1989).

13. *Electronic Text Corpus of Sumerian Literature*, http://etcsl.orinst.ox.ac.uk/cgi-bin/etcsl.cgi?text=t.2.4.2.02#

14. J. N. Postgate, *The First Empires* (Oxford: Elsevier Phaidon, 1977), p. 81.

15. *Electronic Text Corpus of Sumerian Literature*, http://etcsl.orinst.ox.ac.uk/cgi-bin/etcsl.cgi?text=t.2.2.2#

16. *Electronic Text Corpus of Sumerian Literature*, http://www.etcsl.orient.ox.ac.uk/section1/tr171.htm

17. For authoritative examinations of Hammurabi of Babylon and his times, see Dominique Charpin, *Hammurabi of Babylon* (London: I. B. Tauris, 2012); Marc van de Mieroop, *King Hammurabi of Babylon* (Malden, MA: Blackwell, 2005).

18. Martha T. Roth, *Law Collections from Mesopotamia and Asia Minor* (2nd ed.) (Atlanta: Scholars Press, 1997), pp. 76–77.

19. Ibid., p. 77.

CHAPTER 3: CRADLE OF EMPIRES

1. Mogens Trolle Larsen, *The Conquest of Assyria: Excavations in an Antique Land* (London: Routledge, 1996), pp. 52–60.

2. Timothy Larsen, "Austen Henry Layard's Nineveh: The Bible and Archaeology in Victorian Britain," *Journal of Religious History* 33 (2009), pp. 66–81. See also Magnus Bernhardsson, *Reclaiming a Plundered Past: Archaeology and Nation Building in Modern Iraq* (Austin: University of Texas Press, 2005).

3. I. L. Finkel and M. J. Seymour (eds.), *Babylon* (Oxford: Oxford University Press, 2008), pp. 118–123, 208.

4. For an authoritative discussion of the history, society, and institutions of the Neo-Assyrian empire, see Francis Joannes, *The Age of Empires: Mesopotamia in the First Millennium BC*, trans. Antonia Nevill (Edinburgh: Edinburgh University Press, 2004), pp. 27–111.

5. A. T. Olmstead, "The Calculated Frightfulness of Ashur Nasir Apal," *Journal of the American Oriental Society* 38 (1918), pp. 209–263; H. R. Hall, *The Ancient History of the Near East: from the Earliest Times to the Battle of Salamis* (11th ed.) (London: Methuen & Methuen, 1950), p. 445.

6. My thanks to Barbara Nevling Porter for pointing out to me Ashurnasirpal's graphic reliefs on the Ninurta temple walls at Kalhu.

7. Such narratives of destruction abound in the texts known as the "Annals" and the "Standard Inscription of Ashurnasirpal." Translations are to be found in Daniel David Luckenbill, *Ancient Records of Assyria and Babylonia* [A.R.A.B.], Vol. 1. *Historical Records of Assyria from the Earliest Times to Sargon* (London: Histories & Mysteries of Man, 1989 [1926]), pp. 138–173. See also the discussions in Mordechai Cogan, *The Raging Torrent: Historical Inscriptions from Assyria and Babylonia Relating to Ancient Israel* (Jerusalem: Carta, 2008).

8. Daniel David Luckenbill, A.R.A.B., Vol. 2. *Historical Records of Assyria from Sargon to the End* (London: Histories & Mysteries of Man, 1989 [1926]), p. 127.

9. Luckenbill, A.R.A.B., Vol. 2, p. 310.

10. For an engaging and authoritative account of the Israelite encounter with both the Assyrian and Babylonian empires, see Eric Cline, *Eden to Exile: Unraveling Mysteries of the Bible* (Washington: National Geographic, 2007), pp. 154ff.

11. For a recent discussion of the history of the Ten Lost Tribes, see Zvi Ben-Dor Benite, *The Ten Lost Tribes: A World History* (Oxford: Oxford University Press, 2009).

12. Stephen E. Ambrose, *Uncommon Courage: Meriwether Lewis, Thomas Jefferson, and the Opening of the American West* (New York: Simon & Schuster, 1996), p. 90.

13. Michael D. Coogan (ed.), *The New Oxford Annotated Bible* (4th ed.) (Oxford: Oxford University Press, 2010), p. 982.

14. Ibid., p. 563.

15. See, among other sources, David Damrosch, *The Buried Book: The Loss and Rediscovery of the Great Epic of Gilgamesh* (New York: Henry Holt, 2006), pp. 155–160 and passim.

16. For an authoritative account of the history, society and economy, and culture of the Neo-Babylonian empire, see Joannes, *The Age of Empires*, pp. 112–202.

17. F. M. Fales, "Arameans and Chaldeans: Environment and Society," in *The Babylonian World*, ed. Gwendolyn Leick (New York: Routledge, 2009), pp. 288–298.

18. Reidar Visser, *The Sadrists of Basra and the Far South of Iraq: The Most Unpredictable Political Face in the Gulf's Oil-Belt Region* (Norwegian Institute of Foreign Affairs, 2008).

19. Andrew Cockburn, *Muqtada: Muqtada al-Sadr, the Shia Revival, and the Struggle for Iraq* (New York: Scribner, 2008), p. 60.

20. http://www.merriam-webster.com/dictionary/Babylon

21. Much of the information in the following discussion is from Stephanie Dalley (ed.), *The Legacy of Mesopotamia* (Oxford: Oxford University Press, 1998) and Finkel and Seymour, *Babylon*.

22. Along with the Great Pyramid at Giza in Egypt, the statue of Zeus at Olympia in Greece, the temple of Artemis at Ephesus (in modern Turkey), the Mausoleum of Halicarnassus (also in modern Turkey), the Colossus of Rhodes (in Greece), and the Pharos at Alexandria (in Egypt).

23. Quoted in Finkel and Seymour, *Babylon*, p. 107.

24. For a locating of the Hanging Gardens at Nineveh, not Babylon, see Stephanie Dalley, *The Mystery of the Hanging Garden of Babylon: An Elusive World Wonder Retraced* (Oxford: Oxford University Press, 2013).

25. Benjamin R. Foster and Karen Polinger Foster, *Civilizations of Ancient Iraq* (Princeton, NJ: Princeton University Press, 2009), p. 131; Norman Yoffee, *Myths of the Archaic State: Evolution of the Earliest Cities, States, and Civilizations* (Cambridge: Cambridge University Press, 2005), pp. 121ff.

26. Coogan, *New Oxford Annotated Bible*, pp. 2173–2174.

27. Joannes, *The Age of Empires*, p. 13.

28. I am indebted to Nina Nash-Robertson, Central Michigan University School of Music, for this reference.

29. See discussions in Finkel and Seymour, *Babylon*.

30. John V. Tolan, *Saracens: Islam in the Medieval European Imagination* (New York: Columbia University Press, 2002), p. 125.

31. Ibid., pp. 99–100.

32. See John K. Cooley, *An Alliance against Babylon: The U.S., Israel, and Iraq* (London: Pluto Press, 2005), esp. pp. 7–22 for an incisive treatment of the effect the Bible's stories of Babylon have had on American Christians. He notes particularly the impact of the American pioneering film-maker D. W. Griffith's movie *Intolerance*, which featured scenes of a sinful Babylon that were shot on a specially constructed set that was unusually expensive for its time. Cooley also quotes an (uncited) American source ca. 2003: "All false systems of religion began in the land of Babylon and will have their consummation from the spirit of Babylon in the last days."

33. D. T. Potts, "Babylonian Sources of Exotic Raw Materials," in *The Babylonian World*, ed. Gwendolyn Leick (New York: Routledge, 2009), p. 136.

34. Charles Gates, *Ancient Cities: The Archaeology of Urban Life in the Ancient Near East and Egypt, Greece, and Rome* (London: Routledge, 2003), p. 181.

35. Finkel and Seymour, *Babylon*, p. 115.

36. Gates, *Ancient Cities*, p. 181.

37. Finkel and Seymour, *Babylon*, p. 61.

38. Gates, *Ancient Cities*, p. 182; Finkel and Seymour, *Babylon*, pp. 50–51.

39. Gates, *Ancient Cities*, p. 185.

40. Finkel and Seymour, *Babylon*, p. 55.

41. A. R. George, "The Tower of Babel: Archaeology, History, and Cuneiform Texts," *Archiv fur Orientforschung* 51 (2005–6), pp. 75–95.

42. Finkel and Seymour, *Babylon*, pp. 56–57.

43. George, "Tower of Babel," p. 17.

44. For a lively discussion of the role and impact of diviners at the Assyrian court at Nineveh, see David Damrosch, *The Buried Book: The Loss and Rediscovery of the Great Epic of Gilgamesh* (New York: Henry Holt, 2006).

45. Foster and Foster, *Civilizations of Ancient Iraq*, p. 138.

46. William H. Stiebing, *Ancient Near Eastern History and Culture* (2nd ed.) (New York: Pearson Longman, 2009), pp. 347–349.

47. See Francesca Rochberg, *The Heavenly Writing: Divination, Horoscopy, and Astronomy in Mesopotamian Culture* (Cambridge: Cambridge University Press, 2004).

48. Stiebing, *Ancient Near Eastern History and Culture*, pp. 347–349; Eleanor Robson, *Mathematics in Ancient Iraq: A Social History* (Princeton, NJ: Princeton University Press, 2008).

49. David Pingree, "Legacies in Astronomy and Celestial Omens," in *The Legacy of Mesopotamia*, ed. Stephanie Dalley (Oxford: Oxford University Press, 1998), p. 137 [125–137].

50. Foster and Foster, *Civilizations of Ancient Iraq*, p. 135.

51. J. Maxwell Miller and John H. Hayes, *A History of Ancient Israel and Judah* (2nd ed.) (Louisville: Westminster John Knox Press, 2006), pp. 488ff.

52. Mark W. Chavalas (ed.), *The Ancient Near East: Historical Sources in Translation* (Malden, MA: Blackwell, 2006), pp. 428–429.

53. Foster and Foster, *Civilizations of Ancient Iraq*, pp. 143–145.

54. Matthew W. Stolper, *Entrepreneurs and Empire* (Istanbul: Nederlands Historisch–Archaeologisch Instituut, 1985).

CHAPTER 4: CRADLE OF RELIGIONS, CRUCIBLE OF CONFLICTS

1. Finkel and Seymour, *Babylon*, p. 91.

2. Thorkild Jacobsen, *The Treasures of Darkness: A History of Mesopotamian Religion* (New Haven: Yale University Press, 1978).

3. Tikvah Frymer-Kensky, *In the Wake of the Goddesses: Women, Culture, and the Biblical Transformation of Pagan Myth* (New York: Free Press, 1992), p. 57.

4. Jean Bottero, *Religion in Ancient Mesopotamia*, pp. 66–67, quoted in Robert Wright, *The Evolution of God* (New York: Little, Brown, 2009), p. 70.

5. Stephanie Dalley, "The Influence of Mesopotamia upon Israel and the Bible," in *The Legacy of Mesopotamia*, ed. Stephanie Dalley (Oxford: Oxford University Press, 1998), p. 75.

6. For more detail about the following, see ibid.

7. Martha T. Roth, *Law Collections from Mesopotamia and Asia Minor* (2nd ed.) (Atlanta: Scholars Press, 1997), pp. 67, 128.

8. See a number of examples in Benjamin R. Foster, *Before the Muses: An Anthology of Akkadian Literature* (3rd ed.) (Bethesda, MD: CDL Press, 2005).

9. Dan Levene, *A Corpus of Magic Bowls: Incantation Texts in Jewish Aramaic from Late Antiquity* (London/New York: Kegan Paul International/Columbia University Press, 2003); Dan Levene, "Rare Magic Inscriptions on Human Skull," *Biblical Archaeology*

Review, March/April 2009. See also Gideon Bohak, *Ancient Jewish Magic: A History* (Cambridge: Cambridge University Press, 2008).

10. Malise Ruthven, "Divided Iran on the Eve," *New York Review of Books* 56(11) (2009), commenting on Abbas Amanat, *Apocalyptic Islam and Iranian Shi'ism* (New York: I. B. Tauris, 2009).

11. See John Curtis, *The Cyrus Cylinder and Ancient Persia: A New Beginning for the Middle East* (London: British Museum, 2013), upon which much of the discussion here is based.

12. Mary Boyce, *Zoroastrians: Their Religious Beliefs and Practices* (London: Routledge, 2001), pp. 8–9.

13. Paul Kriwaczek, *In Search of Zarathustra: The First Prophet and the Ideas that Changed the World* (New York: Alfred A. Knopf, 2003).

14. Boyce, *Zoroastrians*, pp. 26ff.

15. Ibid., p. 42.

16. Ibid., p. 77.

17. Garth Fowden, *Empire to Commonwealth: Consequences of Monotheism in Late Antiquity* (Princeton, NJ: Princeton University Press, 1993), pp. 17–18.

18. Stephanie Dalley, "Occasions and Opportunities: 2. Persian, Greek, and Parthian Overlords," in *The Legacy of Mesopotamia*, ed. Stephanie Dalley (Oxford: Oxford University Press, 1998), p. 39.

19. Foster and Foster, *Civilizations of Ancient Iraq*, p. 148ff.

20. Susan Sherwin-White and Amelie Kuhrt, *From Samarkand to Sardis: A New Approach to the Seleucid Empire* (Berkeley: University of California Press, 1993), p. 20.

21. George Roux, *Ancient Iraq* (3rd ed.) (London: Penguin, 1992), pp. 414ff; Foster and Foster, *Civilizations of Ancient Iraq*, p. 152.

22. Sherwin-White and Kuhrt, *From Samarkand to Sardis*, p. 200.

23. N. Yoffee, *Myths of the Archaic State: Evolution of the Earliest Cities, States, and Civilizations* (Cambridge: Cambridge University Press, 2005), pp. 155–159.

24. Sherwin-White and Kuhrt, *From Samarkand to Sardis*, pp. 36–37.

25. Maria Brosius, *The Persians: An Introduction* (London: Routledge, 2006), pp. 83–84.

26. Benjamin Foster, Karen Polinger Foster, and Patty Gerstenblith, *Iraq beyond the Headlines: History, Archaeology, and War* (Hackensack, NJ: World Scientific, 2005), p. 109.

27. Ibid.

28. Brosius, *The Persians*, p. 101.

29. Sherwin-White and Kuhrt, *From Samarkand to Sardis*, p. 184.

30. As described in Zainab Bahrani, *Rituals of War: The Body and Violence in Mesopotamia* (New York: Zone Books, 2008), p. 49.

31. Foster and Foster, *Civilizations of Ancient Iraq*, p. 161.

32. Ibid., p. 163.

33. Later used as the backdrop for the opening scenes of the famous movie *The Exorcist*.

34. Roux, *Ancient Iraq*, p. 418f.

35. Caroline Alexander, "Iraqis Find Ancient Mithra Temple in Northern Dohuk Province," 24 June 2009, http://www.bloomberg.com/apps/news?pid=20601117&sid =aRKwP5vWGweE

36. Roux, *Ancient Iraq*, p. 418f.

37. F. E. Peters, *The Harvest of Hellenism: A History of the Near East from Alexander the Great to the Triumph of Christianity* (New York: Barnes & Noble, 1970), p. 289.

38. For an authoritative and engaging treatment of early Christianity which takes into account a number of interpretations, see Geza Vermes, *Christian Beginnings: From Nazareth to Nicaea, AD 30–325* (London: Allen Lane, 2012).

39. Peters, *The Harvest of Hellenism*, pp. 532–537; Anthony J. Saldarini as revised by Amy-Jill Levine, "Jewish Responses to Greek and Roman Cultures, 332 BCE to 200 CE," in *The Cambridge Companion to the Bible* (2nd ed.), ed. Bruce Chilton (Cambridge: Cambridge University Press, 2008), pp. 461ff.

40. Maurice Sartre, *The Middle East under Rome*, trans. Catherine Porter and Elizabeth Rawlings (Cambridge, MA: Belknap Press of Harvard University Press, 2005), pp. 329–330.

41. Foster and Foster, *Civilizations of Ancient Iraq*, p. 168ff.

42. Robert McC. Adams, *Land behind Baghdad: A History of Settlement on the Diyala Plains* (Chicago: University of Chicago Press, 1965).

43. See, for example, Michael G. Morony, *Iraq after the Muslim Conquest* (Princeton, NJ: Princeton University Press, 1984), pp. 280ff.

44. See, for a recent treatment of one of them, Joel Walker, *The Legend of Mar Qardagh: Narrative and Christian Heroism in Late Antique Iraq* (Berkeley: University of California Press, 2006).

45. Foster and Foster, *Civilizations of Ancient Iraq*, 168ff.

46. See Fergus Millar, *The Roman Near East, 31 B.C.–A.D. 337* (Cambridge, MA: Harvard University Press, 1993), p. 497.

47. Morony, *Iraq after the Muslim Conquest*, p. 306.

48. Sartre, *The Middle East under Rome*, p. 332.

49. Foster and Foster, *Civilizations of Ancient Iraq*, pp. 173–175; Morony, *The Middle East under Rome*, p. 314.

50. Morony, *The Middle East under Rome*, pp. 308–311.

51. Foster and Foster, *Civilizations of Ancient Iraq*, pp. 173–175.

52. Morony, *The Middle East under Rome*, pp. 312–331.

53. Saldarini, "Jewish Responses to Greek and Roman Cultures," p. 465.

54. Cited in Millar, *Roman Near East*, p. 463; see also L. Michael White, *From Jesus to Christianity: How Four Generations of Visionaries and Storytellers Created the New Testament and Christian Faith* (New York: HarperCollins, 2004), pp. 389–392.

55. Foster and Foster, *Civilizations of Ancient Iraq*, p. 176; Shams C. Inaty, "The Iraqi Christian Community," in *Iraq: Its History, People, and Politics*, ed. by Shams C. Inaty (Amherst, NY: Humanity Books, 2003), p. 132ff.; White, *From Jesus to Christianity*.

56. White, *From Jesus to Christianity*, p. 443.

57. For a very detailed treatment of these, see Morony's discussion in *Iraq after the Muslim Conquest*, upon which I have relied heavily in much of the following.

58. Giusto Traina, *428 AD: An Ordinary Year at the End of the Roman Empire*, trans. Allan Cameron (Princeton, NJ: Princeton University Press, 2009).

59. Warwick Ball, *Rome in the East: The Transformation of an Empire* (London: Routledge, 2001), pp. 134–135.

60. Karen L. King, "Gnosticism," in *Religions of the Ancient World: A Guide*, ed. Sarah Iles Johnston (Cambridge, MA: Harvard University Press, 2004), p. 653.

61. Kurt Rudolph, "Mandaeism," in *The Anchor Bible Dictionary* [A.B.D.], ed. David Noel Freedman, Vol. 4 (New York: Doubleday, 1992), pp. 500–502.

62. The following discussion draws liberally from Paul Allan Mirecki, "Manichaeians and Manichaeism," in A.B.D., Vol. 4, pp. 502–511, and Guy Stroumsa, "Manicheism," in *Religions of the Ancient World: A Guide*, ed. Sarah Iles Johnston (Cambridge, MA: Harvard University Press, 2004), pp. 647–649.

63. Ball, *Rome in the East*, p. 437.

64. Stroumsa, "Manicheism," p. 649.

CHAPTER 5: IRAQ, ISLAM, AND THE GOLDEN AGE OF THE ARAB EMPIRE

1. One problem with which historians still wrestle is understanding what exactly is meant by the designation "Arab" in early documents. Is "Arab" an ethnic designation – i.e., of Arabic speakers? Or does it designate nomadic pastoralists, or people of nomadic origin? Or both?

2. Millar, *The Roman Near East*, p. 495.

3. Hugh Kennedy, *The Great Arab Conquests: How the Spread of Islam Changed the World We Live in* (Philadelphia: Da Capo Press, 2007), p. 37; C. E. Bosworth, "Iran and the Arabs before Islam," in *The Cambridge History of Iran*, Vol. 3 (1). *The Seleucid, Parthian, and Sasanian Periods*, ed. Ehsan Yarshater (Cambridge: Cambridge University Press, 1983), pp. 598–599.

4. Morony, *Iraq after the Muslim Conquest*, pp. 388f.

5. Ibid., pp. 525–526.

6. Miller and Hayes, *History of Ancient Israel and Judah*, p. 409.

7. See "Hadith," in H. A. R. Gibb and J. H. Kramers (eds.), *The Shorter Encyclopedia of Islam* (Leiden: E. J. Brill, 1995), pp. 116–121.

8. A tradition developed later that while residing at Mecca, before the Hegira, Muhammad was whisked off to Jerusalem in a magical night-time journey, and from there – from the very rock upon which the Hebrew Abraham had almost sacrificed his son at God's command – Muhammad was taken into heaven to visit the earlier prophets and be in the glory of God's presence. That spot lies on the Temple Mount in Jerusalem. In the late seventh century, after the Muslim conquest of Palestine, an architectural masterpiece – the Dome of the Rock – was built to commemorate that sacred spot and signal the establishment of Muslim rule at Jerusalem.

9. For a new interpretation of the origins of Islam as a movement of righteous believers in monotheism which included Jews and Christians, see Fred Donner, *Muhammad and the Believers: At the Origins of Islam* (Cambridge, MA: Belknap Press of Harvard University Press, 2010).

10. See R. Stephen Humphreys, *Islamic History: A Framework for Inquiry* (Princeton, NJ: Princeton University Press, 1991), pp. 71ff; Morony, *Iraq after the Muslim Conquest*; Fred McGraw Donner, *The Early Islamic Conquests* (Princeton, NJ: Princeton University Press, 1981); Hugh Kennedy, *When Baghdad Ruled the Muslim World* (Philadelphia: Da Capo Press, 2005).

11. Kennedy, *The Great Arab Conquests*, pp. 56–57.

12. Ascertaining the facts of the Battle of Qadisiyya remains a thorny problem in the history of the early Arab conquests. For some well-informed treatments, see Donner, *The Early Islamic Conquests*, p. 202ff.; Hugh Kennedy, *The Great Arab Conquests*, pp. 108–115; Hugh Kennedy, *The Prophet and the Age of the Caliphates* (2nd ed.) (Harlow, England: Pearson, 2004), p. 57f.

13. Albert Hourani, *A History of the Arab Peoples* (2nd ed.) (Cambridge, MA: Belknap, 2003), e.g. p. 25.

14. In Egypt, the seventh-century Arab conquerors established a camp city, al-Fustat (city of "the tent"), in the environs of the ancient pharaonic capital at Memphis, near the apex of the Nile delta. Al-Fustat became the nucleus of the city of Cairo (al-Qahira, "the Victorious"), which was founded three centuries later.

15. McGuire Gibson, "Nippur and Archaeology in Iraq," in *Oriental Institute 2004–2005 Annual Report*, pp. 82–87.

16. Kennedy, *The Prophet and the Age of the Caliphates*, p. 68f.

17. Asma Afsaruddin, *The First Muslims: History and Memory* (Oxford: Oneworld, 2008), p. 68.

18. Cockburn, *Muqtada al-Sadr*, p. 22.

19. Quoted in Bernard Lewis (ed.), *Islam: From the Prophet Muhammad to the Capture of Constantinople*, Vol. 1, pp. 23–24, cited in Thabit A. J. Abdullah, *A Short History of Iraq* (London: Pearson Longman, 2003), p. 15.

20. Morony, *Iraq after the Muslim Conquest*, pp. 158–162.

21. Kennedy, *The Prophet and Age*, pp. 116–118.

22. Kennedy, *When Baghdad Ruled*, p. 12.

23. This book went to press shortly after the publication of a superb, accessible treatment of the history of Baghdad: Justin Marozzi, *Baghdad: City of Peace, City of Blood* (London: Allen Lane, 2014).

24. For a recent treatment of the Abbasid caliphs and Abbasid Baghdad, see Amira K. Bennison, *The Great Caliphs: The Golden Age of the 'Abbasid Empire* (New Haven: Yale University Press, 2009). See also Benson Bobrick, *The Caliph's Splendor: Islam and the West in the Golden Age of Baghdad* (New York: Simon & Schuster, 2012).

25. Cited in Bernard Lewis (ed.), *Islam: From the Prophet Muhammad to the Conquest of Constantinople*, Vol. 2. *Religion and Society* (New York: Oxford University Press, 1987), p. 69.

26. Ibid., p. 70.

27. Kennedy, *When Baghdad Ruled*, pp. 152–155.

28. Husein Hadawy (trans.), *The Arabian Nights* (New York: Alfred A. Knopf, 1990); Robert Irwin, *The Arabian Nights: A Companion* (London: Penguin, 1994), p. 2.

29. Jonathan Lyons, *The House of Wisdom: How the Arabs Transformed Western Civilization* (New York: Bloomsbury Press, 2009), p. 61.

30. Irwin, *Arabian Nights*, pp. 122–124.

31. See Philip F. Kennedy, *Abu Nuwas: A Genius of Poetry* (Oxford: Oneworld, 2005).

32. See discussions of his work in Kennedy, *Abu Nuwas* and Robert Irwin (ed.), *Night & Horses & the Desert: An Anthology of Classical Arabic Literature* (New York: Anchor Books, 1999), p. 123ff.

33. William Ochsenwald and Sydney Nettleton Fisher, *The Middle East: A History* (6th ed.) (New York: McGraw-Hill, 2003), pp. 65–66.

34. Lyons, *The House of Wisdom*, p. 61.

35. Michael Axworthy, *A History of Iran: Empire of the Mind* (New York: Basic Books, 2008), p. 79ff.

36. Lyons, *The House of Wisdom*, p. 63.

37. Ibid., pp. 62–63. For much of this discussion, see also John Esposito, *Islam: The Straight Path* (rev. 3rd ed.) (New York: Oxford University Press, 2005), pp. 51–57.

38. Phillip K. Hitti, *History of the Arabs* (10th ed.) (New York: St. Martin's Press, 1970), p. 120.

39. A magisterial treatment of the translation movement under the Abbasids, and the role of the Caliph al-Mamun, is Dimitri Gutas, *Greek Thought, Arabic Culture: The Graeco-Arabic Translation Movement in Baghdad and Early 'Abbasid Society (2nd–4th/8th–10th Centuries)* (London: Routledge, 1998). For the reign of al-Mamun, see Michael Cooperson, *Al Ma'mun* (Oxford: Oneworld, 2005). For other recent treatments of the Abbasids' role in the preservation and transmission of Greco-Roman philosophy and science, as well as the original research conducted by Arab scholars and scientists during this era, see Jim al-Khalili, *The House of Wisdom: How Arabic Science Saved Ancient Knowledge and Gave Us the Renaissance* (New York: Penguin, 2011); reviewed by John Noble Wilford, "The Muslim Art of Science," *New York Times*, 20 May 2011, who highlights Khalili's comparison of Abbasid Baghdad to Periclean Athens and Renaissance Florence. Hans Belting's *Florence and Baghdad: Renaissance Art and Arab Science*, trans. Deborah Lucas Schneider (Cambridge, MA: Belknap Press of Harvard University Press, 2011) provides an original interpretive treatment of how Renaissance artists made use of the eleventh-century Baghdad mathematician Ibn al-Haithan's elucidation of the theory of perspective.

40. It would be remiss not to note that the scholarly activity in Abbasid Baghdad also influenced the centuries-old Jewish rabbinical academies of Iraq, where scholars of the Babylonian Talmud cemented their superiority over the other great pole of Talmudic learning in Palestine after a long history of rivalry. On this issue, and on Jewish cultural and intellectual life under the Abbasids, see Robert Brody, *The Geonim of Babylonia and the Shaping of Medieval Jewish Culture* (New Haven: Yale University Press, 2013).

41. Esposito, *Islam*, p. 52.

42. Cited in Lewis, *Islam*, Vol. 2, pp. 19–20.

43. Esposito, *Islam*, pp. 70–71.

44. William Dalrymple, "The Muslims in the Middle," *New York Times*, 16 August 2010.

45. Much of the following discussion is based on Ahmet T. Karamustafa, *Sufism: The Formative Period* (Berkeley: University of California Press, 2007), pp. 1–60.

46. From Margaret Smith, *Rabia the Mystic and Her Fellow-Saints in Islam* (Cambridge: Cambridge University Press, 1928), p. 30, cited in Esposito, *Islam*, p. 102. See also Karamustafa, *Sufism*, pp. 3–4.

47. Kennedy, *Prophet and Age*, p. 378; Robert M. Adams, *Land behind Baghdad*.

48. Kennedy, *Prophet and Age*, p. 197.

CHAPTER 6: INTERLUDE: FROM CRADLE TO BACKWATER

1. Thabit A. J. Abdullah, *A Short History of Iraq* (London: Pearson Longman, 2003), pp. 26–27.

2. Ibid., pp. 29–30.

3. Amin Maalouf, *The Crusades through Arab Eyes*, trans. Jon Rothschild (New York: Schocken, 1984), pp. 53–55; Carole Hillenbrand, *The Crusades: Islamic Perspectives* (New York: Routledge, 2000), p. 78ff.

4. Maalouf, *The Crusades through Arab Eyes*, p. 55.

5. Hillenbrand, *The Crusades*, pp. 80–81.

6. Ibid., pp. 184–185.

7. Ibid., pp. 240–241.

8. John V. Tolan, *Sons of Ishmael: Muslims through European Eyes in the Middle Ages* (Gainesville: University Press of Florida, 2008), p. 84.

9. Ibid., pp. 82–85.

10. Ibid., pp. 79–100.

11. Ibid., pp. 79–80.

12. See Hillenbrand, *The Crusades*, pp. 118, 184–185, 592–613, for much of this and the following discussion.

13. Hannes Mohring, *Saladin: The Sultan and His Times, 1138–1193*, trans. David S. Bachrach (Baltimore: Johns Hopkins University Press, 2005), pp. 102–103.

14. Hillenbrand, *The Crusades*, pp. 592–613.

15. Mohring, *Saladin*, p. 103.

16. See Ofra Bengio, *Saddam's Word: Political Discourse in Iraq* (New York: Oxford University Press, 2002).

17. Quoted in Jason Goodwin, "The Glory that Was Baghdad," *Wilson Quarterly*, Spring 2003; and in Amina Elbendary, "They Came to Baghdad: Its Famous Names," *Al-Ahram Weekly Online* 634 (2003), http://weekly.ahram.org.eg/2003/634/bo2.htm. I am also indebted to Elbendary's article for some other details of the Mongol conquest of Baghdad as recorded in the account of Ibn Kathir.

18. See, with references, Ross E. Dunn, *The Adventures of Ibn Battuta: A Muslim Traveler of the 14th Century* (2nd ed.) (Berkeley: University of California Press, 2005), pp. 81–82.

19. Erik Hildinger, *Warriors of the Steppe: A Military History of Central Asia, 500 B.C. to A.D. 1700* (Cambridge, MA: Da Capo Press, 2001), pp. 148–149.

20. Justin Marozzi, *Tamerlane: Sword of Islam, Conqueror of the World* (Philadelphia: Da Capo Press, 2004), p. 312.

21. Max Rodenbeck, "The Time of the Shia," *New York Review of Books* 53(13) (2006).

22. Quoted in al-Dhahabi's *Tarikh al-Islam* (The History of Islam), trans. Joseph de Somogyi, cited in Amina Elbendary, "They Came to Baghdad: Its Famous Names," *Al-Ahram Weekly Online* 634 (2003), http://weekly.ahram.org.eg/2003/634/bo2.htm

23. Bernard Lewis, *The Middle East: A Brief History of the Last 2000 Years* (New York: Scribner, 1995), pp. 97–99.

24. David Morgan, *The Mongols* (2nd ed.) (Malden, MA: Blackwell, 2007), pp. 176–177.

25. J. J. Saunders, *The History of the Mongol Conquests* (Philadelphia: University of Pennsylvania Press, 1971), pp. 173–174.

26. Marozzi, *Tamerlane*, pp. 314–315; see also Beatrice Forbes Mainz, *The Rise and Rule of Tamerlane* (Cambridge: Cambridge University Press, 1991), pp. 87–103.

27. Abdullah, *A Short History of Iraq*, p. 52.

28. For the Safavids, see Andrew Newman, *Safavid Iran: Rebirth of a Persian Empire* (London: I. B. Tauris, 2009).

29. See Hala Fattah with Frank Caso, *A Brief History of Iraq* (New York: Checkmark Books, 2009), pp. 119–120, for discussion of the control of silk trade as an important contributor to Ottoman–Safavid tensions.

30. And also the southern coast of the Arabian Peninsula, where in 1839 the British established a foothold in Aden (in what is now Yemen). Aden became a British colony in 1937 and remained so until 1967.

31. Peter Sluglett, *Britain in Iraq: Contriving King and Country* (New York: Columbia University Press, 2007), pp. 2–3.

32. Abdullah, *A Short History of Iraq*, p. 79.

33. Ibid., pp. 81–83.

34. For the impact of the Tanzimat reforms in Iraq, see Ebubekir Ceylan, *The Ottoman Origins of Modern Iraq: Political Reform, Modernization and Development in the Nineteenth-Century Middle East* (London: I. B. Tauris, 2011).

35. The following discussion derives largely from Yitzhak Nakash, *The Shi'is of Iraq* (2nd ed.) (Princeton, NJ: Princeton University Press, 2003), pp. 1–48.

36. Yitzhak Nakash, "The Conversion of Iraq's Tribes to Shi'ism," *International Journal of Middle East Studies* 26(3) (1994), pp. 443–463.

CHAPTER 7: THE CREATION AND ZENITH OF MODERN IRAQ

1. Sluglett, *Britain in Iraq*, pp. 1–2.

2. Marion Farouk-Sluglett and Peter Sluglett, *Iraq since 1958: From Revolution to Dictatorship* (rev. ed.) (London: I. B. Tauris, 2001), p. 7.

3. Sluglett, *Britain in Iraq*, pp. 1–2; Nabil al-Tikriti, "Was There an Iraq before

There Was an Iraq?" *International Journal of Contemporary Iraqi Studies* 3(2) (2009), pp. 133–142; Reidar Visser, "Proto-political Conceptions of 'Iraq' in Late Ottoman Times," *International Journal of Contemporary Iraqi Studies* 3(2) (2009), pp. 143–154.

4. Farouk-Sluglett and Sluglett, *Iraq since 1958*, p. 8.

5. Fisher's role in the conversion of the British fleet to oil propulsion led him to be called "the godfather of oil" – and, by some, the "oil maniac." See Daniel Yergin, *The Prize: The Epic Quest for Oil, Money, and Power* (New York: Free Press, 2008), pp. 134–148.

6. Farouk-Sluglett and Sluglett, *Iraq since 1958*, p. 8.

7. Ibid., p. 8. See also Sean McMeekin, *The Berlin–Baghdad Express: the Ottoman Empire and Germany's Bid for World Power, 1898–1918* (Cambridge, MA: Belknap Press of Harvard University Press, 2010).

8. The Ottoman decision to join Germany and the Hapsburgs in this alliance was not without misgivings; see David Fromkin, *A Peace to End All Peace: The Fall of the Ottoman Empire and the Creation of the Modern Middle East* (New York: Avon, 1989), pp. 49–76.

9. Jack Bernstein, *The Mesopotamia Mess: The British Invasion of Iraq in 1914* (Redondo Beach, CA: Interlingua, 2008), p. 98.

10. The journalist-historian Scott Anderson has argued that by February 1917 Lawrence, against the orders of his superiors, had informed Husayn's son Faisal of the contents of the Sykes–Picot Agreement. See Scott Anderson, *Lawrence in Arabia: War, Deceit, Imperial Folly and the Making of the Modern Middle East* (New York: Doubleday, 2013), p. 270ff.

11. Fromkin, *A Peace to End All Peace*, p. 148.

12. The classic, though pro-Zionist, treatment of this subject is Barbara W. Tuchman, *Bible and Sword: England and Palestine from the Bronze Age to Balfour* (New York: Ballantine, 1984 [1956]). See also Donald M. Lewis, *The Origins of Christian Zionism: Lord Shaftesbury and Evangelical Support for a Jewish Homeland* (Cambridge: Cambridge University Press, 2010).

13. See Piers Brendon, *The Decline and Fall of the British Empire, 1781–1997* (London: Vintage, 2008), p. 314.

14. My thanks to my anonymous reader for this information.

15. Farouk-Sluglett and Sluglett, *Iraq since 1958*, pp. 9–10; Brendon, *Decline and Fall of the British Empire*, p. 316.

16. The French expulsion of Faisal from Damascus occasioned the perhaps apocryphal report of the French general's disrespectful visit to the tomb of Saladin.

17. Later there was some indecision as to whether Mosul should remain in Britain's mandate or be allocated to the new republic of Turkey. A League of Nations commission eventually assigned Mosul to the new Iraq. See Sarah Shields, "Mosul, the Ottoman Legacy and the League of Nations," *International Journal of Contemporary Iraqi Studies* 3(2) (2009).

18. Adeed Dawisha, *Arab Nationalism in the Twentieth Century: From Triumph to Despair* (Princeton, NJ: Princeton University Press, 2003), p. 39.

19. For the impact of the R.A.F. in Iraq during this era, see Sluglett, *Britain in Iraq*, p. 184ff. On the alleged R.A.F. use of chemical gas against Iraqis, see ibid., pp. 279–280 n. 20.

20. Fromkin, *Peace to End All Peace*, p. 508; Brendon, *Decline and Fall of the British Empire*, p. 319.

21. Noted in Adeed Dawisha, *Iraq: A Political History from Independence to Occupation* (Princeton, NJ: Princeton University Press, 2009), p. 155.

22. Toby Dodge, *Inventing Iraq: The Failure of Nation Building and a History Denied* (New York: Columbia University Press, 2003), pp. 34–35, 132, 153–154.

23. See Ebubekir Ceylan, "Carrot or Stick? Ottoman Tribal Policy in Baghdad, 1831–1876," *International Journal of Contemporary Iraqi Studies* 3(2) (2009).

24. Dodge, *Inventing Iraq*, p. 65.

25. Ibid., pp. 43–100.

26. Cited in Fromkin, *Peace to End All Peace*, p. 181.

27. Dodge, *Inventing Iraq*, Chapter 6.

28. Farouk-Sluglett and Sluglett, *Iraq since 1958*, pp. 30–35; Dodge, *Inventing Iraq*.

29. Fromkin, *Peace to End All Peace*, p. 93.

30. Dodge, *Inventing Iraq*, p. 65.

31. Ibid., p. 64.

32. Ibid., p. 11; Fromkin, *Peace to End All Peace*, pp. 144, 326–327.

33. Edward Said, *Orientalism* (New York: Vintage, 1979).

34. Cited in Roger Adelson, *London and the Invention of the Middle East: Money, Power, and War, 1902–1922* (New Haven: Yale University Press, 1995), p. 205.

35. Christopher Catherwood, *Churchill's Folly: How Winston Churchill Created Modern Iraq* (New York: Carroll & Graf, 2004), pp. 64–67.

36. Ritchie Ovendale, *The Longman Companion to the Middle East since 1914* (London: Longman, 1992), pp. 43–44.

37. Fromkin, *Peace to End All Peace*, pp. 534–536.

38. Ovendale, *Longman Companion to the Middle East*, p. 44f.

39. Farouk-Sluglett and Sluglett, *Iraq since 1958*, pp. 13–14; Catherwood, *Churchill's Folly*, pp. 64–67; Phebe Marr, *The Modern History of Iraq* (2nd ed.) (Boulder, CO: Westview Press, 2004), p. 30.

40. Abdullah, *Short History*, pp. 132–133; Ovendale, *Longman Companion to the Middle East*, pp. 43–45. See also Marian Kent, *Oil and Empire: British Policy and Mesopotamian Oil, 1900–1920* (London: Macmillan, 1976).

41. Benedict Anderson, *Imagined Communities: Reflections on the Origin and Spread of Nationalism* (rev. ed.) (New York: Verso: 2006).

42. Farouk-Sluglett and Sluglett, *Iraq since 1958*, p. 15.

43. The classic study is George Antonius, *The Arab Awakening: The Story of the Arab National Movement* (Beirut: Khayat's, 1938).

44. Much of the following discussion is drawn from Farouk-Sluglett and Sluglett, *Iraq since 1958*, p. 17ff; Dawisha, *Arab Nationalism*, pp. 49–74; and Malik Mufti, *Sovereign Creations: Pan-Arabism and Political Order in Syria and Iraq* (Ithaca, NY: Cornell University Press, 1996), p. 28ff.

45. Dawisha, *Arab Nationalism*, pp. 47–48.

46. Hind A. Haider, "Nationalism, Archaeology and Ideology in Iraq from 1921 to the Present," M.A. thesis, McGill University, Montreal, 2001, p. 2. See also Amatzia Baram, "A Case of Imported Identity: The Modernizing Secular Ruling Elites of Iraq and the Concept of Mesopotamian-Inspired Territorial Nationalism, 1922–1992," *Poetics Today* 15(2) (1994), pp. 279–319; Phebe Marr, "The Development of a Nationalist Ideology in Iraq, 1920–1941," *Muslim World* 75 (1985), pp. 85–101.

47. Reidar Visser, "Operation Iraqi Partition," *Gulf Analysis*, posted 1 September 2010.

48. Dawisha, *Arab Nationalism*, p. 90.

49. See Sluglett, *Britain in Iraq*, p. 94ff., for the debate over military conscription during the 1920s.

50. Adeed Dawisha, *Iraq: A Political History from Independence to Occupation* (Princeton, NJ: Princeton University Press, 2009), pp. 166–169.

51. Dawisha, *Arab Nationalism*, p. 119.

52. Ibid., pp. 117–128.

53. Johan Franzen, "Losing Hearts and Minds in Iraq: Britain, Cold War Propaganda and the Challenge of Communism, 1945–1958," *Historical Research* 83(222) (2010), pp. 747–762.

54. Farouk-Sluglett and Sluglett, *Iraq since 1958*, pp. 38–45.

55. For this and much of the following discussion, see Orit Bashkin, *New Babylonians: A History of Jews in Modern Iraq* (Stanford, CA: Stanford University Press, 2012), pp. 7–14. Also see Orit Bashkin, *The Other Iraq: Pluralism and Culture in Hashemite Iraq* (Stanford, CA: Stanford University Press, 2009); Abbas Shiblak, *Iraqi Jews: A History of Mass Exodus* (London: Saqi Books, 2005).

56. Bashkin, *New Babylonians*, p. 12.

57. Charles Tripp, *A History of Iraq* (3rd ed.) (Cambridge: Cambridge University Press, 2007), pp. 103, 119ff.

58. Ibid., pp. 117–118.

59. Farouk-Sluglett and Sluglett, *Iraq since 1958*, pp. 38–45.

60. Ibid., pp. 30–35.

61. Tripp, *History of Iraq*, pp. 132–138.

62. Dawisha, *Iraq*, pp. 166–169, notes that personal gratitude also had a role in the monarchy's ties to the British. The Prince Regent Abd' al-Ilah was always grateful to Britain for its help in saving his family when Abdul Aziz ibn Saud drove them from the Hejaz in the 1920s.

63. Dawisha, *Arab Nationalism*, p. 139.

64. Ibid., p. 183.

65. The incident is described by former Soviet diplomat Yevgeny Primakov in *Russia and the Arabs: Behind the Scenes in the Middle East from the Cold War to the Present*, trans. Paul Gould (New York: Basic Books, 2009), p. 2.

66. Along these lines, see the comments by Dawisha, *Iraq*, pp. 158–165.

67. Marr, *Modern History of Iraq*, pp. 101–110.

68. Tripp, *History of Iraq*, pp. 164–177.

69. Saddam Hussein was earlier known as Saddam Hussein al-Tikriti, which indicated his tribal roots in the region of the city of Tikrit, like those of his predecessor, and uncle, Ahmad Hassan al-Bakr. In the late 1970s, the Baathist government abolished the practice of including such tribal and regional indicators in personal names, probably to hide the fact that so many of the regime's insiders came from the region of Tikrit and the Sunni Arab northwest. See Shahram Chubin and Charles Tripp, *Iran and Iraq at War* (Boulder, CO: Westview Press, 1987), p. 94.

70. Dilip Hiro, *The Longest War: The Iran–Iraq Military Conflict* (New York: Routledge, 1991), p. 148.

71. Fattah, *Brief History of Iraq*, p. 220.

72. Perhaps the most celebrated account of this aspect of Saddam's regime is to be found in Samir al-Khalil (the nom de plume of Kanan Makiya), *Republic of Fear: The Inside Story of Saddam's Iraq* (New York: Pantheon Books, 1990).

73. Marr, *Modern History of Iraq*, p. 90.

74. Ibid., pp. 83–87.

75. Ibid., pp. 108–111.

76. Dawisha, *Arab Nationalism*, p. 174, 294.

77. See the discussions in Eric Davis, *Memories of State: Politics, History, and Collective Identity in Modern Iraq* (Berkeley: University of California Press, 2005), p. 12ff. See also Amatzia Baram, *Culture, History & Ideology in the Formation of Ba'thist Iraq, 1968–1989* (New York: St. Martin's Press, 1991); Amatzia Baram, "Mesopotamian Identity in Ba'thi Iraq," *Middle East Studies* 19 (1983), pp. 426–455.

78. Baram, "Mesopotamian Identity," pp. 26, 134.

79. Marr, *Modern History of Iraq*, pp. 168–170.

80. Ibid., pp. 101–102, 133 f.

81. Ibid., p. 159ff.

82. Ibid., pp. 161–167.

CHAPTER 8: THE LONG DESCENT

1. Stephen Zunes, *Tinderbox* (Monroe, ME: Common Courage Press, 2002).

2. Patrick Cockburn, "Leaving Iraq: The Ruin They'll Leave Behind," *Counterpunch*, 19 July 2010, http://www.counterpunch.org/patrick07192010.html

3. Stephen Kinzer, *All the Shah's Men: An American Coup and the Roots of Middle East Terror* (2nd ed.) (Hoboken, NJ: Wiley, 2008).

4. Marr, *Modern History of Iraq*, pp. 152–158.

5. Peter Harling and Hamid Yasin, "Iraq's Diverse Shia," *Le Monde Diplomatique*, September 2006.

6. Argued by Chubin and Tripp, *Iraq and Iran at War*, pp. 53–67.

7. Cited in Hiro, *The Longest War*, pp. 205 and 241.

8. Ray Takeyh, "The Iran–Iraq War: A Reassessment," *Middle East Journal* 64 (2010), p. 367 and note 6. For another retrospective assessment of the war, see Joost Hiltermann, "Deep Traumas, Fresh Ambitions: Legacies of the Iran–Iraq War," *Middle East Report* 257 (2010), pp. 6–15.

9. Phebe Marr, "One Iraq or Many? What Has Happened to Iraqi Identity?" in *Iraq between Occupations: Perspectives from 1920 to the Present*, ed. Amatzia Baram, Achim Rohde, and Ronen Zeidel (New York: Palgrave Macmillan, 2010), p. 27.

10. Chubin and Tripp, *Iran and Iraq at War*, p. 10.

11. Davis, *Memories of State*, p. 148ff.; Fattah, *Brief History*, pp. 223–228.

12. Davis, *Memories of State*, pp. 187–188.

13. Trita Parsi, "A Campaign for War with Iran Begins," *Salon.com*, 13 August 2010. See also Parsi's treatment of Israel's relations with Iran in *Treacherous Alliance: The Secret Dealings of Israel, Iran, and the United States* (New Haven: Yale University Press, 2007).

14. See Patrick Cockburn, *Muqtada al-Sadr and the Battle for the Future of Iraq* (New York: Scribner, 2008), p. 46f.; Chubin and Tripp, *Iran and Iraq at War*, pp. 53–67; Eric Davis, "Reflections on Religion and Politics in Post-Ba'thist Iraq," *TAARI Newsletter* 3(1) (2008), pp. 13–15; Davis, *Memories of State*, pp. 187–188.

15. Joost R. Hiltermann, *A Poisonous Affair: America, Iraq, and the Gassing of Halabja* (Cambridge: Cambridge University Press, 2007), pp. 29–34.

16. Samantha Power, *"A Problem from Hell": America and the Age of Genocide* (New York: Basic Books, 2002), p. 178.

17. The most recent authoritative treatments of the Anfal campaign are to be found in Power, *"A Problem from Hell,"* pp. 170–245; Hiltermann, *A Poisonous Affair*; and Middle East Watch, *Genocide in Iraq: The Anfal Campaign against the Kurds* (New York: Human Rights Watch, 1993).

18. Middle East Watch, *Genocide in Iraq*, pp. xiii–xiv; see also Hiro, *The Longest War*, p. 201; Power, *"A Problem from Hell"*, p. 188ff.

19. A premier example of how the Halabja incident was thus employed is Jeffrey Goldberg, "The Great Terror," *New Yorker*, 25 March 2002.

20. On the other hand, it is noteworthy that during the war the Reagan administration also secretly attempted to provide arms to Iran (via Israel), as part of a deal whereby the U.S. hoped the Iranian leadership would intercede with Shi'ite militias in Lebanon who had taken Americans hostage there during that country's civil war (1975–91). The scandal that erupted when news of this episode – the "Irangate" or "Iran–Contra" scandal – became public in 1986 and 1987 came close to crippling the Reagan administration. The Reagan administration made a point of emphasizing its support for Iraq for the rest of the war. See Hiro, *The Longest War*, p. 215ff. Also, throughout the war, Israel openly favored – and sold weapons to – Iran, despite U.S. protests. The Israelis regarded Saddam's Arab nationalism as a much greater threat than Khomeini's anti-Israel rhetoric.

21. Ussama Makdisi, *Faith Misplaced: The Broken Promise of U.S.–Arab Relations: 1820–2001* (New York: Basic Books, 2010), p. 334.

22. Takeyh, "The Iran–Iraq War," pp. 376–377.

23. U.S. Senate Committee on Banking, Housing and Urban Affairs, "U.S. Chemical and Biological Warfare-Related Dual-Use Exports to Iraq and Their Possible Impact on the Health Consequences of the Persian Gulf War," May 1994, http://www.gulfweb.org/bigdoc/report/riegle1.html

24. Power, *"A Problem from Hell"*, pp. 188ff, 545 n. 11.

25. Quoted in ibid., p. 235.

26. Quoted in Hiro, *The Longest War*, p. 186.

27. Yergin, *The Prize*, pp. 140, 702, cited in *Wikipedia*, "Carter Doctrine," http://en.wikipedia.org/wiki/Carter_Doctrine#cite_note-2

28. Hiro, *The Longest War*, pp. 186 ff.

29. Takeyh, "The Iran–Iraq War," pp. 374–378.

30. Power, *"A Problem from Hell"*, p. 548 n. 64.

31. Marr, "One Iraq or Many?" p. 28.

32. Power, *"A Problem from Hell"*, pp. 235, 552 n. 148.

33. There was much uncertainty about what Ambassador Glaspie said to Saddam in that meeting until late 2010, when Glaspie's cable to Washington describing the meeting was made public. See also Peter Sluglett, "Iraq under Siege: Politics, Society and Economy 1990–2003," in *From Desolation to Reconstruction: Iraq's Troubled Journey*, ed. Mokhtar Lamani and Bessma Momani (Waterloo, ON: Wilfrid Laurier University Press, 2010), pp. 13–33.

34. Francis Fukuyama, *The End of History and the Last Man* (New York: Free Press, 1992).

35. Note also Makdisi, *Faith Misplaced*, p. 333.

36. According to documents captured by U.S. forces in 2003; reported in Michael R. Gordon, "Hussein Wanted Soviets to Head off U.S. in 1991," *New York Times*, 19 January 2011.

37. Marr, "One Iraq or Many?" p. 28.

38. From transcripts of radio transmissions, as cited in Cockburn, *Muqtada*, p. 69.

39. Ray Takeyh, "Iran's New Iraq," *Middle East Journal* 62 (1968), p. 20 and n. 27, citing (among others) Yitzhak Nakash, *Reaching for Power: The Shi'a in the Modern Arab World* (Princeton, NJ: Princeton University Press, 2006), pp. 72–99; Vali Nasr, *The Shia Revival: How Conflicts within Islam Will Shape the Future* (New York: W. W. Norton, 2006), pp. 185–211; Ali Allawi, *The Occupation of Iraq: Winning the War, Losing the Peace* (New Haven: Yale University Press, 2007).

40. Stephen Starr, "Mandeans in Struggle for Existence," *Asia Times*, 18 August 2010.

41. Saddam had even sought, and been granted, Tehran's permission to send a major portion of his air force to Iran for safe-keeping in the face of the overwhelming might of the U.S.-led forces.

42. The best known of these attacks was Operation *Desert Fox*, carried out over four days in December 1998.

43. Gareth Porter, "From Military-Industrial Complex to Permanent War State," *CommonDreams.org*, 17 January 2011.

44. Jeff Gerth, "Report Offered Bleak Outlook about Iraq Oil," *New York Times*, 5 October 2003.

45. The devastation wreaked on Iraq by the U.N. sanctions is analyzed in Anthony Arnove (ed.), *Iraq under Siege: The Deadly Impact of Sanctions and War* (Cambridge, MA: South End Press, 2000); Joy Gordon, *Invisible War: The United States and the Iraq*

Sanctions (Cambridge, MA: Harvard University Press, 2010); and Andrew Cockburn, "Worth It," *London Review of Books* 32(14) (2010), pp. 9–10. See also Joy Gordon, "Lessons We Should Have Learned from the Iraqi Sanctions," *Foreign Policy Middle East Channel*, posted 8 July 2010; Joy Gordon, "Invisible War: How Thirteen Years of US-Imposed Economic Sanctions Devastated Iraq before the 2003 Invasion," *Open Democracy Now*, posted 1 September 2010. Gordon has especially studied the U.N. records documenting the activities of the 661 Committee. Any member of the committee had the prerogative of vetoing the proposed importing of a specific material. Her analysis suggests that the United States' representative played an especially strong role in blocking the import of materials that might generally have qualified as humanitarian in nature; in ninety percent of cases, they acted unilaterally to block the import of some material on the grounds that it might be of "dual use." It can be argued that the U.S. abused this prerogative, consistently blocking items crucial for maintaining public health, such as chemicals for water purification, replacement equipment for electrical generators, and pipes for water. In what may be regarded as abuse of this prerogative, the 661 Committee blocked the importing of salt, children's bicycles, fabric for making clothes, and even materials for making diapers, and considered blocking children's vaccines, powdered milk, and even egg yolks (reasoning that egg yolks might be used to grow biological cultures as precursors for W.M.D.s).

46. The Clinton administration suffered a major blow in the court of world opinion in 1996: during an interview with the C.B.S. news program *60 Minutes*, U.S. Secretary of State Madeleine Albright, when asked whether she believed that the death of half a million Iraqi children because of the sanctions was worth it, replied, "we think the price is worth it."

47. John Mueller and Karl Mueller, "Sanctions of Mass Destruction," *Foreign Affairs* 78 (1999), pp. 43–53, cited in Peter L. Pellett, "Sanctions, Food, Nutrition, and Health in Iraq," in *Iraq under Siege: The Deadly Impact of Sanctions and War*, ed. Anthony Arnove (Cambridge, MA: South End Press, 2000), p. 197.

48. Davis, "Reflections on Religion and Politics in Post-Ba'thist Iraq," pp. 13–15; see also Marr, "One Iraq or Many?" p. 29.

49. Charles Duelfer, "The Iraqi Who Knew Too Much," www.foreignpolicy.com, 9 August 2010. See also Andrew Cockburn and Patrick Cockburn, *Out of the Ashes: The Resurrection of Saddam Hussein* (New York: HarperCollins, 1999).

50. Hence the concern expressed by Bush's national security advisor (and later secretary of state), Condoleezza Rice, during the run-up to the invasion of Iraq as the U.S. and its allies sought evidence of that program, when she said, "we don't want the smoking gun to be a mushroom cloud."

51. The fourth aircraft crashed into a sparsely populated area of rural Pennsylvania after some of the passengers, alerted by friends and family via cellphone that other planes had been crashed into the World Trade Center and Pentagon, broke into the cockpit and prevented the hijackers from carrying out their mission – which was probably to crash their plane into either the White House or the Capitol in Washington, D.C.

52. Events of this turbulent era in Afghanistan have been discussed in a number of fine sources, including Steve Coll, *Ghost Wars: The Secret History of the CIA, Afghanistan,*

and Bin Laden, from the Soviet Invasion to September 10, 2001 (New York: Penguin, 2004); George Crile, *Charlie Wilson's War: The Extraordinary Story of the Largest Covert Operation in History* (New York: Atlantic Monthly Press, 2003); Lawrence Wright, *The Looming Tower: Al Qaeda and the Road to 9/11* (New York: Vintage, 2007); and Ahmed Rashid, *Taliban: Militant Islam, Oil, and Fundamentalism in Central Asia* (2nd ed.) (New Haven: Yale University Press, 2010).

53. National Commission on Terrorist Attacks upon the United States, *The 9/11 Commission Report: Final Report of the National Commission on Terrorist Attacks upon the United States* (New York: W. W. Norton, 2004).

54. See the account by Bush's counterterrorism adviser, Richard A. Clarke, *Against All Enemies: Inside America's War on Terror* (New York: Free Press, 2004).

55. Israel and its supporters in the U.S. pushed hard for the U.S. to invade Iraq, especially when it became apparent that Bush intended to move against Syria and Iran after disposing of Saddam and that U.S. success in Iraq might compel the Palestinian leadership to acquiesce to Israel's occupation of the West Bank. As early as 2002, Israeli politicians were insisting that Saddam was building a nuclear arsenal, and were passing to the U.S. flawed intelligence about Iraq's alleged W.M.D.s. Israeli leaders also worked to demonize Saddam as a second Adolf Hitler set on inflicting another Holocaust on the Jewish people by using W.M.D.s against Israel. Some U.S. officials – among them Douglas Feith, Paul Wolfowitz, and Richard Perle – likewise raised the specter of a Saddam-inflicted second Holocaust as reason for invading Iraq in 2003. See John J. Mearsheimer and Stephen M. Walt, *The Israel Lobby and U.S. Foreign Policy* (New York: Farrar, Straus and Giroux, 2008), pp. 229–262; Stephen M. Walt, "Bush, Blair, and Iraq (Round II). A Reply to John Judis," *Foreign Policy*, posted 16 February 2010; see also Thomas Ricks, *Fiasco: The American Military Adventure in Iraq* (New York: Penguin, 2006), pp. 16, 77.

56. Some in the U.S. advocated further U.S. military intervention in other Middle Eastern countries in order to ignite a chain reaction of democratization across the Middle East. A battle-cry of the time was, "Real men go to Tehran." When asked about the implications of U.S. military success in Iraq for other Middle Eastern countries, U.S. State Department official Richard Perle replied that it meant, "You're next."

57. For an exploration of various views of why the U.S. decided to invade Iraq, see Jane K. Cramer and A. Trevor Thrall (eds.), *Why Did the United States Invade Iraq?* (London: Routledge, 2012).

58. Paul Rogers, *Iraq: Consequences of a War* (Oxford: Oxford Research Group, 2002), pp. 1–5.

59. National Energy Policy Development Group, *Reliable, Affordable, and Environmentally Sound Energy for America's Future* (Washington: U.S. Government Printing Office, 2001).

60. Jane Mayer, "Contract Sport," *New Yorker*, 16 February 2004.

61. Warren Vieth, "Privatization of Oil Suggested for Iraq," *Los Angeles Times*, 21 February 2003; "Tomgram: Michael Schwartz, the Prize of Iraqi Oil," *TomDispatch. com*, posted 6 May 2007; "Tomgram: Michael Klare on Iraq's Missing Sea of Oil," *TomDispatch.com*, posted 20 September 2005.

62. George Wright, "Wolfowitz: Iraq War Was about Oil," *The Guardian*, 4 June 2003, cited in Slavoj Žižek, *Iraq: The Borrowed Kettle* (London: Verso, 2005), p. 5.

63. Important pieces of the "evidence" of W.M.D.s that was used to support the invasion were supplied by an Iraqi defector who was given the code-name "Curveball." Even at the time, U.S. officials were warned that his information was highly unreliable. In February 2011, "Curveball" admitted to reporters from *The Guardian* that he had lied about evidence of Saddam's W.M.D.s.

64. One observer who accompanied some of the American occupation officials to Iraq noted that they were carrying books about the Allied postwar occupation of Germany and Japan. He also noted that hung on the wall of Bremer's Baghdad office was a chart featuring benchmarks of progress of the U.S. occupation of Germany in 1946. Works that detail some of the missteps of the Coalition Provisional Authority include Rajiv Chandrasekaran, *Imperial Life in the Emerald City: Inside Iraq's Green Zone* (New York: Alfred A. Knopf, 2006); Rory Stewart, *The Prince of the Marshes: and Other Occupational Hazards of a Year in Iraq* (Orlando: Harcourt, 2007); George Packer, *The Assassin's Gate: America in Iraq* (New York: Farrar, Strauss & Giroux, 2005).

65. Anthony Shadid, "U.S. Commander Fears Political Stalemate in Iraq," *New York Times*, 29 August 2010. Shadid's account of an early phase of the fighting (*Night Draws Near: Iraq's People in the Shadow of America's War* [New York: Henry Holt, 2005) provides lyrically eloquent testimony to the effects of the invasion on ordinary Iraqis. For another account of the impact of the U.S. occupation on Iraqis, see Ali Allawi, *The Occupation of Iraq: Winning the War, Losing the Peace* (New Haven: Yale University Press, 2007).

EPILOGUE: "TELL ME HOW THIS ENDS"

1. See Toby Dodge, *Iraq: From War to a New Authoritarianism* (London: International Institute for Strategic Studies, 2012).

2. Among the better accounts of the sectarian and ethnic divisions that beset Iraq during this time are Nir Rosen, *In the Belly of the Green Bird* (New York: Simon & Schuster, 2006); Ahmed Hashim, *Insurgency and Counter-insurgency in Iraq* (New York: Cornell University Press, 2006); and Cockburn, *Muqtada al-Sadr*.

3. Juan Cole, "The Real State of Iraq," *Informed Comment*, posted 22 June 2008.

4. Steven Lee Myers, "With New Violence, More Christians Are Fleeing Iraq," *New York Times*, 12 December 2010.

5. William Dalrymple, "Iraq's Disappearing Christians Are Bush and Blair's Legacy," *The Guardian*, 12 November 2010.

6. That the U.S. may have played an active role in the willful destruction of Iraq's ancient heritage is an issue much debated among experts. See, for example, Zainab Bahrani, "Archaeology and the Strategies of War," in *Cultural Cleansing in Iraq: Why Museums Were Looted, Libraries Burned and Academics Murdered*, ed. Raymond W. Baker, Shereen T. Ismail, and Tareq Y. Ismail (London: Pluto Press, 2010), pp. 67–81. See also Elizabeth C. Stone, "Patterns of Looting in Southern Iraq," *Antiquity* 82 (2008), pp. 125–138; Peter Stone and Joanne Farchakh Bajjaly (eds.), *The Destruction of Cultural*

Heritage in Iraq (Melton, England: Boydell & Brewer, 2008); and John Curtis, Qais Hussein Raheed, Hugo Clarke, Abdulamir M. Al Hamdani, Elizabeth Stone, Margarette Van Ess, Paul Collins, and Mehsin Ali, "An Assessment of Archaeological Sites in June 2008: An Iraqi–British Project," *Iraq* 70 (2008), pp. 215–237.

7. Arabs refer to this group as "Daish," an acronym for "al-Dawla al-Islamiya al-Iraq al-Sham."

8. Patrick Cockburn, "Fragile Iraq Threatened by the Return of Civil War," *The Independent*, 4 December 2011.

9. To his credit, Patrick Cockburn has produced one of the best informed treatments of the emergence of I.S.: *The Jihadis Return: ISIS and the New Sunni Uprising* (New York: O.R. Books, 2014).

10. For an example, see Aref Mohammed, "Dates or Oil? Iraq's Farmers Fear Gold Rush," *Reuters*, 18 August 2010.

11. U.S. Energy Administration Iraq Report, updated 2 April 2013, http://www.eia.gov/countries/country-data.cfm?fips=iz

12. Ibid.

13. Ibid.

Bibliography

Abdullah, Thabit A. J., *A Short History of Iraq*. London: Pearson Longman, 2003.

Adams, Robert M., *Heartland of Cities: Surveys of Ancient Settlement and Land Use on the Central Floodplain of the Euphrates*. Chicago: University of Chicago Press, 1981.

Adams, Robert M., *Land behind Baghdad: A History of Settlement on the Diyala Plains*. Chicago: University of Chicago Press, 1965.

Adelson, Roger, *London and the Invention of the Middle East: Money, Power, and War, 1902–1922*. New Haven: Yale University Press, 1995.

Afsaruddin, Asma, *The First Muslims: History and Memory*. Oxford: Oneworld, 2008.

Alexander, Caroline, "Iraqis Find Ancient Mithra Temple in Northern Dohuk Province," 24 June 2009, http://www.bloomberg.com/apps/news?pid=20601117&sid=aRKw P5vWGweE

Algaze, Guillermo, *Ancient Mesopotamia at the Dawn of Civilization: The Evolution of an Urban Landscape*. Chicago: University of Chicago Press, 2008.

Al-Khalil, Samir [Kanan Makiya], *Republic of Fear: The Inside Story of Saddam's Iraq*. New York: Pantheon Books, 1990.

Al-Khalili, Jim, *The House of Wisdom: How Arabic Science Saved Ancient Knowledge and Gave Us the Renaissance*. New York: Penguin, 2011.

Allawi, Ali, *The Occupation of Iraq: Winning the War, Losing the Peace*. New Haven: Yale University Press, 2007.

Al-Tikriti, Nabil. "Was There an Iraq before There Was an Iraq?" *International Journal of Contemporary Iraqi Studies* 3(2) (2009), pp. 133–142.

Amanat, Abbas, *Apocalyptic Islam and Iranian Shi'ism*. London: I. B. Tauris, 2009.

Ambrose, Stephen E., *Uncommon Courage: Meriwether Lewis, Thomas Jefferson, and the Opening of the American West*. New York: Simon & Schuster, 1996.

Anderson, Benedict, *Imagined Communities: Reflections on the Origin and Spread of Nationalism* (rev. ed.). New York: Verso, 2006.

Anderson, Scott, *Lawrence in Arabia: War, Deceit, Imperial Folly and the Making of the Modern Middle East*. New York: Doubleday, 2013.

Antonius, George, *The Arab Awakening: The Story of the Arab National Movement*. Beirut: Khayat's, 1938.

Arnove, Anthony (ed.), *Iraq under Siege: The Deadly Impact of Sanctions and War*. Cambridge, MA: South End Press, 2000.

Axworthy, Michael, *A History of Iran: Empire of the Mind*. New York: Basic Books, 2008.

Bahrani, Zainab, "Archaeology and the Strategies of War," in *Cultural Cleansing in Iraq: Why Museums Were Looted, Libraries Burned and Academics Murdered*, ed. Raymond W. Baker, Shereen T. Ismail, and Tareq Y. Ismail. London: Pluto Press, 2010.

Bahrani, Zainab, *Rituals of War: The Body and Violence in Mesopotamia*. New York: Zone Books, 2008.

Ball, Warwick, *Rome in the East: The Transformation of an Empire*. London: Routledge, 2001.

Baram, Amatzia, "A Case of Imported Identity: The Modernizing Secular Ruling Elites of Iraq and the Concept of Mesopotamian-Inspired Territorial Nationalism, 1922–1992," *Poetics Today* 15(2) (1994), pp. 279–319.

Baram, Amatzia, *Culture, History & Ideology in the Formation of Ba'thist Iraq, 1968–1989*. New York: St. Martin's Press, 1991.

Baram, Amatzia, "Mesopotamian Identity in Ba'thi Iraq," *Middle East Studies* 19 (1983), pp. 426–455.

Bashkin, Orit, *New Babylonians: A History of Jews in Modern Iraq*. Stanford, CA: Stanford University Press, 2012.

Bashkin, Orit, *The Other Iraq: Pluralism and Culture in Hashemite Iraq*. Stanford, CA: Stanford University Press, 2009.

Belting, Hans, *Florence and Baghdad: Renaissance Art and Arab Science*, trans. Deborah Lucas Schneider. Cambridge, MA: Belknap Press of Harvard University Press, 2011.

Bengio, Ofra, *Saddam's Word: Political Discourse in Iraq*. New York: Oxford University Press, 2002.

Benite, Zvi Ben-Dor, *The Ten Lost Tribes: A World History*. New York: Oxford University Press, 2009.

Bernhardsson, Magnus, *Reclaiming a Plundered Past: Archaeology and Nation Building in Modern Iraq*. Austin: University of Texas Press, 2005.

Bernstein, Jack, *The Mesopotamia Mess: The British Invasion of Iraq in 1914*. Redondo Beach, CA: Interlingua, 2008.

Bobrick, Benson, *The Caliph's Splendor: Islam and the West in the Golden Age of Baghdad*. New York: Simon & Schuster, 2012.

Bohak, Gideon, *Ancient Jewish Magic: A History*. Cambridge: Cambridge University Press, 2008.

Bosworth, C. E., "Iran and the Arabs before Islam," in *The Cambridge History of Iran*, Vol. 3 (1). *The Seleucid, Parthian, and Sasanian Periods*, ed. Ehsan Yarshater. Cambridge: Cambridge University Press, 1983.

Bottero, Jean, *Religion in Ancient Mesopotamia*, trans. Teresa Lavender Fagan. Chicago: University of Chicago Press, 2001.

Boyce, Mary, *Zoroastrians: Their Religious Beliefs and Practices*. London: Routledge, 2001.

Brendon, Piers, *The Decline and Fall of the British Empire, 1781–1997*. London: Vintage, 2008.

Brody, Robert, *The Geonim of Babylonia and the Shaping of Medieval Jewish Culture*. New Haven: Yale University Press, 2013.

Brosius, Maria, *The Persians: An Introduction*. London: Routledge, 2006.

Catherwood, Christopher, *Churchill's Folly: How Winston Churchill Created Modern Iraq*. New York: Carroll & Graf, 2004.

Ceylan, Ebubekir, "Carrot or Stick? Ottoman Tribal Policy in Baghdad, 1831–1876," *International Journal of Contemporary Iraqi Studies* 3(2) (2009).

Ceylan, Ebubekir, *The Ottoman Origins of Modern Iraq: Political Reform, Modernization and Development in the Nineteenth-Century Middle East*. London: I. B. Tauris, 2011.

Chandrasekaran, Rajiv, *Imperial Life in the Emerald City: Inside Iraq's Green Zone*. New York: Alfred A. Knopf, 2006.

Chavalas, Mark W. (ed.), *The Ancient Near East: Historical Sources in Translation*. Malden, MA: Blackwell, 2006.

Charpin, Dominique, *Hammurabi of Babylon*. London: I. B. Tauris, 2012.

Chubin, Shahram and Charles Tripp, *Iran and Iraq at War*. Boulder, CO: Westview Press, 1987.

Clarke, Richard A., *Against All Enemies: Inside America's War on Terror*. New York: Free Press, 2004.

Cline, Eric, *Eden to Exile: Unraveling Mysteries of the Bible*. Washington: National Geographic, 2007.

Cockburn, Andrew, "Worth It," *London Review of Books* 32(14) (2010), pp. 9–10.

Cockburn, Andrew and Patrick Cockburn, *Out of the Ashes: The Resurrection of Saddam Hussein*. New York: HarperCollins, 1999.

Cockburn, Patrick, *The Jihadis Return: ISIS and the New Sunni Uprising*. New York: O.R. Books, 2014.

Cockburn, Patrick, "Leaving Iraq: The Ruin They'll Leave Behind," *Counterpunch*, 19 July 2010, http://www.counterpunch.org/patrick07192010.html

Cockburn, Patrick, *Muqtada al-Sadr and the Battle for the Future of Iraq*. New York: Scribner, 2008.

Cogan, Mordechai, *The Raging Torrent: Historical Inscriptions from Assyria and Babylonia Relating to Ancient Israel*. Jerusalem: Carta, 2008.

Cole, Juan, "The Real State of Iraq," *Informed Comment*, posted 22 June 2008.

Coll, Steve, *Ghost Wars: The Secret History of the CIA, Afghanistan, and Bin Laden, from the Soviet Invasion to September 10, 2001*. New York: Penguin, 2004.

Coogan, Michael D. (ed.), *The New Oxford Annotated Bible* (4th ed.). Oxford: Oxford University Press, 2010.

Cooley, John K., *An Alliance against Babylon: The U.S., Israel, and Iraq*. London: Pluto Press, 2005.

Cooperson, Michael, *Al Ma'mun*. Oxford: Oneworld, 2005.

Cramer, Jane K. and A. Trevor Thrall (eds.), *Why Did the United States Invade Iraq?* London: Routledge, 2012.

Crile, George, *Charlie Wilson's War: The Extraordinary Story of the Largest Covert Operation in History*. New York: Atlantic Monthly Press, 2003.

Crooke, Alastair, "The Shifting Sands of State Power in the Middle East," *Washington Quarterly* 33(3) (2010), pp. 7–20.

Curtis, John, *The Cyrus Cylinder and Ancient Persia: A New Beginning for the Middle East*. London: British Museum, 2013.

Curtis, John, Qais Hussein Raheed, Hugo Clarke, Abdulamir M. Al Hamdani, Elizabeth Stone, Margarette Van Ess, Paul Collins, and Mehsin Ali, "An Assessment of Archaeological Sites in June 2008: An Iraqi–British Project," *Iraq* 70 (2008), pp. 215–237.

Dalley, Stephanie, "The Influence of Mesopotamia upon Israel and the Bible," in *The Legacy of Mesopotamia*, ed. Stephanie Dalley. Oxford: Oxford University Press, 1998.

Dalley, Stephanie (ed.), *The Legacy of Mesopotamia*. Oxford: Oxford University Press, 1998.

Dalley, Stephanie, *The Mystery of the Hanging Garden of Babylon: An Elusive World Wonder Retraced*. Oxford: Oxford University Press, 2013.

Dalley, Stephanie, "Occasions and Opportunities: 2. Persian, Greek, and Parthian Overlords," in *The Legacy of Mesopotamia*, ed. Stephanie Dalley. Oxford: Oxford University Press, 1998.

Dalrymple, William, "Iraq's Disappearing Christians Are Bush and Blair's Legacy," *The Guardian*, 12 November 2010.

Dalrymple, William, "The Muslims in the Middle," *New York Times*, 16 August 2010.

Damrosch, David, *The Buried Book: The Loss and Rediscovery of the Great Epic of Gilgamesh*. New York: Henry Holt, 2006.

Davis, Eric, *Memories of State: Politics, History, and Collective Identity in Modern Iraq*. Berkeley: University of California Press, 2005.

Davis, Eric, "Reflections on Religion and Politics in Post-Ba'thist Iraq," *TAARI Newsletter* 3(1) (2008), pp. 13–15.

Dawisha, Adeed, *Arab Nationalism in the Twentieth Century: From Triumph to Despair*. Princeton, NJ: Princeton University Press, 2003.

Dawisha, Adeed, *Iraq: A Political History from Independence to Occupation*. Princeton, NJ: Princeton University Press, 2009.

Dodge, Toby, *Inventing Iraq: The Failure of Nation Building and a History Denied*. New York: Columbia University Press, 2003.

Dodge, Toby, *Iraq: From War to a New Authoritarianism*. London: International Institute for Strategic Studies, 2012.

Donner, Fred, *The Early Islamic Conquests*. Princeton, NJ: Princeton University Press, 1981.

Donner, Fred, *Muhammad and the Believers: At the Origins of Islam*. Cambridge, MA: Belknap Press of Harvard University Press, 2010.

Donovan, Thomas, "Iraq's Upstream Oil and Gas Industry: A Post-election Analysis," *Middle East Policy* 17(2) (2010), pp. 24–30.

Duelfer, Charles, "The Iraqi Who Knew Too Much," 9 August 2010, www.foreignpolicy.com

Dunn, Ross E., *The Adventures of Ibn Battuta: a Muslim Traveler of the 14th Century* (2nd ed.). Berkeley: University of California Press, 2005.

Elbendary, Amina, "They Came to Baghdad: Its Famous Names," *Al-Ahram Weekly Online* 634 (2003), http://weekly.ahram.org.eg/2003/634/bo2.htm

Esposito, John, *Islam: The Straight Path* (rev. 3rd ed.). New York: Oxford University Press, 2005.

Fales, F. M., "Arameans and Chaldeans: Environment and Society," in *The Babylonian World*, ed. Gwendolyn Leick. New York: Routledge, 2009.

Farouk-Sluglett, Marion and Peter Sluglett, *Iraq since 1958: From Revolution to Dictatorship* (rev. ed.). London: I. B. Tauris, 2001.

Fattah, Hala with Frank Caso, *A Brief History of Iraq*. New York: Checkmark Books, 2009.

Finkel, I. L. and M. J. Seymour (eds.), *Babylon*. Oxford: Oxford University Press, 2008.

Foster, Benjamin R., Before *the Muses: An Anthology of Akkadian Literature* (3rd ed.) Bethesda, MD: CDL Press, 2005.

Foster, Benjamin R. and Karen Polinger Foster, *Civilizations of Ancient Iraq*. Princeton, NJ: Princeton University Press, 2009.

Foster, Benjamin, Karen Polinger Foster, and Patty Gerstenblith, *Iraq beyond the Headlines: History, Archaeology, and War*. Hackensack, NJ: World Scientific, 2005.

Fowden, Garth, *Empire to Commonwealth: Consequences of Monotheism in Late Antiquity*. Princeton, NJ: Princeton University Press, 1993.

Franzen, Johan, "Losing Hearts and Minds in Iraq: Britain, Cold War Propaganda and the Challenge of Communism, 1945–1958," *Historical Research* 83(222) (2010), pp. 747–762.

Fromkin, David, *A Peace to End All Peace: the Fall of the Ottoman Empire and the Creation of the Modern Middle East*. New York: Avon, 1989.

Frymer-Kensky, Tikvah, *In the Wake of the Goddesses: Women, Culture, and the Biblical Transformation of Pagan Myth*. New York: Free Press, 1992.

Fukuyama, Francis, *The End of History and the Last Man*. New York: Free Press, 1992.

Gates, Charles, *Ancient Cities; the Archaeology of Urban Life in the Ancient Near East and Egypt, Greece, and Rome*. London: Routledge, 2003.

George, A. R., "The Tower of Babel: Archaeology, History, and Cuneiform Texts," *Archiv fur Orientforschung* 51 (2005–06), pp. 75–95.

Gerth, Jeff, "Report Offered Bleak Outlook about Iraq Oil," *New York Times*, 5 October 2003.

Gibb, H. A. R. and J. H. Kramers, *The Shorter Encyclopedia of Islam*. Leiden: E. J. Brill, 1995.

Gibson, McGuire, "Nippur and Archaeology in Iraq," in *Oriental Institute 2004–2005 Annual Report*, pp. 82–87.

Gibson, McGuire, "Violation of Fallow and Engineered Disaster in Mesopotamian Civilization," in T. E. Downing and M. Gibson (eds.), *Irrigation's Impact on Society*, pp. 7–19. Tucson: University of Arizona Press, 1974).

Goldberg, Jeffery, "The Great Terror," *New Yorker*, 25 March 2002.

Goodwin, Jason, "The Glory that Was Baghdad," *Wilson Quarterly* (Spring 2003).

Gordon, Joy, "Invisible War: How Thirteen Years of US-Imposed Economic Sanctions Devastated Iraq before the 2003 Invasion," *Open Democracy Now*, posted 1 September 2010.

Gordon, Joy, *Invisible War: The United States and the Iraq Sanctions*. Cambridge, MA: Harvard University Press, 2010.

Gordon, Joy, "Lessons We Should Have Learned from the Iraqi Sanctions," *Foreign Policy Middle East Channel*, posted 8 July 2010.

Gordon, Michael R., "Hussein Wanted Soviets to Head off U.S. in 1991," *New York Times*, 19 January 2011.

Gutas, Dimitri, *Greek Thought, Arabic Culture: The Graeco-Arabic Translation Movement in Baghdad and Early 'Abbasid Society (2nd–4th/8th–10th Centuries)*. London: Routledge, 1998.

Hadawy, Husein (trans.), *The Arabian Nights*. New York: Alfred A. Knopf, 1990.

Haider, Hind A., "Nationalism, Archaeology and Ideology in Iraq from 1921 to the Present," M.A. thesis, McGill University, Montreal, 2001.

Hall, H. R., *The Ancient History of the Near East: From the Earliest Times to the Battle of Salamis* (11th ed.). London: Methuen & Methuen, 1950.

Hashim, Ahmed, *Insurgency and Counter-Insurgency in Iraq*. Ithaca, NY: Cornell University Press, 2006.

Hawling, Peter and Hamid Yasin, "Iraq's Diverse Shia," *Le Monde Diplomatique*, September 2006.

Hildinger, Erik, *Warriors of the Steppe: A Military History of Central Asia, 500 B.C. to A.D. 1700*. Cambridge, MA: Da Capo Press, 2001.

Hillenbrand, Carole, *The Crusades: Islamic Perspectives*. New York: Routledge, 2000.

Hiltermann, Joost, "Deep Traumas, Fresh Ambitions: Legacies of the Iran–Iraq War," *Middle East Report* 257 (2010), pp. 6–15.

Hiltermann, Joost R., *A Poisonous Affair: America, Iraq, and the Gassing of Halabja*. Cambridge: Cambridge University Press, 2007.

Hiro, Dilip, *The Longest War: The Iran–Iraq Military Conflict*. New York: Routledge, 1991.

Hitti, Phillip K., *History of the Arabs* (10th ed.). New York: St. Martin's Press, 1970.

Hourani, Albert, *A History of the Arab Peoples* (2nd ed.). Cambridge, MA: Belknap, 2003.

Humphreys, R. Stephen, *Islamic History: A Framework for Inquiry*. Princeton, NJ: Princeton University Press, 1991.

Inaty, Shams C., "The Iraqi Christian Community," in *Iraq: Its History, People, and Politics*, ed. Shams C. Inaty. Amherst, NY: Humanity Books, 2003.

Irwin, Robert, *The Arabian Nights: A Companion*. London: Penguin, 1994.

Irwin, Robert (ed.), *Night & Horses & the Desert: An Anthology of Classical Arabic Literature*. New York: Anchor Books, 1999.

Jacobsen, Thorkild, *The Treasures of Darkness: A History of Mesopotamian Religion*. New Haven: Yale University Press, 1978.

Joannes, Francis, *The Age of Empires: Mesopotamia in the First Millennium BC*, trans. Antonia Nevill. Edinburgh: Edinburgh University Press, 2004.

Karamustafa, Ahmet T., *Sufism: The Formative Period*. Berkeley: University of California Press, 2007.

Kennedy, Hugh, *The Great Arab Conquests: How the Spread of Islam Changed the World We Live in*. Cambridge, MA: Da Capo Press, 2007.

Kennedy, Hugh, *The Prophet and the Age of the Caliphates* (2nd ed.). Harlow, England: Pearson, 2004.

Kennedy, Hugh, *When Baghdad Ruled the Muslim World*. Cambridge, MA: Da Capo Press, 2005.

Kennedy, Philip F., *Abu Nuwas: A Genius of Poetry*. Oxford: Oneworld, 2005.

Kent, Marian, *Oil and Empire: British Policy and Mesopotamian Oil, 1900–1920*. London: Macmillan, 1976.

King, Karen L., "Gnosticism," in *Religions of the Ancient World: A Guide*, ed. Sarah Iles Johnston. Cambridge, MA.: Harvard University Press, 2004.

Kinzer, Stephen, *All the Shah's Men: An American Coup and the Roots of Middle East Terror* (2nd ed.). Hoboken, NJ: Wiley, 2008.

Klare, Michael, "Tomgram: Michael Klare on Iraq's Missing Sea of Oil," *TomDispatch. com*, posted 20 September 2005.

Kramer, Samuel Noah, *History Begins at Sumer: Thirty-Nine Firsts in Recorded History* (3rd ed.). Philadelphia: University of Pennsylvania Press, 1988.

Kriwaczek, Paul, *In Search of Zarathustra: The First Prophet and the Ideas that Changed the World*. New York: Alfred A. Knopf, 2003.

Larsen, Mogens Trolle, *The Conquest of Assyria: Excavations in an Antique Land*. London: Routledge, 1996.

Larsen, Timothy, "Austen Henry Layard's Nineveh: The Bible and Archaeology in Victorian Britain," *Journal of Religious History* 33 (2009), pp. 66–81.

Lawler, Andrew, "Murder in Mesopotamia?" *Science* 317 (2007), pp. 1164–1165.

Levene, Dan, *A Corpus of Magic Bowls: Incantation Texts in Jewish Aramaic from Late Antiquity*. London/New York: Kegan Paul International/Columbia University Press, 2003.

Levene, Dan, "Rare Magic Inscriptions on Human Skull," *Biblical Archaeology Review*, March/April 2009.

Lewis, Bernard (ed.), *Islam: From the Prophet Muhammad to the Capture of Constantinople*, Vol. 1. *Politics and War*. New York: Oxford University Press, 1987.

Lewis, Bernard (ed.), *Islam: From the Prophet Muhammad to the Conquest of Constantinople*, Vol. 2. *Religion and Society*. New York: Oxford University Press, 1987.

Lewis, Bernard, *The Middle East: A Brief History of the Last 2000 Years*. New York: Scribner, 1995.

Lewis, Donald M., *The Origins of Christian Zionism: Lord Shaftesbury and Evangelical Support for a Jewish Homeland*. Cambridge: Cambridge University Press, 2010.

Luckenbill, Daniel David, *Ancient Records of Assyria and Babylonia*, Vol. 1. *Historical Records of Assyria from the Earliest Times to Sargon*. London: Histories & Mysteries of Man, 1989 [1926].

Luckenbill, Daniel David, *Ancient Records of Assyria and Babylonia*, Vol. 2. *Historical Records of Assyria from Sargon to the End*. London: Histories & Mysteries of Man, 1989 [1926].

Lyons, Jonathan. *The House of Wisdom: How the Arabs Transformed Western Civilization*. New York: Bloomsbury Press, 2009.

Maalouf, Amin, *The Crusades through Arab Eyes*, trans. Jon Rothschild. New York: Schocken, 1984.

Mainz, Beatrice Forbes, *The Rise and Rule of Tamerlane*. Cambridge: Cambridge University Press, 1991.

Makdisi, Ussama, *Faith Misplaced: The Broken Promise of U.S.–Arab Relations: 1820–2001*. New York: Basic Books, 2010.

Marozzi, Justin, *Baghdad: City of Peace, City of Blood*. London: Allen Lane, 2014.

Marozzi, Justin, *Tamerlane: Sword of Islam, Conqueror of the World*. Cambridge, MA: Da Capo Press, 2004.

Marr, Phebe, "The Development of a Nationalist Ideology in Iraq, 1920–1941," *Muslim World* 75 (1985), pp. 85–101.

Marr, Phebe, *The Modern History of Iraq* (2nd ed.). Boulder, CO: Westview Press, 2004.

Marr, Phebe, "One Iraq or Many? What Has Happened to Iraqi Identity?" in *Iraq between Occupations: Perspectives from 1920 to the Present*, ed. Amatzia Baram, Achim Rohde, and Ronen Zeidel. New York: Palgrave Macmillan, 2010.

Mayer, Jane, "Contract Sport," *New Yorker*, 16 February 2004.

McMeekin, Sean, *The Berlin–Baghdad Express: The Ottoman Empire and Germany's Bid for World Power, 1898–1918*. Cambridge, MA: Belknap Press of Harvard University Press, 2010.

Mearsheimer, John J. and Stephen M. Walt, *The Israel Lobby and U.S. Foreign Policy*. New York: Farrar, Straus & Giroux, 2008.

Middle East Watch, *Genocide in Iraq: The Anfal Campaign against the Kurds*. New York: Human Rights Watch, 1993.

Millar, Fergus, *The Roman Near East, 31 B.C. – A.D. 337*. Cambridge, MA: Harvard University Press, 1993.

Miller, J Maxwell and John H. Hayes, *A History of Ancient Israel and Judah* (2nd ed.). Louisville: Westminster John Knox Press, 2006.

Mirecki, Paul Allan, "Manichaeians and Manichaeism," in *The Anchor Bible Dictionary*, Vol. 4, ed. David Noel Freedman. New York: Doubleday, 1992.

Mohammed, Aref, "Dates or Oil? Iraq's Farmers Fear Gold Rush," *Reuters*, 18 August 2010.

Mohring, Hannes, *Saladin: The Sultan and His times, 1138–1193*, trans. David S. Bachrach. Baltimore: Johns Hopkins University Press, 2005.

Morgan, David, *The Mongols* (2nd ed.). Malden, MA: Blackwell, 2007.

Morony, Michael G., *Iraq after the Muslim Conquest*. Princeton, NJ: Princeton University Press, 1984.

Mueller, John and Karl Mueller, "Sanctions of Mass Destruction," *Foreign Affairs* 78 (1999), pp. 43–53.

Mufti, Malik, *Sovereign Creations: Pan-Arabism and Political Order in Syria and Iraq*. Ithaca, NY: Cornell University Press, 1996.

Myers, Steven Lee. "With New Violence, More Christians Are Fleeing Iraq," *New York Times*, 12 December 2010.

Nakash, Yitzhak, "The Conversion of Iraq's Tribes to Shi'ism," *International Journal of Middle East Studies* 26(3) (1994), pp. 443–463.

Nakash, Yitzhak, *Reaching for Power: The Shi'a in the Modern Arab World*. Princeton, NJ: Princeton University Press, 2006.

Nakash, Yitzhak, *The Shi'is of Iraq* (2nd ed.). Princeton, NJ: Princeton University Press, 2003.

Nasr, Vali, *The Shia Revival: How Conflicts within Islam Will Shape the Future*. New York: W. W. Norton, 2006.

National Commission on Terrorist Attacks upon the United States, *The 9/11 Commission Report: Final Report of the National Commission on Terrorist Attacks upon the United States*. New York: W. W. Norton, 2004.

National Energy Policy Development Group, *Reliable, Affordable, and Environmentally Sound Energy for America's Future*. Washington: US Government Printing Office, 2001.

Newman, Andrew, *Safavid Iran: Rebirth of a Persian Empire*. London: I. B. Tauris, 2009.

Nissen, Hans J., Peter Damerow, and Robert K. Englund, *Archaic Bookkeeping: Writing and Techniques of Economic Administration in the Ancient Near East*, trans. Peter Larsen. Chicago: University of Chicago Press, 1993.

Ochsenwald, William and Sydney Nettleton Fisher, *The Middle East: A History* (6th ed.). New York: McGraw-Hill, 2003.

Olmstead, A. T., "The Calculated Frightfulness of Ashur Nasir Apal," *Journal of the American Oriental Society* 38 (1918), pp. 209–263.

Ovendale, Ritchie, *The Longman Companion to the Middle East since 1914*. London: Longman, 1992.

Packer, George, *The Assassin's Gate: America in Iraq*. New York: Farrar, Strauss & Giroux, 2005.

Parsi, Trita, "A Campaign for War with Iran Begins," *Salon.com*, 13 August 2010.

Parsi, Trita, *Treacherous Alliance: The Secret Dealings of Israel, Iran, and the United States*. New Haven: Yale University Press, 2007.

Pellett, Peter L., "Sanctions, Food, Nutrition, and Health in Iraq," in *Iraq under Siege: The Deadly Impact of Sanctions and War*, ed. Anthony Arnove. Cambridge, MA: South End Press, 2000.

Peters, F. E., *The Harvest of Hellenism: A History of the Near East from Alexander the Great to the Triumph of Christianity*. New York: Barnes & Noble, 1970.

Pingree, David. "Legacies in Astronomy and Celestial Omens," in *The Legacy of Mesopotamia*, ed. Stephanie Dalley. Oxford: Oxford University Press, 1998.

Porter, Gareth, "From Military-Industrial Complex to Permanent War State," *CommonDreams.org*, 17 January 2011.

Postgate, J. N., *The First Empires*. Oxford: Elsevier-Phaidon, 1977.

Potts, D. T., "Babylonian Sources of Exotic Raw Materials," in *The Babylonian World*, ed. Gwendolyn Leick. New York: Routledge, 2009.

Pournelle, Jennifer R., "KLM to CORONA: A Bird's-Eye View of Cultural Ecology and Early Mesopotamian Urbanization," in *Settlement and Society: Essays Dedicated to Robert McCormick Adams*, ed. Elizabeth C. Stone. Los Angeles: Cotsen Institute of Archaeology, University of California, 2007.

Power, Samantha. *"A Problem from Hell": America and the Age of Genocide*. New York: Basic Books, 2002.

Primakov, Yevgeny, *Russia and the Arabs: Behind the Scenes in the Middle East from the Cold War to the Present*, trans. Paul Gould. New York: Basic Books, 2009.

Rashid, Ahmed, *Taliban: Militant Islam, Oil, and Fundamentalism in Central Asia* (2nd ed.). New Haven: Yale University Press, 2010.

Ricks, Thomas, *Fiasco: The American Military Adventure in Iraq*. New York: Penguin, 2006.

Robson, Eleanor, *Mathematics in Ancient Iraq: A Social History*. Princeton, NJ: Princeton University Press, 2008.

Rochberg, Francesca, *The Heavenly Writing: Divination, Horoscopy, and Astronomy in Mesopotamian Culture*. Cambridge: Cambridge University Press, 2004.

Rodenbeck, Max, "The Time of the Shia," *New York Review of Books* 53(13) (2006).

Rogers, Paul, *Iraq: Consequences of a War*. Oxford: Oxford Research Group, 2002.

Rosen, Nir, *In the Belly of the Green Bird*. New York: Simon & Schuster, 2006.

Rosen, Nir, "No Going Back," *Boston Review*, September–October 2007.

Roth, Martha T., *Law Collections from Mesopotamia and Asia Minor* (2nd ed.). Atlanta: Scholars Press, 1997.

Roux, George, *Ancient Iraq* (3rd ed.). London: Penguin, 1992.

Rudolph, Kurt, "Mandaeism," in *The Anchor Bible Dictionary*, Vol. 4, ed. David Noel Freedman. New York: Doubleday, 1992.

Ruthven, Malise, "Divided Iran on the Eve," *New York Review of Books* 56(11) (2009).

Saggs, H. W. F., *The Greatness that Was Babylon* (rev. ed.). London: Sidgwick & Jackson, 1988.

Saggs, H. W. F., *The Might that Was Assyria*. London: Sidgwick & Jackson, 1984.

Said, Edward, *Orientalism*. New York: Vintage Books, 1979.

Saldarini, Anthony J. as revised by Amy-Jill Levine, "Jewish Responses to Greek and Roman Cultures, 332 BCE to 200 CE," in *The Cambridge Companion to the Bible* (2nd ed.), ed. Bruce Chilton. Cambridge: Cambridge University Press, 2008.

Salibi, Kamal. *A House of Many Mansions: The History of Lebanon Reconsidered*. Berkeley: University of California Press, 1988.

Sartre, Maurice, *The Middle East under Rome*, trans. Catherine Porter and Elizabeth Rawlings. Cambridge, MA: Belknap Press of Harvard University Press, 2005.

Saunders, J. J., *The History of the Mongol Conquests*. Philadelphia: University of Pennsylvania Press, 1971.

Schwartz, Michael. "Tomgram: Michael Schwartz, The Prize of Iraqi Oil," *TomDispatch. com*, posted 6 May 2007.

Shadid, Anthony, *Night Draws Near: Iraq's People in the Shadow of America's War*. New York: Henry Holt, 2005.

Shadid, Anthony, "Resurgent Turkey Flexes Its Muscles around Iraq," *New York Times*, 4 January 2011.

Shadid, Anthony, "U.S. Commander Fears Political Stalemate in Iraq," *New York Times*, 29 August 2010.

Sherwin-White, Susan and Amelie Kuhrt, *From Samarkand to Sardis: A New Approach to the Seleucid Empire*. Berkeley: University of California Press, 1993.

Shiblak, Abbas, *Iraqi Jews: A History of Mass Exodus*. London: Saqi Books, 2005.

Shields, Sarah, "Mosul, the Ottoman Legacy and the League of Nations," *International Journal of Contemporary Iraqi Studies* 3(2) (2009).

Sluglett, Peter, *Britain in Iraq: Contriving King and Country*. New York: Columbia University Press, 2007.

Sluglett, Peter, "Iraq under Siege: Politics, Society and Economy 1990–2003," in *From Desolation to Reconstruction: Iraq's Troubled Journey*, ed. Mokhtar Lamani and Bessma Momani. Waterloo, ON: Wilfrid Laurier University Press, 2010.

Smith, Margaret, *Rabia the Mystic and her Fellow-Saints in Islam*. Cambridge: Cambridge University Press, 1928.

Starr, Stephen, "Mandeans in Struggle for Existence," *Asia Times*, 18 August 2010.

Stewart, Rory, *The Prince of the Marshes: and Other Occupational Hazards of a Year in Iraq*. Orlando: Harcourt, 2007.

Stiebing, William H., *Ancient Near Eastern History and Culture* (2nd ed.). New York: Pearson Longman, 2009.

Stolper, Matthew W., *Entrepreneurs and Empire*. Istanbul: Nederlands Historisch-Archaeologisch Instituut, 1985.

Stone, Elizabeth C., "Patterns of Looting in Southern Iraq," *Antiquity* 82 (2008), pp. 125–138.

Stone, Peter and Joanne Farchakh Bajjaly (eds.), *The Destruction of Cultural Heritage in Iraq*. Melton, England: Boydell & Brewer, 2008.

Stroumsa, Guy, "Manicheism," in *Religions of the Ancient World: A Guide*, ed. Sarah Iles Johnston. Cambridge, MA: Harvard University Press, 2004.

Takeyh, Ray, "The Iran–Iraq War: A Reassessment," *Middle East Journal* 64 (2010), pp. 365–383.

Takeyh, Ray, "Iran's New Iraq," *Middle East Journal* 62 (2008), pp. 13–30.

Tolan, John V., *Saracens: Islam in the Medieval European Imagination*. New York: Columbia University Press, 2002.

Tolan, John V., *Sons of Ishmael: Muslims through European Eyes in the Middle Ages*. Gainesville: University Press of Florida, 2008.

Traina, Giusto, *428 AD: An Ordinary Year at the End of the Roman Empire*, trans. Allan Cameron. Princeton, NJ: Princeton University Press, 2009.

Tripp, Charles, *A History of Iraq* (3rd ed.). Cambridge: Cambridge University Press, 2007.

Tuchman, Barbara W., *Bible and Sword: England and Palestine from the Bronze Age to Balfour*. New York: Ballantine, 1984 [1956].

U.S. Senate Committee on Banking, Housing and Urban Affairs, "U.S. Chemical and Biological Warfare-Related Dual-Use Exports to Iraq and Their Possible Impact on the Health Consequences of the Persian Gulf War," May 1994, http://www.gulfweb.org/bigdoc/report/riegle1.html

Vermes, Geza, *Christian Beginnings: From Nazareth to Nicaea, AD 30–325*. London: Allen Lane, 2012.

Vieth, Warren, "Privatization of Oil Suggested for Iraq," *Los Angeles Times*, 21 February 2003.

Van de Mieroop, Marc, *King Hammurabi of Babylon*. Malden, MA: Blackwell, 2005.

Visser, Reidar, "Operation Iraqi Partition," *Gulf Analysis*, posted 1 September 2010.

Visser, Reidar, "Proto-political Conceptions of 'Iraq' in Late Ottoman Times," *International Journal of Contemporary Iraqi Studies* 3(2)(2009), pp. 143–154.

Visser, Reidar, *The Sadrists of Basra and the Far South of Iraq: The Most Unpredictable Political Face in the Gulf's Oil-Belt Region*. Oslo: Norwegian Institute of Foreign Affairs, 2008.

Walker, Joel, *The Legend of Mar Qardagh: Narrative and Christian Heroism in Late Antique Iraq*. Berkeley: University of California Press, 2006.

Walt, Stephen, "Bush, Blair, and Iraq (Round II). A Reply to John Judis," *Foreign Policy*, posted 16 February 2010.

White, L. Michael, *From Jesus to Christianity: How Four Generations of Visionaries and Storytellers Created the New Testament and Christian Faith*. New York: HarperCollins, 2004.

Wilford, John Noble, "At Ur, Ritual Deaths that Were Anything But Serene," *New York Times*, 27 October 2009.

Wilford, John Noble, "The Muslim Art of Science," *New York Times* 20 May 2011.

Wright, George, "Wolfowitz: Iraq War Was about Oil," *The Guardian*, 4 June 2003.

Wright, Lawrence, *The Looming Tower: Al Qaeda and the Road to 9/11*. New York: Vintage, 2007.

Wright, Robert, *The Evolution of God*. New York: Little, Brown, 2009.

Yergin, Daniel, *The Prize: The Epic Quest for Oil, Money, and Power*. New York: Free Press, 2008.

Yoffee, Norman, *Myths of the Archaic State: Evolution of the Earliest Cities, States, and Civilizations*. Cambridge: Cambridge University Press, 2005.

Zizek, Slavoj, *Iraq: The Borrowed Kettle*. London: Verso, 2005.

Zunes, Stephen, *Tinderbox*. Monroe, ME: Common Courage Press, 2002.

Index